Coercing Compliance

# Coercing Compliance

## STATE-INITIATED BRUTE FORCE IN TODAY'S WORLD

Robert Mandel

Stanford Security Studies
An Imprint of Stanford University Press
Stanford, California

Stanford University Press
Stanford, California

Printed in the United States of America on acid-free, archival-quality paper

Library of Congress Cataloging-in-Publication Data

Mandel, Robert, author.
    Coercing compliance : state-initiated brute force in today's world / Robert Mandel.
      pages cm
    Includes bibliographical references and index.
    ISBN 978-0-8047-9384-1 (cloth : alk. paper) —
    ISBN 978-0-8047-9398-8 (pbk. : alk. paper)
    1. Military policy. 2. War. 3. National security. 4. Internal security. 5. Security, International. 6. World politics—21st century. I. Title.
    UA11.M27 2015
    355'.0335—dc23

                                  2014032174

ISBN 978-0-8047-9535-7 (electronic)

Typeset by Thompson Type in 10/14 Minion

*The strongest and most effective force in guaranteeing the long-term maintenance of power is not violence in all the forms deployed by the dominant to control the dominated, but consent in all the forms in which the dominated acquiesce in their own domination.*

**Robert Frost**

*People sleep peaceably in their beds at night only because rough men stand ready to do violence on their behalf.*

**George Orwell**

*Speak softly, and carry a big stick.*

**Theodore Roosevelt**

*Nothing made by brute force lasts.*

**Robert Louis Stevenson**

# CONTENTS

## TABLES AND FIGURES

## ACKNOWLEDGMENTS

This study—my twelfth book—is the product of years of deep pondering. I have been fascinated by the theory and practice of brute force on a global scale for as far back as I can remember. Proper examination of this topic requires familiarity with many disparate bodies of literature and thus rarely can be executed successfully without outside help. I wish to thank my two undergraduate student research assistants, Olivia Armstrong and Ugyen Lhamo, for aiding with the case studies and for refining some key ideas. I appreciate the insights received from academic colleagues (including wonderful comments from Tony Burke of the University of New South Wales and encouragement from Heather Smith-Cannoy of Lewis & Clark College) and government defense officials. I wish to thank Geoffrey Burn at Stanford University Press for his usual classy expert shepherding of my manuscript in the long journey from its early stages to its polished final product. However, I take full responsibility for any egregious errors found in this volume.

This book is dedicated to two groups of valiant individuals: soldiers in the battle trenches who both apply force and cope with the devastation it can cause, and government policy makers who spend their lives wrestling with force complexities, especially strategic thinkers who analyze global force dispassionately. Regarding brute force, too often conclusions are reached and then emotionally defended before evidence is even gathered. Given the human and property devastation and moral angst surrounding brute force, impartial clear thinking has never been more essential.

Coercing Compliance

# 1 INTRODUCTION

The Study's Central Thrust

FEW GLOBAL SECURITY ISSUES STIMULATE more fervent passion than brute force. Generally considered "the most extreme instrument of foreign policy," the use of force often dominates security planning.[1] A fierce debate rages about brute force, arguably the most controversial public policy issue in international relations:[2] Some onlookers view force use as the most intuitive way to resolve disputes, a natural and appropriate reaction to perceived threat, while others view force use as primitive, inelegant, uncivilized, barbaric, and illegitimate—and often emotional and irrational[3]—reflecting the failure of more delicate instruments of power. Advocates of the first view pessimistically argue that we now live in an increasingly dangerous world where justified fears and real threats abound and where unruly disruptive state and nonstate players engage in ruthless behavior to attain their power-seeking ends; this global predicament necessitates strong military/police coercion as a management response to such anarchy.[4] Advocates of the second view optimistically contend that we now live in a world characterized by enlightened, democratic, interdependent, peaceful cooperation; civil resolution of differences; and a sense of global community, where ideas of warfare and organized violence are increasingly obsolete; such views see force as superfluous due to the growth and spread of economic interdependence, democracy, and international institutions.[5] Many academic scholars view force as atavistic, a reversion to outmoded behavior from bygone days deserving little attention now.

In a now-famous September 11, 2013, op-ed piece in the *New York Times*, to discourage American military action in Syria, Vladimir Putin stated, "Millions around the world increasingly see America not as a model of democracy

1

but as relying solely on brute force, cobbling coalitions together under the slogan 'you're either with us or against us'; but force has proved ineffective and pointless."[6] Ignoring the irony of this criticism coming from someone who had just authorized brute force use in Georgia (and who later authorized its use in Ukraine, an ongoing crisis at the time of this writing), this remark highlights the centrality of brute force debates in international relations.

## ANALYTICAL FOCUS

This study is the first comprehensive systematic global analysis of major twenty-first-century state-initiated internal and external applications of brute force. The multilayered interpretive context (depicted in Figure 1-1) involves global system transformation, national might misperception, and modern coercion conundrum. Based on extensive case evidence, this investigation assesses the short term and long term; the local and global; the military, political, economic, and social; and the state and human security impacts of state-initiated brute force, explicitly isolating the conditions under which brute force works best and worst by highlighting (1) force initiator and force target attributes linked to brute force success and (2) common but low-impact force legitimacy concerns. Finally, this book provides policy advice for managing global brute force use.

This study comes to two major overarching conclusions: (1) The modern global pattern of brute force futility is more a function of states' misapplication of brute force than of the inherent deficiencies of this instrument itself, and consequently it is not surprising that a mismatch exists between states' brute force application and twenty-first-century security challenges; and (2) the realm for successful application of state-initiated brute force is shrinking, for when facing insuperable security challenges, there are identified circumstances where state-initiated brute force can serve as a transitional short-run local military solution, although not by itself as a long-run global strategic solution or as a cure for human security problems. In the future, brute force used as an instrument of state policy will need much smarter application than in the recent past to avoid pitfalls such as action–reaction cycles or regional contagion effects. This investigation thus calls into question much prevailing wisdom about brute force effectiveness and legitimacy.

By focusing on brute force use, this study is automatically emphasizing those confrontations that occur on the more extreme end of the coercion continuum representing the greatest security challenges state regimes face, ones

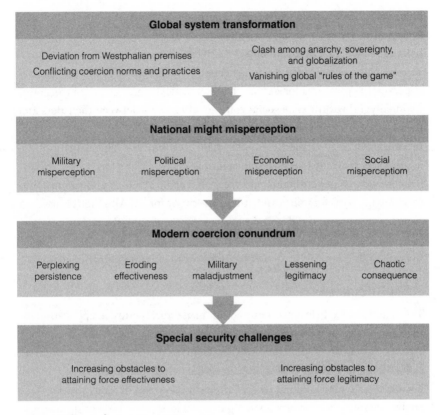

**Figure 1-1.** Brute force interpretive context.

where their very existence or continuity may be at stake or where they deem any other mode of response to be inadequate. These are often cases where diplomacy and economic sanctions have failed and where dire warnings and threats of force have been unable to achieve compliance. Thus this book's scope envelops the most important and "worst-case" security predicaments anyone could imagine occurring in today's world.

Most relevant work does not concentrate on brute force, instead either more narrowly covering warfare or more broadly discussing all forms of coercion, including threats of force and shows of force. Although these broader and narrower studies are valuable for their own purposes, they do not isolate patterns of brute force success and failure. No existing study analyzes the major twenty-first-century state uses of brute force (through the end of 2013) as this book does. Many writings about force in today's world either do not confront the fundamental conceptual paradoxes involved or—in confronting them—take polemical positions defending or attacking the value of applying force in most global predicaments.

This brute force investigation ties in with several other important security concerns: (1) pressures for gun control domestically and arms control internationally; (2) within-state social contract alterations between the rulers and the ruled regarding security responsibilities; (3) sovereignty transformation, reflecting security tensions between state freedom and global integration; (4) fluid global effectiveness and legitimacy norms and practices, including restraint by governments and freedom for individuals and groups; and (5) changing roles for police and military security forces. Although focused on global issues, the findings pertain to other levels of analysis, including interpersonal and intergroup aggression. This study's analysis even links to discussions about human civilization's progress toward enlightened civilized norms.

## SCOPE OF CONCERN

This study is exclusively interested in brute force—direct application of physical strength—in contentious confrontations, not the use of coercive diplomacy, threats and ultimatums, economic sanctions, or shows of force. Considering just brute force applications helps to isolate the security dilemmas this particular kind of physical strength use poses in today's world. This analysis emphasizes the broad strategic context for force use, not specific tactics or training and morale methods.

Because of the distinctiveness of the post-9/11 security setting, this study chooses to cover only twenty-first-century brute force use, not that of earlier time periods. The terrorist attacks on the United States on September 11, 2001, appeared to alter prevailing global interpretations of both force effectiveness and force legitimacy: Although one could easily exaggerate the distinctiveness of this time period,[7] considerable evidence exists that coercion norms and practices have undergone recent transformation. Studying so recent a time period has drawbacks in that this sharply limits the diversity of cases selected and the certainty that these cases have fully played themselves out, but this choice also has benefits in that it fosters homogeneity in the global security context, increasing the chances that this analysis can prioritize situations best and worst for brute force, taking into account the distinctive obstacles and opportunities present in today's world.

As to geographical scope, this study's coverage of brute force is explicitly global, incorporating both Western and non-Western force initiators. There is no special focus on any one particular country or region and no reliance on any one set of narrow security interests. The incorporation of both developed and developing countries' force use captures appropriately the full range of relevant security implications.

This analysis focuses on brute force applications exclusively initiated by state governments, not by private groups or individuals. Within today's global security setting, national governments possess the greatest incentives to use force to keep ruling regimes in power. Even with the proliferation of weaponry to private citizens, and widespread terrorist-initiated violence, state governments still possess the greatest potential for (1) force effectiveness, given their preponderance of lethal firepower; and (2) force legitimacy, given the security-promoting social contract embedded in the Westphalian system. So the greatest international surprise, disappointment, and resentment occur when state-initiated force fails.

This investigation incorporates both internal and external state brute force use. Most studies deal with only one or the other, but not both, because they see the two as so distinctive. In contrast, this study assumes that key commonalities exist between the two in security patterns, and it attempts to link wherever possible what goes on within states to what goes on across states. For example, how conceptually distinct are the Indian crackdown in Kashmir (technically internal) and the Russian invasion of Georgia (technically external)? Recently, internal force uses have had major international implications, and external force uses have had major domestic repercussions.

This book covers only major brute force uses. Major brute force use occurs where political stability threats are centrally involved, unlike minor internal state force uses to put down petty criminal threats with little impact or relevance to national security. So although the most common state use of force may be to crack down on internal criminal violence, that type of application is not the focus of the cases (although it is represented by the Mexican government's use of force against the drug lords).

This study encompasses brute force use during both wartime and peacetime, for "the peaceful uses of military power can have as central an effect on state relations as does its warlike use."[8] Moreover, because recent war–peace distinctions have been difficult—thanks to the frequency of undeclared wars and forceful acts of military intervention that resemble wars—excluding one or the other seems to make little sense. War and peace are on a continuum, representing interconnected but differing phases of statecraft.[9] Furthermore, military confrontations often morph dramatically over the course of the applied coercion, and observers may categorize such confrontations differently. Finally, in terms of global import, occasionally peacetime military interventions or police crackdowns short of full-scale war have more significant security repercussions than highly localized wars.

This study emphasizes brute force security implications—considering human security, state security, and regional and global security—and includes both short-run and long-run military and political, economic, and social impacts. Simply scrutinizing immediate success or failure in force effectiveness and legitimacy is insufficient. Because mission objectives may target the mass public as well as a regime, and force may have collateral damage on civilians, bottom-up human security concerns—including socioeconomic consequences—seem critical in gauging overall force outcomes.

Given this overall scope, this study assumes that brute force use is not random or haphazard, instead exhibiting significant enduring patterns of success and failure. To draw its insights, this book relies on comparative case study analysis incorporating force use description, purpose and rationale of force initiators and targets, force effectiveness, force legitimacy, and future prospects. To overcome the dual obstacles of preconceived biases about brute force and the absence of objective hard data on brute force outcomes, this study relies on the widest range of sources from all perspectives.

## KEY DEFINITIONS

### Meaning of Brute Force

Brute force entails the tangible physical application of military or police strength directly against a designated target for a designated purpose, usually to compel an enemy to submit to or comply with one's will by impeding, constraining, or otherwise altering a foe's behavior. Brute force is typically used against unwilling opponents who would not otherwise follow one's wishes. State-initiated brute force use occurs when "physical actions are taken by one or more components of the uniformed military services as part of a deliberate attempt by the national authorities to influence, or to prepare to influence, specific behavior of individuals"[10] either inside or outside a force initiator's country. On a continuum going from attempts to influence via diplomatic persuasion to attempts to use power via the threat of force to attempts to compel via the application of force, brute force falls on the most severe end of the scale: "To step across the threshold between applying non-violent pressure and using lethal force is a profound act—a step into an arena in which opponents constrained by very few rules are compelled to prevail by inflicting death, destruction, and psychological suffering on one another."[11]

Brute force, constituting the purest kinetic use of the "stick" rather than the "carrot," provides starkly direct avenues for attaining objectives, such as blocking a forceful takeover, destroying a threatening facility, exterminating an enemy, occupying an area militarily, or seizing foreign assets. Brute force is a form of "hard power," entailing the deployment of ground troops and naval and air combat units to attain designated objectives, in contrast to "soft power," involving persuading others about the attractiveness of one's values and ideas.[12] Brute force involves "both the physical means of destruction—the bullet, the bayonet—and the body that applies it."[13] This tool contrasts with (1) cyber-disruption, where the physical effects are downstream rather than direct or immediate; (2) coercive diplomacy, where force is threatened but not applied; and (3) "shows of force," where force is prominently displayed and sometimes demonstrated but not directly attacking an enemy.

The term *brute force* is bandied about pejoratively in many settings. When combined with certain value-laden terminology—such as *political repression, violent crackdown,* or *naked aggression*—reference to brute force may often reflect from the outset highly partial assessments rejecting the desirability of this policy instrument. Outside international relations, even in the field of computer science, brute force generally signals a primitive, inelegant solution.

Due to these nasty connotations, three clarifications seem essential at the outset. First, brute force does not equate with Carl Von Clausewitz's notion of "absolute war," in which the cataclysmic goal is complete annihilation of the target: Absolute war is designed to compel targets to comply without compromise or restraint,[14] applying military strength in an unconstrained manner to obliterate the enemy quickly, completely, and permanently. Instead, brute force can be applied in either an overwhelming or a limited and carefully tuned manner. Second, although brute force use usually involves injuring or killing people and damaging or destroying property, this is not inevitable—a tangible physical application of military strength could occur directly against a designated target for a designated purpose with no human deaths or property damage, such as when a state army invades enemy territory, marches all the way to the capital city, and takes over the country while encountering no forceful resistance. Third, brute force may incorporate either deterrence or compellence elements (or a combination of both).

Regardless of terminology, brutality is usually involved in brute force use, with lethal weapons wreaking incredible death and destruction.[15] Brute force is thus "a blunt instrument" regardless of "how precise and surgical the application of violence."[16] Nonetheless, brute force is distinguished from pure brutality because the application of physical strength may not involve gratuitous violence without purpose. The adjective *brute* is used throughout this study—although it is generally avoided in most force analyses—simply to convey that military or police strength is actually applied (not just displayed or threatened) and that carnage is typically involved.

### Meaning of Force Success

Brute force use success is a function of a combination of its effectiveness and legitimacy. Many studies focus simply on force effectiveness, with some equating effectiveness with overall force success or even having an implicit "might-makes-right" premise that military victors can control perceived force legitimacy. However, sometimes perceived illegitimacy leads to coercive outside intervention, and sometimes enhancing force legitimacy undercuts force effectiveness.

### Meaning of Force Effectiveness

Force effectiveness gauges the degree to which the direct tangible physical application of military or police strength against a designated target achieves designated mission objectives. This often occurs through applying the "capability to impose unacceptable costs"[17] on force targets. Specification of mission objectives is necessary to determine force effectiveness; if these objectives change, then force effectiveness determination would have to fluidly transform as well. Force effectiveness involves some key distinctions: (1) short-term versus long-term force effectiveness; (2) force effectiveness for national security versus for regional or global security; (3) force effectiveness for state security versus for human security; and (4) force effectiveness for military objectives versus for political, economic, or social objectives. Although the alternatives in each of these four areas are not mutually exclusive, they do reflect different emphases that could ultimately produce differences in the way success is measured. The most common force effectiveness errors are to focus just on immediate military outcomes rather than long-range objectives; national security rather than regional or global security; state security rather than human security; and political-military objectives rather than socioeconomic objectives. Force uses cannot be considered effective if target "compliance did not last for long"[18] and failed to accomplish broader strategic objectives.

## Meaning of Force Legitimacy

Force legitimacy gauges the extent to which the direct tangible physical application of military or police strength against a designated target conforms to widely embraced moral and legal principles. Specifically, this usually involves "the compatibility of the results of governmental output with the value patterns of the relevant system,"[19] involving maintenance of fairness/justice, following due process, adherence, and compliance with the popular will in determining leadership and making decisions.[20] With this meaning in mind, it is not surprising that "state use of brute force today raises key legitimacy questions."[21] In practice, however, state political leaders often judge force legitimacy simply by the degree of national and global approval, a somewhat controversial measure because public support for force use may derive simply from its quick and low-cost success even if prevailing norms and principles are violated and dirty tactics are used. The primary error in judging force legitimacy is basing conclusions on one's own standards and values rather than sensitively taking into account those of either force initiators or force targets.

# 2 MODERN COERCION CONUNDRUM

IN THE TWENTY-FIRST CENTURY, global system transformation (shown in Figure 2-1) and national might misperception (shown in Figure 2-2) have led to a modern coercion conundrum. The global system setting sets the tone for acceptable tolerance norms, common practices, and constraints and opportunities surrounding brute force—political leaders who decide whether to apply force do not do so in a vacuum. Within this setting, these leaders often develop distorted views of confrontations, involving overblown expectations about coercive benefits. The modern coercion conundrum consists of five paradoxes (shown in Figure 2-3): perplexing persistence, eroding effectiveness, military maladjustment, lessening legitimacy, and chaotic consequence.

## CONCEPTUAL CONTEXT OF COERCION CONUNDRUM

### Global System Transformation

Recently the presumed global order has been gradually slipping away, with (1) increasing deviations from Westphalian premises; (2) conflicting coercion norms and practices; (3) clashes among anarchy, sovereignty, and globalization; and (4) vanishing global "rules of the game."[1] Together these elements incorporate the security-challenging combination of decreasing state-imposed effective restraint on uncivilized behavior and increasing freedom among disruptive unruly elements. This transformation impedes force success.

The Westphalian system's assumptions are that stability derives from the coercive state with its monopoly on instruments of violence used to maintain social order and that, through coercion, a state can suppress the subnational

*Deviation from Westphalian Premises*

**Original Premises**

Coercive states with monopoly on instruments of violence are supposed to use force to maintain social order.

**Prevailing Realities**

Today globally much of the mass public receives inadequate security protection from their state governments.

*Conflicting Coercion Norms and Practices*

**Changing Coercion Norms**

Cold War's end created expectation of a move away from violent confrontation and toward peaceful cooperation.

**Changing Coercion Practices**

States feel free to use brute force internally and externally.

*Clash among Anarchy, Sovereignty, and Globalization*

**Anarchy**

. An anarchic global security setting has reemerged resembling the Wild West.

**Sovereignty**

State sovereignty concerns increase reluctance to engage in more restrained concerted joint action with other states.

**Globalization**

Globalization may unwittingly increase state brute force use to achieve control and stable predictability.

*Vanishing Global "Rules of the Game"*

**Absence of Universal Rules of Behavior**

In the absence of a universal global rule set, powerful players feel few constraints on their behavior.

**Advantages for Weaker Players**

Violating the presumed rules of the game may be a means for weaker players to escape from a stifling status quo.

**Figure 2-1.** Global system transformation.

*Military Misperception*

**Overestimating Weapons Technology Meaningfulness**
Overstating how weapons capabilities equate with force potential
and force potential with force use
Overstating trust in the value of advanced war-fighting technology

**Overestimating Military Advantage Decisiveness**
Overstating the versatility of soldiers in successfully undertaking
potentially conflicting roles
Overstating the sufficiency of force superiority—a favorable
initiator–target power ratio—for mission success

**Overestimating Strategic Force Effectiveness**
Overstating force effectiveness—ability to overcome decisively
any obstacle
Overstating expectations for a spectacular array of strategic gains

**Overestimating Post-Force Policy Preparedness**
Understating probability of ensuing action–reaction cycles and
regional contagion effects
Understating need for contingency planning in
case of miscalculation

*Political Misperception*

**Overestimating Security Threat Predictability**
Overstating the threatening nature of opponents' political goals
Understating need for political change to cope with differing force
consequences

**Overestimating Universal Political Legitimacy**
Overstating force legitimacy—involving unwavering mass public
support—locally and globally
Overstating other states' admiration for postforce political
arrangements

**Overestimating Global Onlooker Awareness**
Overstating outsiders' accurate recognition of force participants'
political plight and purpose
Overstating global obligations to assist in postforce reparations

**Overestimating Post-Force Target Adaptability**
Overstating the ease of postforce transformation of a force target's
political system
Overstating the ease of postforce transference of power to local force
target authorities

*Economic Misperception*

**Overestimating Favorable Cost-Benefit Ratio**
Overstating the tangible postforce financial benefits accruing to the force initiator
Understating the costs of postforce economic assistance to force targets

**Overestimating Post-Force Economic Resilience**
Understating the obstacles impeding postforce economic reconstruction in force targets
Understating the reluctance of local business people to abandon traditional practices

*Social Misperception*

**Overestimating Post-Force Social Tranquility**
Understating force targets' ensuing social turmoil and ease of movement to a new social order
Overstating human security benefits from force use

**Overestimating Post-Force Value Transformation**
Overstating the chances of force target society adoption of the initiator's social value system
Understating the persistence of traditional local values

**Figure 2-2.** National might misperception.

violence that might ensue when those within national territory disruptively compete over scarce resources and thereby eliminate internal fears about individual and group security within a country. The presumed social contract has citizens remaining loyal to the state and continuing to pay taxes in return for state security protection. Although this Westphalian ideal of complete central government control of all instruments of violence was never fully realized, for centuries it provided a central guiding norm. However, for the first time since the emergence of the nation-state, now more weapons are in the hands of private citizens than in the hands of national governments,[2] and so ongoing threats now operate within a system where states no longer have anything close to a monopoly on instruments of violence.[3] Moreover, many members of the mass public receive inadequate security protection from their states, many citizens disapprove of the ways in which their governments employ

### Perplexing Persistence Paradoxes

Although global violence is declining, brute force recently seems to be persisting and even flourishing—involving both Western and non-Western state initiators—and state military expenditures seem to be robust.

### Eroding Effectiveness Paradoxes

Although both Western and non-Western states employ brute force frequently, the recent record of attaining strategic outcomes seems dismal, with even successful applications of brute force often yielding puny payoffs.

### Military Maladjustment Paradoxes

Although strategic mission futility has been evident, brute force uses, particularly by Western states, recently seem to be halfhearted, without appropriate objectives attainable through force or sufficient staying power.

### Lessening Legitimacy Paradoxes

Although the dynamics of brute force by necessity are anti-democratic and usually involve killing people and destroying property, Western states recently seem to portray their brute force use as an instrument of justice.

### Chaotic Consequence Paradoxes

Although post-force impacts often prove disastrous, both Western and non-Western states recently seem to have done little advance planning for minimizing ensuing action-reaction cycles or regional contagion effects.

Figure 2-3. Modern coercion conundrum.

their coercive capabilities, and many people across the world rely on private rather than public security. From a human security perspective, state force thus could be perceived as irrelevant, ineffective, or even illegitimate.

Coercion norms and coercion practices have been significantly transforming in opposite directions, with norms becoming more restrictive and constrained and practices becoming less restricted and constrained. Over time, the perceived legitimacy of force use declined, yet anticipation of perceived illegitimacy does not always decrease willingness to use force: "Ironically, the declining domain of the legitimacy of military force, and the diminishing discretion accorded over style of military use, render force particularly attractive to some belligerents."[4] A monumental void can exist between force legitimacy resting on sympathy or respect from onlookers and force effectiveness resting on fear or terror by designated targets.

Underlying this inconsistency between coercion norms and practices has been the clash among anarchy, sovereignty, and globalization. Following the end of the Cold War, and especially after the 9/11 terrorist attacks on the United States, a largely anarchic global security setting reemerged where control is low over what transpires within one's territory or across one's borders and where relationships with others become more fluid: "The characteristic features of contemporary world politics—especially the volatility of international alignments and animosities and the difficulty of mobilizing a concerted response to aggression—created a highly permissive environment that tempts aggrieved states and ethnic and religious communities to satisfy their demands with force."[5] Focusing on anarchy can lead to the persistence of "Wild West" security practices: For the rowdiest members of the global community, no form of force seems off limits, and, even for status quo powers, the gloves are off—just as in the old West sheriffs posted wanted posters with cash rewards for notorious outlaws, so in modern times the United States offered a $25,000,000 "wanted dead or alive" bounty on Osama bin Laden's head (prior to his killing). Regarding national sovereignty, territorial jurisdiction, privilege to possess and use weapons and standing armies, and "no-compromise" pursuit of national rights suggest state resort to force without hesitation. Focusing on sovereignty can lead to reluctance to engage in more restrained concerted joint action—that might make force unnecessary—with others facing common threats. Reinforcing unilateral coercive action is the expectation that such force use would be legitimate in the Westphalian system. Regarding globalization, although some observers credit globalization claims that force is not used when complex interdependence prevails under globalization[6] due to cooperation associated with common cross-national interests, globalization often unwittingly increases force use by states seeking control and stable predictability. Focusing on globalization can thus highlight states' considerable vulnerability to disruption.

Regarding vanishing global "rules of the game," with the Cold War bipolar rules largely gone, there appears to be little understanding of—or compliance with—a new set of rules (commonly accepted strategic principles governing force use). In the absence of a uniform universal rule set that is consistently voiced and followed, each party seems freer to behave according to its own idiosyncratic premises. The West assumes its rules are universal and either projects them in a misleading way onto others (interpreting others' behavior in terms of its own rules) or attempts in vain to impose them directly onto others and obtain compliance. With major powers still clinging to a largely outmoded set of rules, weaker states are able to ignore them, and nonstate groups can subvert them. Attempts to establish a more coherent universal set of rules—especially by the West—runs the risk of comparison to the most virulent forms of cultural imperialism: For disenfranchised states, the notion of common rules of the game in today's world is reminiscent of an era where they sacrificed autonomy in their foreign security policy for what they perceived to be an arbitrary and oppressive world order. Resulting frustration by both developed and developing countries can engender force use.

### National Might Misperception

Given this global system transformation, political leaders employing force have often harbored interconnected military, political, economic, and social force misperceptions, distortions, and delusions,[7] enhancing the potential for force failure. Moreover, interactive misperception can cause each side to assume that it is viewing matters relatively accurately and that its foe is misperceiving. The roots of these misperception patterns are so deep that they may persist even in the face of high-quality intelligence collected about adversaries' capabilities and intentions.

Three bodies of psychological theory identify key force misperception processes incorporating the projection of fears or desires onto others: (1) selective attention, ignoring incoming information that contradicts preexisting images;[8] (2) wishful thinking, focusing just on positive outcomes where desires take precedence over expectations;[9] and (3) cognitive bolstering, seeking out evidence to enhance the credibility of preexisting beliefs.[10] Regarding force success, selective attention deemphasizes force use obstacles; wishful thinking exaggerates force use's speed, magnitude, duration, and seamlessness; and cognitive bolstering creates an illusion of force success. Although heads of state often fall prey to the optimistic pattern of projecting desires when applying force, ironically military commanders who implement force often resort to pessimistic fear-driven worst-case analysis because they are responsible for carrying out their mission no matter what roadblocks they face.

Force initiators exhibit a robust mix of misunderstandings. The military misperceptions associated with brute force use are overestimating weapons technology meaningfulness, military advantage decisiveness, strategic force effectiveness, and postforce policy preparedness. The political misperceptions associated with brute force use are overestimating security threat predictability, universal political legitimacy, global onlooker sensitivity, and postforce target adaptability. The economic misperceptions associated with brute force use are overestimating favorable cost–benefit ratios and postforce economic resilience. The social misperceptions associated with brute force use are overestimating postforce social tranquility and postforce value transformation. Together these reflect state exaggeration of military success, exaggeration of achievement of political and diplomatic aims and global approval for doing so, understatement of the effort needed to achieve economic goals tied to force use, and exaggeration of initiator ability to promote human security and foster compliance in target societies.

## PERPLEXING PERSISTENCE PARADOXES

Although global violence and war are declining, brute force recently seems to be persisting and even flourishing—with both Western and non-Western state initiators—and state military expenditures seem to be robust.

An examination of state-initiated force confirms that, despite the apparent decline in interstate warfare and in aggregate global violence, brute force use persists both within and between states. In addition, the expenditure on instruments of force—and the preparation for force application—continues. Thus brute force use is somewhat out of sync with the current global coercive context.

### Continued Force Use despite Reduced Global Violence

A key perplexing persistence paradox is: Why do states employ brute force so much when recently global violence seems to be decreasing? State-initiated brute force generated considerable violence in the twentieth century, when 84 percent of all military and civilian deaths caused by war since 1700 took place.[11] Given that World War II was the most destructive conflict ever, with a staggering 19.4 million people killed in battle, and that in each subsequent decade at least 10 million people died in conflict,[12] many believe that the twentieth century was the most barbaric period in history.[13] During that century, killing of innocent civilians was often intentional rather than accidental:

> The Nazis killed six million Jews in the Holocaust. Millions of Chinese died in the brutal Japanese conquest of the 1930s and 1940s. Between 1975 and 1979, the Khmer Rouge killed two million people in Cambodia. About 800,000 civilians died in the systematic slaughter of men, women, and children in the Rwanda Civil War in 1994.[14]

In World War I, the 13 million civilian deaths outnumbered the 8.5 million military deaths, and the humanitarian organization Save the Children reports that "the percentage of civilians killed and wounded in conflicts has risen from five percent of all casualties at the beginning of the 20th century to 65 percent during World War II to 90 percent toward the end of the century."[15]

Nonetheless, although the overall scope of current global violence is truly staggering,[16] by the twenty-first century aggregate rates of violence had diminished compared to the bloodiest periods of world history.[17] Indeed, today a far smaller percentage of people die violently than a few hundred years ago:[18]

> In the first half of the twentieth century, world wars killed *tens of millions* and left whole continents in ruins. In the second half of that century, during the Cold War, proxy wars killed *millions*, and the world feared a nuclear war that could have wiped out our species. Now, in the early twenty-first century, the worst wars, such as Iraq, kill *hundreds of thousands*.[19]

After the early 1990s, the annual number of armed conflicts has steadily declined,[20] and far fewer people have died in wars:[21] One estimate suggests that in the last thirty years the number of deaths from war violence has decreased by 75 percent.[22] Some observers even conclude that the global violence decline is a sign that humanity is gradually evolving to become more civilized.[23]

At the same time, however, in the twenty-first century states—both developed and developing countries—have persisted in applying brute force externally and internally. Although the exact purposes for using force have changed over time,[24] it seems that state leaders almost out of habit persist in believing that force is effective.[25] Notably, the global community has repeatedly displayed sustained tolerance for state-initiated force, sometimes even providing encouragement to state force initiators. In the end, current global system norms and coercive restraints have been insufficient to prevent

(1) major powers from exercising brute force unilaterally in foreign countries and (2) weaker states from exercising brute force unilaterally against segments of their own domestic populations. In particular, in the twenty-first century great powers have not exhibited the peaceful orientation often attributed to them. Notably, "since the end of the Cold War, the US, and to a lesser but significant extent Britain and France, have used force more often than they did before."[26] Reflecting on recent patterns, "an increasing number of state and non-state actors have displayed an indifference to international norms and law as well as conventional forms of conflict resolution, and have demonstrated a preparedness to adopt offensive strategies that have the potential to challenge the traditional security architecture."[27]

The 9/11 terrorist attacks on the United States seem to have expanded its willingness to use brute force. Persistent political tensions, enduring military rivalries, and residual security fears have thwarted expected post–Cold War military contraction.[28] Despite enlightened Western norms promoting co-operation through negotiation, in the twenty-first century American policy makers have "increasingly turned to the use of limited force" to achieve their goals and seem likely to rely on it for the foreseeable future.[29] Such leaders appear more willing to use force to pursue national interests[30] despite notable failures in Afghanistan and Iraq.[31] Due to American global dominance and frequent use of force, others now feel freer to use force due to the precedent set.[32]

In the twenty-first century, weaker states have also demonstrated a proclivity to use force, especially in violent internal crackdowns. Since the end of the Cold War's violence-dampening bipolar pressures, the lid has opened on long-simmering rivalries within states, and internal divisions—especially ethnic and economic ones—have blossomed, with subnational groups feeling freer to express their desire for autonomy. The result has been a rise in domestic threats to weaker regime control, and in response state coercive repression of internal dissent has expanded. Ethnic and nationalist conflict has blossomed, often involving state brute force use:[33] "Many governments, from the Philippines to India to Colombia, are waging overt or covert wars against resistance movements and government opponents, fostering a climate of fear in which arms and equipment are used for containing domestic dissent and security crackdowns against 'enemies within.'"[34] Domestic "military intervention, and the repression to which it often leads, is frequently treated as a necessary evil required by an inevitably disruptive development process";[35]

and even some established democracies, such as Thailand and Greece, have repeatedly resorted to brute force use despite lip service to civil discourse as a means of resolving internal disputes.

Finally, regardless of global violence's frequency, due to higher global awareness the mass public feels incredibly vulnerable in the twenty-first century. For example, after the Boston Marathon bombing on April 15, 2013, one bystander said, "That's the worst part for me—it can happen anywhere, at any time, and we're not prepared for that."[36] Uncertainty reigns about how to lower this vulnerability.[37] The 9/11 terrorist attacks "have created an atmosphere where it seems as if no new security precaution or security expenditure to protect against threat could be too great."[38]

### Advanced Arms Acquisition despite Negligible Utility

Another perplexing persistence paradox is: Why do states try so hard to acquire state-of-the-art weaponry in preparation for brute force when recently this effort seems so expensive and modern confrontations seem to involve largely small vintage arms? Given the opportunity costs of advanced weapons investment, it is puzzling that many national governments push to acquire advanced weaponry although domestically and internationally force success has at least recently depended more on standard low-level firearms such as the AK-47 rifle. "Victory through technology"[39] assumptions are undercut by the reality that high-tech munitions may not best manage modern confrontations.

Globally, the state capacity to apply brute force remains robust. In 2001, collectively state military expenditures totaled $839 billion, representing 2.6 percent of the global gross domestic product and $137 for every person living on the planet.[40] In 2011, global military spending was about $1.5 trillion, with about 20 million people in regular government armed forces and about 20,000 nuclear warheads stockpiled.[41] Possessing faith in advanced technology, states become concerned that, if they do not keep up in regional or global races, in the future they would be critically disadvantaged relative to enemies.[42] Often arms acquisition is not motivated by intent to deploy them—for example, North Korea and Iran may want nuclear weapons not to use them but for symbolic bargaining purposes.

This pattern of robust military expenditure has been evident outside of great powers. In many developing countries, military capability is based more on advanced weapons systems and highly skilled soldiers than on mass mobilization of "people's armies".[43] Despite the high cost of military expenditures, developing countries engage in them due to "neighborhood arms races or the patronage demands of politically powerful military establishments."[44] Moreover, because developing state governments fear internal revolts and civil wars, they still depend on military force to stay in power and enlarge their defense expenditures to deter such domestic disruptions, whose incidence is high due to the lack of economic development.[45] For these countries, "advanced military technologies . . . have become a measure of status and modernity in the global military culture above and beyond their instrumental value."[46] However, in such cases high military expenditure to enhance force preparedness has often not achieved its goal of deterring internal rebellions, for such expenditure can contribute to poor economic performance, thus increasing the risk of internal violent disruption.[47]

Indeed, today possession of superior military strength does not guarantee success—"Military capabilities are a double-edged weapon in international politics," with "more is better" seriously challenged as a universal rule.[48] At the highest level, pushing to acquire weapons of mass destruction can be seen as a desperate cry for attention, often resulting in states' isolation and decreased status and influence. Advanced weapons acquisition can backfire: Sometimes a military buildup's benefits can be outweighed by other states' negative reactions, and possession of military capabilities can lead to overconfidence and excessive risk taking.[49] In some countries, arms expenditures associate with a callous "might-makes-right"[50] social order, a "police state" mentality involving the societal intensification of militarization, arms races, and diversion of scarce resources to arms procurement.[51]

In the twenty-first century, it is hard for anyone to keep pace in a technological arms race due to the speed of weapons development and the ease of buying arms on the global marketplace. Moreover, prospects of most state government armies attaining large-scale force using state-of-the-art weaponry seem remote because these arms have become prohibitively expensive. The cost of modern military equipment is skyrocketing, so today, for many states with small budgets, defense resources for these expenditures are exceedingly scarce.

## ERODING EFFECTIVENESS PARADOXES

Although both Western and non-Western states employ brute force frequently, the recent record of attaining strategic outcomes seems dismal, with even successful applications of brute force often yielding puny payoffs.

Strategic futility is a common twenty-first-century force outcome, yet states continue to use force due to their emphasis on short-term gains or belief in its deterrence or compellence benefits. The futility may be due to states applying force at the wrong time or in the wrong way. Moreover, states resorting to force may ultimately find it too costly a means to achieve their strategic objectives.[52]

### Force Reliance despite Long-Run Futility

A central eroding effectiveness paradox is: Why do states use brute force so much when recently it has seemed so futile in achieving long-term strategic objectives? Brute force may be successful in the short run but counterproductive in the long run.[53] Today many political leaders seem still convinced that violence is decisive[54] and often exhibit misunderstanding of the force paradox, where superior military capabilities do not yield larger postforce gains.[55] Specifically, states often use force because they overestimate their ability to prevail in armed conflict:[56] They exaggerate the deterrence and compellence benefits attained from military escalation and force use, seeing what they expect to see projecting wishful thinking onto force outcomes.

Brute force outcome expectations have changed considerably over time. In the past, a simple calculus existed—if you possessed superior might, and if your goal was territorial conquest, you were successful. There was little worry about constrained battle modes, postforce reconstruction, or outside opinion, and force initiation yielded respect and glory: "In earlier eras it was commonly believed that war brought out the best in individuals and nations, and that the virtues of discipline, risk-taking, and self-sacrifice that war required were central to civilization."[57] Now, however, prudent states no longer assume that military victory will automatically lead to strategic success, and the link between the military goal and the political aim has become more indirect.[58]

Engaging in violent conflict can become an exercise in futility, failing to achieve the initiator's ideal outcome.[59] For example, the wars in Iraq and Afghanistan have been "defined by strategic stalemate and failure at enormous financial, human and political cost."[60] Specifically, the United States and its allies have not found ways to translate their military superiority into adversary compliance when dealing with foes who violate human rights, commit acts of terror, or pursue weapons of mass destruction:[61] Between 1991 and 2009, American force uses achieved all military objectives just over half of the time, and all political objectives less than 6 percent of the time.[62]

Age-old assumptions about strategic force benefits now seem shaky: "The long-assumed equation between military capability and strategic effect, and between material power and security—where more of one implies more of the other—no longer holds," with often the possession of greater power provoking attack or technological superiority being overwhelmed by an adversary's greater knowledge of battle conditions.[63] Political leaders may cling to outmoded security premises despite disappointing coercive outcomes, ignoring that their force use may result from strategic assumptions that have been rendered invalid by a transformed global security context.[64]

Often winners in confrontations face larger obligations than losers. Many decades ago, a book (and subsequent movie) entitled *The Mouse That Roared* described a tiny fictional state initiating a war against the United States with the express purpose of losing so that this small country could reap substantial economic reparations;[65] this work was in many ways prophetic of modern force's reverse payoff structure. In today's interdependent world, winning a war may be a losing financial proposition, as victory often entails such large economic responsibilities to a defeated party that few net material benefits flow back to the victor. A classic example occurred in the aftermath of World War II: France and Great Britain were on the victorious side, but afterward "never regained their former stature"; while Germany and Japan were vanquished states, yet afterward became major world powers.[66] Military winners now can paradoxically be saddled with huge reparation costs for losers while failing to achieve their own strategic goals—sometimes "it is not so good to win" and "it is not so bad to lose."[67] Moreover, an inverse relationship may exist today between force and mission effectiveness—*The U.S. Army/Marine Corps Counterinsurgency Field Manual* notes that "sometimes, the more force is used, the less effective it is," for "the more force applied, the greater the chance of collateral damage and mistakes."[68]

Nonetheless, some defense analysts contend that force can be just as effective today as in the past: They argue that "overwhelming force is inherently desirable," and militarily superior states "usually win."[69] They contend that "although "victory in battle does not ensure strategic or political success," "defeat all but guarantees failure."[70] Among this crowd, deep skepticism exists that any noncoercive alternative to force would be as effective:

Somehow, numerous smart people in Washington and academe appear to believe that those whom we most need to influence abroad will hear that we plan to co-opt them via soft power and will then happily let us do so. Being charitable, those who think this might work have either not spent enough time among non-Westerners and/or have spent too much time among people skilled at telling them the kinds of things they most want to hear.[71]

Political leaders naturally want to use their state's military power, especially if they are uncreative about thinking of any other reasonable option:[72] For example, as former American Ambassador to the United Nations Madeleine Albright exhorted to Colin Powell, "What's the point of having this superb military that you're always talking about if we can't use it?"[73]

### Quest for Decisive Victory despite Puny Security Payoffs

Another eroding effectiveness paradox arises—why do states so consistently expect substantial security payoffs from decisive military victory when recent brute force outcomes seem to suggest otherwise? Today military force cannot guarantee victory,[74] and even decisive victory has reduced payoffs:[75] Overwhelming defeat of enemies does not always foster the political, economic, and social change force initiators desire. Moreover, successful state force use overseas does not garner large domestic political support gains.[76]

Military victory has dissimilar and often contradictory meanings for winners and losers,[77] with criteria such as material gains and losses and tangibly satisfying stated aims playing less of a role.[78] Victory interpretations differ over (1) the time span needed after battlefield combat ends to gauge postforce payoffs; (2) the postforce ratio of gains to losses; and (3) the proper viewer vantage point for determining if victory is at hand. The proportion of force uses where there is a clear attainment of stated political, economic, and social ambitions has declined.[79] Military victory (success against the enemy on the battlefield) differs sharply from strategic victory (success against the enemy in information control, military deterrence, political self-determination, economic reconstruction, social justice, and diplomatic respect).[80]

Expecting military victory by itself to be sufficient for significant strategic payoffs seems unrealistic within today's global security setting.[81] Although "better armies still tend to win wars,"[82] relying on military superiority for postwar payoffs is decidedly risky. Corrupt local leaders endanger postforce reconstruction,[83] and disaffected local groups sabotage a force target's assets, preventing postforce spoils from flowing to the victor. Military superiority seems particularly unlikely to translate into strategic success in asymmetric confrontations, where a weaker state has more zeal for it than a more powerful state[84] and control over resources does not match willingness to incur costs.[85] The Vietnam War should have taught Americans that military superiority does not automatically produce political victory,[86] but Americans had to relearn this lesson during the 1993–1994 military debacle in Somalia.

## MILITARY MALADJUSTMENT PARADOXES

Although strategic mission futility has been evident, brute force uses particularly by Western states recently seem to be halfhearted, without appropriate objectives attainable through force or sufficient staying power.

Especially in external force uses by the West, states are not adjusting properly to twenty-first-century global challenges. This insufficient adaptation is due to internal constraints within force initiators' government and society, fluid external threats, and changing mission priorities and objectives. Political leaders need to find better ways to develop more nimble responses to the morphing security challenges if these issues are to be effectively addressed.

### Force Application despite Unintended Purposes

A pivotal military maladjustment paradox is: Why do Western states employ brute force recently so much for purposes—such as nation building and humanitarian aid—for which it seems not to be designed? Regarding appropriateness of strategic goals, recently Western states have often used force for ends where it does not possess a clear comparative advantage over other options. This seemingly indiscriminate force use may reflect incomplete acceptance of exactly what tasks force can and cannot accomplish well.

Although military force is explicitly designed to kill humans and destroy property, force faces significant limitations when asked to undertake military missions with unorthodox yet legitimate goals such as peace support, nation building, civil society installation, humanitarian aid, democracy implantation, or social services provision. Many of today's global conflicts center on competing attempts to win the hearts and minds of the people, and force alone cannot be expected to attain this objective, especially given how target populations often resent civilian casualties or excessive force.[87] Many force initiators naïvely expect that quick decisive action would be sufficient to attain effectively and legitimately long-range political, economic, and social objectives.

It may be impossible for soldiers to execute these multiple postforce functions with equal success. Despite the military "can-do" mentality, it is difficult to be adept at both coercive and noncoercive means to address this wide range of postforce needs, as General Anthony Zinni colorfully outlines:

> What is the role of the military beyond killing people and breaking things? Right now, the military in Iraq has been stuck with this baby. In Somalia, it was stuck with that baby. In Vietnam, it was stuck with that baby. And it is going to continue to be that way. We have to ask ourselves now if there is something the military needs to change into that involves its movement into this area of the political, economic, and information management. If those wearing suits cannot come in and solve the problem—i.e., cannot bring the resources, expertise, and organization—and the military is going to continue to get stuck with it, you have two choices. Either the civilian officials must develop the capabilities demanded of them and learn how to partner with other agencies to get the job done, or the military finally needs to change into something else beyond the breaking and the killing.[88]

Even the most optimistic onlookers admit that "expecting the same forces to do both high-intensity warfighting and stability operations requires a grinding shift of mental gears for individual warfighters."[89] As long as soldiers view combat as more heroic than conflict prevention or termination, then peacekeeping will be hampered.[90] Major trade-offs emerge between humanitarian and security challenges within war-torn societies:[91] For example, in the 2001 war on terror in Afghanistan, nongovernmental humanitarian organizations reported friction between their members and government soldiers—having military personnel wearing civilian clothing while carrying weapons "blurred the necessary distinction between members of the military and humanitarian workers, potentially putting the latter at risk."[92]

Even if soldiers could be highly adaptable, after brute force ceases, a force target's citizenry—including those who might eventually become new political leaders—may be understandably hesitant to be involved in any new political arrangement.[93] Postforce regime replacement is extremely difficult, with toppling an enemy leader a lot easier than installing with a force target state a new government "that could run a secure, viable country."[94] For force targets, tensions exist between strong-armed coercion experienced during a violent confrontation and the desire for self-reliance and voluntary participation afterward. Both Afghanistan and Iraq are now struggling with these tensions. Moreover, defeated state citizens' unrealistic high demands on an emerging government about immediate political and economic transformation can be a significant hindrance, leading to disillusionment and lower state credibility.[95]

Nonetheless, the failure rate associated with military force uses for unorthodox purposes may result more from the weaknesses of alternative nonmilitary noncoercive institutions and organizations than from the intrinsic limitations of soldiers and military force. Western states persist in using military force for purposes other than those for which it is designed because there are no other assets that can do the job: No other institutions, such as the Peace Corps or UNICEF, could conduct effectively a strategic lift of huge volumes of materials like food and medical care, across vast distances, and administer it quickly enough to the needy. People may turn to the military for these purposes because they lack anything else that has its reach and scale.

Within the United States, although much of the military is designed for peace support—such as the military police (MPs) who are highly trained for constabulary operations—often commitments for global peacekeeping exceed available resources; as a result, this task may rely instead on infantry troops, whose training is not well suited for that mission, for they are far more aggressive and respond more sharply to provocation. Moreover, the United States does not have superior capabilities for state building, to which it has not paid sufficient attention. The Department of State does try to accomplish this end, but a well-integrated interagency capacity is lacking. The Department of Defense has not sufficiently collected and assimilated lessons from recent mixed state-building experiences. Overall, the West seems far more competent at taking down regimes than at standing up effective replacements.

### Force Implementation despite Halfhearted Resolve

A second military maladjustment paradox is: Why have Western states recently used brute force so much in what seems like a halfhearted manner, lacking narrow/specific objectives and clear commitment or otherwise confused and unfocused? Sometimes force initiators have flimsy rationales, or the mass public, foreign onlookers, and even soldiers themselves lose track of the purposes justifying coercion. This problem can be so severe that those involved may not even be certain when or whether a mission is successfully accomplished. With the advantage of hindsight, many commentators have repeatedly voiced their extreme displeasure at "half-hearted warfare for half-baked reasons that the American people could not understand or support."[96]

Three deficiencies promote halfhearted force resolve: (1) absence of clear well-thought-out objectives; (2) unwillingness to commit sufficient resources in a timely manner; and (3) fear of civilian interference due to casualty sensitivity. These problems, often stemming from disagreements about force desirability, are mutually reinforcing, weakening the "will to fight" so vital to force use.[97] Hesitating in applying force after deciding to use it is usually foolish.

Regarding the first deficiency, internal tensions about where force should be used and for what purposes handicap Western states' force application. Recent force uses have sometimes been confused and poorly tuned to the situation at hand, reflecting "sloppy thinking about how to use force effectively."[98] In a nutshell, "the inability to readily define the precise mission" of a force use is sufficient to indicate that it is "ill-advised."[99] Force use may be unfocused, with vague or changing mission goals, few exit strategies, and little long-term consideration for postforce impacts. News reporting—whose journalists often misunderstand what they are see or try to erode public support for military operations—may amplify this confusion. Although military operations usually have crystal-clear objectives, force use's political aims as articulated by politicians often lack sufficient clarity for mission success.

Regarding the second deficiency, unconventional force use can pose a critical challenge for military resource allocation, involving a choice of whether to coercively intervene "in a big way, to overwhelm the insurgents with the weight of numbers and resources, or in a minimal way to avoid provoking popular resentment and resistance."[100] The United States has had an image of force tentativeness and "irresolution."[101] To compensate for miscalculations and to convey credible commitment, it is generally better to approach force use "with too much rather than too little firepower" because "force will more often fail if it is too light than if it is too heavy."[102] This risk-averse strategic approach can occasionally mean that it is functional to apply force massively from the outset of a confrontation.[103] This logic has led some analysts to inappropriately take a rigid binary "all-in" or "stay-out" position on force use, choosing between a huge well-armed force with a sustained commitment or no military involvement at all.

Regarding the third deficiency, casualty sensitivity—"the quest for bloodless war"—has recently caused Western states sometimes to be worried more about body bags than coercively accomplishing mission objectives.[104] Given the preference for technological firepower over human-to-human combat, "It has long been the American way in warfare to send metal in harm's way in place of vulnerable flesh."[105] To win wars, Western states need to maintain popular support; to maintain popular support, these governments must be sensitive to human casualties; and so casualty aversion seems inevitable due to public upset if lots of citizens die in battle.[106] Media coverage may expand state hesitation to take coercive action, with television especially dramatizing the human costs of brute force.[107] Moreover, the declining birth rates in advanced industrial societies may make families more unwilling to contemplate the loss of a son or daughter in wartime, increasing casualty sensitivity.[108] Although such caution is understandable, such logic is problematic when used against enemies who could not care less about human carnage, ultimately skewing of military force strategies, sacrificing mission effectiveness for force legitimacy through collateral damage minimization.

## LESSENING LEGITIMACY PARADOXES

Although the dynamics of brute force by necessity are antidemocratic and usually involve killing people and destroying property, Western states recently seem to portray their brute force use as an instrument of justice.

Confusion exists in the West, espousing enlightened liberal principles, about the relationship between brute force and justice. In the Wild West, justice was often administered at the end of a gun. In international relations, however, brute force use in internal or external confrontations can often reflect significant injustice. The twenty-first-century global security environment makes it daunting to demonstrate convincingly brute force legitimacy.

### Force Use despite Clash with Democratic Values

An important lessening legitimacy paradox is: Why have Western states recently used brute force so much when it seems to be widely perceived as associating with undermining enlightened democratic values? On the surface, a contradiction—or downright hypocrisy—seems evident: The West continues to use force widely to advance national interests at a time when enlightened values are spreading globally through waves of civil-discourse-oriented democratization and cooperation-oriented interdependence. It seems inherently counterproductive to promote civil discourse through force.

Many democracies experience discomfort when employing brute force for security, for "the concentration of military power that a government feels is required to defend a democracy against its enemies in certain ways poses an inherent threat to the very values it is designed to protect."[109] Valuing the dignity of human life, deeply embedded in democratic traditions, can be associated with brute force being viewed as repugnant. Most Western observers deem diplomacy as always preferable—in terms of fruitful conflict resolution and stability—to coercion. Thus, within democracies some minimum linkage threshold between brute force and justice seems essential for overall success: "Although control can be imposed at gunpoint, it can be maintained only if the security forces have some degree of popular legitimacy."[110]

For Western states, defending brute force legitimacy can certainly be problematic due to an inability "to find a domestically acceptable trade-off between brutality and sacrifice," between expedient and moral tolerance for the costs of war.[111] Externally, despite American President Barack Obama's explicit defense of the morality of the killing of bin Laden as an act of justice, many outsiders perceived the American coercive retaliation for the 9/11 terrorist attacks as an act of vengeance. Yet the United States—possibly motivated by fear, anger, and hatred comparable to that of the terrorists—openly took its gloves off in some circumstances to combat terrorists using the same type of ruthless tactics these groups have used against the West. Through many covert operations, the United States and some of its Western allies have indicated a willingness to circumvent democratic due process abroad in targeted killings and significant property destruction when vital national interests are at stake.

Recently, Western societies' objections have escalated about the morality of brute force. Skeptics contend that force use often violates human rights, national and international law, and prevailing justice norms and that abiding mutual respect and trust have not derived—and cannot derive—from force. This criticism is partially due to (1) growing humanitarian concerns deriving from more direct mass public vulnerability to global actions perceived as unjust; and (2) reflexive opposition to the use of military force where cynics are quick to seize on any evidence that it hurts innocent bystanders. Certainly "policymakers have less latitude to pursue policies that are controversial, uncertain in outcome, and potentially expensive, as military interventions tend to be."[112] For example, the American Department of Defense (as with other democracies' defense ministries) goes to great lengths to minimize collateral damage. As a result, "modern democracies have limited political tolerance for protracted overseas wars against irregular enemies";[113] with American force use displaying "distaste for prolonged occupations as messy, burdensome and corrupting of its own values."[114]

### Force Advocacy despite Minimal Global Status Enhancement

Another lessening legitimacy paradox is: Why do states use brute force so much to gain global status when recent coercion applications have seemed rarely to improve international image? In the past, successful force use directly led to advancement in the global status hierarchy, making it easier to influence other states and get them to comply. In contrast, recently the global status payoff from using force has been minimal, with few states eliciting admiration for using force to resolve internal or external security challenges.

Accumulating and applying force as means to engender admiration, prestige, influence, or domination appears problematic today in terms of international community reactions. Nonetheless, states doggedly pursue status increases through force use, expressing dismay when such increases fail to materialize on cue: If successful, force initiators expect global approval and increases in external political influence—deterrence and compellence—due to outside admiration for their possession and sophisticated use of weaponry and their cunning strategy and tactics on the battlefield. Yet in today's world military weapons buildup and force use appear more likely to generate criticism from international and transnational nongovernmental organizations and declining global status due to engaging in perceived bullying tactics.

For those at the top of the global hierarchy, the direct link between military might and global status appears to be receding. The absence of overarching global security values makes international resentment and "outright hostility" likely to emerge in response to virtually any victory in war by a powerful state[115] (particularly when a sizable power gap exists between winners and losers), no matter how the conflict ends or what terms are imposed. For example, recent American force uses overseas have created a significant foreign backlash.[116] The global influence of major powers is not exclusively a function of either possession or application of force capabilities.

For those at the bottom of this hierarchy, applying brute force may signal weakness to outsiders and result from regime ineptitude at running the country, providing basic services, or employing effectively other means of influence. Moreover, internal coercive repression by developing countries to restore order may not only fail to achieve desired target compliance but also reduce outside respect for initiating regimes. Thus state force use can be both a cause and consequence of fragile and failing states.

However, force use can on some occasions improve global image.[117] Force use may signify the failure of deterrence or diplomacy, not the failure of power. Military power can still enhance political, diplomatic, and economic power. State possession and exercise of superior military force capabilities successfully can sometimes serve to demonstrate state power, an image useful for both deterrence and compellence. States' always-visible military force capacity, undergirded by force use, can make their statements and positions more compelling. For example, China's military prowess not only intimidates Taiwan but also enhances its status as the dominant regional power.

Without military force, to acquire status one is left with a "war of ideas": Regarding the war on terror, former British Prime Minister Tony Blair stated, "My concern is that we cannot win this struggle by military means or security measures alone, or even principally by them . . . we have to put our ideas up against theirs."[118] This approach, originating soon after the 9/11 attacks, derives from the premise that the Western belief system is so far superior to that of terrorists that it will prevail in the global community if given sufficient exposure. However, in such a war of ideas, the West seems in many ways to be losing. Despite reference to Western beliefs in protests such as the twenty-first-century Arab Spring uprisings and the late-twentieth-century prodemocracy Tiananmen Square uprising, Western political, economic, and social ideas are often antithetical to some of those held by much of the non-Western world. When Western ideas are suggested to such countries, they may think that their religion or culture is being attacked, and backfire effects are common. So far the West has had difficulty finding an effective and legitimate way of countering the propaganda broadcasts emerging from sources such as al-Jazeera and al-Arabiya and hundreds of religious schools across the Middle East and the Arc of Instability, where population growth dwarfs that in the West.

## CHAOTIC CONSEQUENCE PARADOXES

Although postforce impacts often prove disastrous, both Western and non-Western states recently seem to have done little advance planning for minimizing ensuing action-reaction cycles and regional contagion effects.

States still plan mostly for how to win in coercive confrontations rather than how to establish stability and order afterward. This shortsightedness can often cause a militarily successful force use to fall flat on its face soon after the confrontation ends, triggering troublesome aftershocks. Although not everything that occurs in the wake of brute force use is either predictable or controllable, a lot more could be done in advance to minimize undesired postforce turmoil.

### Force Promotion despite Ensuing Action–Reaction Cycles

One chaotic consequence paradox is: Why do states employing brute force so consistently anticipate stable orderly outcomes when recently such force applications often trigger action–reaction cycles of violence and instability? When it comes to military capabilities, mutually escalating threats or use of force often directly results from one side's coercive action.[119] The long-term consequences could easily involve spiraling friction, "no-way-out" tit-for-tat entrapment, and ultimately an unending action–reaction cycle:[120] "However carefully planned at the outset, even small doses of violence delivered incrementally can provoke a spiral of retaliation and counterretaliation that escalates to a level of warfare that is disproportionate to the value of the interests essentially at stake."[121]

Especially in the twenty-first century, force use has triggered action–reaction cycles involving negative feedback loops where extreme brutality elicits emotional overreactive coercive responses.[122] Some argue that action–reaction cycles occur just because force initiators use insufficient overwhelming force to achieve their objectives, for if an enemy is completely obliterated with no possibility of regenerating, no action–reaction cycle would follow: For example, in the ongoing Syrian crisis, President Assad had to be willing to kill half of his population if he really wanted to eliminate the threat to his regime and prevent a tit-for-tat cycle of violence between public protesters and government soldiers. However, today limitations due to internal and external pressures usually prevent the kind of draconian action necessary to forestall this cycle. The dangerous escalation spiral can involve high uncertainty[123] and—if mismanaged—can indefinitely intensify. Once states get trapped in a mutual lockstep spiral, strategic thinking erodes, and tensions can eradicate any prospects for stable outcomes.

The action–reaction cycle does not just apply to states. For armed nonstate groups, brute force can often produce a similar escalatory tit-for-tat violent cycle impeding political negotiations,[124] especially if states brutally crack down on them to restore government control.[125] This simple but dangerous reflexive logic can directly apply to coercive counterterrorist responses:[126] When force is used against terrorists, it can trigger "a cycle of violence and counter-violence"[127] that counterproductively evokes mass fears of possible attack and uncertainty about government protection.[128]

Determining whether one side is responding to someone else's force use or instigating it on its own may depend on choice of time period (thus the concept "force initiator" is somewhat controversial). In today's anarchic world, coercive action–reaction cycles underscore the difficulties of pinpointing a clear aggressive initiator and a clear innocent victim. The global prevalence of action–reaction cycles also makes it difficult to get any meaningful sense of when a particular force interaction started or ended or whether a particular force use is offensive or defensive: For example, Islamic extremists may view al-Qaeda not as an offensive threat but rather as a response to threats/actions from the United States, and China may view its offensive military forces along the Straits of Taiwan (which the United States sees as an offensive threat) as a defense against Taiwan wanting to assert its independence. Labeling cycle initiators is particularly tricky when relevant parties transform, such as through regime change. So engaging in finger-pointing, trying to isolate who did what first and to punish the presumed guilty party, can be futile because such "eye-for-an-eye" retaliation requires tightly confirming instigator actions.

### Force Promotion despite Ensuing Regional Contagion Effects

A related chaotic consequence paradox is: Why do states employing brute force so consistently anticipate contained outcomes when recently coercion applications have frequently triggered regional contagion effects? For some time, it has been evident that "contagion of violence appears to be a universal phenomenon."[129] Often today violence spreads from perpetrators not only to victims but also to onlookers.[130] This contagion process helps to explain the spread of terrorism among neighboring countries, increasing the challenge of identifying indigenous sources of terrorism.[131]

Among the elements responsible for postforce violence contagion within a region are failing states, diffusion of instruments of violence, weak economic structures, widespread poverty, and a large refugee flow from nearby states.[132] External disruptive forces can play postforce divisive roles,[133] throwing their support behind a social faction that otherwise might have had to cooperate with others; as disgruntled groups in the force target society seek and receive support from outside, the chances of regional contagion of turmoil can esca-

late. Regarding internal brute force confrontations, ethni(
refugee flows can cause civil wars to spill over boundaries.¹
and alienated peoples in one area refer explicitly to trends i
source of justification and hope for their non–status quo a
states scrutinize each other's brute force use, and its security ~.....,..., w
see what is acceptable. The proliferation of transnational nonstate groups with
common interests serving as transmission belts across nearby areas makes violence patterns in one state seem likely to spread to another. Moreover, within
a globalized interdependent world, geographically isolating brute force effects
is difficult, for they dramatically increase the likelihood of disruptive revolutionary ideas spreading quickly across disgruntled populations in neighboring countries, as evidenced by the Arab Spring uprisings in the Middle East.

## CONCLUDING THOUGHTS

The identified coercion conundrum paradoxes are decidedly difficult to resolve. Opposing interpretations based on contrasting premises emerge about
what works and what is appropriate regarding the use of force. To address
this problem, this study will investigate for the twenty-first-century global security setting the circumstances most likely to promote success in achieving
specified mission objectives.

The nontransparent nature of force dynamics as an element of influence in
today's world makes states' tendency to misapply brute force easier to understand. Making state brute force use more coherent requires first and foremost
making the perplexing persistence, eroding effectiveness, military maladjustment, lessening legitimacy, and chaotic consequence dilemmas more understood and widely acknowledged in resulting transformed state policies. Being
cognizant of coercion conundrum paradoxes seems essential to any forward
movement in refining both the conceptual comprehension and the practical
application of brute force in international relations.

# 3 CASES OF STATE EXTERNAL BRUTE FORCE USE

THIS CHAPTER EXAMINES MAJOR twenty-first-century external state-initiated brute force incorporating political stability threats. The ten cases are the American drone strikes in Pakistan and Yemen, American killing of Osama bin Laden, American invasion of Afghanistan, American invasion of Iraq, French intervention in Mali, Israeli destruction of a Syrian nuclear facility, Israeli invasion of Lebanon, NATO coercion in Libya, North Korean sinking of a South Korean ship, and Russian invasion of Georgia. Major powers (except North Korea) have tended to project force internationally. Each case includes the description of the force use, the purpose and rationale of force initiators and targets, force effectiveness, force legitimacy, and future prospects.

## AMERICAN DRONE STRIKES AGAINST PAKISTAN AND YEMEN

### Force Description

Although President George W. Bush first began using drone strikes against terrorists in November 2002 in Yemen, it was President Barack Obama who massively escalated the program in 2009.[1] Since that time, the United States has initiated a major campaign of unmanned aerial drone strikes, primarily against targets within Pakistan and Yemen but also against Afghanistan and Somalia. For the United States, "no president has ever relied so extensively on the secret killing of individuals to advance the nation's security goals."[2] From 2009 to 2013, the United States initiated over 400 drone strikes as the centerpiece of its counterterrorism campaign, with strikes killing an estimated

3,300 al-Qaeda, Taliban, and other jihadists in Pakistan and Yemen (including over fifty senior leaders).[3] Through the drone campaign the United States constructed a very extensive apparatus to carry out targeted killings of suspected terrorists and covert tracking of other foes.[4] In implementing these strikes, usually the Central Intelligence Agency has managed most of them outside recognized war zones, such as in Pakistan, while the Defense Department has headed most of the operations in established theaters of conflict, such as in Iraq, Afghanistan, and Libya, but in some cases, such as in Yemen, the drone operations of the two agencies are integrated.[5]

### Purpose/Rationale

The primary purpose of the drone strikes is deterrence, killing pivotal al-Qaeda terrorists so as to pursue those responsible for the 9/11 terrorist attacks and to prevent future terrorist attacks on the United States.[6] The perceived advantage of this reliance on drones is that they are significantly cheaper than traditional fighter aircraft, so their usage not only potentially saves American lives but also saves money.[7] Nonetheless, President Obama's justification and action regarding the drone strikes reveal a significant rhetoric–reality gap: "When President Obama came into office, he pledged to end the 'war on terror' and to restore respect for the rule of law to America's counterterrorism policies"; but since that time "he has been just as ruthless and indifferent to the rule of law as his predecessor."[8] This hypocrisy, painfully visible to global observers, suggests that "American counterterrorism policy operates at cross-purposes: it provides a steady flow of arms and financial resources to governments whose legitimacy it systematically undermines by conducting unilateral drone strikes on their territory."[9]

Ironically, American heads of state have sought to defend the legality of the international drone strikes:

> The Bush and Obama administrations have sought to justify targeted killings under both domestic and international law. The domestic legal underpinning for U.S. counterterrorism operations and the targeted killing of members of the Taliban, al-Qaeda, and its affiliates across the globe is the 2001 Authorization for the Use of Military Force (AUMF), which the U.S. Congress passed just days after 9/11. The statute, which lawmakers reaffirmed most recently in the 2012 National Defense Authorization Act, empowers the president "to use all necessary and appropriate force" in pursuit of those responsible for

the terrorist attacks. . . . The White House maintains that the U.S. right of self-defense, as enumerated in Article 51 of the UN charter, may include the targeted killing of persons such as high-level al-Qaeda leaders who are planning attacks, both in and out of declared theaters of war. The administration's posture includes the prerogative to unilaterally pursue targets in states without their prior consent if that country is unwilling or unable to deal effectively with the threat.[10]

Underlying this legal defense is the assumption that the United States remains in a state of armed conflict with al-Qaeda.[11] However, cynical observers believe that American drone strikes occur because the country has no other effective options at its disposal to disrupt terrorist operations.[12]

### Force Effectiveness

The American drone strikes have had short-term military effectiveness, killing over half of al-Qaeda's identified leaders and making their replacement difficult:[13] "By killing key leaders and denying terrorists sanctuaries in Pakistan, Yemen, and, to a lesser degree, Somalia, drones have devastated al Qaeda and associated anti-American militant groups."[14] The drone strikes lower the morale and terrify, unnerve, and anger targeted groups.[15] Even with short-term effectiveness, drone strikes' efficiency remains relatively low, as only one out of every seven U.S. drone attacks in Pakistan kills a militant leader, and most of those killed are low-level fighters and innocent bystanders.[16]

Despite the immediate success of the attacks, the long-range impact remains murkier. Some analysts argue that they are effective here as well, claiming that, even taking into account long-range repercussions, the drone strikes on Pakistan and Yemen represent a sound example of effective force, denying the enemy shelter and protection and security and demonstrating that the United States can reach out and kill adversaries wherever they are.[17] However, killing suspected terrorists eliminates the possibility of extracting useful intelligence from them and can create outside sympathy—a former CIA general counsel said, "If they're dead, they're not talking to you, and you create more martyrs."[18] The strikes may thus backfire by "creating sworn enemies out of a sea of local insurgents" and may be thwarted due to al-Qaeda's speedy replacement of dead operatives.[19] Moreover, the scarcity of accurate current intelligence on alleged terrorists "remains a weak link" in the drone campaign.[20]

In the long run, drone strikes do not seem to stabilize targeted areas. First, despite the intensity of the strikes, Afghanistan and Pakistan still experience very high levels of terrorist violence.[21] The U.S. National Counterterrorism Center has acknowledged that violence in Pakistan has risen sharply since the initiation of the drone campaign.[22] Although local violence minimization is not the expressed goal of drone strikes, this increase in disorder is an ominous sign for force effectiveness. Second, these strikes "have not deterred Western would-be terrorists from traveling to Pakistan's tribal regions for training in militant camps."[23] Third, despite their number, drone attacks cannot stop a movement—they are so narrowly targeted, relatively so small in number, and so circumscribed by the self-imposed need to minimize collateral damage that many terrorist elements are spared. Fourth, in a related matter, the drone program frequently "neither ruptures group cohesion nor ideological commitment."[24] When performing an overall assessment of force effectiveness, the growing American reliance on drone strikes has "adverse strategic effects that have not been properly weighed against the tactical gains associated with killing terrorists," for "drone strikes corrode the stability and legitimacy of local governments, deepen anti-American sentiment and create new recruits for Islamist networks aiming to overthrow these governments."[25] Furthermore, questions continue about the extent to which drone strikes have really handicapped al-Qaeda: Due to these strikes, the al-Qaeda terrorist network may have become more decentralized, with the group's regional affiliates in Yemen, Iraq, Somalia, Nigeria, Mali, and elsewhere in North Africa "increasingly self-reliant and independent."[26]

### Force Legitimacy

For some observers, the reaction to this global use of force has been decidedly positive. Proponents of drone strikes contend that (1) drones' resulting civilian death toll is exaggerated for political purposes; (2) drones are the most discreet way to pursue militant leaders and their networks; and (3) drones "put fewer Americans in harm's way and provide a low-cost alternative to expensive and cumbersome conventional forces."[27] The American drone campaign has never attracted as much scrutiny as its terrorist detention or interrogation programs, and so public debate—at least about foreign drone strikes—"remains muted":[28] A *Washington Post*/ABC News poll revealed that 83 percent of respondents approved of the Obama administration's use of drones against terror suspects overseas.[29]

Among vocal critics, three persistent major concerns—(1) collateral damage, (2) backfire effects, and (3) sovereignty violation—have emerged as a result of the American campaign of antiterrorist drone strikes. Regardless of which al-Qaeda leaders are killed, critics continue to condemn the lethal tactic on moral, legal, and political grounds.[30] Heightening skeptics' accountability worries is that the "convergence of military and intelligence resources has created blind spots in congressional oversight."[31] Making matters worse is the veil of secrecy surrounding the drone program: "The most glaring problem is that the whole world knows about U.S. targeting practices but the U.S. government cannot talk about them openly—because the operations are either covert (which means they cannot be officially acknowledged) or classified (which means they cannot be discussed publicly), or both."[32]

Regarding collateral damage suffered by innocent civilians in the targeted areas, regardless of their precision in isolating targets, the drone attacks risk killing innocent civilians and fueling anti-Americanism overseas.[33] Estimates of the extent of the collateral damage vary widely.[34] Although civilian deaths have reportedly been declining recently, due to better intelligence and more precise weaponry,[35] "blowback from civil liberties and human rights groups is likely to grow in direct proportion to any increase in targeted killings."[36]

Regarding drone strikes' backfire effects, a major security worry is that, due to sympathy for those killed and anger toward the United States as a force initiator, al-Qaeda may be able through these actions to recruit more terrorists—albeit less experienced ones—than the drone strikes kill.[37] Within Yemen, for example, a leader in a major political party claims that the drone strikes are spawning more militants there.[38] Within Pakistan, unsurprisingly, almost 90 percent of the respondents located within the drone strikes' region oppose American military operations there:[39]

> The United States' unannounced and unacknowledged war against Pakistan in the form of drone attacks launched from sites in Afghanistan and Pakistan continues to be a source of political unrest in the region. It has fortified opposition to the United States among the people of Pakistan, especially in the hinterland, where it has become a symbol of what many consider an unequal partnership between the United States and the government of Pakistan. Compounding the confusion about the legality of such attacks and the anger directed against them is the behavior of the Pakistani authorities, who publicly condemn these attacks and privately condone them.[40]

In Pakistan, little doubt exists that civilian deaths caused by the drones have aided local Taliban recruitment efforts,[41] with Pakistani media fanning the flames of discontent and anti-Americanism:[42] "Every one of these dead non-combatants represents an alienated family, a new desire for revenge, and more recruits for a militant movement that has grown exponentially even as drone strikes have increased."[43] Recent media revelations suggesting "the categorising of all military-age males in a strike zone of a target as militants," outraged human rights organizations.[44] Relations between the American and Pakistani governments have visibly deteriorated due to the drone strikes, compounding "the chronic mistrust that pervades the U.S.–Pakistan relationship."[45]

Regarding the drone strikes' arbitrary violation of national sovereignty, despite covert support for these strikes from the governments of both Pakistan and Yemen,[46] to many outsiders these American attacks appear unjustified because neither country is in an armed conflict with the United States.[47] Among Yemen's citizenry, for instance, emotional resentment is escalating: "These strikes are not acceptable, and we should not take the help of infidels to kill Muslims . . . al-Qaeda might be just an excuse to interfere in our internal affairs."[48] The United Nations has categorized the American drone strikes as "targeted killings"—"premeditated acts of lethal force employed by states in times of peace or during armed conflict to eliminate specific individuals outside their custody"—and thus has opposed the strikes: A UN representative claimed that "if other states were to claim the broad-based authority that the United States does, to kill people anywhere, anytime, the result would be chaos."[49]

### Future Prospects

The future prospects for American use of drone strikes appear to be quite bright. A recent study by the Congressional Budget Office reported 775 Predators, Reapers, and other medium- and long-range drones in the U.S. inventory, with hundreds more in the pipeline.[50] Most observers anticipate that the United States will expand drone strikes in the near future "as military technology improves and the public appetite for large-scale, conventional armed intervention erodes."[51] Increased future American reliance on special operations and covert action may ramp up this reliance even further.[52] One trigger of drone strikes' future growth—possibly entailing target adjustment—is the rise of disruptive armed nonstate groups, organized in transnational networks and posing a principal national security threat.[53] Overall, the drone campaign has "spawned a multibillion dollar industry"[54] not likely to vanish anytime soon.

However, fitting with tensions embedded within the coercion conundrum, in undertaking these drone strikes the U.S. government is going to have to walk a tightrope in balancing several opposing interests, including "asserting broad war powers while assuring critics that they are limited; justifying actions that remain covert; and promoting government transparency while protecting sensitive intelligence programs."[55] In particular, political leaders need to find ways to convince the public that there is a sound basis for determining who is targeted by drone strikes.[56] Due to the need for secrecy, the mass public's incomplete understanding of the drone strike campaign seems likely to continue.

In terms of the broader security impact in South Asia and the Middle East, the drone campaign seems likely to increase regional instability.[57] In November 2013, drone strikes dramatically strained American relations with Afghanistan and Pakistan.[58] Rather than calming affected areas, the target killings have inflamed affected populations, destabilized institutions that drive regional development, and complicated American strategic coordination and pursuit of national interests in the region.[59]

Globally, American drone strikes could set a negative precedent for unrestrained violence by other states—such as China and Russia—acquiring this capacity, for worldwide spending on drone aircraft is projected to double over the next decade to $11.4 billion and grow by 2021 to over $94 billion:[60]

> As with most military programs, the United States is far and away the leader in developing drone technology, and the country is projected to account for 77 percent of drone R&D and 69 percent of procurement in the coming decade. Nevertheless, estimates of how many other countries have at least some drone capability now range from 44 to 70, for an estimated 680 drone programs around the world, up greatly from 195 in 2005. China is escalating its drone program, with at least 25 types of systems in development. Iran has also touted its program, including the armed "Ambassador of Death" drone, which President Mahmoud Ahmadinejad unveiled by declaring: "Its main message is peace and friendship."[61]

In November 2012, Israel successfully used a drone strike to kill the commander of Hamas forces in Gaza.[62] Even the terrorists themselves have used American drone strikes as an excuse for violence:

> On 21 June 2010, Pakistani American Faisal Shahzad told a judge in a Manhattan federal court that he placed a bomb at a busy intersection in Times

Square as payback for the US occupations of Afghanistan and Iraq and for its worldwide use of drone strikes. When the judge asked how Shahzad could be comfortable killing innocent people, including women and children, he responded: "Well, the drone hits in Afghanistan and Iraq, they don't see children, they don't see anybody. They kill women, children, they kill everybody. It's a war and in war, they kill people. They're killing all Muslims."[63]

For some states or armed nonstate groups, continuing drone attacks could even "suggest that it's acceptable behavior to assassinate people."[64]

## AMERICAN INVASION OF AFGHANISTAN

### Force Description

The American invasion of Afghanistan opened with Operation Enduring Freedom, which began on October 7, 2001, four weeks after the September 11 terrorist attacks on the World Trade Center and the Pentagon in the United States. The explicit mission was to defeat in Afghanistan the Taliban and al-Qaeda forces, identified as the perpetrators. Most of the bombing had ended by late 2001, at which point the Taliban were apparently defeated and a new more amicable government regime in Afghanistan was inaugurated. However, since summer 2006, "there has been a rising tide of Taliban violence,"[65] at least in part because the Taliban interpreted the American announcement to transfer command of coalition forces to NATO and to undertake a troop drawdown as a sign of its intention to withdraw.[66]

Afterward, an increasing number of soldiers began to be needed for this task, and by June 2010 there were 91,775 U.S. troops there.[67] A coalition of Afghan Northern Alliance fighters, air sorties by American planes, Western special operations forces and intelligence operatives, and a small contingent of Western ground forces participated in the military action. The killing of bin Laden on May 4, 2011, did little to change the ongoing pattern of instability. In 2011, the Obama administration entered into direct secret talks with senior Afghan Taliban leaders to explore possibilities for peace to end the decade-long war,[68] and in 2012 these efforts went public.[69] American troops began withdrawing from Afghanistan in July 2011, and NATO handed over control to the Afghan forces on July 18, 2013. Although initial domestic expectations were that the United States would pull all of its military troops quickly out of Afghanistan, with the stability of the country left completely to local forces, the plan now is to hand over security responsibilities to Afghan police and soldiers by the end of 2014, with the United States keeping between 8,000 and

15,000 troops there until at least the end of 2024. By 2013, the longest war in American history had resulted in 2,144 U.S. military personnel dead[70] along with many thousands of civilian deaths.

### Purpose/Rationale

The motivation for American invasion of Afghanistan fits into the compellence category of force use. The West has long associated Taliban rule with the spread of transnational terrorism and consequently has sought to undermine it. In retrospect it is ironic that the United States had supported the Taliban from 1994 to 1996 because the American government viewed the Taliban as anti-Iranian and potentially pro-Western.[71] However, the United States quickly changed its policy as it began to realize that, from the time the Soviets withdrew from Afghanistan in 1989, "a chaotic, Taliban-dominated Afghanistan and adjoining areas of Pakistan became hospitable venues for the continued training, recruitment, indoctrination, and team-building of violent jihadist groups whose resentments would be focused elsewhere."[72] In August 1998, as the Taliban began its takeover of the country, American military might destroyed camps near Kabul run by Osama bin Laden, accused of instigating the 1998 bombings of the American embassies in Kenya and Tanzania.[73] Although Pakistan's position changed somewhat after the 9/11 terrorist attacks on the United States, and although the Pakistani government is formally an American ally in the war on terror, the border areas between Afghanistan and Pakistan—especially North Waziristan—have turned into safe havens and training grounds for Taliban and al-Qaeda forces.[74]

After the 9/11 terrorist attacks on the United States, President George W. Bush demanded that the Taliban turn over Osama bin Laden and the al-Qaeda leadership; when the Taliban refused, the United States and its allies began military operations against the Taliban on October 7, 2001. The Taliban soon joined al-Qaeda forces in waging continuous guerrilla warfare against the coalition forces.[75] Before its formal ouster by U.S.-led forces in December 2001, the Taliban controlled some 90 percent of Afghanistan's territory, although it was never officially recognized by the United Nations.[76] After the Taliban was defeated, chaotic warlord politics reemerged,[77] with the Taliban insurgents fighting the American-backed government regime in Kabul. Since 2005, fighting between remnants of the ousted Taliban regime and the Afghan government has continued to escalate.[78]

As with the 2003 Iraq War, the purpose of the Afghanistan War changed midstream, posing additional obstacles to successful mission accomplishment. Initially the stated goals of the invasion were elimination of Osama bin Laden, removal of the Taliban from power, dismantling of al-Qaeda, and prevention of Afghanistan from being used as a base for terrorists to strike either its neighbors—especially Pakistan—or the United States and its allies.[79] However, in 2005, following the American government's recognition that "failed and failing states are breeding grounds for terrorists and insurgents,"[80] the American mission statement changed, and the objective for the war in Afghanistan transformed into "stability operations," elevated "as a core mission comparable to combat operations."[81] The range of immediate and long-run dangers to be confronted here included not only terrorism but also extremism, weak and corrupt governments, poverty, and deep-seated regional rivalries.[82]

### Force Effectiveness

The initial phase of the U.S. force use in Afghanistan was highly successful militarily: Not long after the October invasion of Afghanistan, the Taliban regime was overthrown, and a new government was installed. Many analysts assert that the early stunning military successes may have been a bit misleading, as American airpower was essentially unopposed[83] because the Taliban lacked the know-how to undertake deception or camouflage and the technology to implement electronic jammers and air defense systems.[84] Moreover, when facing a more difficult foe—the al Qaeda terrorists, whose unbridled passion for their cause and their apparent unwillingness to accept defeat made victory against them a real challenge—American military success has been a lot less decisive.

In the long run, however, the positive outcome was short lived, as soon "the Taliban regrouped, top al-Qaeda leaders managed to elude justice, and terrorist violence in Pakistan and Afghanistan spiked."[85] The war has not yet achieved anything close to strategic victory:

> In Afghanistan, the Taliban insurgency is more violent than at any point since the U.S. invasion after 9/11. NATO forces are paying a heavy toll. Afghan public enthusiasm for the government is waning after years of unmet expectations. The economy, devastated by more than thirty years of war, has not recovered sufficiently to provide for the people, while the government remains largely ineffective and riven by corruption.[86]

Although the United States thought "that the same men who caused Afghanistan so much misery in the past will somehow lead it to democracy and stability in the future," the evidence "suggests that the opposite is happening," as "key warlords have returned to power" and "opportunities have been lost, goodwill squandered, and lessons of history ignored."[87] The rapid military victory of the Alliance and the collapse of the Taliban "released centrifugal tendencies throughout Afghanistan, giving warlordism, banditry, and opium production a new lease on life."[88] Indeed, the export of illicit drugs from Afghanistan to the rest of the world has dramatically escalated after the war reduced Taliban control. Perversely, "Operation Enduring Freedom's severing of al-Qaeda's symbiotic relationship with the Taliban and destruction of its training bases in Afghanistan have provoked even more decentralised modes of operation that are even more difficult to detect and target."[89] Even among American government officials, the longer the war progressed, the more their hopes and expectations for a stable postwar Afghanistan fell.[90]

In terms of managing the terrorist threat emanating from Afghanistan, the war has had mixed results:

> U.S.- and NATO-led military operations have cleared the vast majority of international terrorist training camps in Afghanistan. But top al-Qaeda leaders and other international terrorists fled to Pakistan, where they continue to plan attacks against the United States and its allies. Since 9/11, there have been more than a dozen serious attempts—some successful, some thwarted—to attack the United States and American allies that were planned or supported by groups on the Afghanistan–Pakistan border. These include the Times Square bomber in 2010; the plot against the New York subway system in 2009; the plan to attack the Barcelona metro system in 2008; the effort to bomb airliners in flight over the Atlantic in 2006; the attack on the London subway system in 2005 in which 52 civilians died; the Madrid attack in 2004 in which 191 civilians died; the Bali bombings in 2002 that killed 202 civilians; and other plots known and unknown to the general public.[91]

There is little doubt that the war on terror in Afghanistan has degraded al-Qaeda and the Taliban leadership, but the security threat is still present.[92] As of late 2013, after NATO withdrawal, "the Taliban's re-emergence is not out of question and they still rule the roost in many provinces while Afghan security forces are not yet capable enough to take them on."[93]

This war ended up highlighting key limitations against a hard-to-identify target. Despite "the adulation of Operation Enduring Freedom (OEF) as a 'finely-tuned' or 'bulls-eye' war, the campaign failed to set a new standard for precision in one important respect—the rate of civilians killed per bomb dropped; in fact, this rate was far higher in the Afghanistan conflict—perhaps four times higher—than in the 1999 Balkans war."[94] A key obstacle to success has been the difficulty in distinguishing between civilians and the informally clad terrorist combatants. The costs of the war for the United States—in terms of deaths and injuries—have been high without many benefits to compensate for them: "The underlying dynamics in Afghanistan remain stubborn—pervasive corruption that breeds the insurgency; weak governance that creates a vacuum; Taliban resilience that feeds an atmosphere of intimidation; and an erratic leader whose agenda may not be the same as that of the United States."[95] This dismal cost–benefit ratio was in no way anticipated at the outset of the American invasion of Afghanistan in 2001.

Unfortunately, the Afghan government stabilization goal has been "making only slow progress, particularly in the southern provinces."[96] The overwhelming hurdle has been that "decades of war had destroyed civilian and military institutions, deprived young Afghans of education, and sent many of the country's most talented people into exile."[97] Stabilization efforts have been unsatisfactory in terms of how quickly these gains have been achieved and how vast the resource expenditures have been to achieve these modest gains. Stability operations in Afghanistan have brought comfort to some civilians, but improvements are neither widespread enough in terms of geographical coverage nor permanent enough in terms of long-run durability to be considered an effectively-executed mission: A 2010 Defense Department report to Congress admits that stability has not increased in all areas of the country and that violence has not only persisted but actually increased.[98] American military officials have been unable to announce a "winning" situation in the country.[99]

As in Iraq, while eventually the military has cleared out several areas in Afghanistan and achieved a fragile "freedom" for some citizens, the American government seemed to lack forethought about durable stability and to have forgotten about the maintenance—involving painstaking reconstruction, trust building, and other human security improvements—that needs to follow the fight. Although the American and NATO International Security Assistance Force (ISAF) has provided some needed social services for Afghan citizens, a key report states that this in reality has been "undercutting the confidence of the local population in their government's ability to provide essential services."[100] If most Afghan citizens are left out or believe that the Taliban can provide for them better, then stability operations fall short of their goals.

The goal switch to stability operations did afford the American military a small buffer between itself and those who oppose the war by emphasizing helping the Afghan people rebuild, not engaging in combat. Nonetheless, stability operations have seemed doomed from the outset because the underlying original instability causes were not rectified and any temporary stability gains would not be self-sustaining after American withdrawal. Moreover, "vague mission, vague roles, and insufficient resources created significant civil–military tensions,"[101] leading to doubts about the ability of the military to create strong enough bonds with villagers to make a meaningful impact.

### Force Legitimacy

As the war in Afghanistan has dragged on, public support has diminished. Most Americans have grown weary of the conflict[102] and just want withdrawal as quickly as possible:[103]

> Beyond the troop numbers, debate has intensified over the purpose of the U.S. deployment in Afghanistan, heightened by the killing of Osama bin Laden in neighboring Pakistan. Mounting concern over the U.S. debt crisis has also focused new attention on spending in the Afghan war theater, estimated at about $2 billion per day.[104]

Global opposition to the war, especially within predominantly Muslim countries, has also plummeted, along with enthusiasm for the American war on terror,[105] with objectives in both cases not seen as attainable.

Even the specter of free and open elections—a signal usually promoting domestic and international legitimacy—has generated mixed reactions in Afghanistan. Although the first presidential election in October 2004 was an uplifting national experience, the second attempt five years later was a fiasco, lowering the international community's confidence in the legitimacy of President Karzai and his government.[106] Without strong domestic approval of the government in Kabul, little hope exists to stabilize Afghanistan.[107]

### Future Prospects

Thus the future prospects in Afghanistan do not appear bright. Specific concerns have emerged about insufficient spending on postwar reconstruction and an inability to constitute a solid international peacekeeping force,[108] along with continuing worry about violence and the pace of progress toward democracy. Sadly, it looks increasingly as if it will be difficult to remedy in the future Afghanistan's many problems, what with "its flourishing drug trade, widespread insecurity, sluggish disarmament, and insufficient international aid."[109] Unfortunately, the principal war victims have been ordinary Afghan citizens, a group that "has grown disappointed and disillusioned with the international community, which it increasingly blames for failing to deliver the lofty promises that preceded the U.S. attack on the Taliban."[110] In the end, American combat troops seem likely to leave behind "a grinding stalemate" between the Afghan government and the Taliban,[111] and it is difficult to demonstrate convincingly that the overall conditions in the country or the region have dramatically improved as a result of the war.

The effects on Afghanistan of the impending American military withdrawal could be dire: "Pulling back U.S. troops too early could overwhelm Afghan forces and undermine tenuous negotiations with the Taliban."[112] The outcome of being overwhelmed seems highly likely because Afghan and Pakistani security forces lack the numbers, skills, equipment, and motivation to fully uproot al-Qaeda.[113] Furthermore, Taliban fighters seem "confident in their return to power" after the United States leaves.[114] Finally, in the long run this withdrawal could jeopardize the antiterrorist thrust: "A rapidly deteriorating security environment could cause a highly strategic and potentially volatile part of the world—with a nuclear-armed Pakistan and an increasingly isolated Iran—to plunge into turmoil."[115]

In terms of broader regional security implications, the long Afghanistan conflict has had spillover effects in neighboring countries in Asia and negative international stability impacts.[116] Specifically, the continuing turmoil endangers the stability of the Central Asian republics, which are especially worried about the rise of antiregime Islamic movements—"These threats led Tajikistan to allow Russian deployment along its border with Afghanistan, to prevent any possible Taliban incursions and to rein in the smuggling of opium and heroin into Tajikistan."[117] The Taliban's harboring of terrorist elements has also posed a threat to regional stability, allowing a base of disruptive operations that could easily affect neighboring countries as well as the world at large.

## AMERICAN INVASION OF IRAQ

### Force Description

This case involves the United States preventively initiating force against Saddam Hussein's oppressive regime in Iraq. On March 19–20, 2003, the invasion of Iraq—called Operation Iraqi Freedom—commenced. Despite American claims that its coalition included forty-nine nations, the initial land coalition force consisted of about 200,000 Americans, 50,000 Britons, 2,000 Australians, and 200 Poles (Denmark and Spain helped in sea-based naval operations). The primary campaign reached a speedy conclusion, with the capital city Baghdad controlled on April 9, followed by the collapse of the Iraqi government, signified by the fall of Saddam Hussein's stronghold Tikrit on April 15. On May 1, 2003, President George W. Bush declared that major combat operations were over. In December 2003, after much searching, U.S. troops captured Saddam Hussein himself, a step of huge symbolic importance to both the American government and American citizens. However, small-scale fighting continued for years afterward. It was not until December 2011—under great adverse domestic pressure from both Congress and the American people—that the U.S. government finally withdrew its last troops from Iraq and the war officially ended.

Operation Iraqi Freedom was designed to be quick and surgically effective against designated targets. The campaign involved a simultaneous launch of a massive air campaign and limited ground attack, with a key role for special operations troops: There was heavy use of precision-guided weaponry—including satellite-guided bombs and unmanned aerial vehicles—designed to nullify the capacity of the enemy to fight back. An initial phase of this campaign involved "shock and awe," aimed at reducing the enemy's will to fight through a display of overwhelming force using superior technology.

### Purpose/Rationale

The American invasion of Iraq began in the deterrence category of force use and then later changed to the compellence category. The American preventive military strategy in Operation Iraqi Freedom was designed to eliminate the perceived threat with minimum loss of American soldiers' lives. The perceived incoming threat prompting the American preventive response was that the Iraqi government had weapons of mass destruction—possessing chemical weapons and making biological and nuclear weapons—and ties to the terrorist group al-Qaeda. President George W. Bush specifically feared that Saddam Hussein could provide these arms to terrorists for use against the United States.[118] As a result, the primary initial goal was to rid the country of these arms and free the Iraqi people from the oppressive Saddam Hussein regime. White House Press Secretary Ari Fleischer specifically stated that the two victory benchmarks were on changing the Hussein regime and finding and destroying the chemical and biological weapons presumed to be in Iraq.[119]

Later on, however, when no weapons of mass destruction were found and no link to al-Qaeda could be confirmed, the goals of the American preventive action changed considerably. Implicit regional instability threats associated with an authoritarian hostile state led the United States to emphasize simply bringing democracy and freedom to the Iraqi people to pave the way for peace and democratization of the Arab world.[120] Specifically, "after toppling Saddam in 2003, U.S. policy aimed to create a democratic state that enshrined civil liberties; national reconciliation; a fair, apolitical judiciary; and freedom of speech."[121] The huge change in rationale was never officially acknowledged.

American leaders exaggerated the ease of promoting democracy and civil society in Iraq, expecting that grateful cheering Iraqis would greet their forces:

> Overoptimism in the planning of the war—about how many troops were needed and what they were likely to face after a military victory—spawned several failures of the occupation phase. Rumsfeld's doctrine of using small, highly maneuverable forces plus overwhelming aerial bombardment proved successful in achieving quick military victories (both in Afghanistan and in Iraq), but it contained a hidden overoptimism about what these same forces would face the day after victory. In the planning phase, officials played down potential postwar problems partially in order to garner support for launching the war.[122]

American planners underestimated the potential for postwar violence, supply line vulnerability, local guerrilla-style resistance, and reconstruction costs.[123] There was also significant resistance to changing fighting tactics:

> The reasons for the missteps by U.S. troops can be traced to an ingrained Pentagon tradition of training and fighting for conventional war, with well-plotted battle lines and an easily distinguished enemy. The U.S. force in Iraq was slow to recognize the emergence of the Iraqi insurgency in 2003 and it has been reluctant to adopt counterinsurgency tactics. Commanders trained in heavy artillery assaults bristled at the notion of exposing troops on street patrols, interacting with Iraqi citizens and gathering intelligence on likely insurgents.[124]

This overoptimism did not end when major fighting ceased: In May 2004, General Richard Myers, chair of the Joint Chiefs of Staff, stated, "I think we are on the verge of success here."[125] To many analysts, "Iraq proves again, hard on the heels of Afghanistan, that the United States chronically underestimates the difficulties of nonmilitary aspects of foreign interventions and wildly inflates nonmilitary goals without committing the resources required to achieve them."[126] Thus some U.S. government officials exhibited a highly unusual combination of perceptual distortions regarding ongoing threat: (1) perception of a sharp religious divide between Christianity and Islam, demonization of the Iraqi regime, hypersensitivity to threat after the 9/11 terrorist attack, and massive and escalating capacity to retaliate; and (2) overconfidence about the adequacy of the American military response to incoming threat. In assuming that the Iraqis would readily accept Western democracy, American leaders displayed classic moralistic black-and-white thinking, "with the United States symbolizing 'good' and its enemies embodying 'evil,'" reflecting a "chasm of suspicion and hostility" between Westerners and Muslims.[127]

In retrospect, a clear deficiency was evident in the Iraq War planning in concentrating on winning the war rather than on winning the peace. A Joint Chiefs of Staff report issued well into the war revealed that Operation Iraqi Freedom emphasized military operations to defeat the Iraqi military too much at the expense of political transition planning.[128] With the benefit of hindsight, many analysts now agree that "the U.S. occupation of Iraq is a debacle not because the government did no planning but because a vast amount of expert planning was willfully ignored by the people in charge."[129] The American emphasis on military rather than political priorities, however misguided, was in some ways to be expected:

> Translating a military triumph into a political success—that is, a peace better than that of the pre-war situation—is an inherently difficult enterprise, especially for a country that has historically viewed war as a suspension of politics and military victory as an end in and of itself; this view was reflected in Operation Iraqi Freedom's virtually exclusive focus on the first half of the regime-change challenge—toppling the old regime—at the expense of the second and far more difficult challenge—creating a new political order amenable to US interests.[130]

The planning involved was decidedly short term, ignoring the complexities of the long-term strategic mission. In the end, it would be difficult to imagine a postforce security predicament in the twenty-first century that more starkly contrasted the disjuncture between speedy military victory—forceful overthrow of an oppressive regime—and agonizingly slow accomplishment of the long-term political objective of establishing a more open political system.

### Force Effectiveness

The American invasion of Iraq did succeed in defeating Iraq's army and toppling the Saddam Hussein regime. Moreover, it improved the plight of a number of groups within Iraq:

> If we start the inventory of gains and losses inside Iraq itself, the war was unquestionably worth it to the Kurds who gained a state within a state and look set to gain still more from oil and gas development on their territory. The Shias in the south, always repressed under Saddam, have made gains too, though they face the menace of continuing sectarian violence. For many Sunnis too, fear of continuing sectarian violence has to be balanced against the gains in freedom, large and small, that have been won since the destruction of Saddam's "republic of fear."[131]

Finally, the United States had hoped that the Iraq War would trigger a chain of events "that would eventually democratize the entire region,"[132] and to some degree this hope was fulfilled with the Arab Spring bottom-up revolutions in some countries in the Middle East and North Africa. However, "the 'Arab Spring' indicates that regimes that only offer their people repression and delusion eventually collapse under the weight of their incompetence, corruption, and self-deception," so it is unclear whether the American invasion of Iraq was necessary to free the Iraqi people from Saddam Hussein and to stimulate dissatisfaction with regional repressive regimes.[133]

Soon after the United States initially declared military victory in May 2003, a secondary threat appeared: "U.S. troops stood by helplessly, outnumbered and unprepared, as much of Iraq's remaining physical, economic, and institutional infrastructure was systematically looted and sabotaged."[134] Anarchic violence produced interruptions in basic social services (including power plants, oil pipelines, communication lines, water purification facilities, and bridges), thievery in many cities (particularly Baghdad), guerrilla insurgency, and suicide bombings. The sources of postwar insurgency included the lack of American advance planning for postwar developments, the violent power struggle among those in Iraq vying for control, and jihadists' choice to make Iraq a key platform in their war against the United States.[135] Many insurgent attacks aimed not at Iraqi security forces or at civilians but rather at American and coalition troops,[136] with insurgents determined to kill as many Americans as possible in the hope that lots of casualties would prompt American withdrawal,[137] frighten Iraqis into refusing to cooperate with American forces, perpetuate disorder, and prevent the formation of a legitimate and democratic Iraqi government.[138] The insurgents' effectiveness has not depended on beating Americans on the battlefield; rather, they "win merely by making Iraq ungovernable."[139] Over four years after the invasion, Iraq was as violent as ever,[140] a pattern that not only caused popular support for the war to wane in both Iraq and the United States but also perversely delayed the exit of occupying American troops from Iraq.

Even before the end of major combat operations in May 2003, the costs of the war had risen sharply. Within this early phase of the war, despite the speed of military operations, the protection of the oil wells, and American casualty counts far lower than those in the Gulf War, there were already signs not only of unexpectedly massive American expenditures but also of significant collateral damage to Iraqi people and property:

> As the battles dragged on week after week, it became evident that the unrelenting mathematics of war had reached a tipping point. American and British forces had used such a high number of smart bombs that the normal miss rate of the Joint Direct Attack Munitions (JDAMs) and Tomahawk cruise missiles had produced an inordinate number of civilian casualties.
>
> The most ominous sign, clearly documented on Al-Jazeera, but not on U.S. news networks, was the daily growing number of women and children with missing limbs . . . Doctors in Baghdad were so overwhelmed with casualties that they had neither the time, anesthetics nor antibiotics to repair complex injuries.[141]

Moreover, by the war's end in December 2011, the costs escalated even farther:

> Saddam Hussein has gone, but at a cost to his own people of almost nine years of war, civil strife, terrorism and occupation that left more than 100,000 Iraqi civilians dead and millions displaced from their homes, infrastructure destroyed (water and electricity supplies in Iraq remain patchy even now) and the country's social fabric torn apart. Of the 1.5 million American soldiers that cycled through Iraq, 4,487 were killed and tens of thousands left with debilitating physical and psychological scars. And the war has cost the United States some $1 trillion and counting.[142]

Although American casualties were substantially lower than most previous American wars, the war ended up being quite costly on both sides.

After the United States withdrew from Iraq in 2011, the internal situation quickly unraveled. Earlier concern had surfaced that, if the United States could not leave well-functioning governance infrastructure behind in Iraq, then the roadblock to withdrawal would be that acceptable governance requires a minimal level of security.[143] In fulfillment of this fear, after the American military withdrawal reports emerged that "the fragile governing coalition that has teetered between dysfunction and collapse for the past year appears to be splintering, strained by personality clashes, governance disagreements and sectarian rivalries coming to a head."[144] This long-term failure was apparently due to (1) the premature withdrawal of all American troops from Iraq well before key political institutions had gelled and (2) the plethora of unresolved political issues.[145] Recently, "historic and seemingly dormant affiliations—to sect, tribe, or ethnicity—have apparently reasserted themselves as local populations take increasingly partisan positions," evidenced by increased Kurdish agitation in Syria, Turkey, and Iran.[146] In retrospect, the new Iraqi political institutions may have survived as long as they did in significant part due to perception that the United States was standing behind them.[147]

Due to continuing violence and instability, it would be difficult to classify the Iraq War outcome as a strategic victory exhibiting long-run force effectiveness. In a blunder of epic proportions, the United States inadvertently seems to have squandered "a decisive, potentially historic military victory":

Mistakes were made at virtually every turn, and as the principal nation promoting the conflict and managing its aftermath, the United States bears the chief blame. In the weeks leading up to and following the war, the Bush administration depicted a liberated Iraq welcoming our invading troops as liberators, quickly stabilizing the political order, regaining economic vitality, and making the momentous transition to freedom—a transition that would, in turn, set off pressures for democratic change throughout the Middle East. But from the moment the war ended, Iraq fell into a deepening quagmire of chaos, criminality, insurgency, and terrorism, which, even in the months following the January 2005 elections, showed no prospect of ending anytime soon. During the period of occupational rule, Iraq became a black hole of instability and a justification for neighboring regimes that insisted their societies were not culturally suited or politically ready for democracy.[148]

The harsh lessons for the United States in the aftermath of the fall of Baghdad include

> ... that occupying the country is much more difficult than conquering it; that a breakdown in public order can jeopardize every other goal; that the ambition of patiently nurturing a new democracy is at odds with the desire to turn control over to the Iraqis quickly and get U.S. troops out; that the Sunni center of the country is the main security problem; [and] that with each passing day Americans risk being seen less as liberators and more as occupiers, and targets.[149]

The Americans continuously faced local roadblocks in inducing Iraqis to manage their own affairs, including dealing with insurgents and running government institutions.[150] Thanks to fresh intelligence, once the American focus in the Iraq War shifted away from dealing with weapons of mass destruction and terrorism toward promoting democracy and freedom, the chances of a purely military strategy succeeding in achieving long-term strategic objectives declined precipitously due to a series of mistakes including injecting inadequate American military forces, liquidating the existing Iraqi military, and purging Baath Party members from civilian ministries.[151]

### Force Legitimacy

Throughout the war, skepticism has abounded about the American government's underlying assumptions, especially the presence of weapons of mass destruction and the link between Hussein and al-Qaeda: Most American foreign policy experts and members of the international community agree now that the threat assessments used to justify the Iraq war "were greatly exaggerated, and on some dimensions wholly baseless."[152] Despite fluctuations in observer reactions throughout the war, a marked disconnect emerged within the United States about the war between the perceptions of the general public and those of many so-called opinion leaders.[153] International criticism of the war was widespread, particularly from Europeans—who viewed Middle Eastern dangers quite differently than Americans did[154] and generally did not see Iraq as an immediate threat—and from Russia, China, and the Arab League. Indeed, some critics saw the United States rather than Iraq as the threat source, rejecting any justification for preventive attack.

Within the postwar field operations themselves, American forces felt torn between competing demands—on the one hand promoting freedom and open civil society and on the other hand maintaining order and deterring acts of violence. The inherent conflict between these mission tasks became so severe that ultimately "America's ability to win the peace is in doubt":

> U.S. forces are struggling to balance the doctrinal principles of security and legitimacy. Furthermore, they are doing it without a strong doctrinal foundation that prescribes important post-war practices. Consequently, victory appears distant, despite President Bush's declaration of the end of major combat operations in Iraq. Coalition forces continue to encounter resistance. This, however, is not surprising. Undeniably, U.S. efforts are handicapped. Winning the peace in Iraq has been elusive because of a failure to win Iraqi hearts and minds, friction between security and legitimacy, and a failure of doctrine to underscore important post-war practices.[155]

Existing guidance to soldiers in terms of standard operating procedures for dealing with these mission tensions appeared to have been inadequate. Sensing increasing risk, American soldiers were forced to operate with increased caution (for example, not removing helmets or leaving vehicles) and with growing suspicion of Iraqi citizens, in turn increasing local disenchantment with U.S. soldiers and decreasing the positive interactions necessary for strategic victory.

The international community was divided on the legitimacy of this invasion, and the United States has received heavy criticism for the war from Belgium, Russia, France, China, Germany, and the Arab League. This global criticism was particularly noteworthy because, before the war started in 2003, there was practically universal global disapproval of the Saddam Hussein regime in Iraq. As the war progressed, the international reactions became more intensely negative, and the pressures for speedy American withdrawal escalated.

### Future Prospects

The long-term postwithdrawal future prospects for the United States achieving its political objectives in Iraq look dim. Toward the end of the American occupation of Iraq, the writing was on the wall, with "the continued attacks on the U.S. military, other coalition forces, Iraqi recruits and police, and civilians (including U.N. staff), plus the soaring costs and controversial progress toward democracy."[156] Many observers believe that the abrupt American military pullout in December 2011 dramatically escalated "the prospects of a catastrophic failure."[157] The postwithdrawal political situation in Iraq appears truly bleak:

Nine years after U.S. troops toppled Saddam Hussein and just a few months after the last U.S. soldier left Iraq, the country has become something close to a failed state. Prime Minister Nouri al-Maliki presides over a system rife with corruption and brutality, in which political leaders use security forces and militias to repress enemies and intimidate the general population. The law exists as a weapon to be wielded against rivals and to hide the misdeeds of allies. The dream of an Iraq governed by elected leaders answerable to the people is rapidly fading away.[158]

With democratic stability continually eluding Iraq,[159] a quick future reversal of fortune seems unlikely.

Given that one of the initial purposes of the American Iraq invasion was terminating the presumed link to al-Qaeda, the backfire effect of rising terrorism and anti-Americanism[160] seems particularly troubling in the future. For example, in April 2004, a closely spaced series of terrorist acts hitting Damascus, Syria; Riyadh, Saudi Arabia; and Amman, Jordan, stimulated Arab fears that the war in Iraq triggered exactly the kind of extremist violence it was supposed to curtail.[161] Domestic and international terrorist dangers within Iraq have been deepening over the years:

The U.S.-led military intervention in and occupation of Iraq, as well as the ensuing armed resistance, has successfully intertwined Iraq with the war on terrorism. Although terrorist acts in postwar Iraq (politically motivated attacks intentionally directed against civilians and civilian objects, both local and foreign) have been coupled with and at times even overshadowed by acts of guerrilla warfare (attacks by insurgents against coalition forces and pro-coalition Iraqi security targets, such as the "new" Iraqi military and police), terrorism generated by conflict in Iraq remains a long-term security problem. The continuing presence of coalition forces in Iraq also has further motivated forces ready to employ terrorist means in the fight against the United States and its allies worldwide.[162]

The war seems to have "bred a new generation of religious extremists, dangerously heightened sectarian tensions in the Islamic world, strengthened Iran's hand in Iraq and in matters of nuclear diplomacy, and created the most serious threat to world's oil supply since the OPEC embargo—all the while undermining American authority in the region and straining the U.S. military to the breaking point."[163] These extremist dangers threatened security both within Iraq and outside of the country.

Regionally, the American willingness to exit from Iraq before achieving its stated goals has left Middle Eastern states wondering about the credibility of future U.S. commitment and caused some to open up to adverse outside influences:

> Uncertainty about U.S. intentions and capabilities in the region has increased local states' receptivity to assistance from China and Russia. Post-invasion disarray in the Arab world was accompanied by a corresponding erosion of confidence in the United States as a security guarantor, stemming from the perception of U.S. entanglement in Iraq, which some viewed as limiting both U.S. capabilities and willingness to intervene elsewhere. The net effect has been the increased willingness of traditional U.S. Arab allies to consider patronage from other extraregional powers—most notably Russia and China.[164]

The recent American reluctance to intervene militarily in the Middle East to promote stability, particularly in Syria, has confirmed these fears. Moreover, war-related refugee flows have exacerbated these worries by Middle East states:

> The influx of an estimated 2 million Iraqi refugees has created socioeconomic stresses in Syria and Jordan; the resulting public discontent and demographic changes could challenge stability in these states over the long term. The Iraq War created the largest refugee crisis in the Middle East since the 1948 Arab–Israeli War, potentially jeopardizing the long-term stability of Jordan, Syria, and—to a lesser extent—Lebanon.[165]

Furthermore, the war has indirectly augmented Iran's regional power,[166] highly troubling given its nuclear program and regional hegemony aspirations:

> The war has affected new shifts in the regional balance-of-power equation that, in the minds of Arab regimes and their publics, have assumed almost seismic qualities; much of this stems from the perceived disappearance of Iraq as the Arab world's "eastern flank" and, since 1979, as a military bulwark against a seemingly expansionist and predatory Iran.[167]

Globally, some analysts contend that, after the initial rationale for the war was deemed erroneous, the American invasion of Iraq signals an end to future moderation by the United States of its military power: "Central to that legacy has been Washington's decisive and seemingly irrevocable abandonment of any semblance of self-restraint regarding the use of violence as an instrument of statecraft."[168] In the long run, "the damage that mendacious claims about

WMD did to U.S. credibility"[169] was quite significant across a wide range of observers.

## AMERICAN KILLING OF OSAMA BIN LADEN

### Force Description

On May 1, 2011, after a nearly decade-long manhunt, the United States finally located in Pakistan and killed Osama bin Laden, founder of the al-Qaeda terrorist network responsible for the September 11, 2001, terrorist attacks. President Barack Obama personally authorized this mission, described by many as the defining moral victory of the U.S. war on terror. Observers have alternatively either cheered this action's gutsy quality or bemoaned its depravity, with a primary focus in these reactions on its tangible short-term implications for the power and status of the United States and for the fate of the states in the immediate area (Afghanistan and Pakistan). What have not received sufficient attention are the broader intangible long-term implications for the international system.

The American killing of bin Laden demonstrated willingness, indeed determination, to do whatever was necessary to accomplish the desired end. In response to the 9/11 terrorist attacks, President George W. Bush had vowed on September 20, 2001, to "direct every resource at our command—every means of diplomacy, every tool of intelligence, every instrument of law enforcement, every financial influence, and every necessary weapon of war—to the destruction and to the defeat of the global terror network."[170] In President Obama's May 1, 2011, speech, he said, "We will never tolerate our security being threatened"; and "We are once again reminded that America can do whatever we set our mind to."[171] He may have issued a direct "kill" order—not a "capture or kill" order—consistent with his vow on October 7, 2008, as a candidate for president that "we will kill bin Laden; we will crush al-Qaeda."[172] In executing a mission involving uncertainty about bin Laden being at the designated location, the United States kept its allies, including and especially Pakistan, completely in the dark:[173] The American government neither secured the permission of the Pakistani government to undertake the mission nor gave the Pakistani government any form of advance notice about it. Although serious concerns about possible mission-aborting leaks made this noncommunication understandable from an intelligence perspective, the strategy inadvertently stimulated a diplomatic nightmare in American–Pakistani relations.

## Purpose/Rationale

First and foremost, the killing of bin Laden was systemically motivated by a desire for deterrence through the application of punishment—to retaliate in response to the 9/11 terrorist attacks and al-Qaeda–sponsored violence over the years opposing the interests of the United States and its Western allies all over the world. This successful retaliation was designed to satisfy angry Americans and to foster more national unity, pride, and support at a time of economic recession and uncertainty about the country's future security. The tone of President Obama's May 1 speech illustrates this pattern:

> Let us think back to the sense of unity that prevailed on 9/11. I know that it has, at times, frayed. Yet today's achievement is a testament to the greatness of our country and the determination of the American people.[174]

This speech was full of patriotic bravado, aimed at the domestic audience, and designed to highlight strong leadership in the face of peril.

Secondarily, systemically influencing the killing of bin Laden was a desire to demonstrate that the global war on terror could successfully accomplish what is defined as its most important objective, thereby highlighting prodigious American military and intelligence capabilities. It was designed to showcase that the country could execute a precise coercive mission, removing a major threat and returning unscathed (in contrast to, for example, President Jimmy Carter's failed helicopter rescue of American hostages in Iran on April 24, 1980). The killing revealed that American intelligence is fully capable of pinpointing a threat source and—crucial in today's porous world—keeping that information secret until completion of the mission. It illustrated the capacity of the United States, when an opportunity presents itself, to act decisively and to avoid being bogged down by bureaucratic obstacles. Finally, it highlighted the country's dogged persistence in pursuing a critical security goal regardless of roadblocks encountered.

For many Americans it had been exasperating that, for almost a decade, the greatest military power with the most advanced surveillance and intelligence capabilities had not been able to locate and take out a single individual it blamed for masterminding the deadliest terrorist attack in history on American soil. For these Americans, the bin Laden killing was deeply satisfying. After numerous foreign military actions had produced mixed results—including President Bill Clinton's humiliating American military intervention in Somalia in 1992–1993—the United States wanted to demonstrate that it had not lost its security bite in international relations. This attempt to repair the American post–Cold War security image is in some ways parallel to President Ronald Reagan's relatively successful Cold War attempt through the American invasion of Grenada on October 25, 1983, to reestablish American credibility after the embarrassing terrorist suicide bombing of the American embassy in Beirut, Lebanon, on April 18 earlier that year.

The long-range strategic goal of the killing of bin Laden was the establishment of systemic deterrence against any future state or nonstate threat. Through the demonstration of resolve—combining will and capability—to execute such a successful lethal strike anywhere in the world, the aim was to create fear and trepidation among those seeking to do harm to America and the West, to signal to violent disruptive parties that they will be on the losing side of future confrontations. This killing occurred in the context of a largely unrestrained counterterrorist thrust involving (1) putting every kind of military pressure possible on the terrorist system; (2) keeping the pressure on for a sustained period; (3) changing countermeasures continually to keep terrorists off balance and to keep pace with their own changes in behavior; and (4) conducting aggressive intelligence operations against this system, particularly on apprehending leaders and key operatives. This thrust consisted of a flexible and versatile toolbox of approaches in confronting transnational terrorists on all fronts, including their sources of supply and demand, their modes of transport, their safe havens, and the advanced technologies on which they rely.

President Obama defended the essential morality of killing of bin Laden by arguing in his May 1 speech that "justice has been done."[175] The official framing of this action thus explicitly rejected the rationale of practical expediency, which would have entailed an admission that it might not reflect the most principled action but that it was absolutely necessary under trying circumstances. This was truly a "fight fire with fire" approach (ironic because President Obama in his May 1 speech called the operation a "firefight") in which the United States—possibly motivated by fear, anger, and hatred comparable to that of the terrorists—took its gloves off to combat terrorists using the same type of ruthless tactics these groups have used against the West. This bold American action is not unprecedented: Through many covert and semicovert operations, the United States and some of its Western allies have over time displayed a willingness in foreign settings to undertake targeted killings and significant property destruction when they perceive direct threats to their national security.

## Force Effectiveness

In terms of the immediate military objective, this force use was an absolute success. The head of the most feared terrorist organization in the world was killed, confirmed by DNA evidence. There was absolutely minimal collateral damage in the surrounding area in Pakistan. Although an American helicopter crashed, there was no loss of American life.

In killing Osama bin Laden, the United States behaved like a global security hegemon, demonstrating conclusively the kind of command of effective force in the current global security setting. Although the deterrent effect seemed likely to be short, especially given that zealous armed nonstate groups willing to undertake suicide bombings are difficult to restrain, the killing makes a statement that will not soon be forgotten and might, due to fear of retaliation, at least temporarily dampen the frequency and intensity of global terrorist violence. After all, the killing of bin Laden demonstrated "what U.S. Special Forces are able to do—it sends a clear message to terrorists that they are at least as vulnerable as those they would seek to hurt."[176] The anticipated result is that "some terrorists, one hopes, will decide to become former terrorists—and some young radicals might now think twice before deciding to become terrorists in the first place."[177] The caveat in Obama's May 1 speech about how those executing the mission "took care to avoid civilian casualties"[178]—designed to pacify those with moral qualms about such collateral damage, especially because the target compound was in a residential neighborhood—did little to reduce the stern embedded global signal. As long as American military strength is the greatest in the world, it will be capable of effectively projecting force abroad, but at the same time that strength may make the United States the top target of violent disruptive global elements.

The long-term dangers surrounding bin Laden's killing center primarily on the reactions of global violent extremists, who at some point may endeavor to formulate and execute international acts of reprisal:

Osama bin Laden died the death he wanted: that of a "martyr." He was a mass murderer, but as we celebrate his killing in the West, we should not forget muted reactions in the East and how this is bringing a new generation of jihadists to the fore. Although the jubilation in New York and outside the White House is understandable, it risks sending the message of another premature "Mission Accomplished" moment. To put it simply, Osama bin Laden is dead, al Qaeda is not.[179]

Despite improved and vigilant Western defenses, at least a few of these retaliation attempts would succeed: For example, on May 13, 2011, suicide bombers linked to the Taliban attacked a Pakistani paramilitary training center and killed eighty people in the deadliest militant attack that year in retaliation for bin Laden's killing. Al-Qaeda confirmed shortly after bin Laden's death that his blood "will not be wasted" and that it will continue attacks on the United States and its allies as "the blood of Osama will give birth to thousands of other Osamas."[180] Even world leaders who welcomed the news of bin Laden's death "warned that al-Qaeda's willingness to wreak havoc was undimmed and that the possibility of reprisal attacks meant vigilance was more important than ever,"[181] and Central Intelligence Agency director Leon Panetta said that "terrorist groups 'almost certainly' would try to avenge bin Laden."[182]

Thus the American killing of bin Laden could eventually trigger an escalating pernicious violent action–reaction cycle of mutual retaliation. This act could also plant the seeds for future terror: It has already served as a popular terrorist recruitment tool, as his followers portray him as a martyr and thereby try to rally more support. Those who base their actions on virulent anti-Americanism could find themselves unified and even significantly strengthened by this naked and brutal exercise of American power overseas.

### Force Legitimacy

When the United States uses force in a speedy and effective manner with minimal collateral damage, and the public is convinced that the target was a threat, then the government approval rating among American citizens usually soars. So there is little doubt that, at least for domestic audiences, this bold American action has reconfirmed a wide bandwidth of legitimate action in foreign military missions if they prove successful, regardless of moral and legal principles violated. Immediately after the killing of bin Laden was made public, "outside the White House, a crowd of about 200 people has gathered with American flags; they are singing 'The Star Spangled Banner' and chanting 'USA USA'";[183] and "another large crowd gathered at Ground Zero in New York, singing 'God Bless America.'"[184] Indeed, "More than any other manufactured or authentic feel-good moment in the past decade—more than the toppling of Saddam Hussein's statue in Baghdad, the purple-stained fingers of Iraqis at ballot boxes, or the smiling faces of Afghan girls at school ribbon-cutting ceremonies—the raid that killed Osama bin Laden stands, to date, as the defining moral victory of America's war on terror."[185]

In undertaking the mission to kill bin Laden, the U.S. government strongly felt that it was legitimate. From an American security perspective, the anarchic nature of the global security environment and the masterminding by bin Laden of the deadly 9/11 terrorist attacks more than justified the military intrusion into Pakistan. In this view, this was decidedly not an issue warranting cross-national consultation, due process deliberation, adherence to the rule of law, noninterference in the internal affairs of other countries, or concerns about respect for individual dignity and the sanctity of human life. Like President Obama, some American analysts even attempted to provide legal justification for the killing:

> The U.S. killing of Osama bin Laden in Pakistan was lawful under both U.S. domestic law and international law. The U.S. government's legal rationale will be similar to arguments used by both the Bush and Obama administrations to justify drone strikes against other al-Qaeda leaders in Pakistan and elsewhere. The Authorization to Use Military Force Act of September 18, 2001, authorizes the president to use "all necessary and appropriate force" against persons who authorized, planned, or committed the 9/11 attacks.[186]

This logic renders any form of due process unnecessary.

However, despite such arguments and American force effectiveness, U.S. global legitimacy took a hit. Given that, when the American government deems any person anywhere in the world to be a direct threat to its security, the United States may now feel empowered to enter the country where this person is located and kill him or her without the slightest hesitation, weaker states may not like some of the security implications of this American mandate to undertake coercive unilateral intervention wherever and whenever it pleases. Within much of the Arab world, the response was sadness and anger: "In sharp contrast to the celebrations in America, on the streets of Saudi Arabia, bin Laden's native land, there was a mood of disbelief and sorrow among many; the Palestinian Islamist group Hamas mourned bin Laden as an 'Arab holy warrior'";[187] and "Arab readers' responses from across the Middle East to news of bin Laden's death on mainstream websites such as Al-Jazeera have been overwhelmingly condemnatory of America and full of praise for Osama bin Laden, the 'martyr,' the 'warrior,' the 'hero.'"[188] Moreover, American–Pakistani relations were further eroded:

> The operation could complicate relations with Pakistan, a key U.S. ally in the battle against militancy and the war in Afghanistan. Those ties have already

been damaged over U.S. drone strikes in the west of the country and the six-week imprisonment of a CIA contractor earlier this year. Pakistani authorities were told the details of the raid only after it had taken place, highlighting the lack of trust between Washington and Islamabad. "For some time there will be a lot of tension between Washington and Islamabad because bin Laden seems to have been living here close to Islamabad," said Imtiaz Gul, a Pakistani security analyst.[189]

The unabashed and highly visible emotional gushing by Americans over this killing only served to make matters worse in these parts of the globe.

Many observers strongly rejected the notion that the killing of bin Laden was a just act and instead asserted that in many ways the killing was a premeditated act of revenge by the United States. Specifically, "the killing of Osama bin Laden when he was unarmed has raised concerns the United States may have gone too far in acting as policeman, judge and executioner of the world's most wanted man."[190] For example, from a U.S. ally, former West German Chancellor Helmut Schmidt contended that "it was quite clearly a violation of international law."[191] Australian human rights lawyer Geoffrey Robertson went even further in his indictment of the American action:

> It's not justice. It's a perversion of the term. Justice means taking someone to court, finding them guilty upon evidence and sentencing them. . . . This man has been subject to summary execution, and what is now appearing after a good deal of disinformation from the White House is it may well have been a cold-blooded assassination.[192]

Although both the United Nations and global humanitarian nongovernmental organizations have remained relatively quiet in reaction to bin Laden's killing, on May 6, 2011, U.N. human rights investigators—stressing that all counterterrorism operations must respect international law—called on the United States to disclose full details about the killing of Osama bin Laden, especially revealing whether or not there had been any plan to capture him.[193] Furthermore, "For several Muslim leaders, the more unsettling issue is whether the al Qaeda leader's burial at sea was contrary to Islamic practice"—"if the US can't explain that, then it appears just like dumping an animal and that means there is no respect for the man . . . and what they did can incite more resentment among Osama's supporters."[194] To such skeptics, justice maintaining the moral high ground would associate with a trial, not a killing, and the pursuit of terror would never involve violating the tenets of international law. The killing to them legitimizes a form of vigilantism involving guns and explosives where a government takes the law into its own hands.

### Future Prospects

The death of Osama bin Laden significantly disrupted al-Qaeda's operations but by no means ended global terrorism:

> Terrorism is a decentralized phenomenon—in its funding, planning, and execution. Removing bin Laden does not end the threat. There are successors in al-Qaeda—and successors in autonomous groups operating out of Yemen, Somalia, and other countries. So terrorism will continue. Indeed, it could even grow somewhat worse in the short run as there are sure to be those who will want to show that they can still strike against the West.[195]

Moreover, "The terrorist challenge has metastasized—sanctuary is found more in decentralization, franchising, the Internet, and anonymity than massing in austere locations."[196] So the bin Laden killing is "a milestone, not a turning point" in an ongoing struggle.[197] The al-Qaeda movement itself is likely to survive the death of bin Laden because many al Qaeda affiliates are so financially and operationally autonomous that their day-to-day activities will not be significantly affected by bin Laden's removal; al-Qaeda's narrative that Islam is under attack still resonates with many disaffected people, and several states in the Middle East, South Asia, and North Africa continue to serve as "lifelines" for al-Qaeda.[198]

In terms of image and signaling, the American killing of bin Laden serves to provide a vivid and memorable reminder for the future of how far the United States and other major powers may be willing to go to protect strategic interests. The circumstances promoting such unilateral sovereignty-thwarting military action include the presence of extremely high perceived foreign threat, the location of the threat being within a weaker country, and the emergence of a narrow window of opportunity to execute a successful mission that can be portrayed as defensive. Thus, in addition to violent armed nonstate groups and rogue states, major powers may use brute force when they possess the capacity and will both to execute the mission successfully and to minimize the disruptive impact of negative repercussions. Bin Laden's killing puts the rest of the world on notice that coercive force may be applied anywhere when there is perceived threat to its national security, and vulnerable states now have every reason to be fearful not just of armed nonstate group and rogue state violence but also of great power intervention if they harbor someone deemed to be an enemy.

As a result of glow surrounding the killing of bin Laden, limitations on future counterterrorist operations may plummet. Specifically, there may be more willingness to fund intelligence (given how pivotal the Central Intelligence Agency was to the successful mission), to undertake covert operations (given how sheltered this mission was from conventional democratic checks and balances), and to increase the use of Special Forces (given how the elite squad of Navy Seals was so crucial to mission success). Special Forces have already assumed major roles often in covert missions in the war in Afghanistan, and their use may be expanded all over the world.[199] Enhanced interrogation procedures may be tolerated more than in the past, and objections to torture may now be more easily overridden.

As with the drone strikes' security impact, American–Pakistani relations are likely to continue at a low ebb, for the U.S. government feels that Pakistani security should have located and apprehended bin Laden, and the Pakistani government feels that the United States should have notified it and received permission prior to undertaking such a sovereignty-violating action. Because a Pakistani physician (Shakil Afridi) running a fake vaccination program provided critical confirmation to the Central Intelligence Agency about bin Laden's location, after bin Laden's death medical aid workers in Pakistan administering polio vaccines have been harassed and even killed due to suspicion of being American spies.[200] Beyond the United States and Pakistan, the norms fostered by this American action could very well be contagious and cause other countries to feel freer now to use irregular coercive techniques to extract information and to pursue their objectives abroad using force aimed at foreign targets they perceive as dangerous due to the tacit global acceptance of American tactics to locate and kill bin Laden. Given the proliferation of long-range precision-guided munitions, the future prospects seem to be rising for this kind of unrestrained force use.

## FRENCH INTERVENTION IN MALI

### Force Description

In March 2012, mutinous soldiers with links to al-Qaeda, angry over the government's mishandling of a revolt by nomadic Tuareg rebels in Mali's northern desert, launched a coup in Bamako, Mali, overthrowing the democratically elected government of President Amadou Toumani Tour. Soon afterward, the Tuareg rebels seized much of the north. On January 10, 2013, Islamist extremists captured the town of Konna, and on January 14 they captured the town of Diabaly in a move south toward the capital Bamako designed—in the words of the rebels—to "strike at the heart of France."[201]

Mali's government was reluctant to act on its own, and so it called on France (its former colonial ruler) for help. Having been involved in 2011 in conflicts in Libya and the Ivory Coast, France responded to Mali's request "with a swift and affirmative response"[202] and began a military intervention in Mali in January 2013. The French government ordered into action fighter jets and attack helicopters, employing warplanes based both in France and in Chad.[203] On January 11, France initiated Operation Serval, designed to support Mali government troops fighting advancing armed Islamist extremists. After air strikes failed to dislodge the rebels, on January 15, French ground troops became involved in the fighting for the first time, preparing for a potentially lengthy effort to retake the country's north. Some 2,900 French troops, accompanied by a thousand-plus Malians, carried out a swift assault on the three big towns in Mali's vast desert reaches that had been occupied by al-Qaeda–led rebels since April 2012. When French soldiers marched into the northern city of Gao on January 26, they won the decisive victory of a three-week-old campaign to dislodge the jihadists. On February 22, the United States deployed several unarmed Predator drones from a new base in Niger to fly surveillance missions supporting French forces in Mali. In March 2013, France announced that "a large part of its task in Mali is already done,"[204] with plans announced to further scale back its military deployment, which had ballooned to nearly 4,000—the number France once deployed in Afghanistan—along with nearly 3,800 African soldiers.[205] On May 25, after suffering very few casualties, France began to withdraw its troops. During an interview on May 31, 2013, French President François Hollande "confirmed that only 1000 of the over 4000 French troops who participated in Operation Serval would be left at the end of the year" (many of the departing troops stayed in the region in French military bases in Chad, Senegal, and Côte d'Ivoire).[206]

## Purpose/Rationale

Officially, the dual deterrence/compellence purposes of the French intervention in Mali were fighting "Islamic terrorism" and reestablishing Mali's "territorial integrity."[207] President Hollande stressed that the Mali intervention "is not a neo-colonial move, but rather the result of one sovereign nation asking another for help."[208] Unofficially, France intervened in Mali in part because it was concerned about "the protection of French interests in the region and is an attempt to promote France's presence in an area that was traditionally considered a centre of special influence due to its former colonial presence"; the coveted natural resources within Mali, including large oil, gas, and mineral resources, were "much coveted by the French."[209] However, narrow economic interests in a former colony appeared not to be the root of the French intervention: "Anyone who wishes to understand the conflict in Mali must recognise that this is not a resource grab by the French . . . the idea that socialist President François Hollande, a man who was welcomed into office eight months ago promising a 75 per cent tax for France's rich, is embarked on a final push into West Africa on behalf of French corporations is bonkers to put it mildly."[210]

France's intervention addressed worries about a potential safe haven for terrorists emerging—to prevent "the establishment of a terrorist state"[211]—and by isolating the radical elements of Mali's population: "The aim of the French and their Malian allies is to separate the religious zealots, hailing mainly from Algeria and beyond, from native Malians and the less fanatical rebels."[212] The frustration of the Tuareg rebels has deep roots:

> The territorial integrity of Mali is threatened above all by Tuareg groups in the north of the country, who consider themselves, rightly or wrongly, to have been ignored by successive Malian governments run largely by black Africans from the south. These are long-standing grievances, going back more than 30 years, and are the consequence of the colonial division between North Africa, which is mostly in the hands of Arabs, and Central Africa, largely in the control of black Africans. The Tuaregs have been the losers in this partition, and are now concentrated in Chad, Mali and Niger.[213]

The rebel forces' goals are multifaceted—autonomy, reduced French postcolonial influence, and imposed Islamic Sharia law—"while some wish for an Islamic state in Northern Mali, others aim for a global jihad and the rest are just keen to get a share of the lucrative drug trade and kidnapping business which makes the groups millions of dollars every year."[214] A former captor even reports that these rebels' aspirations were to create "an Islamic emirate that spanned Africa" and "to spread chaos from the Atlantic to the Pacific."[215]

### Force Effectiveness

The French intervention involving a ground and air offensive in Mali constituted a short-term military success. On February 7, 2013, U.N. Secretary-General Ban Ki-moon announced that the military operation "so far has been effective and successful."[216] Most of the world concluded that by February 2013 French forces had succeeded in driving Islamist rebels out of northern Mali, where there was an African al-Qaeda stronghold.[217] At the same time, the French military in Mali did acknowledge that "there is a risk of 'residual presence' of terrorists mixed among the population."[218]

However, in terms of long-run security consequences, the impacts of the military invasion are murkier: When France announced its intervention in Mali, "at that moment young Muslims in France heard that Shariah is in force in northern Mali and they wanted to go there to defend this 'real Islam' against an announced intervention."[219] Safety for Malian civilians did not seem to improve much after the military action. Moreover, the French victory caused the Islamic extremists to change their tactics in a manner undesired by the French: After having begun by using conventional army tactics involving "taking and holding cities, travelling along roads in vehicles that presented a clear target for French jets, now they will revert to what they do much better—surviving as guerrillas in the desert."[220]

### Force Legitimacy

The immediate response to the French invasion of most Malian people was very positive, punctuated by "scenes of joy and excitement":

> In driving out the Islamists, a French socialist politician has provided Malians with sanctuary from the fanatical whims of the Islamists; hence the celebrations. Most Malians want their lives dictated by the totalitarian edicts of religious fanatics about as much as they want lectures from Western cultural relativists about the "legitimate grievances" of those who would chop off their hands for stealing a loaf of bread.[221]

Widespread gratitude existed in Mali that the French were willing to bear the expenditure to undertake the military intervention, although "in northern Mali the price of food and fuel is rocketing up as a result of the conflict."[222]

Within France, the enthusiasm of its citizens for this foreign invasion was also quite high. Unlike earlier action in Libya, the Mali invasion had considerable support in France, with much talk of it being a "just" or "necessary" war.[223] In the popular French view, it was a fight to defend "the values of the Enlightenment and territorial integrity against Islamic terrorists who enforce sharia law, force women to wear the veil, and kill westerners."[224]

Global approval for France's military intervention was high because of (1) the Malian government's direct request for France's assistance; (2) the real danger that Mali was becoming a terrorist haven; and (3) the evidence that the Islamic extremists had taken over northern Mali, which had severely infringed on the rights of the people. Regarding the second point, many observers concluded that "what the intervention *did* do . . . *was* drive out of Mali some of the most unpleasant people on earth."[225] Regarding the third point, the rebels had "imposed sharia law and everything that goes with it, including amputations, the banning of music, and the reduction of women to the status of chattel."[226] American Vice President Joe Biden praised France's invasion by noting that the "decisive action was not only in the interest of France but of the United States and everyone."[227] Further legitimizing the French intervention was a U.N. Security Council resolution passed on December 20, 2012, establishing an international force to support Mali in its fight to restore stability in its north.[228] Although "many people in the Muslim world criticized France for intervening in a Muslim country,"[229] international praise was high—"For those at a safe distance from the reach of the jihadists, one can welcome the liberation of the Malian people from this stark nightmare."[230]

France had a couple of missteps trying to increase its action's legitimacy. At least partially in response to a January 23, 2013, report by a Paris-based human rights group claiming that Malian government soldiers had carried out multiple summary executions during the French invasion,[231] France agreed to work with a European Union (EU) training team being dispatched to teach Malian forces to respect human rights.[232] However, Amnesty International reported in June 2013 that the Malian security forces' human rights record since January was "simply appalling, violating human rights with apparently no fear of being held accountable," and engaging in torture and execution of dozens of people while in detention.[233] Moreover, France portrayed the military intervention as multilateral (with African forces), although it was largely unilateral because French soldiers did not wait for the African forces to arrive.[234]

### Future Prospects

What is most needed to address the Malian turmoil is the establishment of a strong national government, but this is unlikely after the French invasion:

Meanwhile, Mali's politics is still a mess. "Stabilisation requires an election," said a Western diplomat, adding that a fair poll is as important as the army's reconquest of the country's northern half. After a military coup nearly a year ago, no decent government emerged. But on January 25th a council of ministers endorsed a plan that laid out a series of steps leading, with luck, to an election—and included proposals for talking to the rebels. Few people in Bamako, the capital, are confident that such worthy ideas will be put into practice soon. The hard part of putting Mali back together has barely begun.[235]

As is typical, little advance planning occurred for political reconstruction, jeopardizing the Malian regime's capacity to manage the instability:

> Even if the Islamists do leave Mali there was still a conflict and tension raging between various different groups before they arrived. Mali was already a failed state and until it is repaired will always be a breeding ground for Islamists and the criminal groups which work from within their ranks. Before the Islamists even began to be a threat, Tuareg rebels were fighting against the Malian government leading to the coup which helped create the power vacuum in the north.[236]

The extremist rebel violence seems likely to continue for the foreseeable future, as "the diehard types are likely to carry on the fight."[237] So the idea of a postinvasion peaceful Mali seems remote.

The future stability in Mali is very much in question, in part because France reduced its military role, with the Malian army and the foreign African forces primarily responsible for long-term national stability.[238] Considerable doubt exists that these local forces have the training or the equipment to be able to handle the challenge. Fears are rampant within the affected population—"The population of Timbuktu is anxious, worrying that the departure of French troops will open the door for the Islamists to return."[239] Widespread skepticism surrounds the ability of local Malian government forces to handle the security challenges—"Even after years of American training, the ill-disciplined Malian army on its own is no match for the rebels."[240] The predicament is unlikely to improve in the future, as relations between the Malian army and the Tuareg minority are likely to remain poor.[241] Ultimately the insecurity "could push Mali down the road to being a failed state."[242] As with the United States in its invasion of Iraq and Afghanistan, domestic pressures have not allowed French troops to stay in Mali very long after the initial invasion, and the French government was quick to label the use of force as a success; yet the actual predicament has proven to be sufficiently unstable as to warrant a much longer coercive commitment.

The Mali invasion may even inadvertently trigger major future backfire effects, due to misdiagnosing prevailing threat as focused on Islamic terrorism:

> In truth, the Tuareg question is a matter of ethno-national tensions and has little to do with Islamism. It is a problem that can only be resolved by political negotiation that aims to establish a more equitable balance of power. In order to re-establish Mali's territorial integrity, a solid and stable central state is required (for the moment, such a thing does not exist). Rather than restoring a viable state for all Malians, the French intervention risks exacerbating ethnic tensions by handing power back to a particular faction that is unwilling to share it.[243]

In addition, "the French military intervention in Mali has increased the threat of domestic terrorism, with some French citizens of black African ancestry becoming more willing to fight under the banner of jihad"—"The concerns of the French authorities were once largely limited to residents of North African Arab ancestry, like Algerians and Tunisians, but attention has broadened to include those French with roots in Mali, Senegal, Nigeria and Niger."[244]

The French invasion in Mali involved regional violence contagion while the fighting was still going on, and it seems likely to cause even more in the future. On January 16, 2013, in retaliation for the French intervention, Islamic extremists seized hundreds of Algerian and foreign workers as hostages at an internationally managed gas field in Algeria's southeastern desert; when on January 19 Algerian special forces recaptured the gas complex, at least thirty-seven foreign hostages, one Algerian hostage, and twenty-nine kidnappers were killed, creating fears of broader North African conflict. Moreover, as a result of the French intervention, "several thousand jihadists threaten to de-stabilize Mali, Niger, Nigeria, and Algeria; beyond the human rights abuses, their attacks will discourage foreign investment, paralyze local economies and produce vast numbers of refugees."[245] Furthermore, although the French invasion disrupted the cocaine supply to Europe, drug smugglers have already creatively discovered new routes through Angola, the Republic of Congo, the Great Lakes region of eastern Africa, and Libya,[246] potentially expanding the reach of violent criminal activity to Mali's neighbors. Overall, "through a domino effect, there is a risk of state fragility spreading throughout the region, across the Sahel, in turn exerting dangerous pressure on the Maghreb and

Europe; fragility leaves the whole region prone to the further emergence of weapons, drugs and cross-border trafficking, providing income for jihadists and other criminal organisations."[247]

## ISRAELI ATTACK ON SYRIAN NUCLEAR FACILITY

### Force Description

On September 6, 2007, in a surprise attack shortly after midnight, seven Israeli Air Force fighter jets executed "Operation Orchard" and destroyed a covert site of a future nuclear reactor near al-Kibar in northeast Syria. The planning for this brute force act had begun months earlier: In mid-May 2007, Prime Minister Ehud Olmert contacted American government officials asking if Mossad chief Meir Dagan could share intelligence that Syria was building a nuclear reactor, with North Korea providing both the design and the technical assistance.[248] This force use was later confirmed by the CIA as a nearly completed gas-cooled, graphite-moderated nuclear reactor secretly under construction since 2001.[249] Apparently, the unit may have been part of an Iranian-led multinational nuclear weapons effort, with both Syria and North Korea as collaborators.[250]

Given the location selected and the absence of an electrical grid connection, it was clear that this reactor served a nuclear-weapons program rather than electric power production.[251] Importantly, after the attack follow-up investigations revealed that Namchongang Trading, a North Korean firm, smuggled in key materials for the Syrian reactor from China and possibly Europe.[252]

An American deputy national security adviser reports that Syria building a nuclear reactor was surprising to both Israel and the United States:

> Initially, there were doubts that Bashar al-Assad could be so stupid as to try this stunt of building a nuclear reactor with North Korean help. Did he really think he would get away with it—that Israel would permit it? But he nearly did; had the reactor been activated, striking it militarily could have strewn radioactive material into the wind and into the nearby Euphrates River, which was the reactor's source of water needed for cooling. When we found out about the reactor, it was at an advanced construction stage, just a few months from being "hot."[253]

As security officials from the two countries plotted the response together, intense secrecy was maintained[254] so as not to promote panic.

In April 2008, American intelligence authorities released a video revealing that the Syrian facility had concealed construction of a graphite-cooled
nuclear reactor similar to North Korea's Yongbyon reactor, generating plutonium for the North Korean nuclear weapons program. In April 2011, the
International Atomic Energy Agency (IAEA) confirmed that the Syrian target
was indeed a nuclear reactor site.[255] ABC News reported that, prior to the air
strike, Israel had recruited a spy to take ground photographs of the nuclear
reactor's construction from inside the complex.[256] After the destruction of the
facility, "Syria moved quickly to cover up its covert nuclear activities by de-
molishing and burying the reactor building and by removing incriminating
equipment":[257] Soon after the bombing, the Syrian government bulldozed the
reactor site; when a 2008 IAEA site visit found uranium traces, Syria never
permitted a return visit.[258] Despite frequent opportunities to do so, the Syrian
government was not willing at any point later to admit details about the true
nature of this facility.

### Purpose/Rationale

The motivation for the Israeli action was deterrence—a senior Israeli official
stated that it was designed to "re-establish the credibility of our deterrent
power," signaling that Israel had zero tolerance for even a potential Syrian
nuclear weapons program.[259] Beyond preventing the Syrians from developing
a weapon of mass destruction that could be used against it, Israel wanted to
reinforce deterrence broadly in the Arab world: "Israel's failures in its 2006
war with Hezbollah weakened the perceived deterrent that it held over its
neighbors; the al-Kibar strike may have been an attempt to reestablish the
supremacy of Israel's military apparatus in its enemies' eyes."[260] In every respect, this action represented classic preemptive military action to eliminate
the possibility that an existing major threat would be actualized. Israel could
not afford to wait to act until the reactor was fully functional because doing
so would risk spreading contaminated radioactive material.[261] Ultimately Israel's greatest fear was getting a hostile "nuclear neighbor," "particularly one
with which Israel has been in a constant state of war since the Jewish state's
independence in 1948"; and it is even possible that the attack on al-Kibar may
have served as a warning to Iran or as a practice run for a future raid on an
Iranian nuclear site.[262]

Diplomatic options were considered instead of the destruction of the Syrian nuclear reactor, with the idea that if they failed then the military option

could be executed: informing the International Atomic Energy Agency of the situation, demanding immediate inspections and cessation of work on the reactor, and then—if Syria refused—going to the U.N. Security Council and demanding action.[263] However, diplomacy was quickly rejected, as Israel never trusted the United Nations: Syria's allies in the United Nations—especially Russia—would protect it, and the IAEA was known to have a leaning against meaningful sanctions in such cases.[264] Moreover, force use as a last resort after the failure of diplomacy appeared to make little sense in this case:

> The argument that there would always remain a military option as a last resort was misleading at best. Once we made public our knowledge of the site, Syria could put a kindergarten right next to it or take some similar move using human shields. Military action required secrecy, and once we made any kind of public statement about al-Kibar, that option would be gone.[265]

Thus a strike destroying the nuclear site seemed to be the only viable option.

The motivation for Syrian construction of the nuclear facility is still clouded in mystery because the Syrian government has denied that the al-Kibar plant was designed to build nuclear weapons. However, there is informed speculation about this matter:

> Although the precise motives behind Syria's nuclear activities are unknown, a primary impetus was likely the Assad regime's obsession with obtaining a deterrent against Israel. Syria's nuclear program was the capstone of one of the Middle East's most active chemical and biological weapons programs. This program, together with Syria's extensive surface-to-surface missile capabilities, is a major source of potential contention and conflict between Syria and Israel.[266]

Given this rationale's enduring nature, outside fears persist that Syria might try this effort again, possibly with North Korean or Iranian help.

### Force Effectiveness

The immediate outcome of this strike was military success—Syria could not develop nuclear weapons, and a key threat potential was eliminated.[267] Moreover, Syria has made no clear nuclear move since that time—"There is nothing to suggest that Damascus will or is even able to play with fire once again."[268] Diplomatically, it seems that the Israeli attack "made the Syrians more, not less, desirous of talking to the Israelis because it made them afraid of Israeli power."[269] Furthermore, the attack thwarted any plans Iran may have had to build a backup plutonium facility in Syria.[270] So Israel accomplished its deterrence purpose, as in its mind "this incident is a reminder that there is no substitute for military strength and the will to use it."[271] For the long run, however, a decisive impact is difficult to specify. Over time, Israeli–Syrian relations showed no sign of thawing and have remained quite hostile, as verbal barbs have been exchanged without forceful confrontation.

However, three major negative repercussions remain at least potential concerns. First, the attack could have inadvertently encouraged illegal nuclear weapons facilities to be built in much harder-to-detect locations, such as the secure underground tunnels where the centrifuges Iran is using for uranium enrichment are now located:[272] This dispersed subterranean positioning of nuclear facilities could make any future demolition operation much more complex, creating much greater vulnerability to counterattacks.[273] Second, if the Israeli action hoped to uncover Iran's air defense weaknesses, the strategy may have backfired, for the apparent system failure prompted Iran in December 2007 to purchase the more advanced Russian S-300 air defense system.[274] Third, the possibility of retaliation was not completely eliminated: Hezbollah commander Imad Mughniyah, a "notorious terrorist mastermind," reportedly had planned to avenge the Israeli strike on al-Kibar with an attack on an Israeli embassy in Baku, Cairo, or Amman but was killed in Damascus on February 12, 2008, before this plan could be carried out.[275] These concerns reveal that the Israeli attack risked an action–reaction cycle of violence between the state of Israel and Hezbollah, Syria, or Iran.

**Force Legitimacy**

The global verbal reactions to the Israeli strike on the Syrian nuclear power plant were decidedly underwhelming:

> What was particularly notable about this attack was what occurred afterward: the near total lack of international comment or criticism of Israel's action. The lack of reaction contrasted starkly to the international outcry that followed Israel's preventive strike in 1981 that destroyed Iraq's Osiraq reactor. To be sure, foreign governments may have reserved comment because of the lack of information after the attack. The Israeli and U.S. governments imposed virtually total news blackouts immediately after the raid that held for seven months, and Syria was initially silent on the matter and then subsequently denied that the bombed target was a nuclear facility. Yet, the international silence

continued even after the CIA on April 24, 2008, provided a 12-minute video and an extensive briefing that made a strong case that the target was a North Korean–built reactor designed for producing weapons-usable plutonium.[276]

Stunningly, after the strike "no Arab government commented on the Israeli raid, much less pressed for retaliation against Israel, diplomatic or otherwise"; and the matter was not raised at the U.N. Security Council or the General Assembly.[277] Indeed, "to this day, Syria and Israel, two countries that have technically been at war since the founding of the Jewish state in 1948, have largely adhered to a bizarre policy of downplaying what was clearly an act of war."[278] Even much later, Syria's position remained unchanged:

> "The facility that was bombed was not a nuclear plant, but rather a conventional military installation," Syrian President Bashar Assad insisted . . . at his palace near Damascus in mid-January 2009. "We could have struck back. But should we really allow ourselves to be provoked into a war? Then we would have walked into an Israeli trap."[279]

This silence in many ways has been deafening.

What little criticism of the Israeli action came mainly from the Egyptian Director General of the IAEA, Mohamed ElBaradei, who learned of the Israeli attack only from media reports. He forcefully condemned both the United States and Israel for their "shoot first and ask questions later" strategy.[280] vehemently argued that the Israeli action was "a violation of international law," and claimed that, if Israelis and the Americans had intelligence about an illegal nuclear facility, the IAEA should have been immediately notified.[281] This censure went unheeded.

Considering its complicity in planning the strike, after initial hesitation the United States was supportive of the Israeli force use, believing that the Syrian reactor "was not intended for peaceful activities" and asserting that "the Syrian regime must come clean before the world regarding its illicit nuclear activities."[282] The Israeli strike was in the end "a model both of U.S.–Israel collaboration and of interagency cooperation without leaks."[283] The United States had itself considered launching an attack on the Syrian nuclear facility, but President George W. Bush had decided that "bombing a sovereign country with no warning or announced justification would create severe blowback," adding that a covert attack to be too risky.[284]

Israeli citizens viewed this action very positively—the BBC reported that "the apparent strike on the reactor, deep inside Syria, was seen by many in

Israel as a sign of their military prowess."[285] The global image of high-quality Israeli intelligence was thus reinforced. However, due to pervasive public fear of attack in Israel, no sense of complacency emerged afterwards.

### Future Prospects

Given ongoing tensions between Iran and both Israel and the United States, some speculation has occurred about whether the 2007 Israeli strike on Syrian nuclear facilities could be repeated in the future with an attack on an Iranian nuclear site.[286] To many observers, the key question is, "Was the destruction of the Al Kibar complex meant as a final warning to the Iranians, a trial run of sorts intended to show them what the Israelis plan to do if Tehran continues with its suspected nuclear weapons program?"[287] Considerable regional and global fears have emerged about a possible future Israeli–Iranian confrontation over nuclear facilities, and these fears have been heightened by the revelation that "Western intelligence agencies report that the Iranian leadership is demanding that Syria return—in full and without compensation—substantial shipments of uranium, which it no longer needs now that its nuclear program has been destroyed."[288]

The weakness of today's global nuclear nonproliferation norms was highlighted by Syria's ability to progress so far on its nuclear facility. The reality that within the Middle East alone there are "about a dozen states with at least nascent nuclear programs" turns the existence of al-Kibar into a serious warning about the dysfunction of the current global non-proliferation regime.[289] In light of this concern about nuclear proliferation, in response to the Israeli strike a debate began among American policy makers about whether the intelligence prompting the Israeli attack on the Syrian facility should harden the U.S. approach to Syria and North Korea.[290]

More questions emerge about brute force utility:

> Can bomb attacks and hit squads against real or presumed terrorists bring about progress in the Middle East? Is it true that Arabs and Israelis only understand the language of violence, as many in Tel Aviv are now saying? Did the operation against the Al Kibar complex, which violated international law, bring the Syrian president to his senses, or did it merely encourage him to harden his position?[291]

The root causes of Syria's action and Israel's forceful response—deep Arab–Israeli tensions, religious antagonism, and enduring distrust—remain unresolved despite external diplomatic attempts to forge a lasting peace. Although—like the United States—Israel feels that it "can act whenever and wherever it wants to protect vital interests," "how much deterrence does Israel need to dissuade enemies from attacking?"[292]

Determining whether one assumes a future atmosphere in the region filled with mutual violence depends on if the deterrence value for Israel of its attack on the Syrian nuclear facility outweighs the value for Israel's adversaries of justifying future attacks on Israel and exacting violent revenge against an enemy hated and feared for centuries. Tensions between Israel on the one hand and Syria and Iran on the other hand have never been higher, and nuclear fears exacerbate centuries-old religious hatreds. However, since 2011, the instability promoted by the Arab Spring uprisings, which Arab states feel Israel has taken advantage of, has appeared to reduce at least temporarily the negative anti-Israel energy among Middle Eastern states. Due to the intensity of the ongoing Syrian civil war, for the foreseeable future the Assad regime appears to have its hands so full with managing internal rebellion that concerns about Israel have been marginalized.

## ISRAELI INVASION OF LEBANON

### Force Description

On July 12, 2006, hours after Hezbollah guerrillas in Lebanon had killed three Israeli soldiers and captured two others, Israel declared war on Lebanon. Israel launched massive air strikes, an air and naval blockade, and a ground invasion from the south. After the initial stages of the conflict, Israel dispatched thousands of additional ground troops into southern Lebanon to destroy Hezbollah rocket-launching sites prior to the imposition of a U.N. cease-fire.[293] In the course of the fighting, both sides were accused by human rights organizations of causing needless civilian casualties, with Israel accused of using cluster bombs in the last days of the war and Hezbollah accused of showering Katyusha rockets on northern Israeli cities with no strategic military targets. Hostilities ceased on August 14, when the United Nations did impose the cease-fire, and Israel lifted its naval blockade on September 8. In the end, the war's casualties included 119 Israeli soldiers and over forty Israeli civilians killed, and over 1,000 Lebanese killed, mostly civilians.[294] Hezbollah also reportedly suffered enormous losses,[295] although it survived as a force in the region.

The 2006 war had its most devastating impact in southern Lebanon:

The 33 day war that followed Hezbollah's capture of two Israeli soldiers in July 2006 was widely considered to be more destructive than previous Israeli invasions or occupations of Lebanon. Approximately 1,200 Lebanese were killed, one million were displaced and direct war damage was estimated at US $4 billion, with an additional $6 billion in indirect costs. Israel's response went far beyond an operation to rescue its two soldiers, though it was goaded by Hezbollah rocket attacks deep into Israeli territory that killed 43 civilians. Roads, bridges and public utilities were targeted, and thousands of housing units were destroyed or damaged, particularly in the Shia-dominated areas of Beirut Southern Suburbs (BSS) and southern Lebanon. Most civilians returned home within hours of the cessation of hostilities in mid-August 2006 (thus averting the humanitarian problems associated with long-term displacement), but returnees faced hazards from enormous quantities of unexploded ordinance.[296]

The horrendous devastation of civilian lives and property made this "one of the most devastating wars in Lebanon's recent history,"[297] highly significant given the frequency of violent conflict within Lebanon over many decades. Not coincidentally, given the location of Hezbollah's fighters and equipment, the damage was most severe in parts of southern Lebanon where Hezbollah's support has been the greatest, although notably this pattern did not lead to reduced popular support for Hezbollah.

### Purpose/Rationale

The primary motivation for the Israeli action was deterrence of future Hezbollah attacks on Israel through punishment of Hezbollah for capturing the Israeli soldiers. By implication, Lebanon was to be punished for providing Hezbollah a safe haven and deterred from doing so in the future. Israelis expected to secure the release of the two captured soldiers as well.

Hezbollah's immediate motivation for undertaking the action triggering the Israeli invasion—the capture of the Israeli soldiers—was the hope of negotiating a prisoner exchange. More specifically, "Hezbollah's July 12 raid into Israel, backed by Iran, was intended to entangle Israel in a limited skirmish on its northern border and a drawn-out prisoner exchange at a time when Iran was facing mounting pressure over its nuclear program."[298] However, instead of a limited skirmish, a full-scale war with Israel ensued. Hezbollah's overall goals call for "Islamic rule in Lebanon, an end to Western imperialism, and the destruction of the state of Israel."[299]

As with the Israeli attack on the Syrian nuclear facility, the roots of this war run a lot deeper than simple tensions between Israel and Hezbollah. Although Hezbollah's capturing of the two Israeli soldiers triggered the conflict, more fundamentally "the fighting was the combined result of the unresolved Arab–Israeli conflict and the struggle between the forces of modernization and those of extremism within the Muslim world—two issues that are linked by the radicals' exploitation of the Arab–Israeli conflict for their own political ends."[300] Hezbollah ("party of God") emerged as a Shi'a Muslim organization in 1982 as a response to the Israeli invasion of Lebanon.[301] Since its October 1983 attack on the American embassy in Beirut generated 250 casualties, Hezbollah has carried out over 179 attacks, killing more than 800 and injuring over 1,500 people.[302] During the 1990s, Hezbollah made a concerted effort to expel Israel from Lebanon, given Israel's 1985 establishment of a "security zone" in southern Lebanon. Hezbollah has also given money, weapons, and personnel to the Palestinian freedom movement in Israel.[303]

Hezbollah relies on diverse international sources for funding and support, with Iran having helped to create, finance, and train Hezbollah:[304]

Both Hezbollah's terrorist actions and its guerrilla warfare are facilitated by the group's extensive international network. Hezbollah operatives have been found in France, Spain, Cyprus, Singapore, the "triborder" region of South America, and the Philippines, as well as in more familiar operational theatres in Europe and the Middle East. The movement draws on these cells to raise money, prepare the logistical infrastructure for attacks, disseminate propaganda, and otherwise ensure that the organization remains robust and ready to strike.[305]

Among these highly diverse foreign sources for Hezbollah are Colombian drug traffickers,[306] reinforcing the global reach of Hezbollah's funding network.

Hezbollah is unusual among armed nonstate groups in that it actively participates in legislative governance by holding seats in the Lebanese parliament. Despite previously labeling the electoral system as corrupt, Hezbollah decided to officially enter the political arena in 1992. As of 2009, Hezbollah holds twenty-eight seats in the Lebanese parliament and "enjoys the status of a political organization that negotiates directly with governments, both its own and foreign."[307] The group "operates as a political party, but at the same time it is a terrorist organization, a highly trained militia, and a clandestine criminal organization with illegal enterprises in Lebanon and abroad."[308] Hezbollah's ability to project multiple faces aids its successful global functioning:

> By mixing religion, ideology, social welfare, politics, and occasional violence, Hezbollah has gained legitimacy with local communities and developed sophisticated institutional practices, which give it strength and resilience. The movement is at once a religious organization, an aid organization, a political party, and a paramilitary force. This makes it hard for governments to know how to categorize and confront it. The U.S. government, for example, considers Hezbollah a terrorist organization and has banned its television programs, financial arms, and charity activities from operating in the United States. The British government proscribes only Hezbollah's military wing, including its External Security Organization, but allows the group's political, social, and welfare elements to proceed unhindered. The disparities between countries' domestic counterterrorism legislation helps Hezbollah because it inhibits a consistent, unified Western response to its activities.[309]

These remarkable hybrid qualities provide for Hezbollah's incredible operational flexibility and an ability to manipulate their image in the global community.

### Force Effectiveness

The Israeli invasion was not successful in its primary objective to punish and weaken Hezbollah and deter it from further offensive action. Although Israeli analysts have asserted that the 2006 Lebanon War "enhanced deterrence," dangerous friction persists.[310] Israel specifically did not secure the release of the two captured soldiers or destroy Hezbollah's military wing,[311] and Hezbollah has maintained its powerful influence in southern Lebanon.[312] A postwar Israeli review panel concluded that the country's "inconclusive 33-day war with Hezbollah fighters in Lebanon undermined the military deterrence Israelis consider indispensable to their survival" and found that the war "was a big and serious failure" for Israel.[313] The identified reasons for this military failure included "failures in preparedness, strategic thinking and decision-making by civilian and military leaders."[314]

Part of the explanation for the Israeli failure lies in its apparent military overconfidence and its surprise at the strength of the Hezbollah resistance, stocked with sophisticated Syrian-made and Iranian-made missiles:

Hezbollah is a militia trained like an army and equipped like a state, and its fighters "are nothing like Hamas or the Palestinians," said a soldier who just returned from Lebanon. "They are trained and highly qualified," he said, equipped with flak jackets, night-vision goggles, good communications and sometimes Israeli uniforms and ammunition. "All of us were kind of surprised."[315]

Having a fighting force numbering between 2,000 and 4,000, Hezbollah had studied and prepared for asymmetrical warfare, possessed the advantage of fighting in their own territory, and purposely made it difficult to attack them without bombing civilian areas.[316] Over time, Hezbollah has proved to be "the single most effective adversary Israel has ever faced": With their "combination of skilled operations, willing sacrifice, and emphasis on long-term struggle," Hezbollah's "fighters and leaders have demonstrated exceptional dedication and an ability to learn from mistakes and innovate quickly."[317] Hezbollah sees itself as the winner in the war with Israel[318] and now has solid organization under a charismatic leader, strong finances, effective education, welfare, and emergency aid, and a military able to deploy advanced weapons systems.[319]

### Force Legitimacy

Within Lebanon, the reactions of the people to the war were decidedly mixed:

For the south, which suffered for more than a decade under Israeli occupation, Hezbollah's leader, Sheik Hassan Nasrallah, is a folk hero who helped drive out the Israelis; but many middle-class Lebanese who have worked for the past decade to generate an economic revival are tired of war and resent Hezbollah's capture of two Israeli soldiers in a cross-border raid on July 12.[320]

Nonetheless, the net effect of Hezbollah's success in delivering significant aid to displaced, destitute, and homeless people was to mute Lebanese citizens who might have otherwise criticized Hezbollah for triggering a conflict that devastated much of southern Lebanon[321] and to cause Lebanese people benefiting from Hezbollah-sponsored aid to approve of the organization. After the war, "the mood in Beirut's southern suburb on September 22, 2006 was one of unrestrained jubilance; Hizbullah's 'divine, historic, and strategic victory against Israel' was being celebrated by a gathering of more than a million people."[322] As a direct result of Hezbollah's massive postwar reconstruction effort,[323] it "won the loyalty of many Lebanese":[324] Its broad-based Lebanese support encompassed 96 percent of Shiites, 87 percent of Sunnis, 80 percent of Christians, and 80 percent of Druze.[325] Given the diversity of groups residing within Lebanon, this level of domestic popular support for an armed nonstate group is impressive.

Despite American approval of Israeli action and widespread disapproval of Hezbollah, Israel did not receive much support for its invasion of Lebanon:

> Israel's operations against Hezbollah in Lebanon and Hamas in Gaza have been widely condemned in Europe, the Arab world and at the United Nations as violations of international law. Some of the critics seem to deny that Israel has any legitimate right to use force. Others, while acknowledging its right to self-defense, nevertheless regard its exercise in these cases as illegal. Israel's alleged offenses include treating mere "terrorist" attacks as an excuse to attack Lebanon, using disproportionate force, causing excessive civilian casualties and refusing to contemplate an immediate cease-fire.[326]

The most common criticism of the Israeli force use was that it overreacted to the capture of two of its soldiers. After the war ended, with many in Israel interpreting the invasion as "a debacle," the country found itself having to cope with the resulting humanitarian crisis.[327] Because of its steadfast support for Israel during the war, the image of the United States overseas was also "badly battered, in part due to prolonged negotiations widely perceived in the Arab world as deliberate to allow Israel to pursue its military agenda."[328] Moreover, American–Israeli relations worsened after the war, as American Secretary of State Condoleezza Rice indicated that the Israelis had "mishandled both the military and the diplomatic sides of the conflict."[329]

In terms of postwar aid to war victims (which can affect perceived legitimacy), the Lebanese government did little more in the aftermath of the 2006 war than to pay some financial compensation to those who had lost their homes.[330] As usual, "European states and Western-backed financial institutions focused their attention on providing aid primarily in the form of programmes for better governance."[331] Indeed, many states providing assistance in the war-torn area tended "to be slow paced, wedded to bureaucratic procedures and prone to attaching conditions to financial assistance."[332] In an unsuccessful attempt to discredit the success of Hezbollah's reconstructive assistance, Western media expressed worry that Hezbollah's apparent reconstruction efficiency was due to Iranian funding,[333] as both Iran and Syria have close ties to Hezbollah.[334]

### Future Prospects

For Israel, the war's dismal outcome generated some long-run backfire effects that seem likely to continue into the future. In addition to the strengthening of Hezbollah's reputation, "Israel's disproportionate response to Hezbollah is only likely to increase the hatred most Lebanese, even non-Shiites, now feel toward Israel; while more and more civilians die in Lebanon, Hezbollah's appeal and recruiting are only likely to increase, while reducing the likelihood that it will be willing to compromise and disarm in the future."[335] Perhaps most important, the military setbacks that the Israeli ground invasion encountered had the hugely negative regional security impact of "puncturing the aura of invincibility long projected by the Israel Defense Forces."[336] This loss of the Israeli aura of invincibility appears to be particularly important given subsequent developments in the region: In June 2007, Hamas took over Gaza, and Israel has since fought two indecisive wars in that area in December 2008/January 2009 and in November 2012. Hezbollah has more recently become fully rearmed, with a growing international reputation for military effectiveness, and Iran is on the verge of becoming a nuclear power. When outsiders consider the implications of these developments together, they serve to highlight the vulnerability of the state of Israel.

Despite its positive security impact within southern Lebanon, Hezbollah's action has been—and is likely to continue to be—devastating for regional stability. Aside from the direct regional effects of the 2006 war with Israel, "Hezbollah has provided guerrilla training, bomb-building expertise, propaganda, and tactical tips to Hamas, Palestinian Islamic Jihad, and other anti-Israeli groups."[337] This expanding external outreach allows Hezbollah to disrupt the Middle East peace process at little cost to itself, and "exporting its model of conflict while limiting actual attacks allows the movement to continue its fight without alienating its Lebanese constituents (many of whom fear an Israeli backlash) or its backers in Tehran and Damascus (who fear U.S. retaliation)."[338] These internationally disruptive efforts by Hezbollah seem only to have been emboldened by its tangible success in the 2006 war with Israel, as recently evidenced by its extensive coercive efforts to help prop up the embattled Assad regime in Syria.

## NATO INTERVENTION IN LIBYA

### Force Description

Beginning on February 17, 2011, as part of the regional Arab Spring movement, antigovernment protesters in Libya began working to overthrow the long-standing forty-two-year government regime under the brutal dictator Colonel Muammar el-Qaddafi. Emotional mass uprisings occurred in Libya's eastern port cities, especially Benghazi. The trigger for violence was protestors assembling there around outside city police headquarters to protest the detention of human rights activist Fethi Tarbel. Some observers hoped that the nonviolent protests would end up in a manner similar to uprisings in Tunisia and Egypt, peacefully resolving differences between the government and the protesters. However, Qaddafi responded by initiating a brutal government crackdown applying overwhelming force against the rebels.

In late February, the U.N. Security Council imposed an arms embargo and an asset freeze on Libya and referred Qaddafi's alleged crimes against humanity (in terms of barbaric acts committed on Libyan citizens) to the International Criminal Court. The United States was the first state to terminate Qaddafi's funding, freezing $32 billion in Libyan assets, and soon other countries followed suit.[339] On March 17, in response to a request from the Arab League, the U.N. Security Council approved the implementation of a no-fly zone over Libya and authorized "all necessary measures" to protect civilian lives.[340] On March 19, with U.N. authorization, the United States launched "Operation Odyssey Dawn," in which Britain and France participated under American strategic command: The coalition initiated air and missile strikes that "obliterated Libya's air defense system within 72 hours" and targeted Libyan forces, "including against a large concentration of armored vehicles approaching Benghazi, the headquarters of the revolution and home to 750,000 people whom Qaddafi had labeled as 'rats' when he threatened to 'cleanse Libya house by house.'"[341]

On March 31, 2011, the North Atlantic Treaty Organization (NATO) agreed to take command of the military operation in Libya—called "Operation Unified Protector"—providing air power enforcing the arms embargo and a no-fly zone, supporting the rebel movement, attacking government air defense and military installations around the country, and engaging in actions to protect civilians from attack or the threat of attack. Overall, a coalition of European, North American, and Arab forces participated in the military operation: Belgium, Canada, Denmark, France, Greece, Italy, Jordan, the Netherlands, Norway, Qatar, Spain, Sweden, Turkey, the United Arab Emirates, the United Kingdom, and the United States. The intervention encompassed over 26,500 sorties, including over 9,700 strike sorties, and at its peak involved 8,000 troops, over 260 aircraft, and twenty-one ships.[342] Despite playing a decidedly secondary role, the United States supplied 75 percent of the intelligence, surveillance, and reconnaissance data used for protecting Libyan civilians and enforcing the arms embargo.[343] British and French forces accounted for 75 percent of all NATO air operations in Libya, flew over 40 percent of the sorties, and destroyed over a third of the targets.[344] By August 21, with substantial NATO assistance, rebel forces had captured the capital of Tripoli. On October 20, 2011, Qaddafi was captured—begging for mercy in a sewer drainage pipe in his hometown of Sirte—and then angry rebels severely beat and killed him, completing their national takeover. The rebels declared victory on October 23, and Operation Unified Protector officially ended on October 31, 2011.

### Purpose/Rationale

The dual overarching purposes of NATO force use in Libya were deterrence—to protect innocent Libyan citizens' lives—and compellence—to force regime change so as to oust a repressive dictator and allow citizens of the country to choose their own form of leadership. The specific NATO military objectives were (1) ending all attacks against civilians, (2) withdrawal of Qaddafi's military forces back to their bases, and (3) immediate humanitarian access to needy Libyans.[345] An explicit humanitarian motivation for NATO military intervention was the "responsibility to protect" doctrine, prompting intervention by the international community when state governments fail to safeguard their own citizens' lives: "Attempts by Gaddafi loyalists to ruthlessly quash the rebellions compelled the West to take action in forums such as the UN and NATO under the justification of a 'responsibility to protect' ('R2P')."[346] Heightening this humanitarian worry by the West was Qaddafi's willingness to employ the plentiful arms available "in the name of terror."[347] Western human rights values were directly at stake in the NATO military intervention because during the conflict with the rebels Qaddafi had threatened to kill all the "cockroaches . . . house by house" in the rebel stronghold of Benghazi.[348]

A crucial yet largely unstated motivation for NATO intervention in Libya revolved around the vital economic interests of the alliance's member states:

European activism in Libya is completely understandable: Europe has the most to gain economically and to lose politically. Before the conflict, Italy and France received approximately 80 percent of Libya's oil supply. Libya pumped 1.6 million barrels a day, or about 1.8 percent of the world oil output. The oil imported from Libya accounted for 22 percent of Italy's supply, 16 percent of France's supply, and 13 percent of Spain's supply.[349]

This worry applied more to Libya than to any of the other Arab Spring protests.

A third rarely mentioned motivation was more cultural in nature. Specifically, "if post-conflict reconstruction in Libya were to fail, Europe could expect 200,000 to 300,000 immigrants; if Libyan and third-country refugees wash upon Europe's shores in the coming weeks, anti-immigrant sentiments in Europe will grow substantially, strengthening far-right parties."[350] Fears surrounding an undesired flood of North African immigrants have long been rampant in Western Europe, and unmanaged political instability in North Africa could easily be viewed as causing these fears to be realized.

### Force Effectiveness

Certain force effectiveness obstacles hampered the NATO intervention. First, NATO forces overestimated the speed of the military operations in Libya, as across time unexpected loyalist perseverance forced scale-ups in NATO's military capacity.[351] Second, because NATO's air and sea mission in Libya was the first major military engagement after the 2008 global financial crisis and European NATO allies had drastically reduced their defense spending, there was widespread fear that at this point they could not afford to respond effectively.[352] Third, intra-alliance coordination roadblocks existed—the mission was "hampered by a lack of cohesive action within the alliance as well as significant operational shortfalls," as "the burden of the Libya operations is increasingly borne by a small number of countries."[353] Fourth, little evidence existed that air power alone could induce regime change.[354] Fifth, especially in the NATO intervention's early stages, the proximity of the Qaddafi regime's personnel, equipment, and facilities to civilian infrastructure made the Libyan opposition's defense difficult and—due to casualty aversion—slowed down the military operation to the point where sometimes it looked like a stalemate.[355]

Nonetheless, in the short term many observers judged the NATO operation as a smashing military success and "a historic milestone" for the international organization:[356]

NATO'S operation in Libya has rightly been hailed as a model intervention. The alliance responded rapidly to a deteriorating situation that threatened hundreds of thousands of civilians rebelling against an oppressive regime. It succeeded in protecting those civilians and, ultimately, in providing the time and space necessary for local forces to overthrow Muammar al-Qaddafi. And it did so by involving partners in the region and sharing the burden among the alliance's members.[357]

In retrospect, the evidence suggests that the Libyan rebels could not by themselves have overthrown the Qaddafi regime without NATO support.[358] Moreover, the costs of the NATO operation in Libya were relatively small:

> It conducted an air campaign of unparalleled precision, which, although not perfect, greatly minimized collateral damage. It enabled the Libyan opposition to overthrow one of the world's longest-ruling dictators. And it accomplished all of this without a single allied casualty and at a cost—$1.1 billion for the United States and several billion dollars overall—that was a fraction of that spent on previous interventions in the Balkans, Afghanistan, and Iraq.[359]

In the words of a senior NATO official, Operation Unified Protector "was the kind of multilateral, affordable, effective endeavour that any foreign policy initiative aspires to."[360] In the end, NATO action "prevented a brutal massacre in Benghazi, helped the Libyan opposition to route Gadhafi and his regime from Tripoli, and thereby enhanced the prospects that Libya's future will be decided by its citizens."[361] Fears that the NATO intervention would turn into a costly and indecisive quagmire turned out to be misplaced.

However, achieving long-term political stability in Libya has been challenging, given nonexistent functional national political infrastructure:[362]

> If the economic and political stakes are high for Europe, the challenges of successfully transforming Libya are equally so. Forty-two years of Qaddafi's violent and mercurial rule has ensured that Libya has no institutions or foundation upon which to build its future. With no functioning parliament, no unified military command, no political parties, no unions, no civil society, and no nongovernmental organizations, Libya is composed of multiple factions and tribes, unlike its more homogenous Mediterranean neighbors, although the emergence and initial work of "local councils" have been encouraging.[363]

Over two years following the fall of Qaddafi, there is still no stable functioning national government, as the country is ruled by ruthless armed
militias.[364] In the long-run, this intervention may not be a model for political—as opposed to military—success: "It is not at all clear that the specific characteristics of the Libya campaign—a low-intensity, air-to-ground
campaign with a limited set of objectives—should serve as a benchmark for
the future of NATO's burden-sharing."[365] According to some skeptics, the
intervention highlighted "NATO's limitations rather than its power,"[366] for
despite NATO capabilities, American military power and expertise proved
to be absolutely essential.

### Force Legitimacy

Despite the military success of NATO's intervention in Libya, serious internal
unity concerns emerged. U.S. Secretary of Defense Robert Gates noted that
the NATO mission in Libya had "widespread political support" but that of
NATO alliance members "less than half have been willing to participate in
the strike mission."[367] Several member states that did not directly participate
in the military operation lacked the resources to do so, highlighting "a decade
of European underinvestment in defense" because "after over two decades of
reduced defense budgets, Europe appears incapable of sustaining even a small
war against a weak opponent located practically next door"; but some other
NATO members—notably Germany and Poland—"decided not to participate
even though they could have."[368] NATO's intervention in Libya ultimately
heightened intra-alliance tensions between (1) states feeling that they carried
too much of the burden in Afghanistan and Libya and (2) states not willing to
shoulder much political or military risk.[369]

On the other hand, having NATO rather than the United States take the
lead in the operation in Libya may have increased the intervention's legitimacy among some of the participants. Specifically,

> Some countries hesitated to place NATO in charge of a military action, fearing
> that the alliance would not garner enough support in the region; but it turned
> out that Arab states preferred to work through NATO; several of them, such
> as Jordan, Morocco, and the United Arab Emirates, had already participated
> in NATO-led operations in Kosovo and Afghanistan, and others had fostered
> closer relations with NATO through the Mediterranean Dialogue and the Is-
> tanbul Cooperation Initiative.[370]

The military intervention's truly multilateral nature, where the United States chose to take a backseat and "lead from behind,"[371] prevented it from being widely characterized as self-serving on the part of the participants. However, although the U.N. "responsibility to protect" mandate supported NATO actions to protect civilians, some analysts felt that operations aimed at overthrowing Qaddafi constituted "an illegal use of force."[372]

Legitimacy concerns revolving around fear of civilian casualties, linked to worries about eroding public support, severely limited NATO's military options. NATO established "an extremely high threshold for avoiding civilian casualties, a laudable policy, but one that has tradeoffs in terms of lethality, particularly as Qaddafi has been reported as using human shields and positioning military assets in civilian areas, as well as cultural heritage sites such as the UNESCO protected Roman ruins of Leptis Magna."[373] Military options that would have proven highly effective had to be avoided because of these concerns.

Legitimacy worries also surround the post-Qaddafi regime in Libya. Months after the NATO operation ended, Amnesty International reported that the militia ruling Libya "are forcing whole communities to flee as they impose a regime of torture and violence."[374] In late 2013, Human Rights Watch contended that "the failure to investigate systematic executions [mass murders carried out by Libyan rebels on the day of Qaddafi's death] helped to set the stage for the militia lawlessness in Libya today."[375] From a global legitimacy standpoint, the postintervention improvement in Libya was thus minimal.

### Future Prospects

A central postwar Libyan concern is reconstruction of the country.[376] Because the postintervention humanitarian situation in Libya is grave, to have any chance of future stability the country would require sustained foreign postintervention assistance:[377] Initially, hope existed that this aid would come from the European Union and specifically from the United Kingdom, France, and Italy,[378] but this foreign reconstruction assistance has largely failed to materialize due to lack of safety in the country.[379] Specifically, international assistance organizations may be reluctant to send out aid workers until a requisite level of security and operability exists within Libya.[380] Internally, there is hope that restoring oil production and resuming oil exports to Europe could help fund Libyan postwar reconstruction,[381] but Libyan oil production has been shut down many times since the overthrow of Qaddafi due to "a plethora of security troubles that include kidnappings, assassinations, and militia violence."[382] For this reconstruction effort to be successful, political divisions and social tensions among the tribes within the country will have to be overcome[383]—"those conflicts need to be sorted out before you have any kind of effective reconstruction," and consequently "this reconstruction will take years."[384] This challenge is compounded by the reality that "the leadership vacuum in Libya is not likely to be filled anytime soon."[385]

The prospects for regional stability involving Libya's neighbors—Algeria, Chad, Egypt, Niger, Sudan, and Tunisia—are dependent on how the post-Qaddafi transition works out. Bumps in the road could easily negatively affect these neighbors, most of which have their own fragile political infrastructure and societal instability problems. Because these political difficulties are compounded by extreme regional economic poverty, even if the political transition in Libya goes smoothly—by no means assured—considerable regional turmoil could emerge due to the unpredictability of the change.

In broader strategic terms, the NATO operation in Libya seems likely to reinforce the strength of transatlantic ties between Europe and the United States: "When Washington needs military support from allies in the world's most explosive strategic location—the Middle East—it can realistically turn only to Europe for help, both in securing UN legitimization for the action and in carrying it out."[386] Moreover, the Libyan intervention appears likely in the future to increase pressure on NATO to improve its burden-sharing arrangements.[387] At the same time, the NATO action underscored the importance of NATO members' openness to undertaking military operations through partnerships with non-NATO allies:

> Looking to the future, partnerships with non-NATO allies are likely to be increasingly important for the alliance. Sweden, which is not a member of NATO, contributed to the air campaign. The political and military efforts of Morocco, Jordan, Qatar and the United Arab Emirates were very much a product of the Mediterranean Dialogue and the Istanbul Cooperation Council, NATO's outreach to North Africa and the Persian Gulf. In an age when NATO has to be prepared to undertake complex expeditionary operations farther afield than Libya, partnerships around the globe can offer needed military capabilities as well as valuable intelligence and political support.[388]

Especially due to increasingly fruitless calls by the United States for its European allies to increase their defense spending,[389] NATO's future success may depend on its strategic flexibility using existing military resources.

## NORTH KOREAN SINKING OF SOUTH KOREAN SHIP

### Force Description

On March 26, 2010, at 9:22 PM, a 1200-ton South Korean naval vessel, ROKS *Cheonan*, was allegedly sunk off the country's west coast by a North Korean torpedo near Baengnyeong Island in the Yellow Sea. Out of a total of 104 people on the ship, forty-six South Korean sailors lost their lives in the incident. The location of the attack was an area of tension and contested territorial claims between North and South Korea. The timing of the attack coincided with joint naval antisubmarine warfare exercises being conducted by the United States and South Korea seventy-five miles away from the incident. In response to this incident—"an act of war and a clear violation of the armistice agreement that has kept a tenuous peace on the peninsula since 1953"[390]—South Korea boosted its military preparedness for possible future provocations from North Korea. As expected, security tensions between North and South Korea escalated due to the incident, and on May 24, 2010, South Korea stopped virtually all trade with North Korea and restricted the country from using its shipping channels.[391]

On May 20, 2010, despite the denial of any form of involvement by North Korea, a South Korea–led international investigative team of civilian and military experts—including representatives from the United States, the United Kingdom, Canada, Australia, and Sweden—issued a comprehensive report concluding that the sinking of the warship was indeed the result of a North Korean torpedo attack. Although some analysts responded with skepticism to the report and issued alternative explanations—including possibilities of an accidental mine explosion and an accidental act by an American submarine in the area[392]—the majority of global onlookers accepted the report's findings.

### Purpose/Rationale

Because North Korea has never accepted responsibility for the sinking of the South Korean ship—calling the results of the final investigative report "sheer fabrication"[393]—and because North Korea is such a closed society, identifying North Korean motivations necessarily involves some speculation. In the context of other provocative security-oriented statements and actions by North Korean political leaders over the last few years, it appears as if muscle flexing—showing their military strength and willingness to use it—and deterrence were probably at the root of this offensive action. More specifically, retaliation for an earlier incident may have been involved in the North Korean rationale for this brute force action:

From the North's perspective, it was a strike in retaliation for another naval clash in November 2009 in the West Sea, when an undetermined number of North Korean sailors were killed. Pyongyang's military doctrine, North Korea watchers in Seoul say, has always stressed retaliation for anything that smacks of defeat in an individual skirmish, and indeed there have been South Korean media reports since the *Cheonan* sinking that those military officers who pulled it off have been promoted.[394]

To this day, the exact strategic mission objectives by this force initiator have not been definitively established.

### Force Effectiveness

The sinking of the South Korean warship did not serve to accomplish the presumed deterrence purposes but rather simply to escalate tensions more between North and South Korea. A month and a half after the incident, during an East Asian visit, American Secretary of State Hillary Clinton took up the question with her counterparts in China, Japan, and then South Korea of what resulting punishment North Korea should suffer; but from the outset there was "little chance of any retaliatory strike from Seoul" because "while there may be 'genuine fury' amid the highest echelons of the South Korean government," South Korea "knows well that it can't risk this getting out of hand—there is no appetite in South Korea for a war."[395] The incident did temporarily derail the six-party talks aimed at denuclearizing North Korea, which began under the American George W. Bush administration and have continued intermittently under the Obama administration.[396]

On November 23, 2010, North Korea shelled the border island of Yeonpyeong, an attack that killed two South Korean marines and two South Korean civilians and "sent inter-Korean relations to one of its lowest levels in decades," as the two countries still technically remain at war.[397] Ever since the sinking of the *Cheonan*, South Korean negotiations with North Korea over North Korea's nuclear weapons program have been stalled: In April 2011, South Korean President Lee Myung-bak stated that a North Korean apology for the sinking would most likely be a prerequisite for progress in any further talks between the two countries.[398]

On October 28, 2011, over a year and a half after the incident, South Korean Defense Minister Kim Kwan-jin told reporters at a joint news conference with American Secretary of Defense Leon Panetta that "next year, I believe that the possibility of North Korea conducting additional provocations is . . .

very high."[399] On March 25, 2013, the South Korean Navy carried out maritime drills in the tensely guarded western sea right before the third anniversary of the sinking of the *Cheonan* warship by North Korea, "amid high tensions with the communist country that has issued repeated threats of war": The drills "occurred during a time of escalating tensions on the Korean Peninsula, with multiple threats from the North of an armed response to joint South Korea–U.S. military drills and to U.N. sanctions imposed after its nuclear test."[400] Neither South Korea nor North Korea appears to have benefited from these post-*Cheonan* developments, making the security predicament even more volatile than prior to the incident.

### Force Legitimacy

Despite widespread international verbal condemnation of North Korea's action, the policy response from the international community to the sinking of the South Korean corvette was decidedly underwhelming. The United States openly supported the South Korean trade sanctions on North Korea[401] and conducted joint naval exercises in the area with South Korea but otherwise did nothing. The U.N. Security Council condemned the attack but purposely did not identify the attacker.

Perhaps the most important nonreaction came from China, North Korea's closest ally:

> How Beijing reacts . . . will be critically important, since China remains North Korea's de facto economic lifeline. China accounts for fully one-third of North Korea's total external trade . . . A cutoff of critical Chinese oil shipments, much less a complete trade embargo, would bring the country to its knees. Which is why it's unlikely to happen. Beijing to date has never evinced any serious interest in bringing the economic hammer down on Pyongyang. It values stability over anything else, and the death of 46 South Korean sailors is unlikely to change that view. It took China a month, in fact, to offer Seoul its condolences after the attack.[402]

Thus North Korea escaped largely unscathed in terms of global sanctions, although no state openly pronounced that its attack was in any way legitimate.

### Future Prospects

The prospects seem high for future escalating tensions between North and South Korea in the wake of this incident. The strongly worded verbal responses from both sides indicate the high likelihood of a future violent action–reaction cycle: Right before the third anniversary of the *Cheonan* sinking, South Korean Defense Minister Kim Kwan-jin told soldiers, "We have to thoroughly prepare so as not to allow such unprovoked attacks (on the South) again . . . if (the North) provokes again, we have to strongly retaliate to prevent them from even thinking about attacks in the future."[403] Tensions on the Korean peninsula "remain high as North Korean leader Kim Jong-un has made frequent visits to military units and front-line artillery troops urging soldiers to stay on high alert to prepare for an all-out battle with the South"; the South Korean Defense Minister claimed that these frequent North Korean front-line military inspections "are aimed at creating a war-like situation" that "could stir conflicts in the South and result in a real provocation."[404]

Moreover, these ominous future prospects look even worse when considering the regional arms race, as both sides have recently upgraded their warfighting capabilities: The North Korean government has recently "increased operations of its submarine fleets and training of coastal artillery units, and may have even beefed up secret infiltration missions targeting the South"; just since 2012, the North Korean military has "intensified amphibious training involving ground, naval and air force elements, and focused on tactics to attack the group of South Korean border islands lying along the maritime border."[405] Reports have also emerged that "as many as 1,000 North Korean artillery pieces may be targeting the Seohae Islands that can do considerable damage," for "threats of provocations targeting the five border islands have been steadily intensified."[406] In parallel fashion, in response to the escalating risk of North Korean naval provocations, South Korea has "upgraded its defense capacities along the Yellow Sea border, with advanced torpedo countermeasures as well as additional aircrafts that can deal with anti-submarine and surface threats."[407] The South Korean government military "is also moving to secure Spike missile system from Israel to better eliminate North Korea's coastal artillery."[408]

As long as North Korea continues its recent highly bellicose pattern of repeated threats regarding the United States and on South Korea, and as long as mutual arms escalation by both sides continues without any signs of abating, the security situation on the Korean peninsula will be one of the most volatile in the world. Since the sinking of the *Cheonan*, neither side has let up on its verbal barbs. For example, in March 2013, after North Korea threatened military action if joint "hostile" American–South Korean drills continued, South Korea responded that it would strike back if this happened.[409]

## RUSSIAN INVASION OF GEORGIA

### Force Description

This case involves a major military power using brute force to crush a neighboring country attempting to assert its political autonomy. Long-standing tensions going back to the early 1990s have existed within Georgia, with two areas—Abkhazia and South Ossetia—wanting to separate and highly partial to Russian rule: Russia's growing dominance in South Ossetia and Abkhazia "transformed the separatist conflicts into essentially Russia–Georgia disputes"; and most Abkhazia and South Ossetia residents were granted Russian citizenship and passports and seemed to want to be part of Russia.[410] When Mikheil Saakashvili was elected president of Georgia in 2004, he pledged to institute democratic reforms and to regain control over the separatist regions. Georgian forces and South Ossetian separatists clashed in summer 2004 when the Georgian government attempted to clamp down on widespread smuggling operations in the area; in September to October 2006, Georgia expelled six Russian intelligence agents accused of espionage, and Russia responded with a full economic embargo of Georgia, including the severance of all transportation and communication links; in July 2008, the Georgians and the South Ossetians exchanged artillery fire, and Russia launched a large-scale military exercise near the Georgian border.[411]

On August 7, 2008, these tensions escalated between Russia-leaning South Ossetia and more democratically oriented Georgia, with each accusing the other of launching hostile artillery barrages, and "on August 8, as world leaders gathered in Beijing to watch the opening ceremony of the Olympic Games, Russian tanks rolled across the border into Georgia."[412] The specific trigger of the escalating state-initiated violence could have turned out under other circumstances to be a relatively small and isolated incident:

> Two massive shootings at Georgian villages in the Georgian-controlled part of South Ossetia on 7 August, which entailed casualties, provoked Georgian forces to launch a retaliatory attack on the South Ossetian capital Tskhinvali. The Georgians attacked the positions of the separatist military forces and government buildings (the shootings also entailed civilian casualties), and then, following an order from the Georgian president Mikheil Saakashvili, started a military operation (which had probably been planned in advance) to seize the whole or part of the separatist region. As a result, Russia was able to present Georgia as having initiated the armed conflict, and had a pretext to start the

armed offensive in South Ossetia in the morning of 8 August, which two days later became a land invasion of Georgia proper.[413]

Georgia claims that South Ossetian forces did not respond to a cease-fire appeal but intensified their shelling, "forcing" Georgia to send in troops, whereas Russia claimed that its forces entered the area simply as a "peacekeeping" operation. On August 8, Russia launched massive air attacks throughout Georgia, and Russian troops engaged Georgian forces in South Ossetia. By August 10, Russian troops occupied most of South Ossetia, and they later occupied several Georgian cities. Russian warships landed troops in Georgia's Abkhazia region and took up positions off Georgia's Black Sea coast. On August 26, Russia officially recognized the two breakaway regions of Abkhazia and South Ossetia.

As a result of the Russia–Georgia conflict, nearly 1,000 people died, and tens of thousands of Georgians had to flee their homes;[414] in October 2008 the World Bank reported that about 127,000 persons were displaced by the fighting in Georgia, South Ossetia, and Abkhazia.[415] This Russian military action was possibly "the most significant challenge to European Security since the Cold War's end" in that "it constituted Moscow's first military aggression against a neighboring state since the invasion of Afghanistan in 1978; and it took place, this time, against a member state of European institutions such as the OSCE [Organization for Security and Co-Operation in Europe] and the Council of Europe, and to that a country on track to integration with NATO."[416]

In mid-August, French President Nicolas Sarkozy, serving as the European Union president, helped Georgia and Russia to agree to a peace plan calling for both sides to cease hostilities, pull troops back to preconflict positions and play a greater international role in peacekeeping. Later, on September 8, 2008, President Sarkozy negotiated a follow-up agreement with Russia stipulating that Russian forces would withdraw from areas near the borders of Abkhazia and South Ossetia; Georgian forces would return to their barracks; U.N. and OSCE observers already in place would remain; and the number of international observers would be increased.[417]

### Purpose/Rationale

Deterrence of further unruly behavior through punishment of an act of defiance was a core purpose for Russia's invasion of Georgia:

President Medvedev's vow on August 8 to "punish" Georgia denoted Russian intentions beyond restoring control over South Ossetia. When he announced on August 12 that Russian troops were ending their offensive against Georgia, he stated that Russia's aims had been accomplished and the aggressor punished. Various observers have suggested several possible Russian reasons for the "punishment" beyond inflicting casualties and damage. These include coercing Georgia to accept Russian conditions on the status of the separatist regions, to relinquish its aspirations to join NATO, and to depose Saakashvili as the president. In addition, Russia may have wanted to "punish" the West for recognizing Kosovo's independence, for seeking to integrate Soviet successor states (which are viewed by Russia as part of its sphere of influence) into Western institutions such as the EU and NATO, and for developing oil and gas pipeline routes that bypass Russia.[418]

More specifically, the Russian military action sought to punish Georgia for its pro-Western foreign policy and to unseat the Georgian government,[419] with Vladimir Putin famously saying that "he wanted to hang up Georgia's President Mikheil Saakashvili by the genitals."[420] Russian motivations went well beyond simple maintenance of its sphere-of-influence: Aside from border and political influence issues, Russia was concerned about control of vital oil and gas natural resources.[421]

Both Russia and Georgia campaigned to convince global observers that the other party initiated the conflict. However, most analysts surmised that rather than spontaneously reacting to the Georgian attack on South Ossetia, Russia launched "a carefully calculated and prepared operation."[422] An independent commission after sustained review concluded that "Georgia's military action in South Ossetia on August 7–8 was a response to a plan set in motion by Russia over a period of months that culminated in an invasion by more than 40,000 Russian troops."[423]

Beyond the deterrence motive, Russia also used force for compellence purposes to change and constrain Georgian behavior. The intended message from Russia to Georgia was extremely harsh. The negative signals included that (1) Georgia's pro-Western policy had caused it political and economic losses; (2) Moscow could undo most of the President Saakashvili's political accomplishments; (3) Georgia cannot protect its citizens and is at the mercy of Russia; and (4) Georgia cannot count on sizable political or military support from the West, making Georgian efforts to join NATO "pointless."[424]

As a broader compellence objective for the Georgian invasion, reinforcing regional hegemony was a key Russian motivation. Russia was determined to protect its influence in the area, and the invasion was "intended to demonstrate both Russia's status as a world power and the weakness and helplessness of the West (particularly the USA) to the countries of the region and the Russian political classes";[425] for Russia, "The war was a firm rejoinder to a reckless Georgian leadership and a chance to stand up to U.S. influence in Moscow's backyard."[426] A wide range of intended compellence outcomes was in all likelihood involved in the Russian invasion of Georgia, with the minimum expectation being to seize South Ossetia and Abkhazia and to bomb Georgia proper, and the maximum expectation being to occupy Georgia and overthrow President Saakashvili.[427] The coercive goals involved doing as much damage as possible to the Georgian military, including intentional seizure and destruction of Georgian military bases and facilities; promoting fear among Georgian civilians; stimulating widespread looting of Georgian stores and private apartment; enhancing Georgian transport and communication problems by destroying the telecommunications network and interrupting a key railway line); and reinforcing the Russian forces' ability to do what they wish.[428] It was clear that Russia wanted to use force in such a way that there would be absolutely no chance that Georgia or any other nearby hostile parties would dare take similar upstart action in the near future.

### Force Effectiveness

Russia certainly achieved a decisive military victory over Georgia, but the payoffs may have been less than it expected:

> According to some observers, the recent Russia–Georgia conflict harms both countries. In the case of Georgia and South Ossetia, the fighting reportedly resulted in hundreds of military and civilian casualties and large-scale infrastructure damage that set back economic growth and contributed to urgent humanitarian needs. Tens of thousands of displaced persons added to humanitarian concerns. The fighting appeared to harden anti-Georgian attitudes in both South Ossetia and Abkhazia, making the possibility of re-integration with Georgia—which is still hoped for by the Saakashvili government even in the face of Russia's recognition of the regions' independence—more remote. Georgia also appeared even less eligible by some NATO members for a Membership Action Plan (MAP), usually considered as a prelude to membership, because of the destruction of some of its military capabilities and the heightened insecurity of its borders. In the case of Russia, its seemingly disproportionate military campaign and its unilateral declaration of recognition appeared to harm its image as a reliable and peaceable member of the

international community. Russia also reported that its military operations and pledges to rebuild South Ossetia were costing hundreds of millions of dollars.[429]

Moreover, hampering postwar prospects for thawing Russia–Georgia relations was Russian refusal to negotiate directly with President Saakashvili, and on August 12, 2008, Georgia filed a case against Russia at the International Court of Justice for alleged crimes in Abkhazia and South Ossetia between 1990 and 2008.[430] Furthermore, showing the Bush administration's strong support for Georgia was the U.S.–Georgia Charter on Strategic Partnership, signed in January 2009 and stating that the "two countries share a vital interest in a strong, independent, sovereign, unified, and democratic Georgia."[431]

For achieving its short-term military objectives, Russia also appears to have been successful through the invasion. In addition to subduing Georgia, Russia's status as a global power was reinforced.[432] Russia was able to undertake coercion in Georgia with impunity, and, from Russia's perspective, the costs of the invasion seemed to be substantially less than the gains.

Nonetheless, in the end, an important element of strategic weakness was evident in the Russian invasion of Georgia:

> Russia's decision to wage a war of aggression in Georgia may be a sign of might, but not one of strength; in fact, it indicates that Russia for years failed to reach its political objectives in the South Caucasus with political instruments, and saw no other option but to employ war, the ultimate and most costly instrument to its international reputation, to achieve these objectives.[433]

With the huge military strength disparity between Russia and Georgia, had years of Russian diplomacy worked properly to achieve its strategic objectives among its neighbors, an actual invasion should not have been necessary to ensure political compliance.

### Force Legitimacy

Given earlier aggressive policies and provocations, the Russian invasion of Georgia should have been anticipated by the international community but instead "took the world by surprise."[434] A key reason is that "the United States and Europe misjudged their ability to help Russia's neighbors slip into the Western orbit without a full-blown international crisis; now that there has been a test of strength, and Russian strength has prevailed, many of the tools of Western policy are severely damaged."[435] Subtle verbal encouragement to those near Russia sympathetic to the West has proven to be inadequate, and Western states do not seem willing to go much further than that.

Within Russia, the military intervention in Georgia was "wildly popular": Almost 80 percent of the Russian people approved of the invasion, and over half blamed Georgia for starting the war and "identified the United States' desire for influence in the Caucasus and the greater Black Sea region as the root cause."[436] This support from the Russian people reflects deep popular suspicion about American aims in the Black Sea region and about democratic values.[437] The manner in which the Russian people learned of the war was not balanced in terms of exposure to competing interpretations and thus was not conducive to the development of any sympathy by them for the Georgians' aspirations. For example, Russia launched a sophisticated internal disinformation campaign claiming that the Georgian military committed widespread human rights violations in South Ossetia.[438]

Nonetheless, global condemnation emerged of the Russian invasion of Georgia, with Russia warned that it risked complete global isolation by engaging in behavior denounced by the international community.[439] European and other global leaders were overwhelmingly critical of (1) Russia's refusal to comply with the six-point peace plan calling for its immediate military withdrawal from Georgia and (2) Russia's recognition of Abkhazia and South Ossetia as independent states.[440]

From a worldwide perspective, the Russian invasion of Georgia blatantly violated international norms. Russia was perceived as having "embarked on a new era of muscular intervention" by having tried "to bypass established channels of conflict resolution and unilaterally change the boundaries of another UN member state."[441] Moreover, in undertaking the invasion Russia made no attempt to obtain international support, made no apologies for its unilateral attack on Georgia, and did not even try to develop any form of public relations strategy to mollify the obviously displeased international community.[442] Furthermore, human rights violations undermined any legitimacy associated with Russia's invasion: "International media reported that Russian troops and paramilitary forces were widely looting, destroying infrastructure, detaining Georgians, and placing mines throughout the country."[443] And despite Russia's claim that its intervention was based on humanitarian concerns, "its forces subsequently permitted or endorsed the systematic ethnic cleansing of ethnic Georgians from South Ossetia."[444]

The United States was particularly harsh in its verbal reaction to the Russian invasion, with it transforming "relations between Russia and the United States to their lowest point since the dark days of the Cold War."[445] President George W. Bush declared that "Russia has invaded a sovereign neighbouring state and threatens a democratic government elected by its people—such an action is unacceptable in the 21st century."[446] Secretary of State Condoleezza Rice asserted that "Russia is 'becoming more and more the outlaw in this conflict,' and that by 'invading smaller neighbors, bombing civilian infrastructure, going into villages and wreaking havoc and wanton destruction of this infrastructure,' Russia is isolating itself from the 'community of nations.'"[447] This criticism persisted long after the war ended, exemplified by Vice President Joe Biden's comments in February 2009:

> The United States will not recognize Abkhazia and South Ossetia as independent states. We will not recognize a sphere of influence. It will remain our view that sovereign states have the right to make their own decisions and choose their own alliances.[448]

Although on September 30, 2008, the U.S. Congress passed legislation providing $365 million in added humanitarian and rebuilding assistance for Georgia for 2009, tangible American military or economic sanctions against Russia did not follow this barrage of verbal attacks.

Ultimately, the reactions of Western states and international organizations to the Russian invasion of Georgia were "limited to statements, diplomatic efforts and humanitarian aid."[449] The European Union was internally divided, with France, Germany, and Italy developing close economic ties to Russia, and thus not capable of a firm unified reaction to the Russian invasion.[450] The clever timing of the invasion—President George W. Bush was near the end of his last term in office, the European Union was in crisis following the Irish referendum, and the Olympic Games were just beginning in Beijing—may have contributed to this tepid international response.[451]

For Georgia, the Russian invasion was truly jolting. Specifically, "the Russian tanks that scarred the lush countryside were an affront to all that had been achieved since the Rose Revolution of 2003, including the creation of passably democratic institutions and the implementation of an unwaveringly pro-U.S. foreign policy."[452] The absence of military intervention on Georgia's behalf was stunningly disappointing in its eyes, especially given that international observers confirmed that after the war Abkhazia and South Ossetia would be permanently outside of full Georgian control.[453]

### Future Prospects

The August 2008 Russia–Georgia conflict seems likely to have a major disruptive regional security impact in the future. Russia seems now to have a long-time military presence through bases in Georgia's breakaway Abkhazia and South Ossetia regions; because Georgia's military capabilities were degraded by the conflict, Georgia will need substantial U.S. and NATO military aid.[454] In mid-2013, five years after the military conflict with Russia ended, "Georgia now wants to make friends with the Kremlin" but "is also keen to integrate fully with the West" by pursuing admission to NATO and the EU.[455] Former Soviet satellite states feel decidedly intimidated, and the likelihood that they will be able to engage in political self-determination in the future seems low. Tensions in the region seem likely to persist in the long run.

There are still long-term dangers of further Russian aggression in the region, especially given a long-standing awareness of "Russia's proclivity to see hard power as the true currency of international relations."[456] Indeed, "the Russian tanks and planes rolling into the sovereign country of Georgia (eerily reminiscent of Afghanistan in 1979) serve as a reminder that Russia continues to exert economic and military pressure to strong-arm her former prisoners into a less formal, but no less real, subservience."[457] Overall, Russia appears to be moving on an increasingly confrontational course, "powered by a bristlier conception of its interests than at any time since the end of the Cold War, by domestic political arrangements that appear to feed on international tension, and by an enhanced ability to stand its ground."[458] Given the tepid reaction of the West to the Russian invasion, it appears as if it signals "the beginning of an offensive phase in Russia's effort to rebuild its influence in Eurasia."[459] Furthermore, some observers worry that Russia has not given up its ambition to control Georgia, as "Russia's repeated claims that Georgia is massing troops and equipment near South Ossetia (claims that monitors from the European Union find groundless) may be cover for a new Russian attack."[460] Russia has shown its staunch determination not to allow any form of progressive change nearby that would threaten its national interests.

The surrounding region now seems to becoming much less stable due to the Russia invasion of Georgia:

Terrorism and insurgency are spreading in Russia's North Caucasus region. Russian military occupation of Abkhazia, South Ossetia, and adjacent areas in Georgia heightens strains. Renewed hostilities are increasingly possible between Armenia and Azerbaijan over the ethnic Armenian enclave of Nagorno-Karabakh in Azerbaijan.[461]

Despite the Russian recognition of Abkhazia and South Ossetia as independent states, "they are effectively being integrated into Russia"; "in the North Caucasus, popular alienation and militant violence are increasing."[462] Longstanding intraregional tensions have by no means subsided, and vital natural resource access has suffered as a result.

# 4 CASES OF STATE INTERNAL BRUTE FORCE USE

THIS CHAPTER EXAMINES MAJOR twenty-first-century internal state-initiated brute force incorporating political stability threats. The ten cases of internal state force use are the Bahraini crackdown on dissidents, Chinese repression of dissidents, Egyptian repression of dissidents, Greek repression of dissidents, Indian repression of Kashmir separatists, Mexican coercion against drug lords, Myanmar repression of dissidents, Sudanese repression of dissidents, Syrian repression of rebels, and Thai repression of dissidents. Weaker governments (the strongest of which are China, Greece, and India) tend to use force domestically. Each case explicitly includes the description of the force use, the purpose and rationale of force initiators and force targets, force effectiveness, force legitimacy, and future prospects.

## BAHRAINI REPRESSION OF DISSIDENTS

### Force Description

Inspired by the Arab Spring uprisings begun in 2010, on February 14, 2011, Bahraini demonstrators began peaceful unarmed protests in the capital city of Manama against their government, demanding the creation of a constitutional monarchy, free and open elections, and equality for all citizens.[1] This was quickly followed by "brutal" state repression,[2] and within a month the protesters were driven from the square by force: Because Bahraini government armed forces are "highly patrimonial" and "largely detached from the local population,"[3] unlike in Egypt they did not hesitate in the crackdown. The regime was so jolted that it asked the Saudis to intervene, and on March 14,

2011, Saudi soldiers invaded, with the acquiescence of the U.S. government.[4] Because the Bahraini regime received backing from these powerful allies, it faced little pressure to give in to any of the protesters' demands.[5]

Possibly due to this intransigence, as the confrontation progressed, the confrontations became more violent: In September and October 2012, Bahraini security services killed two teenage dissidents, and a police officer died in an alleged attack; a second police officer was killed in April 2012 in what the government called a "domestic terrorist attack."[6] Indeed, to alter the image of an indigenous grassroots uprising, "Bahrain's government, like the dictatorial regimes in Egypt, Syria and Libya, tried to blame outsiders, claiming that it had found weapons and flags from the radical Lebanese group Hezbollah" and later "blaming Iran for the unrest."[7]

During the confrontation between the state regime and the protesters, the Bahraini government severely sanctioned free speech. For example, citing recent violence, on October 30, 2012, the Bahraini regime banned all public rallies and demonstrations.[8] During that same month the Bahraini government prosecuted activists for postings on social media and jailed doctors who treated protesters, charging them with illegal gathering and other crimes.[9]

This "dangerous standoff" involved a protest movement that was "unable to wrest freedoms from a government that opposition activists say is methodically blocking all avenues for dissent."[10] Overall, the death toll from the protests is at least eighty-seven people killed by government forces,[11] with about 3,000 people arrested[12] and over 4,400 people fired from their jobs for supporting the prodemocracy movement and over forty mosques and religious sites demolished for allegedly sheltering prodemocracy activists.[13] In the end, "of the popular pro-democracy civil insurrections which swept the Middle East in 2011, none were as large—relative to the size of the country—as the one which took place in the island kingdom of Bahrain; and, while scattered resistance continues, none were so forcibly and thoroughly suppressed."[14]

### Purpose/Rationale

The goal of the ruling Bahraini regime was to stay in power and to deter demonstrations inspired by the Arab Spring movement from disrupting the status quo. Concern about oil is at the center of American and Saudi Arabian support for Bahrain, with the United States reluctant to antagonize such a large supplier of a vital natural resource.[15] Saudi Arabia's two crucial fears regarding

Bahraini developments were (1) that Bahrain might move toward becoming a constitutional monarchy[16] and (2) that the large Shia population in its eastern province, where the oil is located, might become disloyal; in light of these two concerns, Saudi Arabia "was certainly not going to tolerate a democracy—which it thinks would be a 'Shia' democracy, and therefore a hostile regime—in Bahrain, right next door."[17]

The Bahraini protesters against the government have concentrated on opposing the ruling Sunni monarchy's monopoly of political power, undergirded by frequent complaints from the majority Shiite population about "systematic, apartheidlike discrimination."[18] Shiite protesters have expressed resentment at their treatment as second-class citizens, excluded from many state jobs.[19] The protesters' specific demands included "the resignation of the prime minister, greater civil liberties, a unicameral elected legislature, a government elected by the people rather than by royal appointment, fair electoral districts based on one person one vote, an independent judiciary, and an army and security apparatus representative of the country's population."[20] The protesters' objectives widened as the confrontation proceeded: The political aims began with expanding the rights and freedoms for the oppressed Shia population,[21] then moved to focus on instituting a constitutional monarchy accountable to the will of the people,[22] and finally directly sought the overthrow of the existing Bahraini government regime.[23]

### Force Effectiveness

In the short run, the Bahraini government crackdown coercively kept in power the ruling regime but did not solve long-run problems. "They don't want people to express their opinions, their anger," bemoaned Sayed Hadi al-Mosawi, a member of Al-Wefaq, the largest opposition group, "This will not take the country to stability."[24] On February 14, 2012, the first anniversary of the confrontation, hostilities recommenced:

> Armored vehicles patrolled Bahrain's capital, Manama, on Tuesday in a security clampdown to deter protesters after overnight clashes outside the city on the first anniversary of a forcibly suppressed pro-democracy uprising. Youths threw gasoline bombs at police cars during skirmishes before dawn, prompting the authorities to send police reinforcements backed by helicopters into Shiite villages around Manama. The police fired tear gas at two dozen protesters near the former Pearl Roundabout, the focal point of last year's protests, nearly hitting several people as canisters bounced off cars. About 30 people

were arrested, some of them dragged from their cars apparently on suspicion of being protesters aiming to block the highway near the roundabout. The prominent activist Nabeel Rajab, who led the protesters, was detained, as were six American activists in the country as part of a Witness Bahrain group to monitor how the police handle demonstrators.[25]

On March 9, 2012, one of the largest antigovernment demonstrations occurred, involving hundreds of thousands of protesters. Even two full years after the demonstrations began, the same pattern persisted, with violent crackdowns and jailing of activists.[26] Thus state force use against the people had few lasting deterrence effects.

### Force Legitimacy

Global verbal criticism of Bahraini force use against its own people has been high. After Bahraini state police stormed a protest camp and killed three people, American Secretary of State Hillary Clinton phoned her Bahraini counterpart to express "deep concern," urge future restraint, and recommend political and economic reforms on behalf of Bahraini citizens;[27] on May 19, 2011, American President Barack Obama stated that "we have insisted publicly and privately that mass arrests and brute force are at odds with the universal rights of Bahrain's citizens, and will not make legitimate calls for reform go away."[28] Moreover, both the European Union and NATO urged Bahraini government authorities "to refrain from violence and settle the escalating crisis through political dialogue."[29] U.N. Secretary Ban Ki Moon similarly asked Bahraini leaders not to use violence against civilians and journalists, labeling the government's coercive action as "deeply troubling."[30] However, the international criticism turned out to be just lip service; for example, evidence eventually emerged that "despite Bahrain's bloody crackdown on pro-democracy protesters, the US has continued to provide weapons and maintenance to the small Mideast nation."[31] Parallel to the reaction of Georgians fighting against Russia in 2008, the United States "disappointed pro-democracy activists" in Bahrain by failing to provide tangible support to the antigovernment protesters, to censure Saudi military support for the regime, and to accept without question the Bahraini regime's claims of Iranian interference.[32]

Human rights groups strongly condemned the ban on public demonstrations, asserting that "it was intended solely to stifle criticism of the ruling monarchy in the tiny Persian Gulf nation."[33] On October 30, 2012, Amnesty International argued that the ban violated the right to freedom of expression and peaceful assembly and "must be lifted immediately."[34] Human Rights Watch stated that "the government shifted from talking about reforms to silencing critical voices, banning demonstrations, and restricting access to independent journalists and rights organizations," serving to "thoroughly discredit claims by Bahraini authorities of respecting human rights,"[35] and in June 2013 the organization urged the European Union to pressure the Bahraini regime to free political prisoners detained for exercising their rights.[36] A November 23, 2011, Bahraini state-commissioned report, "designed to help heal sectarian divisions between the island kingdom's Sunni rulers and majority Shi'ites," reported that five people had been tortured to death and found that "in many cases security agencies in the government of Bahrain resorted to excessive and unnecessary force" (to which the Bahraini government responded that such abuses were "isolated incidents").[37]

### Future Prospects

The prospects for future resolution of grievances in Bahrain seem dim:

> The shadows of Iran and Saudi Arabia hover over Bahrain. There is no mass terror, but the political order is not pretty. There is sectarian discrimination and the oddness of a ruling dynasty, the House of Khalifa, that conquered the area in the late years of the eighteenth century but has still not made peace with the population. Outsiders man the security forces, and true stability seems a long way off.[38]

The Bahraini government and the protest movement have both been digging in their heels, preparing for a long struggle. Although compromise should have been an option because Bahrain is "one of the more liberal monarchies in the region" and the protesters are mostly moderate and middle class, the confrontations have elevated hard-line over moderate voices.[39] In 2013, the confrontation between the government and the protesters worsened: Following crude bomb attacks on police patrols in July, in September the government expanded security measures designed to curtail the activities of Bahrain's dissidents, including tougher punishment for "terror instigators" and banning all protests, rallies, and sit-ins in the capital Manama.[40] For the foreseeable future, "even if it gets a great deal worse in Bahrain, no Western government is going to condemn the country's rulers,"[41] for Saudi Arabia's strong stance seems likely to continue to prevent major outside powers from intervening on behalf of the prodemocracy dissidents.

## CHINESE REPRESSION OF DISSIDENTS

### Force Description

In recent years, there have been at least two separate strands of Chinese government coercive repression of internal political protesters. First, since 2008, there have been government crackdowns on protesters trying to free Tibet. Second, since early 2011, there has been a government crackdown against protests in major Chinese cities that claim to be part of the "Jasmine Revolution" emulating the Arab Spring uprisings elsewhere in the world.

Concerning the Chinese crackdown in Tibet, the repression of a prominent ethnic and religious minority has been brutal and unrelenting. The government response to the political protests has been unequivocal coercion: Since Tibetan mass rioting in spring 2008, the Chinese government has imposed martial law in Tibet, and mostly ethnic Han security officers undertook a brutal crackdown, particularly in monasteries,[42] where at least ten Tibetans were shot dead near the Kirti Monastery in Sichuan Province[43] and at least twenty-two people have died overall. The Chinese government described these dissidents as "terrorists in disguise," thereby attempting to discredit their cause.[44]

Despite this government crackdown, the popular protests in Tibet continued and escalated. Between 2009 and mid-2012, at least thirty-eight Tibetans—including many Buddhist monks and nuns—have protested by setting themselves on fire.[45] Since the self-immolations began, Chinese authorities have begun rounding up many Tibetans, with as many as 600 people having been expelled from Tibet or held in detention centers.[46] In January 2012, in the worst violence between ethnic Tibetans and the Chinese authorities since 2008, thousands of Chinese security forces flooded into an ethnically Tibetan area in Sichuan Province in southwestern China following large protests fueled by "anger and despair over Chinese rule" that led to violent clashes with the police in anticipation of the Tibetan New Year on February 22.[47]

Regarding the brute force used to suppress the "Jasmine Revolution," in the wake of popular revolts against authoritarian governments in early 2011 in the Middle East and North Africa, calls by "a small but stubborn" national protest movement within China escalated despite a government "campaign of arrests and censorship."[48] This prodemocracy effort came to a head when an anonymous posting on the Internet on February 18 called for antigovernment protests in thirteen major cities across China on February 20, at 2:20 PM, "taking its cue from the successful revolts in Tunisia and Egypt and branding itself the Jasmine Revolution."[49] The source of the anonymous Internet posting turned out to be the United States, from the Chinese-language news site (based in Durham, North Carolina) boxun.com, whose "leading figures are veterans of Chinese pro-democracy movements going back to the anti–Gang of Four demonstrations in Tiananmen Square in 1976, the Democracy Wall Movement of 1978, and the protests in Tiananmen Square in 1989."[50] Due to the instability wrought by Arab Spring protesters, Chinese authorities reacted strongly to the threat and "interrogated, arrested and detained at home dozens of people suspected of fomenting the anti-government movement."[51] These security forces even "deployed a SWAT team, attack dogs and scores of plain-clothes security agents" to manage the situation[52] and detained a man who simply "placed a jasmine flower near a McDonald's restaurant near Wangfujing."[53] A Chinese government warning stated that websites refusing to censor comments about parallels to the Arab Spring uprisings would be "shut down by force."[54]

International journalists quickly got caught in the middle of this confrontation. More than a dozen journalists were subjected to the violence, and local government officials admitted that they could not guarantee these reporters' safety unless they stopped recording the protests.[55] The outcome was that "what started as a whisper on the internet—an anonymous call for protest across China, a so-called Jasmine Revolution—has quickly become the biggest showdown between Chinese authorities and foreign media in more than two decades":

> In less than two weeks, the situation has deteriorated into violence against reporters by police and threats by Chinese immigration police that they would revoke visas for correspondents and their news organisations who did not follow tough new rules. Dozens of journalists' emails have been hacked and viruses sent to their computers. Chinese staffs of foreign news groups have been harassed and landlords have been co-opted to send warnings.[56]

Stephen McDonell, president of the Foreign Correspondents Club of China and China correspondent for the Australian Broadcasting Corporation, said, "Now we have had a taste of the bullying from the provinces right in the heart of the nation's capital; reporters [are] being bashed up by plainclothes thugs in the middle of the city—and the government claims it can do nothing about this."[57] In the end, "the crackdown on foreign media is just one arm of a far broader operation against perceived dissident elements in China including activists, writers, human rights lawyers and local media, as paranoia about Middle-East-style protests spreading to China has gripped Beijing."[58]

### Purpose/Rationale

The Chinese state use of internal force was oriented toward deterrence, with the central government striving to prevent the dissidents' disruption from overturning the status quo. More specifically, the rationale of the Chinese government for using coercive repression against the Tibetans and the proponents of the Jasmine Revolution was to maintain internal order, force compliance to its regulations among all of its citizens, and integrate into the country as a whole a province that has long desired separatist autonomy.

The motive of the protesting Tibetans is more cultural than political—to "protect their religious and cultural integrity" in the face of what they perceive as an illegitimate "continuing occupation" by the Chinese central government.[59] The dissidents' "actions are seen as protests against Chinese rule over Tibet and calls for the return of the Dalai Lama who has been in exile in India since 1959."[60] Indeed, "many Tibetans resent Beijing's heavy-handed rule and the large-scale migration of China's ethnic Han majority to the Himalayan region; while China claims Tibet has been under its rule for centuries, many Tibetans say the region was functionally independent for most of that time."[61] Tibetans often accuse the Chinese regime of trying to "erode their culture and faith"[62] and "silence their voices and erase their identity."[63]

The motive for those promoting the Jasmine Revolution seems to be more political than cultural—to pursue the expansion of freedom and democratic rights within China. Just as with the Tiananmen Square protesters of 1989, their focus has consistently been on the achievement of "political reform."[64] In addition, these dissidents aim "to protest corruption and unjust rule,"[65] with greater checks on the authority of government officials whom protesters feel have exceeded their proper limits of authority.

### Force Effectiveness

In the short term, the brutal Chinese government response coercively prevented political upheaval. For example, state police "easily quashed" the call on February 20, 2011, for protests all over the country.[66] Indeed, "the authorities, never shy about baring their teeth, have also rolled out a formidable show of force, cordoning off parks and public squares with paramilitary police and threatening to dismiss government workers who join the rallies."[67] Revolutionary activity is unlikely in such a fortified setting.

However, in the longer run the Chinese government repression has high-lighted to the world the shaky foundations of the regime's authority:

> While the heavy-handed response has succeeded in stifling protest, it illustrates how concerned China's leaders are about the potential for social unrest, at the same time drawing domestic and international attention to the extent of the Internet and social controls those leaders rely on to remain in power.[68]

The offensive and defensive tactics employed by the Chinese government indicated uneasiness about the Arab Spring comparison: "Officials have used state-run media outlets to dismiss any comparisons of those regimes with China; at the same time, they have stepped up public comments on the need to address 'social conflict' and to tackle problems such as the growing income disparity between the rich and poor."[69] Such a response highlights regime insecurity—"This shows just how nervous and how insecure the Chinese government is," for "it is aware of how many forms of grievances are in society that are simmering despite the prosperity on the surface."[70] Although Chinese authorities have usually been able to suppress news regarding protesters exposing official abuses,[71] Chinese government authorities "have been spooked by the popular protests sweeping the Middle East"[72] and are "incredibly terrified and paranoid" about any antigovernment movement forming in China.[73]

Moreover, at least in Tibet, Chinese government coercion has generated some backfire effects. In particular, "The crackdown seems to have fueled a renewed sense of Tibetan national identity," and there is now "a growing sense of nationalism among Tibetans."[74] Indeed, "the India-hosted administration that claims to speak for all Tibetans says the protests may increase if Beijing favors using bullets rather than dialogue for its regional security."[75]

A bit of a cat-and-mouse game seems to be playing out between the Chinese central government and the internal dissidents, and in this game the regime is not always the clear-cut winner. Chinese government authorities routinely restrict Internet access when they feel that protesters are gaining traction, but they do not completely cut off such access because they know that could backfire and damage the overall Chinese economy.[76] At the same time, dissidents have gradually developed new subtler forms of online and off-line protest, including informal "strolls" where "Chinese activists challenge, embarrass or shame the authorities through provocation rather than direct confrontation."[77] Often "this kind of activism is effective," for "even as the government tightens control, it also takes steps to mollify public concerns."[78]

### Force Legitimacy

To the Tibetan people, the Chinese force use in Tibet has been utterly illegitimate. For example, between March and November 2011, eleven Tibetans—of whom six have died—set fire to themselves in eastern Tibet, signaling the deepest form of protest against Chinese rule:

> The reality is that their desperate acts were a scathing indictment of the People's Republic of China's rule in occupied Tibet. They highlight the dramatic struggle for survival as a people with a unique culture and identity. The monks and nuns who immolated themselves were sacrificing their bodies to draw the world's attention to Chinese repression in Tibet. The immolators acted on behalf of Tibet and the Tibetan people, and their intention was to harm no one else. This painful and sad action emerges from their anguish; they live in a climate of fear and have no other means of expressing themselves.[79]

Because of the brutality of the Chinese government response, Tibetan leaders in exile do not encourage self-immolation or internal demonstrations, although—when they occur—these leaders do try to ensure that the international community hears about the confrontations because they recognize their "responsibility to make sure that the calls those Tibetans for restoration of freedom are heard, and their sacrifices are not in vain."[80] Tibetan leaders have requested U.N. fact-finding missions be sent to investigate the situation in Tibet firsthand so that they can "press the government of the People's Republic of China to restore freedom and resolve the issue of Tibet through dialogue for the mutual benefit of the Tibetan and Chinese peoples."[81]

Foreign governments have verbally criticized the Chinese government for its crackdown on dissidents. For example, on March 6, 2011, the Australian government "added its voice to the growing wave of international condemnation over the situation," saying that it has been "extremely concerned by recent reports of attacks on journalists, the detention of lawyers and activists, and the tightening of already strict controls on social media in China."[82] American and European diplomats have also condemned government intimidation of foreign journalists: On February 28, 2011, Jon Huntsman Jr., the departing American ambassador to China, said, "I am disappointed that the Chinese public security authorities could not protect the safety and property of foreign journalists doing their jobs," and "I call on the Chinese government to hold the perpetrators accountable for harassing and assaulting innocent individuals and ask that they respect the rights of foreign journalists to report in China."[83] Furthermore, in incidents not involving foreign journalists, the U.S. government complained on March 8, 2011, about the apparent detention and disappearance of some of China's best-known human rights lawyers and activists;[84] criticized China in April 2011 for its alleged beating and torture of monks at the Kirti Monastery after a twenty-year-old monk killed himself on March 16 to protest Chinese government policies in Tibet;[85] and again "expressed concern" in response to a call for international intervention by the Tibetan government-in-exile after the January 2012 crackdown.[86] Even the president of Taiwan "urged Chinese authorities to adopt 'new concepts' and 'accelerate efforts on democratic political reform to safeguard human rights'" in the wake of Chinese government crackdown response to the Jasmine Revolution.[87]

Global human rights organizations have been very active and vocal in identifying fundamental human rights violations in China. For example, Amnesty International stated that the "string of self-immolations by Tibetans has been fuelled by years of repressive policies that violate fundamental freedoms in the region"; brought Chinese coercive repression against the Tibetans to the U.N. Human Rights Council and asked that "the Chinese authorities loosen their stranglehold over Tibetan culture"; and demanded that the Chinese government undertake a comprehensive review of the human rights situation in Tibet and end human rights violations.[88] In July 2010, a comprehensive Human Rights Watch examination of the Chinese government crackdown in Tibet between March 2008 and April 2010 found a higher than expected scale of human rights violations; "Chinese forces broke international law—including prohibitions against disproportionate use of force, torture and arbitrary detention, as well as the right to peaceful assembly—despite government claims to the contrary"; and "violations continue, including disappearances, wrongful convictions and imprisonment, persecution of families, and the targeting of people suspected of sympathizing with the protest movement."[89] In late February 2011, the international director of Chinese Human Rights Defenders asserted that "in the matter of a few days, we have seen more cases of prominent lawyers subjected to prolonged disappearances, more criminal charges that may carry lengthy prison sentences for activists, more home raids, and a heavier reliance on extralegal measures."[90] China "has denounced the accounts of the violence by the rights groups as 'ill-intentioned hype' by 'overseas secessionist groups attempting to distort the truth and discredit the Chinese government.'"[91]

## Future Prospects

Although little visible political change has occurred so far in China due to internal prodemocratic protests, there may be at least some hope for significant transformation in the future. For example, one observer argues that "while it's true that sudden, radical change is not likely to happen in China, that's no reason for despair: change has been under way in China for years, but in forms more subtle than most people outside the country understand."[92] Reflecting on the Tiananmen Square uprising in 1989, one reporter provides a context for optimistically interpreting future trends:

> After the government crackdown on protesters in Tiananmen Square in 1989, it was widely assumed that Beijing had quashed any chance for meaningful dissent. But protests have become more common since then, over everything from wages and polluted land to dam-building and animal rights. They have involved workers, villagers, migrants, environmentalists and public-interest lawyers. Protest is also increasingly common on the Internet. I recently counted 60 major cases of online activism, ranging from extensive blogging to heavily trafficked forums to petitions, in 2009 and 2010 alone. Yet these protests are reformist, not revolutionary. They are usually local, centering on corrupt government officials and specific injustices against Chinese citizens, and the participants in different movements do not connect with one another, because the government forbids broad-based coalitions for large-scale social movements. Because of those political limits, protesters express modest and concrete goals rather than demand total change.[93]

Thus, despite China's extensive brute force use, evolutionary rather than radical political change may be inevitable for this emerging world power.

Nonetheless, China seems to be still doing everything it can to slow down the pace of future change in response to continuing protests.[94] This government policy seems likely to persist because—in the words of a prominent Chinese dissident—"behind the pride and conceit of the Chinese government there's a great sense of crisis and vulnerability."[95] Chinese authorities have been increasing their brute force efforts used to spy on and harass dissidents.[96] In March 2013, China's parliament "approved $124 billion for domestic security," including "surveillance and harassment of activists," representing "the third year that spending on perceived domestic threats has exceeded the military budget."[97] Furthermore, unlike many antigovernment dissident movements elsewhere, the Chinese Jasmine Revolution failed to transform into an influential popular movement largely because the protests have remained scattered, diffused, and focused on limited local issues.[98]

In terms of the regional impact, any granting by the Chinese government of increased autonomy or political rights to its people in the future could send shock waves through the region. Several closely aligned states, such as Myanmar and Cambodia, could find their own political stability directly affected by such a transformation. However, as mentioned earlier, in this part of the world bottom-up democratization processes work very slowly, and in most of these countries there are significant obstacles to reforms—whether violently or peacefully achieved—that would dramatically jolt them in the direction of being much more open societies.

## EGYPTIAN REPRESSION OF DISSIDENTS

### Force Description

As part of the popular uprising against long-standing dictators throughout much of the Middle East and North Africa, widespread popular protests emerged in early 2011 against Egyptian President Hosni Mubarak, who had ruled the country for almost thirty years. The immediate trigger was Tunisia's Jasmine Revolution in mid-January, demonstrating that "sustained and broad-based popular mobilization can lead to political change."[99] The uprising started on January 25, after years of frustration by prodemocracy activists trying to oust President Husni Mubarak:[100] "For 18 magical days in January and February, Egyptians of all walks of life came together in Tahrir Square demanding to be rid of him."[101] The protesters who sparked this uprising encompassed "elite activists, formerly apolitical, disenfranchised Egyptians, the working class, and politicized reformist constituents of the old regime."[102] An estimated one million people filled Cairo's Tahrir Square, as well as Alexandria and other major Egyptian cities, chanting anti-Mubarak slogans and demanding that he relinquish power.

On February 11, 2011, "after weeks of dramatic sit-ins, clashes with security forces, and resistance against agent provocateurs,"[103] the largely nonviolent revolution finally ousted President Mubarak. In this effort, Mubarak's security forces had killed over 800 people and seriously injured many thousands of activists.[104] Afterward, however, for several months those who had protested against him were frustrated about the pace of reform and were concerned that Egypt's military leadership was purposely delaying the transition to civilian rule.[105] Finally, on June 30, 2012, Mohammed Morsi (of the Muslim Brotherhood's political wing, the Freedom and Justice Party) was sworn in as the first democratically elected president of Egypt and the first Islamist to rule an Arab state, after six decades of militarily supported autocracy. At the time the Muslim Brotherhood was the only organization within Egypt dedicated to mass protest.[106] However, fears persisted about Egypt's economic capability to construct a successful modern Islamic state.[107] These fears were realized when, on July 3, 2013, Egyptian General Abdul Fatah al-Sisi in a military coup suspended the Egyptian constitution and overthrew President Morsi, placing him under house arrest.

### Purpose/Rationale

The motive for the government force use in Egypt was simple maintenance of power, with deterrence of politically destabilizing action through punishment for the dissidents at the core of its rationale. President Mubarak enjoyed the power that accompanied being head of Egypt and wanted to continue in that position. The country had no tradition of orderly democratic transition among leaders, so force use was expected to prevent change.

The motives for the dissidents in Egypt creating the uprising against the government were poverty, misery, hopelessness, and the huge gulf between the people and the government. The regime's dismal basic needs performance was a core concern: "The government's deteriorating ability to provide basic services and seeming indifference to widespread unemployment and poverty alienated tens of millions of Egyptians, a feeling that was exacerbated by growing conspicuous consumption among a business elite connected to Mubarak's son Gamal."[108] Indeed, "consent had drained out of public life; the only glue between ruler and ruled was suspicion and fear."[109] In Egypt, "six decades of military rule robbed them of the experience of open politics,"[110] and the population has felt considerable resentment about that and a strong desire to have more influence over their own fate. Within Egypt, "the anger of the protesters is largely directed inwards—at a bankrupt Arab order—rather than outwards at Israel, the United States or the West."[111]

### Force Effectiveness

The effectiveness of Egyptian government coercion against the dissidents was a failure, as the Mubarak regime was eventually overthrown. Through this failure President Mubarak (and the rest of the world) learned something about the limits of relying solely on military force to maintain power:

When unrest overtook the country in January 2011, President Husni Mubarak quickly discovered that the state he presided over was not his fiefdom. When his security services were unable to quell the unrest, he learned that the army would not. The generals abandoned him, unwilling to sacrifice the welfare of 82 million for one man.[112]

With his rule in jeopardy, "Mubarak had to hire armed thugs to disperse the protesters bent on his defeat; but with their fealty only to their wages, they disappeared into the crowds they were hired to disperse within two days."[113]

Key Egyptian government coercion tactics failed along the way to defeat. One of these tactics was the shutdown of Egyptian Internet access:

Mubarak's regime was able to shut down the internet on January 26, presumably to reduce activists' ability to communicate with one another about how events were unfolding. But this action backfired, as tens of thousands of people, no longer glued to their computers, went outside and joined the demonstrations. For the next several days, the crowd gathered at Cairo's Tahrir Square swelled to include millions of people, who set up tents, refreshment stations, and even portable latrines, to give the gathering staying power. Meanwhile, Egypt's other major cities, including Alexandria, saw mobilization increasing despite deadly repression by security forces.[114]

Thanks to the news media, the rest of the world was still able to witness the uprising in the country. A second unsuccessful tactic was an allegedly staged attack on the protesters in Tahrir Square on February 2 by pro-Mubarak demonstrators, "riding into the Square on camels and horses, swinging sticks, swords, and clubs through the crowd":

The army stood by while mayhem ensued. Hundreds were hurt, and for a rattling 24 hours, the fate of the uprising hung in the balance. But many immediately sensed that Mubarak was relying on agent provocateurs, whose violence was meant to sow divisions within the opposition and cause some to retaliate with violence, giving the army a good excuse to surround and attack the demonstrators. Mubarak's strategy backfired. Instead of intimidating the crowd and dividing the opposition, on February 4, hundreds of thousands of people descended on Tahrir Square to show their unity and solidarity with those who had been attacked.[115]

So the Mubarak regime's coercive choices proved to be deficient in coping with the critical security challenge.

Despite the military victory of the rebels, in many ways the political payoff in Egypt was underwhelming and did "not match the sacrifices made by the Arab peoples who revolted for the sake of freedom, social justice and human dignity."[116] Quite a bit of dissatisfaction emerged over the provisional military rule before the mid-2012 elections, and during its short time in office the new leadership was not able to promote peaceful stability, let alone freedom, justice, or democracy. The military coup that deposed Mohammed Morsi on July 3, 2013—less than a year after he assumed power—portended poorly for long-term Egyptian political stability satisfying the primary thrust of the internal dissident movement.

## Force Legitimacy

There was a high level of popular support within Egypt for the January protests leading to Mubarak's overthrow. For example, in March 2011, 83 percent of Egyptians said they supported protesters who called for Mubarak's resignation.[117] Although Egyptian security forces engaged in coercive repression against their countrymen for a while, they were unwilling to do so indefinitely:[118] "Throughout the demonstrations, the Egyptian Armed Forces acknowledged the legitimacy of the protesters' demands," and they "ultimately sided with the protesters against the country's President."[119] Notably,

> The [Egyptian] Army's refusal to engage in a Tiananmen Square-style massacre in Tahrir Square came not because the generals were on the protesters' side—indeed, they had long been the bedrock of Mubarak's regime—but because they could not trust their own soldiers, disproportionately from the poor and disenfranchised sectors of society, to obey orders to fire on their own people.[120]

A key reason for widespread popular support within Egypt for the uprising was unity among the protesters: Although "from the very beginning the government marked the protestors as traitors for foreign mercenaries, a common 'recipe' of challenged strongmen," the united Egyptian dissidents sent this clear message to Mubarak—"We are Egypt. This is our country. We stay, you go."[121] This unity "opened up the eyes of Western audiences" and increased their sympathy for the uprising.[122]

Although Mubarak had "for decades been one of the closest U.S. allies in the Arab world, playing a key role in mediating peace talks between Israel and the Palestinians and seeking to drum up Arab support for a tough line towards Iran," the United States eventually ended up on the side of the rebels;

indeed, during the latter stages of the conflict President Obama "bluntly told the Egyptian leader not to run for another term."[123] However, as with other Arab Spring uprisings, American support for the rebels was not immediate: Right before the overthrow of Mubarak, U.S. Secretary of State Clinton "insisted that the country was stable and that the government of President Husni Mubarak was 'looking for ways to respond to the legitimate needs and interests of the Egyptian people,' despite the miserable failure of the regime in its nearly 30 years in power to do so."[124] The context for this American hesitation to support the peaceful mass uprising in Egypt was that in many ways "the West is complicit in Arab autocracy," as "for decades, American and European leaders chose stability over democracy."[125] This initial American government hesitation to support a prodemocracy insurrection that "caught Washington completely off-guard" has "not endeared many in these largely youthful movements—who will likely eventually find themselves in positions of power—to the United States."[126]

The type of state brute force applied by the Egyptian government against the dissidents reinforced the global community's perception of its illegitimacy. The government repression included "war crimes and human rights violations committed against democracy advocates,"[127] making these abuses seem even more flagrantly unacceptable to the international community. The protest movement's nonviolent tactics garnered significant outside sympathy:

> In Egypt . . . the vast majority of activists refused to respond to violence with violence, even though the regimes deliberately attempted to provoke them into taking up arms. Because the protesters avoided violence, they did not physically threaten the police and military, allowing the military to remain neutral. Moreover, they were able to maintain the moral high ground domestically and internationally. In addition, Egyptian . . . people were outraged when the regimes cracked down violently against unarmed civilians. People who had been "on the fence" about the movements soon saw that the regime was out of bounds and began to support the uprisings.[128]

The Western media had a tendency to idealize the uprising in Tahrir Square, making Mubarak's coercive response appear even more inappropriate.[129]

### Future Prospects

Within Egypt the lines of future internal conflict are readily evident: "When the dust settles, three forces will contest Egypt's future—the army, the [Muslim] Brotherhood, and a broad liberal and secular coalition of those who want a civil polity, the separation of religion and politics, and the saving graces of a normal political life."[130] The violent July 2013 military coup overthrowing Mohammed Morsi signals future instability and suggests a possibility of an unending action–reaction cycle among contending Egyptian factions. Moreover, the 2013 military coup may suggest that Egyptian popular commitment to nonviolent protest—evidenced in the 2011 demonstrations—may have ceased. The new army-backed regime has been accused of trying "to intimidate anyone likely to question the idea that the army's heavy-handed governance is the only alternative to Morsi's Muslim Brotherhood."[131] Indeed, many Egyptians feel that they are now receiving the same treatment, involving government corruption and police brutality, received under the Mubarak regime.[132]

After the July 2013 military coup, the unpredictability of the future course of the country could negatively affect long-term regional stability. Within a region as volatile as the Middle East, "what is also certain is that the consequences of ending democratisation in Egypt won't be limited to the country itself."[133] The future prospects for Israeli–Egyptian relations appear to be mixed:

> In the short-term the demise of the Muslim Brotherhood is good news for Israel—especially since it further isolates Hamas in the Gaza Strip—however, with uncertainty about the political future of Syria and Lebanon in the north and now Egypt again in the south, Israel finds itself surrounded by political forces that it can neither control nor predict.[134]

Moreover, Egypt's relationship with the West is likely to be more complex than under Mubarak. Although initially analysts trumpeted that the dramatic bottom-up transformation of power in Egypt challenged both the realist assumption that "power rests with whoever runs the government and whoever has the guns" and the neoconservative assumption that "only by Western invasion and occupation could Arab dictators be toppled and democracy take hold,"[135] the fleeting nature of the Morsi regime indicates that this cheering may have been a bit premature. The broader lesson here is that, when reflecting on Arab Spring political transformations, one should not jump the gun to make a quick assessment based on immediate security outcomes.

## GREEK REPRESSION OF DISSIDENTS

### Force Description

On May 5, 2010, Greek protesters commenced a series of demonstrations set off by national government plans to cut public spending and raise taxes in exchange of a European Union bailout to address the severe Greek debt crisis. Three protesters were killed in the demonstration. On May 25, 2011, these demonstrations spread to major cities across the country. On June 25, 2011, there were renewed violent clashes between the government police and protesters in anticipation of the Greek parliament's approval of the European Union's austerity measures on June 29 and June 30, 2011. The reaction of government police was particularly brutal: "Shock grenades were thrown every other minute during the demonstrations for the general strike of June 2011 (in Syntagma), even inside buildings, and new chemical gases were unleashed on an unprecedented scale."[136] On February 12, 2012, half a million protesters in Athens demonstrated against further government austerity measures required by the European Union and International Monetary Fund loan. In January 2013, a series of bomb attacks occurred targeting the country's largest shopping mall, government offices, banks, and journalists who had defended the Greek government's efforts to cope with the financial crisis.[137] Since the beginning of 2013, "strikes have continued, prompting the government to take more extreme measures against demonstrators."[138]

These antigovernment protests were often but not always nonviolent:

> Many of the anti-austerity demonstrations that have taken place in recent years were peaceful, such as the sit-ins staged by the "Indignant movement" in the main squares of the capital Athens and the city of Thessaloniki between May and August 2011. On other occasions, including several times in June 2011, the otherwise peaceful demonstrations became violent when a minority of rioters clashed with police. A few of the demonstrations had more serious consequences. On 5 May 2010, three bank workers died during a demonstration in Athens against the austerity measures after some rioters threw a petrol bomb at the bank. On 10 February 2012, the largely peaceful demonstration taking place while Parliament voted a second bail-out agreement turned into a riot, which resulted in extensive fire damage to many buildings including banks and shops. Police also reported a large number of injuries to their officers in some of these demonstrations or protests.[139]

However, Greek state officials often misperceived the protests as entirely violent. Even when the protesters were violent, they did not employ sophisticated weaponry, often preferring to throw bottles, marble chunks, and rocks at the police.

## Purpose/Rationale

The root cause of the Greek demonstrations was socioeconomic frustration. In the words of one protester, "Those who govern are the ones who brought this country into the crisis, and made people poor; we are from two directly opposite worlds that will never stop clashing."[140] The combination of poverty and social exclusion, along with increasing police brutality, made a popular uprising virtually inevitable.[141] As of early 2013, "three years of unrelenting austerity have been devastating; unemployment is nearly 27 percent and rising, one in three Greeks lives on or below the poverty line, and more wage and pension cuts are yet to come."[142] For example, even back in early May 2010, there were increased taxes on company profits and on luxury and "vice" expenditures, as well as government pay cuts and pension reductions.[143]

Motivating the Greek government response to these protests was a desire to deter disruption and promote economic survival. A senior government official said, "We want to present ourselves as successful, to start legitimizing Greece again in the eyes of the international community."[144] Between 1995 and 2007, Greece had one of the European Union's highest economic growth rates, but "a substantial portion of the country's population was partially excluded or had a very unfair share of the material benefits that were linked to that growth."[145] The Greek government had run up a large debt when the economy had been strong at the start of the twenty-first century, and then, when recession hit in 2008, Greece suffered tremendously because its two main industries—shipping and tourism—were highly sensitive to the economic downturn. On April 23, 2010, to address increasing concern about a sovereign default on debt, the Greek government requested activation of a bailout package offered by the European Union and the International Monetary Fund.

## Force Effectiveness

The Greek government's security strategy is "to crack down on lawless behavior and to press a safety agenda" to restore law-and-order.[146] In the short run, within each demonstration this was relatively effective in preventing the disruptions from escalating too far. However, this coercive repression has generated significant long-run backfire effects: "In its bid to restore order, the government is provoking exactly the violence it says it is trying to quash."[147] Indeed, "escalating political violence from both the left and right is raising fears of political instability in debt-burdened Greece," with protesters saying that government authorities are focusing on a violent crackdown "to divert people's attention from growing poverty and despair."[148]

### Force Legitimacy

Most of the global reaction to the Greek government crackdown on the protesters was supportive of the regime (with the longest tradition of democracy anywhere), generally accepting its need for austerity measures for economic survival. At the same time, the protests were widely accepted due to the severity of the government economic cuts: Even a representative from the International Monetary Fund expressed understanding for the intensity of the protests.[149] So this was a rare case where the international community generally approved of both the force initiator and the force target.

However, an internal financial scandal has hurt the external legitimacy of the Greek state's response to the protests. This growing tax scandal "threatens the stability of the shaky government coalition" involving accusations that the ruling regime "failed to pursue rampant tax evasion by the wealthy and well-connected," many of whom have large Swiss bank accounts.[150] The tax scandal appears to be so deeply rooted that it just will not go away.

Human rights groups have accused the Greek government of excessive force to quell the protests, evidenced by this Amnesty International report:

> Manolis Kypreos, a journalist, suffered a total loss of his hearing after a police officer reportedly threw a stun grenade at him while he was covering a demonstration in Athens on 15 June 2011. Yiannis Kafkas sustained near-fatal head injuries when he was beaten by riot police during another demonstration, on 11 May 2011. He was among a large group of peaceful protesters against whom riot police reportedly used excessive force that day.[151]

Reports abound of torture and ill-treatment of imprisoned Greek protesters.[152] The Greek government has not curbed overreactions by its police; although it acknowledges their human rights violations, it classifies them as "isolated incidents" to avoid dealing with the depth of the issue.[153] Human rights violations have grown particularly since the government has imposed austerity measures in the wake of the financial crisis.[154]

### Future Prospects

Future prospects for Greece look dim—in the words of a protester, "If they think they will stop a growing movement of resistance, they are wrong."[155] Given "widespread poverty engulfing the country's vast middle class and the political establishment's loss of credibility, escalating violence can only endanger Greece's fragile political stability."[156] Today "in Greece the homeless line up at soup kitchens, pensioners commit suicide, the sick cannot get prescription medicines, shops are shuttered, and scavengers pick through dustbins—conditions almost reminiscent of the 1940s."[157] The Greek economy could take up to ten years to get back on its feet,[158] and Greece's debt-to-GDP ratio climbed from 106 percent in 2007 to 170 percent in 2012.[159] Moreover, xenophobic Greeks have found a scapegoat for rising joblessness and crime:[160] "Greece has already been grappling with an intensification of violence by the far right, where sympathizers of a neo-fascist political party, Golden Dawn, have carried out a series of brutal attacks against immigrants, often with the police standing by."[161] Worker unrest has spread to Italy and Spain.[162] Until Greece's economic situation improves, the clashes seem likely to continue.

## INDIAN REPRESSION OF KASHMIR SEPARATISTS

### Force Description

Kashmir is a mostly Muslim Himalayan region north of India, created in the 1947 British partition of Hindu India and Muslim Pakistan. The region has been since claimed by both India and Pakistan, which have fought over control of the area, where Indian soldiers are now seen as an occupying force.[163] Although back in 1972 India and Pakistan had agreed to forego force use to settle their Kashmir dispute, in the late 1980s emerging in Kashmir was a militant Muslim separatist movement opposed to Indian control, and consequently "Indian paramilitary forces have remained in the region since they were deployed to fight a brutal, Pakistan-backed insurgency that swept across the Kashmir Valley in the 1990s."[164]

During three successive summers from 2008 through 2010, deadly clashes occurred in Kashmir between stone-throwing protesters and heavily armed Indian government troops. In 2008, the largest number of anti-India protests occurred since 1980, with "several hundred thousand protesters spilling out onto the streets demanding freedom from India."[165] In response, Indian armed forces brutally suppressed the protests, with forty unarmed civilians killed.[166] From 2009 to 2010, militant activity significantly escalated in Kashmir, with significant instigation from Pakistan.[167]

During the summer of 2010, the turmoil hit its peak. A series of nearly 900 clashes[168] dubbed "Kashmir's stone war"[169] between the Indian government and the residents of Kashmir proved to be most lethal, as Kashmir's demand for self-determination became stronger "than it has been at perhaps any other time in the region's troubled history."[170] Beginning on June 11, 2010, over two weeks of increasingly strident mass protests occurred in Kashmir, with police and paramilitary troops firing on thousands of anti-India protesters and killing eleven people. This confrontation was triggered "when a 17-year-old student, Tufail Mattoo, was killed by a tear-gas shell that shattered his skull, making him an instant martyr."[171] On September 13, 2010, a report that a Koran had been desecrated in the United States caused demonstrations to erupt, but they quickly changed into protests against the Indian military presence.[172] This particular "stone-pelting intifada-like street revolt" was part of "the most serious crisis in Kashmir in decades."[173] On September 18, 2010, thousands of mourners violated a curfew to march in a funeral procession honoring a ten-year-old boy whose body was recovered from a nearby river after he was "reportedly being chased by officers," and Indian officers brutally responded by firing "without provocation on the procession."[174] In 2010 as a whole, the violent confrontation between Indian government forces and the Kashmir protesters took on "a new intensity as the protesters have become less willing to obey the curfew and more willing to confront the security forces" and ultimately "spiraled into a broad, unarmed popular revolt that Indian authorities have struggled to control."[175]

The carnage from these government–protester clashes was significant. In 2010 incidents alone, over 100 protesters were killed[176] (many of whom were youth, who comprise over 70 percent of Kashmir's population[177]) and at least 145 people were injured,[178] along with 194 students in police custody for throwing stones and fifty-one for violating the Public Safety Act, a special law that grants broad purview to soldiers and security officers.[179] Ironically, although over 1,200 soldiers were wounded by rock-throwing protesters, not one was killed, leading to questions as to "why Indian security forces are using deadly force against unarmed civilians."[180] Although the protests largely subsided in 2011, as of late 2013 still about 500,000 Indian troops and paramilitary police patrol rebellious Kashmir, and due to the protests over the last decade 40,000 to 50,000 Kashmiris are believed to have been killed.[181]

Notably, throughout the turmoil from 2008 through 2010, there was an absence of meaningful dialog between the protesters and the Indian government. A moderate Muslim leader in Kashmir complained vociferously that the Indian government response to the desire for free political expression by the people was simply force:

The sad part is that all summer, people were being killed for expressing political sentiment. Now they are killed for expressing their religious sentiments. It seems the answer to their sentiments is just bullets.[182]

There was a widespread feeling that the Indian government had overreacted to a protest where stones were the only weapon used by the mass public.

During most of protest, diplomatic efforts to help calm Kashmir remained "stalled" due to "a trust deficit" between opposing parties.[183] However, in summer 2011, there was no mass violence due to "visible improvement in the situation" in Kashmir "in terms of the relationship with the Indian government, the relationship between India and Pakistan, and the quality of governance people are enjoying."[184] Nonetheless, the underlying tensions behind this dispute remain unresolved.

### Purpose/Rationale

India's interest in Kashmir is motivated by a desire to maintain order and its control of the region, deterring destabilizing disruptions. Fear of terrorist attacks is certainly part of this rationale, as "India has suffered hundreds of terrorist attacks on its soil every year, with the impetus behind the majority of these attacks coming from recalcitrant insurgents in the Kashmir region of the country, who desire autonomy from New Delhi."[185] Although the Indian government's brute force use has generally operated on "counterinsurgency" premises, in the last couple of years Indian security forces "have received new training and equipment that allows them to control restive crowds without resorting to lethal force": In the summer of 2011 "'the government security machinery is a lot better at handling situations that could arise out of protests than we were at the same time last year, in terms of equipment, in terms of training and in terms of mind-set as well,' said Omar Abdullah, the chief minister of the Indian state of Jammu and Kashmir."[186]

The 2008 violence was at least partially due to cultural insensitivity and mismanagement of the region by the Indian government:

Much of the unrest the Indian government has faced here in the past few years was self-inflicted. After record turnout in elections in 2008, senior Indian politicians crowed that Kashmiris had essentially voted for union with India. This angered many who felt their vote had meant nothing of the sort—they were voting for local representatives to help with basic governance issues, not making a broad statement about their national identity.[187]

This kind of misunderstanding makes force even less likely to achieve a successful outcome.

The armed rebels, who are also accused of being linked to terrorist acts in India, are seeking independence and complete autonomy from India. Given that the uprising in Kashmir is led by Muslim militants, some have in the past been open to a merger with Pakistan,[188] but recently "the idea of joining Pakistan holds less attraction than it used to" due to "the problems just across the border."[189] Regardless, the primary immediate thrust of the revolt remains to force India to withdraw its troops from Kashmir.

### Force Effectiveness

The respite from popular protests and mass uprising since summer 2010 signifies at least short-term military effectiveness of the Indian government's force use in Kashmir. However, even in the short run, the Indian government's violent crackdown created some negative repercussions that have impeded the emergence of stable order in Kashmir. For example, the 2010 confrontations involved a government-imposed curfew that "was the strictest in memory," where "many residents were not allowed out for medical care or to buy food."[190] This situation "has turned a once prosperous region into a locked-down war zone, with Indian security forces posted in bunkers on nearly every street."[191] The immediate economic impact included "education, health care, and business at a standstill"[192] and many Kashmir residents suffering "devastating" financial losses through not being able to get agricultural produce to the market.[193]

In the long run, the stability of Kashmir remains uncertain. For many residents of Kashmir, the drive for independence fuels a continuous struggle:

> Syed Ali Shah Geelani, the aging separatist leader who led the calls for strikes and protests over the last few years, said this lull was not true peace. "This is a forcible peace that has been made at the point of a gun," he said. "People are under very grave slavery." Maqbool Rishi, a student of zoology at the University of Kashmir who took part in protests last year, said that the struggle for self-determination would continue. "It is just a cycle," he said. "The protest will come again and again. It is the inner voice of Kashmir."[194]

Moreover, given Indian government reforms instituted in 2011, residents of Kashmir have wondered why so many Indian troops are still present and given so much power; "with violence on the wane, the chief minister of Jammu and

Kashmir says the mainly Muslim people of his state deserve to see a 'peace dividend,' in the form of a limited withdrawal of the rules that grant soldiers the right to shoot to kill, with virtual immunity from prosecution."[195]

Over the years, an action–reaction cycle has been evident in the battle between the dissidents and the Indian government. Specifically, "each [protester] death prompted a fresh set of angry demonstrations that prompted even tougher crackdowns, leading to more bloodshed."[196] During these violent confrontations, "poorly trained and ill-equipped security forces use live ammunition to fend off angry, stone-throwing crowds; the resulting deaths have only fed the protests, and the state government has called in more troops to try to wrest control of the streets from the protesters."[197]

### Force Legitimacy

Because Indian paramilitary forces in Kashmir operate under a special "draconian" law that shields them from prosecution yet still allows them to arrest anyone suspected of disturbing the peace,[198] many residents of Kashmir say that "this has led to many human rights violations in the region."[199] The controversial law, known as the Armed Forces Special Powers Act, "gives the army widespread power to search houses, arrest people without warrants and detain suspects indefinitely; as a result of the impunity it grants, the armed forces routinely torture suspects, Human Rights Watch says, calling the law 'a tool of state abuse, oppression and discrimination.'"[200] Even more fundamentally, local politicians in Kashmir continue to feel that the violent clashes between Indian government troops and Kashmir constitute "an attack on the rights of citizens to protest peacefully."[201]

However, beginning in late 2010, the Indian government has increased the legitimacy of its control by minimizing many of the triggers for violence in Kashmir. On September 25, 2010, the Indian government announced a major policy shift in Kashmir, "calling for the release of jailed student protesters, easing security strictures in major cities, reopening schools and universities, and offering financial compensation to the families of the more than 100 civilians killed since the restive region erupted in protests in June."[202] India took a series of highly visible actions in 2011 to signal this new attitude: "Dozens of bunkers that scarred the streets of downtown Srinagar have been removed, lifting the sense of siege that has hung over the city for years"; "nighttime checkpoints, a humiliating nuisance to many Kashmiris, have been sharply curtailed"; and "heavily armed paramilitary forces," which used to infest many city neighborhoods "with deep-seated separatist leanings," have been reduced.[203] Moreover, the Indian government "has appointed a trio of interlocutors who have been traveling around the Kashmir Valley, speaking to communities and trying to come up with ways to address their grievances."[204] In tandem with this action,

> Palaniappan Chidambaram, India's powerful home minister, who is the country's top security official, has visited Kashmir several times, seeking to soothe anger over last summer's violence; he declared on the floor of Parliament that because the way in which Kashmir became part of India (by decree from its Hindu sovereign more than 60 years ago) was unusual, Kashmiri demands required a unique solution.[205]

A concrete example of this new more conciliatory legitimacy-enhancing government approach occurred at the beginning of 2012. One day after Indian security forces killed a Kashmiri teenager in a dispute over electricity shortages, government authorities acted quickly to forestall disruptive protests:

> The chief minister of the state of Jammu and Kashmir, Omar Abdullah, visited the family of Altaf Ahmad Sood, 18, on Tuesday and then denounced his killing on Twitter, calling the circumstances "tragic, shocking and inexcusable." Five security officers—an inspector and four constables—were arrested Monday in connection with the shooting of Mr. Sood.[206]

In earlier years, the Indian government would have probably completely ignored such incidents, often leading to mass riots.

Although in 2002 Pakistani President Pervez Musharraf ordered a decrease in his country's open support for the militants in Kashmir,[207] there is little doubt that Pakistan is pleased at the protests by largely Muslim people in Kashmir against the Indian government. Indeed, "according to the Pakistani Ministry of Foreign Affairs, India has no legitimate claim on the Kashmir territory, as even if one accepts the [1947] accession as lawful, there has never been a plebiscite as proposed in the agreement."[208] Over time, Pakistan has used "allegations of human rights abuses by Indian troops in Kashmir to help justify its claim over the territory."[209] Although on December 5, 2006, Musharraf said that Pakistan might be willing to give up its claim on Kashmir if India formally accepted certain conditions,[210] there has been little progress made.

Global responses to the turmoil in Kashmir have been largely muted. Perhaps because "the territory itself has no economic or strategic value,"[211] the violent confrontation in Kashmir seems to have been largely off the radar of Western states, as they have spoken little about it. Those in Kashmir wonder "why there is so little international outcry" about the government violence in their homeland—"The world is silent when Kashmiris die in the streets," said Altaf Ahmed, a thirty-one-year-old schoolteacher.[212] Indeed, the protesters themselves rely on low-level violence—the use of stones—explicitly to promote global legitimacy and to attract global support:

> "If we take up arms, the world will call us terrorists. Stone pelting is the only way to fight for our freedom," said Sajid Shah, a.k.a. Lion of Allah, who was editing his videos in hiding Wednesday. "It makes India think. It makes the world think: What's happening in Kashmir? We will get our freedom with the stone."[213]

However, some outside analysts argue that the United States—which has at least pressured Pakistan to shut down the pipeline of militants entering Kashmir[214]—ought to be more actively concerned with Kashmir and "pursue a path to peace" due to worries about preventing nuclear warfare, "precluding global instability in both markets and security" and minimizing the impact of Kashmir developments on American mission success in Afghanistan.[215] Notably, al-Qaeda and Taliban members may be helping organize terror tactics in Kashmir to promote India–Pakistan conflict.[216]

**Future Prospects**

The turmoil in Kashmir is globally significant, as the area "sits astride one of the world's most dangerous nuclear flash points,"[217] with hostile India and Pakistan governments both possessing weapons of mass destruction. For the foreseeable future, "expanded military responses are unlikely to end the conflict over Kashmir."[218] For India, the world's largest democracy, Kashmir is not only "a political and security crisis," but also "a major embarrassment" in its quest to become a respected world power within the international community.[219] Any granting by India of more autonomy to Kashmir would be likely to have unsettling regional repercussions in South Asia. Sporadic clashes continue in Kashmir; on July 18, 2013, Indian forces killed four protesters and injured dozens more when firing into a crowd demonstrating against alleged desecration of the Koran,[220] and on September 20, 2013, at least seven people were injured in clashes between anti-India protesters and government forces that prevented hundreds of people from marching to a southern town.[221] Even today, "gunfire is common on the 1947 cease-fire line known as the Line of Control (LOC) that divided the beautiful mountain kingdom of Kashmir into Indian- and Pakistani-controlled portions," and "fighting in that tense region always has the potential to quickly escalate into a major war—or even nuclear conflict."[222]

## MEXICAN COERCION AGAINST DRUG LORDS

### Force Description

In 2007, Mexican President Felipe Calderón declared Mexico's war on its powerful drug cartels—the primary suppliers of cocaine, marijuana, and methamphetamine to the United States (which brings in about $38 billion a year in illicit drugs).[223] As of mid-2013, the fighting has killed 90,000 people.[224] About 60,000 Mexican police and soldiers are combating several major drug cartels, which struggle to maintain security control of key areas of the country and "have shown a determined willingness to fight Mexican law enforcement and security forces and an increasing ambition to control other illicit and informal economies in Mexico and to extort legal businesses."[225]

Triggering the Mexican regime's action has been a dramatic recent upsurge in illicit drug runner activity, inadvertently resulting from the American war on drugs ongoing since the early 1970s:

What has changed in recent decades is the scale of Mexico's narcotics operations. U.S. demand has grown and diversified, and Mexico has increasingly become the primary supplier. While in 1990, 50 percent of U.S.-bound cocaine came through Mexico, today the figure is 90 percent. It's also important to note that the power base of the hemisphere's drug trade has shifted from Colombia to Mexico. After four decades and billions of dollars, the U.S. "war on drugs" has pushed the epicenter of these illegal criminal networks closer to the U.S. border. The sheer amount of money that has accompanied this fundamental shift to transportation and smuggling just south of the U.S. border has upped the stakes. More resources have transformed the cartels into increasingly sophisticated organizations—with more professional enforcement arms.[226]

Today, according to American government estimates, 450,000 people in Mexico are employed in the cultivation and trafficking of illegal drugs, with possibly millions more indirectly involved, and annual revenues are estimated at $25 billion.[227] The scope of this unsavory activity grew to the point where the Mexican government felt compelled to take stern coercive action to interdict it.

Although drug trafficking organizations have operated in Mexico for more than a century,[228] the scope of violent turmoil in Mexico has been escalating. Over the last two decades, "Mexican drug cartels have acquired unprecedented power to corrupt and intimidate government officials and civilians."[229] Although Mexican drug violence is highly concentrated, with two-thirds of drug-related homicides occuring in just five of the thirty-two Mexican states, it continues to spread[230] and is primarily directed toward law enforcement personnel—"Dozens of elected officials, hundreds of police and military personnel, and intelligence agents working with U.S. law enforcement in the fight against organized crime have been murdered."[231] So, although parts of the country are free from this problem, "currently violence dominates the political and social context in Mexico," and "organized crime and in particular activities related to drug trafficking constitute the main threat to national security in Mexico."[232]

The nature of the Mexican drug cartel violence is truly grotesque and has been getting progressively worse over time:

> The macabre nature of the violence ratcheted up too, featuring heads rolling across an Acapulco disco floor, a "stewmaker" admitting to dissolving some 300 bodies in acid and a dead man's face stitched onto a soccer ball. The drug cartels openly taunt the authorities and each other, hanging *narcomantas*, or banners, over major thoroughfares boasting about their latest kills and threatening future violence if not left alone. Both the number of the attacks and their brazenness—particularly in states such as Sinaloa, Chihuahua and Michoacán—are unprecedented.[233]

Despite government interdiction efforts, there appears to be no end in sight for these barbarous acts, involving tactics that "often resemble those of terrorists and insurgents, even though their objectives are profit seeking rather than politically motivated."[234] Overall, "although violence has been an inherent feature of the trade in illicit drugs, the character of the drug trafficking-related violence in Mexico seems to have changed recently, now exhibiting increasing brutality."[235] The impact on the public has been huge: "For most Mexicans, rich and poor, a psychological leap into a state of generalized fear and a perception of acute vulnerability coincided with an increase in gruesome displays of barbarism since the spring of 2006."[236]

Although since the early 1980s Mexican presidents have repeatedly used force to combat drug traffickers, this effort has been stepped up in recent years as a full-scale internal war has been declared by the government:

Just days after his new administration began work in December 2006, Calderón declared a war on narco-trafficking—making the establishment of law and order the signature policy for his administration. Over the past three-and-a-half years, he has sent some 45,000 soldiers onto Mexico's streets, spent billions of dollars annually to upgrade their equipment and training and launched a broad process of police and judicial reform. He also increased the operations of both the police and the military, leading to record numbers of interdictions, arrests and extraditions to the United States.[237]

Under President Calderón, there has been a dramatic militarization of the war on drugs, with government troops visible everywhere.[238] Throughout his administration, his zeal in this mission never seemed corrupted either by the lure of drug money or the fear of violent reprisals from the drug cartels.

Unfortunately, the susceptibility to bribes of many Mexican police, law enforcement, and judges has impeded resolution of the crisis:[239]

Mexico's main problem is not control of its territory, which was the principal challenge that Colombia faced. Mexico's dilemma is corruption. Without clean cops, clean courts and clean politicians, Mexico's war will never be won. Instead, Mexico's challenge is to remake its law enforcement, judicial and government institutions to work transparently, effectively and fairly.[240]

Specifically, "The cash generated by drug sales and smuggled back into Mexico is used in part to corrupt U.S. and Mexican border officials and Mexican law enforcement, security forces, and public officials to either ignore DTO [drug-trafficking organizations] activities or to actively support and protect them."[241] However, after American help, Calderón's government "has made great strides in professionalizing the federal police force."[242]

After ignoring the problem for a while, recently the American government became concerned with the instability and the escalation of the violence due to the Mexican drug dilemma's direct security impact on the United States, as the country "has much to gain by helping strengthen its southern neighbor and even more to lose if it does not."[243] The violence of Mexico's drug war is now beginning to spill over the border, and for the United States "border patrols are already costing the country more than $3 billion per year and obstructing billions more in legitimate trade."[244] The problem is exacerbated by Mexico and the United States being highly economically and culturally interdependent, with over $300 billion in annual cross-border trade, tens of millions of American and Mexican citizens in binational families, and over 14 million people residing near the almost 2,000-mile shared border.[245]

In March 2007, Presidents George W. Bush and Calderón agreed to the Mérida Initiative, formally passed in June 2008 by the U.S. Congress, launching a $1.4 billion multiyear security package primarily destined for Mexico: "With an ambitious mandate to break the power of organized crime, strengthen the U.S. southern border, improve Mexican institutional capacity, and reduce the demand for drugs, Mérida encompassed technology and military equipment, as well as law enforcement training and support for judicial reforms."[246] On March 24, 2009, the United States announced plans for a massive crime-fighting operation targeting the Mexican drug cartels "on a scale not seen since the battles against the US mafia": Besides sending more than 100 customs officers to the border, the United States is giving $700 million dollars to the Mexican government for five new helicopters, a surveillance aircraft, and other crime-fighting equipment.[247] Despite these joint initiatives, many Mexican citizens bemoan the disappearing civic order and the growing illicit drug transfers due to the strength of the cartels.

### Purpose/Rationale

The rationale for the Mexican government crackdown on the drug lords was a mixture of (1) deterrence of violent groups creating political and economic instability and (2) compellence of groups and individuals involved in illicit drug running to change their line of business and comply with the law. The state feels that it cannot progress by improving its security and socioeconomic development without this effort. Mexicans involved in the illicit drug industry do so—despite the risks—because it is so incredibly lucrative.

Belatedly, the United States recognized its role in the Mexican drug problem and provided major assistance in this crackdown. During her first official visit to Mexico in March 2009, American Secretary of State Clinton admitted coresponsibility for the problem because the United States has such high demand for the illicit drugs and is a source for much of the drug cartel's weaponry.[248] The United States is "the largest illegal drug market in the world," with an estimated market size of about $70 billion a year,[249] and constitutes "the world's largest supplier of weapons, which fuel the drug war in a more direct way—fully 10 percent of America's gun dealers line the Mexican border, and the country's permissive gun laws make it an inexpensive and convenient source of powerful guns, ammunition, and explosives."[250]

## Force Effectiveness

The Mexican crackdown on the drug lords has not achieved its goals:

> Finding Mexican police forces pervaded by corruption and lacking the capacity to effectively deal with organized crime, President Felipe Calderón dispatched the military into Mexico's streets; yet while scoring some successes in capturing prominent drug traffickers, the military too has found it enormously difficult to suppress the violence and reduce the insecurity of Mexican citizens.[251]

Calderón's frontal assault failed because "the flow of drugs across the border did not diminish to any meaningful extent," major trafficking cartels gained territory and influence, and many of these groups "branched into migrant smuggling, kidnapping, extortion, and other crimes."[252] Some analysts criticized Calderón for declaring war on the drug traffickers without having "a clear definition of success" or "the tools necessary to win."[253] Nonetheless, on more than one occasion "the government of Mexico has argued that its battle against Mexican drug trafficking organizations (DTOs) is effective."[254]

Ironically, government interdiction of high-value targets may increase Mexican violence by destabilizing the existing balance of power among the Mexican drug cartels,[255] evidenced by the reality that "ninety percent of the homicides have involved members of one drug cartel killing members of another."[256] An accusation has even emerged that "the fracturing of Mexico's criminal establishment in the government-led crackdown on drug traffickers created between 60 and 80 new cartels."[257] Moreover, kidnapping and extortion have skyrocketed in Mexico as a by-product of Mexico's crackdown on its drug gangs, as traffickers explore new sources of income.[258]

One of the reasons that the Mexican government crackdown has been ineffective in restraining both drug lord violence and ongoing drug running is the persistent pattern of long-term retaliation in an action–reaction cycle involving state and society:

> If officials, especially at the state and local level, threaten to interfere with criminality, their days may be numbered. In general, though, drug-connected torture, hanging, and decapitations appear to follow a tit-for-tat (or tit-tit-for-

tat-tat) rhythm. . . . Ildefonso Ortiz, an intrepid crime reporter who follows the drug war for *The Monitor* (McAllen, Texas), says that "absolutely, revenge drives the carnage that takes place along the border." . . . Sometimes the targets of revenge are opposing criminal organizations. Other times they involve banks, public buildings, police headquarters, and innocent people whose demise enables brigands like the beastly Los Zetas to maintain credibility— "cartel cred"—as vicious actors in the Mexican underworld. Such a reputation enhances their success in accomplishing extortion, kidnappings, human smuggling, contraband sales, loan-sharking, and more than a dozen other felonies.[259]

Responding to the crackdown, the drug runners "have fought back strongly, refusing to allow law enforcement actions to take place or go unpunished."[260] Recently this violent cycle seems to be escalating rather than diminishing.

Like the Mexican government crackdown, American government action regarding Mexican drug running seems to be unsuccessful. Specifically, "while the United States has supplied funding and labor to increase Mexico's institutional capacity to address drug trafficking, its primary focus has been on cross-border policing and targeting U.S. drug users," and most analysts "agree that the U.S. war on drugs is a failure and necessitates a new approach."[261] Despite the escalation of brute force, target compliance has not followed.

### Force Legitimacy

The Mexican public reaction has been mixed to the state crackdown: "Although many ordinary Mexicans welcome the army's intervention, certain that things would be far worse without it, approval has been far from universal."[262] Moreover, public approval for the war on drugs "is rapidly dwindling" because "most Mexicans believe that the government is outmatched by the narco-traffickers, who enjoy at least some complicity, support, and even sympathy from other members of society."[263] In a January 11, 2011, poll, more than 70 percent of respondents believed that since 2009 national security had worsened—a huge "disconnect exists between what the government thinks it is achieving and what the public perceives as happening."[264] Furthermore, the Mexican drug war has spawned not only more military corruption but also—as Human Rights Watch notes—"a sixfold increase from 2006 to 2009 in accusations of serious human rights abuses by members of the military," which when combined with the high desertion rate among Mexican armed forces (around 20,000 troops per year) reduces force legitimacy.[265]

## Future Prospects

The Calderón regime in battling drug lords prioritized "reducing the power of Mexican drug trafficking organizations" over "a determination to reduce the violence."[266] Mexico's new president, Enrique Peña Nieto, has changed this priority since taking office in December 2012, arguing that he "would focus on public safety and on bringing down the number of homicides."[267] This priorities change seems crucial because "for many Mexican citizens, the primary sign of success" by the Mexican government in its drug crackdown "would be a significant reduction in the violence."[268]

Mexico's crackdown on drug trafficking has been regionally destabilizing. Just as the Colombian drug crackdown earlier led drug operations to shift to Mexico, so the Mexican crackdown is shifting operations elsewhere:

> As Mexico has cracked down on the drugs trade, it was virtually inevitable that Central America would be exploited by traffickers seeking more permissive environments to move their products. As a result, the region has become more violent than Mexico and one of the most dangerous places on earth. In Honduras, there were 77 murders per 100,000 inhabitants in 2010; El Salvador and Guatemala had "only" 66 and 50 per 100,000 respectively.[269]

The disastrous effects of drug violence in Mexico on its southern neighbors have gone largely unnoticed:

> Drug mafias such as the Sinaloa and Zetas cartels, in search of new territory and looking to escape the Mexican government's crackdown, are increasingly setting up shop in the politically fragile states of Central America; with the addition of Belize and El Salvador this year, all seven countries in Central America are now on the White House's list of major drug-trafficking states.[270]

In the end, managing the security challenge posed by the Mexican drug lords is absolutely central to the future of Mexico, but the future looks bleak. The Mexican drug cartels "do not have an ideology other than a ruthless pursuit of profit, but their corruption and intimidation have challenged the state's monopoly on the use of force and rule of law."[271] Mexican central government sovereignty is at stake, as in parts of the country drug cartels are in the process of taking over government roles.[272] Unfortunately, unless somehow there is a substantial decrease in the illegal drugs demand and "the southbound flow of weapons, cash, and drug-making chemicals, the United States will keep feeding the flames that threaten to consume the basis for civilized life in Mexico."[273] In Mexico and throughout Central America, "drug cartels and criminal gangs are challenging the legitimacy and solvency of the state."[274] Perhaps even more dramatically, experts warn that "if the cartels are not contained, Mexico could become a failed state and the U.S. could find itself with an Afghanistan or a Pakistan on its southern border."[275] In response, in 2013 private Mexican self-defense vigilante organizations proliferated "to restore order to Mexican communities," fed up with incompetent or corrupt local police and having "lost faith in the government's willingness or ability to protect them."[276]

## MYANMAR REPRESSION OF DISSIDENTS

### Force Description

In Myanmar (formerly Burma) huge antigovernment peaceful demonstrations—named the "Saffron Revolution"—occurred beginning on August 19, 2007, and lasting through September. This mass uprising, ostensibly triggered by a fuel price hike, was led by Buddhist monks. Around 100,000 people marched in protest in the largest antigovernment demonstrations since March 1988,[277] at which time government security forces killed around 3,000 peaceful demonstrators.[278] After watching fast-growing protests in major cities for over a month, on September 26 the government in Myanmar, ruled by generals since 1962, began a brutal crackdown, "clubbing and tear gassing protesters, firing shots into the air and arresting hundreds of the monks and their supporters";[279] "Buddhist clergy and common citizens were quickly beaten back with batons and bullets"[280] as Myanmar soldiers fired automatic weapons into crowds of antigovernment protesters.[281] A U.N. human rights report indicated that thirty-one people died as a result, although the government acknowledged only fifteen deaths.[282]

Even a few months after the Saffron Revolution ended, the coercive impact lingered. Of the many thousands arrested, 700 were left in jail, adding to 1,150 political prisoners already being detained.[283] More people awaited trial under a wide assortment of highly questionable political charges. Moreover, "many monasteries in the main city, Yangon (formerly Rangoon), have emptied out," with "new arrests are reported almost every day."[284]

### Purpose/Rationale

The government brute force use in Myanmar falls into the deterrence category, with a desire through quick coercive action to forestall any sizable revolt. The regime's aims in undertaking this crackdown were to maintain power and preserve the status quo hierarchy in the country. At a graduation of military students in Yangon on January 9, 2012, the commander in chief of Myanmar's army warned that, to prevent "recurrences of past bitter experiences," there needed to be a renewed focus on "non-disintegration of the Union of Myanmar, non-disintegration of national solidarity, and perpetuation of sovereignty."[285] Resisting any foreign interference is still a primary concern among government officials in Myanmar.

The mass uprising in Myanmar, which is one of the poorest countries in the world due to government corruption despite its "vast natural gas reserves, minerals, teak and the finest rubies, jade and sapphires,"[286] was "a social upheaval" largely "sparked by a rise in fuel prices," with protesters hoping "that a chapter would be closing on the world's longest-running military regime."[287] However, political frustration was the underlying source of the prodemocracy mass uprising—some dissidents shouted, "Give us freedom, give us freedom!" at soldiers during the protests.[288] In the Myanmar public's mind, the continuing political repression by the military junta trumped ongoing popular economic hardships—as the British ambassador to Myanmar stated, "The government must also understand what this is about—not fuel prices, but decades of dissatisfaction."[289]

### Force Effectiveness

In the short run, the Myanmar government force use seems effective:

> The streets are quiet in Myanmar. The "destructive elements" are in jail. The international outcry has faded. The junta's grip on power seems firm.[290]

The government of Myanmar initially trivialized this predicament as not meriting much of a policy response:

> Information Minister Kyaw Hsan belittled the protests as the work of a few agitators and dissident monks who were acting with the support of foreign powers. "Actually, the August–September protests were trivial for the whole country and in comparison to other events in other countries," he said. They dissolved quickly, he added, "because the general public did not take part and our security forces were able to make pre-emptive strikes."[291]

Indeed, "the generals who rule Myanmar have reason to feel relief" because "it seems they have ridden out their most difficult challenge in two decades and are set to maintain control through force and fear, offering only small concessions to the demands of their critics abroad."[292] These ruling generals in Myanmar have openly expressed their intention to perpetuate the status quo:

> As the attention of the world shifts elsewhere, the generals have made it clear that they intend to follow their own course, as they have through a half-century of self-imposed isolation. . . . they signaled their defiance by announcing that a constitutional drafting committee had begun its work and was not going to listen to outside voices. The constitution is one step on what the junta calls a "road map to democracy." Many analysts call it a dodge to evade genuine reform.[293]

The protests clearly did not precipitate meaningful immediate political change.

Whatever initial concessions the Myanmar government made to the protesters were both trivial and cosmetic. As in the past, when facing international pressure, the junta "offered small gestures of compliance; but analysts say that whatever happens, the generals are not about to give real ground to the demands of the United Nations."[294] For example, in one concession, the regime allowed a U.N. envoy to visit the country so as to promote constructive dialog between the government and the dissidents, but this follows "a half-dozen other United Nations envoys over the past 17 years who have failed to moderate the behavior of the junta"; in another concession, a government official met three times with Daw Aung San Suu Kyi, the prodemocracy leader who had spent twelve of the last eighteen years under house arrest, but these meetings also had little impact.[295] Frustrated by these concessions, a Western diplomat in Myanmar confided that "this is not what the Security Council has called for, a genuine process to heal the country."[296]

Overall, for quite some time there was little long-run evidence of bottom-up change in Myanmar, as "the spirit of protest is almost silent," evidenced by the lack of activity due to disillusionment during the uprising's first anniversary.[297] One year after the uprising, the military government in Myanmar seemed even stronger, having profited from high global food and fuel prices, and "business with China is booming . . . partly because tighter Western sanctions have made the junta more dependent on China for diplomatic support, as well as arms and consumer goods."[298]

However, in 2011, the Myanmar government took some seemingly genuine steps toward transformation. In March, President Thein Sein installed what was at least a nominally civilian government. In line with a surprise earlier release on November 13, 2010, of the country's most prominent human rights activist, Aung San Suu Kyi, on October 12, 2011, Myanmar released about 150 of its more than 2,000 political detainees—"the mass amnesty, which authorities say will eventually free 6,300 prisoners, has helped fuel hope for change in one of the most repressive states in the world."[299] During his visit to the White House on May 20, 2013, President Sein talked openly about the release of these political detainees in return for Western concessions.[300] In July 2013 President Sein guaranteed that all prisoners of conscience would be released by the end of the year.[301] This leniency, especially significant since Myanmar denied for decades that political prisoners even existed, represents "the latest in a series of moves that could help the isolated nation normalize relations with the West"; the Myanmar government now claims that it "is striving for emerging good governance and clean government, flourishing of democratic practices, ensuring rule of law, making economic reform and motivating environmental conservation in building a new peaceful, modern, and developed discipline-flourishing democratic nation."[302]

Aiding this change was the consistent media access within Myanmar. Although the closed military regime attempted to censor popular access to the Internet, "signs posted openly, even in small towns, explained how to circumvent government censors through proxy servers."[303] Indeed, "more than ever, satellite TV and the Internet are making people aware of their government's glacial pace of progress": Participants in the 2007 uprising were able the next day to watch "the blood-soaked crackdown live on Al Jazeera television."[304]

### Force Legitimacy

Within Myanmar, there was a great deal of public support for the "Saffron Revolution," albeit with great trepidation. Unlike in the prodemocracy demonstrations in 1988, when monks were not directly targeted, during the 2007 protest there was a dramatic change: The level of "fear, but also anger" among the general population was "unprecedented, as even religious leaders are now clearly not exempt from such violence and repression."[305] A real emotional intensity emerged in this mass uprising, leading to great disappointment when real political change did not immediately follow.

The coercive crackdown by the Myanmar government was heavily criticized by global human rights groups. A Human Rights Watch report complained that "during the crackdown, security forces fired into crowds, beat marchers and monks, and arbitrarily detained thousands of people."[306] Moreover, Myanmar is one of the only countries to be publicly denounced for human rights abuses by the International Committee of the Red Cross, and Amnesty International confirmed that more than 2,100 political prisoners languish in Myanmar's jails, about 1,000 having been locked up in the year since the uprising.[307] Repressive actions in Myanmar have also alienated some global religious groups, as in January 2012 the regime "increased restrictions on Christian activity in the capital city of Rangoon and surrounding areas, including the closure of several churches"; "Christians are often singled out for specific attack or repression because of their perceived connections with the West" and because the regime openly promotes Buddhism.[308]

The Myanmar government crackdown, "witnessed abroad in smuggled photographs and on videotape," elicited verbal condemnation from countries around the world.[309] Transparency International, a Berlin-based nongovernmental organization, has consistently listed Myanmar as one of the world's most corrupt countries.[310] Myanmar and Western states "have been at odds for years because of Myanmar rulers' ongoing clampdown on their political foes."[311] Europe responded to the crackdown by tightening visa restrictions and other sanctions against Myanmar's military regime.[312] British Prime Minister Gordon Brown said, "The whole world is watching Burma now, and the age of impunity is over for anyone in that regime who commits crimes against individuals or the people of Burma."[313] In December 2007, India expressed its displeasure by halting all arms sales and transfers to Burma.[314] The U.N. Security Council discussed the crackdown in Myanmar, but from the outset it was unlikely that any criticism or sanctions would result "due to veto-wielding China, Burma's chief economic and political patron."[315]

The United States joined in the vocal disapproval of the 2007 crackdown and imposed financial and travel restrictions. As violence against the protesters was occurring in 2007, "the United States called on Myanmar's military leaders to open a dialogue with peaceful protesters and urged China to do what it can to prevent further bloodshed"; "'We all need to agree on the fact that the Burmese government has got to stop thinking that this can be solved by police and military, and start thinking about the need for genuine reconciliation with the broad spectrum of political activists in the country,' said U.S. Assistant Secretary of State Christopher Hill in Beijing."[316] Later, the top American diplomat in Myanmar argued that the continuing state repression "raises questions about the sincerity of the military in pursuing what we will consider to be a genuine dialogue leading to national reconciliation."[317]

Southeast Asian neighbors have so far refused to be very vocal or active regarding the repression in Myanmar. Indeed, "in what seems to be a sign of the United States' waning influence in the region, China, India and Myanmar's Southeast Asian neighbors have brushed aside Washington's calls for an economic embargo and the diplomatic isolation of the junta."[318] Although the Association of Southeast Asian Nations (ASEAN) has said that the Myanmar crackdown has "evoked the revulsion of people throughout Southeast Asia and all over the world," at a November 2007 meeting of all ten members in Singapore, the regional organization canceled an invitation at Myanmar's request to a U.N. envoy, changed the language of a new charter to weaken its section on human rights, and argued that "we don't want to come across as being too confrontational in a situation like this."[319]

However, after Myanmar took some progressive steps in 2011, American Assistant Secretary of State Kurt Campbell said in early October that "there are dramatic developments under way" in Myanmar that could prompt the United States to improve ties to it,[320] and in early December Secretary of State Clinton concluded her Myanmar visit by stating that "she was 'cautiously hopeful' that Myanmar was emerging from decades of military dictatorship."[321] In April 2012, the European Union lifted all nonmilitary sanctions on Myanmar. Indeed, following the 2011 amnesty, many outsiders concluded that President Sein "is willing to make more concessions in order to get sanctions lifted and get more international legitimacy."[322]

**Future Prospects**

In the future, some version of the status quo seems likely to be preserved in Myanmar, involving "a military-dominated, civilianized government."[323] Regarding political transformation, "if change is coming in Myanmar," then "it is likely to be a long process and to emerge from within the power structure."[324] However, the liberalization steps taken in 2011—"including talks between new President Thein Sein and pro-democracy icon Aung San Suu Kyi, a relaxation of media censorship, and the release of some political prisoners—have stunned many foreign observers and sparked speculation that the historically military-run country is on the verge of a new era of democracy and openness."[325] Public dissatisfaction and internal bottom-up pressures for change seem likely to continue, and recently the Myanmar government has indicated more receptivity to Western business and economic assistance. Future political reform would affect regional stability, potentially opening the door to improved relationships between Myanmar and its neighbors. For example, in January 2013, Myanmar and the International Committee of Red Cross (ICRC) pledged increased cooperation in distributing humanitarian aid to conflict areas in the country,[326] and on August 20, 2013, Myanmar announced its plan to expand its cooperation with China in a broad range of economic areas, including agriculture, trade, and tourism.[327]

## SUDANESE REPRESSION OF DISSIDENTS

### Force Description

As with China, there have been two separate strands of Sudanese government force uses against internal dissidents. First, from 2003 to 2010, there was a central government crackdown in Darfur against two rebel movements. Second, in mid-2012, a peaceful mass protest began in the capital city of Khartoum demanding a change in regime and significant economic reforms. These two strands of state brute force use in the country are distinct but reflect some of the same kinds of popular dissatisfaction against a regime that is "the most oppressive and violent of those that have come under the winds of the Arab Spring."[328]

Addressing the first government crackdown, in February 26, 2003, rebels comprised of the Sudan Liberation Movement/Army (SLM/A) and Justice and Equality Movement (JEM) in the western region of Darfur attacked Sudanese government garrisons in the region, demanding greater autonomy and resolution of land rights disputes. The Sudanese government responded with a massive counterinsurgency campaign, destroying entire villages and torturing, raping, or killing many civilians. The historical context for this revolt is that Sudan has a legacy of popular revolts bringing down the central government, including in October 1964 and in April 1985.

In this counterinsurgency campaign, the government of Sudan relied heavily on private militias known as "Janjaweed" as its principal counterinsurgency ground force in Darfur: "With government aerial support, arms, communications, and other backing, and often alongside government troops, the Janjaweed militias have been a key component in the government's military campaign in Darfur, a campaign that has resulted in the murder, rape and forced displacement of thousands of civilians."[329] Because of the destruction of hundreds of villages in Darfur through bombing and ground attacks, over a million people were forced from their homes and over 158,000 refugees fled Darfur for neighboring Chad. By June 2004, the conflict had killed about

10,000 people and left several hundred thousand in danger of starvation.[330] As of December 2005,

> More than half of Darfur's six million people—Arabs and non-Arabs, pasto-
> ralists and farmers—now suffer the effects of a collapsed economy, little or no
> freedom of movement, and the loss of livelihoods from looted and destroyed
> property; more than two million displaced victims of "ethnic cleansing" in
> Darfur remain confined in camps, some for more than two years, where they
> are almost entirely dependent on foreign assistance and remain vulnerable to
> violence.[331]

In January 2005, the Sudanese government and the Sudanese People's Liberation Army (SPLA) signed a comprehensive peace agreement to end the war.
However, in February 2008, the Sudanese government initiated a large-scale
attack on towns in rebel-held areas of West Darfur in "a vicious reprise of
'scorched earth' counterinsurgency tactics" undertaken from 2003 to 2005.[332]
The Sudanese government and the Justice and Equality Movement signed
a ceasefire agreement in February 2010. By the time the conflict ended that
month, about 2.7 million people had fled their homes and about 300,000 had
died, mostly from disease.[333]

Moving to the second government crackdown, just months following
South Sudan's secession and becoming an independent state in July 2011,
in January 2012 the country was "plagued by ethnic violence at home and
ongoing tensions with its previous rulers in Sudan."[334] In that same month,
landlocked South Sudan shut down its oil production because of disagreements with Sudan about oil fees, "throwing both nations into turmoil" due to
both countries' heavy dependence on crude oil exports for foreign currency to
import food and fuel.[335] In April 2012, Sudanese and South Sudanese armies
fought each other for weeks along their disputed border "in the worst violence
since South Sudan seceded in July 2011."[336]

In mid-June 2012, a new more peaceful mass uprising commenced. Thousands of Sudanese dissidents "braved police batons and tear gas to rail against
the government."[337] The first stage began on June 16 and involved students
at the University of Khartoum rising up to protest, with the unrest spreading "deep into middle-class neighborhoods, where people blocked roads with
burning tires."[338] Then came what the protesters called "Sandstorm" Friday
on June 22, by which point the protests involving hundreds of people had

spread to dozens of other locations in Khartoum, Omdurman, Madani, Sennar, Gedarif, Port Sudan, Hasahisa, and other towns across Sudan. On June 29, "Licking the Elbow" Friday protests (a clever reference to doing the impossible) occurred after regular prayer in Khartoum, at which time ten regional towns received large numbers of antiriot police units and plainclothes security agents of the National Intelligence and Security Services using tear gas, batons, and rubber bullets. On July 6, the "Vagabonds" Friday demonstrations (a taunt directed at President Omar al-Bashir, who has ruled Sudan since 1989 and who had described the protesters in a speech as "agitators" and "vagabonds"[339]) involved clashes after regular prayer between police officers and a crowd of about 500 antigovernment protesters in greater Khartoum and other Sudanese cities. Generally, the Muslim day of prayer on Friday was "the easiest time to mobilize people to hit the streets."[340] The Sudanese government once again quickly and brutally responded with "a fierce crackdown from riot police officers, who have routinely swatted the protesters in the head and have even shot tear gas into hospital courtyards."[341] Sudan security forces "have arrested scores of protesters, opposition members, and journalists; beat people in detention; and used rubber bullets and even live ammunition to break up protests."[342] Since June 2012, the government crackdown has injured hundreds of protesters,[343] and Sudanese security forces have detained 2,000 people linked to youth-led protests in major Sudanese cities.[344] In March 2013, South Sudan and Sudan finally reached agreement on cross-border petroleum flows, and in April 2013 South Sudan restarted oil production.[345]

### Purpose/Rationale

The rationale in both of the two phases of force use against the internal rebels by the Sudanese government, as controlled by the National Congress Party and President Omar Hassan al-Bashir (an army officer who had seized power from democratically elected Prime Minister Sadiq al-Mahdi and instituted a military dictatorship on June 30, 1989), was to maintain control of the country, impose order, and put down the armed rebellion. This motivation falls squarely in the deterrence category. The chosen means by this military regime to achieve its ends was "violence and intimidation to silence dissenters."[346] Negotiation with protesters was not considered a viable option.

The Sudanese dissidents in both of the two revolts had political aims to gain autonomy from the oppressive military regime, to end the current government, and to achieve economic reforms. When the SLA and JEM began attacking government targets in early 2003, they accused the Sudanese government in Khartoum "of oppressing black Africans in favour of Arabs," particularly in terms of the division of "land and grazing rights between the mostly nomadic Arabs, and farmers from the Fur, Massaleet and Zaghawa communities."[347] Thus political, economic, and racial, and cultural elements triggered the revolt.

On June 22, 2012, after Friday prayers dissidents in Khartoum demanded the overthrow of President al-Bashir: "'Leave, Bashir, leave!' they chanted; 'Khartoum, people, please revolt against humiliation and dictatorship.'"[348] On July 6, 2012, protesters' placards read, "Down, down military rule," and they shouted, "No, no to high prices!,"[349] "Revolution is the choice of the people—freedom, peace and justice!," and "The people want to bring down the regime!"[350] Rioting intensified "because of the failures of this regime to realise people's aspirations for democracy"[351] involving "a repressive, autocratic regime that has been in power 23 years; a dire economic crisis; heavily armed insurrection in several corners of the country; and a fired-up protest movement that goes beyond the usual suspects of students and unemployed youths to shopkeepers and homemakers, all willing to take a beating."[352]

The economic crisis, in which the Sudanese government faces a $2.4 billion budget deficit with a weakening currency and rising prices for food and other goods (many of which are imported),[353] revolves around oil:

> Sudan's nose-diving economy is the ostensible fuse. In mid-June, the government announced that it could no longer afford to subsidize gas. As a result, fuel prices shot up 60 percent, making everything drastically more expensive. The Sudanese economy has been in a free fall since the start of the year, when the newly independent nation of South Sudan, which split off a year ago, completely shut down oil production. Most of the oil in the Sudans lies in the south, but the pipeline runs through the north. The two sides have yet to agree on a formula to share oil profits and are locked in brinkmanship as economic troubles build on both sides of the border.[354]

President Bashir defended the new decision to cut fuel subsidies by contending that "the secession of South Sudan turned the country from an oil exporter to importer, but political parties and activists believe mismanagement, corruption and government policies have been responsible for the economic collapse."[355]

## Force Effectiveness

The short-term military force effectiveness in the two phases of revolt seems high, as the Sudanese government remains in power. Indeed, many Sudan analysts are skeptical that the protests would cause the regime to fall.[356] One reason is the military strength of the regime, as "Bashir has built a force of as many as 30,000 special security troops, drawing significantly from his own Arab tribe, with underground barracks and hidden arsenals, who are ready to 'defend the regime street by street', as a last line of defense."[357] Another reason is the lack of cohesion and spatial visibility of the protesters, for "unlike in Egypt, as of yet, the Sudanese lack an organized and disciplined party, like the Muslim Brotherhood, that can form the core of the protest movement," and "unlike protesters in Egypt, Libya or Bahrain, the Sudanese have not been able to occupy anything, not even a single public square."[358]

The long-term prospects for Sudanese government force effectiveness are considerably cloudier. Despite the military might of the regime, and some "hardcore" regime supporters, now "Bashir is facing what some describe as unprecedented popular dissent"[359] involving "the most serious challenge to the ruling National Congress Party in many years."[360] The mass uprising intensity seems to be in direct proportion to the regime intractability.[361] In the long run, "it is unclear whether the divided and fractured opposition can close ranks, mobilise large masses, and lead a revolution."[362]

## Force Legitimacy

The legitimacy of the Sudanese government's force use has been low among outside states. In the 2003 uprising, the global community quickly became antagonistic toward the military regime, eventually leading in 2009 to President Omar Hassan al-Bashir being indicted by the International Criminal Court on war crimes, crimes against humanity, and genocide charges for the massacres in the western region of Darfur.[363] The U.N. undersecretary general for humanitarian affairs has called Darfur probably "the world's greatest humanitarian catastrophe."[364] Human Rights Watch reports that, since July 2003, Sudanese government forces and militia forces have committed crimes against humanity and war crimes "on a massive scale"—"civilians have suffered direct attack from land and air, summary execution, rape, torture, and the pillaging of their property."[365] The United States has imposed economic sanctions on Sudan since 1997. In the Darfur conflict, the Sudanese government's illegitimacy was heightened by its denial at the beginning of the conflict that the

Janjaweed ethnic militias even existed and its denial later in the conflict that it had any official links with these private militias, although Human Rights Watch obtained copies of Sudanese government documents that describe an official policy of support to the Janjaweed militia.[366] Moreover, thousands of people associated with a joint African Union–U.N. peacekeeping mission have witnessed the carnage firsthand,[367] although the Sudanese government "has allowed no news reporters into the region and has severely restricted humanitarian access."[368]

International verbal attacks on the Sudanese government were quite common. In response to the 2012 uprising, Canadian Foreign Minister John Baird said, "We condemn the arrests of bloggers, journalists and political activists that have taken place over the last week and call for their immediate release."[369] Britain's minister for Africa Henry Bellingham expressed concern "at growing levels of censorship and restrictions on the media and on the political opposition" in Sudan and called for "the immediate release of those detained while engaged in peaceful protest, and for the security forces to act with restraint and avoid the use of force in responding to peaceful demonstrations."[370] On June 26, 2012, American State Department spokeswoman Victoria Nuland criticized the crackdown on dissidents in Sudan, noting that "the heavy-handed approach adopted by Sudanese security forces is disproportionate and deeply concerning."[371] On July 17, 2012, American Assistant Secretary of State for African Affairs Johnnie Carson urged Sudan and South Sudan to resolve their differences quickly or face "extremely bleak economic futures" and a "rapid downward economic spiral."[372]

Global human rights organizations have been consistently opposed to Sudanese government repression. U.N. High Commissioner for Human Rights Navi Pillay "has urged the government to avoid 'heavy-handed suppression' of protests and to immediately release those detained for exercising their rights to freedom of assembly and expression."[373] On June 26, 2012, the Africa director at Human Rights Watch stated that Sudanese government "authorities should call off their security forces and vigilantes, end the violence immediately, and respect the right of the people to protest peacefully."[374] On July 11, 2012, both Amnesty International and Human Rights Watch called on Sudanese authorities "to immediately release people arrested for participating in recent peaceful protests and demanded that torture and ill-treatment of detained protesters stop."[375] These international groups contend that "Sudanese security forces have repeatedly used excessive force to disperse the demonstrations and arrested scores of peaceful protesters including students, youth activists, and journalists."[376] In some cases, Sudanese activists "have been detained from their homes before they even join the protest as a precautionary measure" by government security forces.[377] Moreover, global antagonism toward the Sudanese regime has been exacerbated in the 2012 crisis because the government has arrested and detained Sudanese and international journalists while trying to report on the protests;[378] prevented Sudanese newspapers from publishing or distributing copies reporting on antigovernment uprisings;[379] and "routinely censored newspapers, removing articles about sensitive topics and seizing entire print runs of specific issues."[380]

In response to these criticisms, the Sudanese government has dismissed the significance of the mass protests and blamed them on "foreign elements." Sudan's information minister called the protesters "'rioters' who threaten the country's stability."[381] A government spokesman complained that "Zionist institutions inside the United States and elsewhere are exploiting the latest economic decisions to destabilise the security and political situation."[382] Because state officials have "played down the protests," they plan to "press ahead with spending cuts which they say are needed to heal the ailing economy"[383] and not even consider stepping down. President Omar al-Bashir himself "has played down the demonstrations as small-scale and not comparable to the Arab Spring uprisings in Egypt and elsewhere, maintaining that he himself remains popular."[384]

Sudanese dissidents ultimately garnered considerable legitimacy. They generally renounced force use, as they hoped "to change the regime using peaceful means,"[385] although on occasion low-level violence has been used, "with people throwing stones at police, burning tires and police trucks, and cutting off roads."[386] The United States and other Western nations have long supported and poured billions of dollars into the South Sudan government, led by leader of the Sudan People's Liberation Army Salva Kiir, "to try to turn a destitute land, with oil reserves but a long history of violence and little in the way of institutions, into a viable country."[387] Moreover, the international community has generally come to view Sudanese protesters as impoverished victims of violence rather than as rowdy perpetrators of turmoil.

### Future Prospects

The Sudanese rebels are hoping for a smooth power transition. In spring 2013, in light of a widening antiregime offensive, for the first time since 2011 the

Sudanese government began direct talks with the Sudan People's Liberation Movement North.[388] Long divided in the past, now "the opposition factions are working on a document that would administer the country in a post-Bashir Sudan"—as an opposition leader explains, "We need to prevent chaos and a power vacuum once the regime falls, so that is why we are working on agreeing on a transitional phase."[389]

One way or another, political change could well be in the offing in Sudan. One foreign journalist insightfully called eastern Sudan "a volcano waiting to erupt."[390] But for such change to be lasting, internal military challenges will have to be effectively managed. Regardless, the violent turmoil within Sudan could promote regional instability among its neighbors through both large refugee flows and spreading transformational ideas. In particular, "the conflict in Sudan's Darfur region increasingly threatens two neighboring countries—Chad and the Central African Republic."[391]

## SYRIAN REPRESSION OF REBELS

### Force Description

As part of the popular uprising against dictators throughout much of the Middle East and North Africa, since March 15, 2011, popular protests have escalated against Syrian President Bashar al-Assad.[392] Boosted by the collapse of the Qaddafi regime, in October 2011 protests erupted across Syria, with most of the civilians killed in Homs, Syria's third-largest city, which quickly became the hub of antiregime activity: Demonstrators were filmed chanting "Qaddafi is dead, prepare yourself Bashar."[393] As the demonstrations grew, the slogans became bolder—"The people want to overthrow the regime."[394]

The Syrian government quickly engaged in massive retaliation "on a no-holds-barred basis"[395] against the protesters. The regime "has not shied away from using the army for violent repression, with high numbers killed, missing, or detained; as opposed to Egypt and Tunisia, in which security forces largely held back from overt or widespread violent tactics, there seems to be little restraint from direct action against protests" in Syria.[396] The net result was truly brutal repression:

> The main response from Syrian security and intelligence services has been to use live ammunition to silence growing protests, arbitrarily detain hundreds of protestors, and subject them to torture and ill-treatment. Security forces have also detained a number of journalists, activists, and lawyers who have

reported on the protests or called for further protests. Moreover, Syrian security forces in at least two towns prevented medical personnel and others from reaching wounded protestors and prevented injured protestors from accessing hospitals, as reported by Human Rights Watch.[397]

Having learned valuable lessons from the successful Tunisian and Egyptian uprisings, "The Syrian government expelled foreign journalists and prevented international news networks like CNN and al-Jazeera from broadcasting live coverage of the protests."[398] In late October 2012, the United Nations tried to impose a cease-fire, but both Assad's troops and rebel forces violated it.[399] By September 2013, about 120,000 people had been killed in more than two years of civil war, and two million people had fled Syria,[400] with about half of the country's 22 million citizens displaced.[401] Syria refugees fled to Turkey, Jordan, Lebanon, and Iraq.

A number of issues have hampered the effectiveness of the dissidents in Syria. First, rather than a unified national uprising, the protests in Syria have been relatively small and scattered over local grievances.[402] Second, while demonstrations have involved thousands of Syrians, they have not yet reached the critical mass of huge protests movements such as in Egypt.[403] Third, residents of Damascus and Aleppo—Syria's major cities—joined the protests only in July 2012. Fourth, the Syrian protests have had little quality leadership and were quickly "infiltrated by violent elements and were soon dominated by Sunni Muslim fundamentalists viewed with suspicion by secularists and minority Christians, Alawites, Druze, and Kurds."[404] Thus the rebel movement has been plagued by infighting and inexperience.

### Purpose/Rationale

As in other Arab Spring uprisings, the motive for the government force use in Syria was simple maintenance of power, incorporating deterrence of politically destabilizing action through punishment for the insurgents. As with his father before him, Bashar Assad has coveted the position of Syria's president and has not yet showed any sign that he is willing to relinquish it. In Syria, as with most of the Middle East, there is no tradition of orderly democratic transition of government authority.

The Syrian dissidents had multifaceted motives: "The revolt fused a sense of economic disinheritance and the wrath of a Sunni majority determined to rid itself of the rule of a godless lot."[405] In particular, "in Syria the revolt has been largely fuelled by resentment felt by the urban and rural poor against the regime rich."[406] So both religion and economics play a role in this crisis.

### Force Effectiveness

Although so far the government force use in Syria has prevented the overthrow of the Assad regime, long-run force effectiveness is dubious:

> Syria remains in chaos. Hamas left Damascus in December [2011] because it feared being left on the wrong side of the mounting Arab consensus against the Syrian regime. "No Iran, no Hezbollah; we want rulers who fear Allah," has been one of the more meaningful chants of the protesters. Alawite rule has been an anomaly, and the regime, through its brutal response to the uprising, with security forces desecrating mosques, firing at worshipers, and ordering hapless captives to proclaim, "There is no God but Bashar," has written its own regional banishment.[407]

By mid-2012 the rebels had developed strongholds in many outlying areas, with government forces focusing on the major cities.

In November 2012, six Gulf States composing the Gulf Cooperation Council—Saudi Arabia, Bahrain, the United Arab Emirates, Oman, Qatar, and Kuwait—officially recognized the National Coalition for Syrian Revolutionary and Opposition Forces—a new coalition united the various factions opposing the Assad regime—as "the legitimate representative of the brotherly Syrian people."[408] Western states and Turkey had earlier welcomed the creation of this new coalition, as they had in previous weeks "put pressure on a hitherto fractious Syrian opposition to create a unified, credible body that could become a conduit for all financial and possibly military aid."[409] This unification represents a real challenge to the Syrian government.

The popular uprising in Syria has followed the violent Libya pattern rather than the nonviolent Tunisia pattern. Since late 2011, "the Syrian revolt has been taken over by armed rebels seeking to replicate the Libyan model by drawing outside powers into the struggle to topple the regime by force."[410] Although some peaceful activists there are also protesting the regime,[411] their efforts have been overshadowed. So the confrontation is perceived globally as armed conflict—often labeled a "civil war"—rather than peaceful protest.

The Syrian government's attempt to keep its brutal force use away from the global spotlight has not succeeded. Syrian authorities have harassed or expelled foreign journalists, shut down electricity, and disabled cellular and

Internet services, but dissidents have found alternative means of communicating abuses, including video recordings of brutal government violence.[412] In today's interconnected world, it is extremely difficult for an authoritarian regime to effectively shut down any form of external communication. However, unlike in Libya, no foreign troops are likely to invade Syria to help the rebels,[413] at least in part due to adamant Russian and Chinese opposition to foreign interference in the country.[414]

**Force Legitimacy**

The Syrian government's force use against its own people has generated global outrage and condemnation.[415] Despite continued support from Russia, China, and Iran, whom Assad has relied on to block international action preventing the violent crackdown,[416] most of the global community has expressed horror at the carnage, especially after the 2012 revelation of large-scale massacres: On May 25, a government attack on the village of Houla killed 108 people, forty-nine of them children, with most "shot at close range or stabbed."[417] In May 2012, a U.N. independent panel probing abuses in Syria found that "gross" human rights violations continue unabated there.[418] The United States quickly imposed financial sanctions on the Assad government, and in 2013 American Secretary of State John Kerry "said that it is the United States' hope to change Mr. Assad's 'calculations' about his ability to hold on to power so that he will allow negotiations for a political solution to the conflict."[419] The violence in Syria has "prompted even the Arab League, which has a history of overlooking the follies of its members, to suspend Damascus' membership"[420] on November 12, 2011. Ten days after that decision, Prime Minister Recep Tayyip Erdogan of Turkey called on Assad to "remove [himself] from that seat," accusing him of "cowardice"; shortly afterward, the Arab League imposed sanctions on Syria, including freezing its assets, ending all dealings with the Central Bank of Syria, and halting financial interaction with the Syrian government.[421] To many observers, Assad's days in power seem numbered.

Following Assad's June 2012 threat to use chemical weapons in the conflict, American President Obama concluded that Assad's government forces had indeed used these unsanctioned arms against Syrian rebel fighters.[422] After a team of U.N. chemical weapons inspectors confirmed that the Assad regime had used the nerve agent sarin on August 21, 2013, killing more than 1,300 people—including many small children and babies—U.N. Secretary General Ban Ki-moon told the U.N. Security Council that the attack constituted a war crime.[423] As a result—what President Obama called the crossing of a "red line"—he decided to supply direct military assistance (though not American "boots on the ground") to the opposition. Nonetheless, partly due to "the arrival of thousands of seasoned Iran-backed Hezbollah Shi'ite fighters to help Assad combat the mainly Sunni rebellion," the momentum keeps shifting in the conflict, with "outgunned rebel forces desperate for weapons" often overwhelmed;[424] in contrast to hard-line Islamist rebel groups that "enjoy free-flowing streams of money from donors in oil-rich Persian Gulf states," moderate rebel groups in particular find themselves short on funding and weapons, for an American–Russian agreement to destroy Syria's chemical weapons stockpile prevented a promised substantial increase in Western support from materializing.[425]

Although in the early stages of the conflict the Assad regime commanded sufficient loyalty from the military "for the unleashing of lethal force against civilians" on behalf of a dictator,[426] this support has recently eroded. The obscure Islamic sect Alawis, to which Assad belonged but which comprises only 12 percent of the Syrian population, has remained so far fiercely loyal to the Syrian regime.[427] Nonetheless, despite 90 percent of Syrian military commanders being Alawis,[428] cracks have lately been emerging here in this military loyalty: American Secretary of State Clinton noted that "those with the closest knowledge of Assad's actions and crimes are moving away—we think that's a very promising development."[429]

Nonetheless, Assad consistently overestimated his imperviousness to outside criticism. In January 2011, he "granted an interview to The Wall Street Journal in which he claimed that, because he was so close to the beliefs and aspirations of his people, Syria was 'immune' to the revolutionary fever of nearby Arab lands."[430] Before the uprising in Syria, Assad mistakenly had this idea because, unlike Tunisia, Egypt, or Libya, Syria's leader "was young, not old" and its "regime had more legitimacy because it had confronted Israel rather than collaborated with it"; after the uprising, with the fighting still raging on, still "the embattled ruler appears convinced that he can resist the laws of gravity."[431] Moreover, "from the outset of the peaceful uprising that began more than two years ago, to the eruption of violence and civil war that now grips the country, Assad has blamed the unrest on foreign terrorists."[432] He refuses to recognize the dramatically changed Syrian realities, and in the end "Syria has the same preconditions for revolution as Tunisia and Egypt—poverty, unemployment, corruption, and repression."[433] Indeed, "Syria's ruler has embraced his image as a global pariah; he will not flee and will not bend to foreign pressure, he has said publicly and privately."[434]

## Future Prospects

Regardless of the ultimate outcome in Syria, the security state that "rested on fear" is gone—"in Syria, the bonds between the holders of power and the population have been irreparably broken."[435] Although "governments in the Middle East and North Africa have long relied on repression to intimidate, harass, and punish political opponents," in Syria inadvertently "government repression has not destroyed the movements and, indeed, may have breathed new life into them."[436] Syria could eventually devolve into a failed state.[437]

At the same time, Russia and China show no signs of abandoning their firm support for the Syrian regime in power. In March 2013, Russia "sent advanced antiship cruise missiles to Syria, a move that illustrates the depth of its support for the Syrian government."[438] With the United States on one side and Russia on the other in the Syrian crisis, this confrontation resembles the old Cold War proxy wars between the superpowers.

Extreme brutality by both sides prevents long-term reconciliation:

Syrian soldiers slowly stab a man to death, puncturing his back dozens of times. A rebel commander bites an organ ripped out of an enemy combatant. A young boy hacks the head off a prisoner. A soldier mutilates the genitals of a corpse. These are the images of Syrian conflict, the first war in which the prevalence of camera phones and Internet access has allowed hundreds of gruesome war crimes to be broadcast, spreading hatred and fear. They are defining the war that is spilling across Syria's borders and making reconciliation an ever more distant prospect. Brutality has been used as a tool since the revolt began two years ago, when videos emerged of government soldiers torturing pro-democracy protesters. In response to the crackdown, the opposition took up arms and now fighters from both sides are filming themselves committing atrocities.[439]

There is no end in sight to the gruesome carnage.

Significant fears persist about the future impact of the Syrian predicament on the Middle East. With regard to regional stability, the fall of Assad could "unleash a cataclysm of chaos, sectarian strife and extremism that spreads far beyond its borders, threatening not only the entrenched rulers already battling to hold at bay a clamor for democratic change but also the entire balance of power in the volatile region."[440] Although "Qatar, Saudi Arabia and Kuwait favour providing the rebels with arms and money and are already doing so, it is feared that militarisation will simply prolong Syria's agony and could destabilise neighbouring Turkey, Iraq, Lebanon and Jordan."[441] The flood of Syrian refugees into these neighboring countries has overwhelmed their ability to assimilate them. Of all the countries neighboring Syria, Lebanon "is the most vulnerable to spillover from the Syrian conflict: the state is weak, sectarian tensions are high, and the main political coalitions have chosen sides, either explicitly backing or opposing the regime of Bashar al-Assad."[442] If the Assad regime collapses and a new regime better reflects the Sunni majority, "it will deliver a blow to Iran, Assad's closest regional ally, and undermine the so-called 'axis of resistance' that unites countries and groups opposed to Israel and Western interests in the Middle East."[443] Economically, if due to Syria the Arab Spring uprisings spread to a major Middle Eastern oil exporter such as Saudi Arabia, the global oil price could skyrocket. Finally, "the meltdown of the Syrian state is empowering terrorist groups,"[444]—it is "a magnet for global jihadists, including al-Qaeda-linked groups, fighting for the establishment of an Islamist state."[445]

## THAILAND REPRESSION OF DISSIDENTS

### Force Description

During the spring of 2010, although Thailand "has been embroiled in political chaos for years,"[446] its "worst political unrest in nearly two decades" erupted.[447] On March 14, 2010, following the court-ordered confiscation of about $1.4 billion of popular former Prime Minister Thaksin Shinawatra's assets, tens of thousands of Red Shirt protesters—known for the clothes they wear and constituting the United Front for Democracy against Dictatorship—converged on Bangkok, Thailand. The initially nonviolent uprising began by holding its first major rally and occupying the government district. The Red Shirt protesters included not only the rural and urban poor but also some Bangkok bankers.[448] Behind barricades made of bamboo stakes and car tires, protesters pitched their tents in a one-square-mile area dubbed the Red Zone, surrounding the Ratchaprasong business district and sealed off on all sides by the government army.[449]

On March 16, a few hundred liters of the protesters' blood collected the day before were "ceremonially splashed" on the four gates of Government House, the office of Prime Minister Abhisit Vejjajiva, and over the headquarters of the ruling Democrat party "in a ritual aimed at bringing down the government."[450] On March 30, a round of talks between the dissidents and the Thai government ended in deadlock. On April 7, the Prime Minister declared a "state of emergency," with the royalist government and the army on one side and a broad coalition of antigovernment protesters on the other.[451] Ultimately, at the peak of the demonstrations, around 120,000 Red Shirt protesters[452]—including women and children—amassed and ended up paralyzing the center of the normally bustling capital city.

On April 10, 2010, government troops tried to clear out the protesters, with twenty-five people killed and hundreds injured. In May, the Bangkok authorities "cut off water and electricity to the camp"; troops "set up roadblocks to prevent further protesters from entering the camp";[453] and Thai authorities "imposed the curfew initially on the capital, but later extended it to 21 provinces—about a third of the total—after outbursts of unrest in seven regions, particularly in the north, a 'red shirt' stronghold."[454] Once the military crackdown began and "the soldiers attempted to clear the demonstrators, they left a trail of casualties—they fired live ammunition at Red Shirts who were barely armed": "Young people crouched behind sand bags and fired on the soldiers with homemade fireworks and slingshots," and "the soldiers returned fire with pump guns, sniper rifles and M-16 assault rifles."[455] The turmoil reached its zenith on May 19: The military completed its brutal crackdown while, as a last-gasp effort, the once relatively docile protesters set twenty-seven buildings including the stock exchange ablaze in Bangkok in the "most widespread and most uncontrollable" political violence Thailand has ever seen.[456] The Thai government declared on May 20 that "it had mostly quelled 10 weeks of violent protests in the capital."[457] Overall, in the entire bloody confrontation from March to May, at least ninety people died,[458] most of them unarmed civilians,[459] and over 2,000 were wounded, in clashes between state forces and the Red Shirt protesters.[460]

## Purpose/Rationale

The goal of the Thai government force use was maintenance of regime power and authority. The rationale was the deterrence—"keen to show no one is above the rule of law," Prime Minister Abhisit Vejjajiva felt that he could not allow the defiant protest to continue.[461] The ruling regime repeatedly stated that its crackdown was defensive rather than offensive, undertaken to restore order after all other options were exhausted. In political leaders' minds, allowing the protest to continue would highlight regime weakness.

The goal of the Thai protesters was primarily political in nature, involving a change of government leadership that in their minds would come if parliament were dissolved and fresh elections were held.[462] The specific desire was for Abhisit's government to resign "because it has not been elected by the people and is only supported by the military, which staged a coup [in 2006] to oust the former Prime Minister Thaksin Shinawatra—the hero of the poor"[463] living in self-imposed exile in Dubai. Protesters wanted Thaksin to return but more fundamentally yearned for a more democratic and socially just Thailand "where the elite no longer have all the power and others also share in the wealth." Indeed, the relatively high turnout by protesters "has underlined divisions in Thailand between the rural poor and the Bangkok establishment."[464] Most of the protesters "never thought that the government would so brutally crack down on its own people"[465] because their strategy was apparently "to disrupt the functioning of government for as long as possible, in the hope that the prime minister blinks."[466]

### Force Effectiveness

The Thai mass uprising constituted a major challenge to Thai government authority, as "the pro-government Bangkok Post had called it 'anarchy' and the opposition spoke of 'civil war.'"[467] Although brute force against the Red Shirt protesters reestablished order in the short run, it was not an unmitigated success:

> Even as the government declared victory in quashing a debilitating protest that had shut down parts of Bangkok for two months, the rampage across Bangkok and in at least three provinces in the country's populous northeastern hinterland raised concerns about the conflict's spreading and the future of the current government.[468]

The manner in which the violent confrontation played out does not seem conducive to long-run stability in the country. In many ways, the Thai government crackdown left the country "more divided than perhaps at any time since it became a constitutional monarchy in 1932."[469] As Red Shirt leader Somyos Prueksakasemsuk said after handing himself in to police, "The (ideological) consciousness will survive; there will be more hatred [toward the regime] and they [Thai citizens] will express it in whichever way they can."[470]

The Thai army was "an amateurish force"—"if they had cleared the street protests at the outset, the conflict would have never escalated" to the bloody extent that it did.[471] Indeed, "outside analysts and diplomats said the military appears to have underestimated the resolve of thousands of 'red shirt' protesters barricaded" in the Red Zone.[472] This force underestimation led to the need for a state-initiated brutal crackdown as a short-term solution.

In reality, though, Thai government coercion was inevitable, as government authorities on May 16 "ruled out negotiations with the Red Shirt protesters"[473] by "rejecting demands for U.N.-supervised talks" and calling on Red Shirt leaders "to surrender."[474] A violent action–reaction cycle also seemed predetermined, because when in May 2010 one of the Red Shirt leaders said that "there would be a 'civil war' if the army did not pull back and declare a cease-fire," the Thai army responded by making parts of Bangkok "live-fire zones," "warning that anyone found entering certain roads in the capital would be shot on sight."[475] As the confrontation was evolving, "moderate voices on both sides have lost ground to hard-liners bent on a head-on collision."[476]

### Force Legitimacy

Global response to the crackdown focused on minimizing bloodshed. U.N. Secretary General Ban Ki-moon "urged both protesters and the authorities to avoid further violence": His office said he "strongly encourages them to urgently return to dialogue in order to de-escalate the situation and resolve matters peacefully."[477] The United States also urged military restraint and encouraged the two sides "to find a way to work peacefully through these differences."[478] International sympathy emerged for captured protesters, facing terrorism charges with maximum penalty of death, raising the stakes in a crisis that "stifled Southeast Asia's second-biggest economy and choked investment in one of Asia's most promising emerging markets."[479]

A comprehensive study of the mass uprising by Human Rights Watch was decidedly skeptical about the legitimacy of Thai government coercion, accusing security forces of "excessive and unnecessary lethal force."[480] Moreover, the aftermath of the uprising—involving high-level corruption, human rights abuses, and widespread economic disparities—caused Human Rights Watch to be unconvinced that justice has been restored, with key protest leaders charged with serious criminal offenses and government forces implicated in abuses continuing to enjoy impunity.[481]

The internal mass public feelings about the Red Shirt protest and the government crackdown were mixed. Some residents sympathized with the protests, and others were against the disruption and just wanted everything to return to normal. In addition, "the emergence of divided loyalties among members of the security services transformed the stand-off with Thailand's Red Shirt opposition into a crisis for the government."[482] Mass reactions within Bangkok were complicated by the existence of a small contingent of militant Red Shirt protesters, known as the "Black Shirts," who were armed and dangerous and more willing to use violence to achieve their ends than the Red Shirts.[483] The existence of the Black Shirts allowed the Thai government to falsely claim that its crackdown was aimed exclusively against them.

Initially, the Thai government maintained that "it has nothing to do with liquidations, and that the demonstrators are shooting each other dead," but eyewitness accounts proved that claim to be completely false.[484] Later on, a Thai military officer asserted that "the military had been restrained in its use of deadly force"—"if we had the intention to attack civilians, the death toll would have been much higher."[485] However, collateral damage against civilians was extensive. The legitimacy of the Thai government action was hampered by confirmed reports that several foreign journalists being killed or injured in the military crackdown. Furthermore, during the military crackdown, a local news blackout was imposed, and "local TV ran programs of dancing and flag-waving Thais, periodically interrupting them for government statements."[486]

**Future Prospects**

In the future, Thai government action could lead to continuous dangerous violent insurgency, as former Prime Minister Thaksin Shinawatra said the crackdown could spawn guerrilla warfare: "A military crackdown can spread resentment and these resentful people will become guerrillas."[487] After the confrontation ended in May 2010, a former Red Shirt leader said that "rather than solving the crisis, the government has further polarized the country and pushed it toward more violent clashes."[488] Considering the regime as a whole, "Thailand's social contract has frayed, posing a future challenge to an entrenched hierarchical system with a constitutional monarch at its core."[489]

Tourism was negatively affected by the uprising, and it is unclear how quickly that industry will recover in the future. This "lifeblood of the Thai economy" "draws visitors to the temples of Bangkok, the beaches of Andaman Sea and the mountains of northern Thailand," accounts for almost 7 percent of Thailand's GDP, and is a key source of employment.[490] Tourism immediately declined in March 2010 after the turmoil began when more than forty countries issued travel warnings amid reports of thousands of tourists canceling trips, and the Thai Ministry of Finance estimated that gross domestic product growth "will decline by 0.2 to 0.5 percent" due to the unrest.[491]

More broadly, this confrontation could promote regional instability in Southeast Asia:

> If the divisions in Thailand can't be healed it could lead to a deteriorating security situation which would have wider implications for the region. Thailand's relations with Cambodia are especially frosty since Thaksin was appointed economic adviser to Cambodian Prime Minister Hun Sen. The worst case scenario would see Cambodia drawn into the dispute, with Thaksin using the country as a political base, adding to the already considerable tensions on the border.[492]

Forceful suppression of dissent within what is supposed to be a model democracy—without significant outside intervention on behalf of force targets—could have dire political implications for less open neighboring countries.

Two violent incidents in 2013 provide tangible evidence of political volatility in Thailand. On June 14, 2013, 200 Red Shirts beat up a small group of white-masked demonstrators in the northern city of Chiang Mai, reflecting worsening political divisions among Thai citizens.[493] In late November and early December 2013, in the largest protests since 2010, around 30,000 anti-government protesters in Bangkok attacked the Government House, trying to unseat Prime Minister Yingluck Shinawatra, with government troops responding with rubber bullets, tear gas, and water cannons. Although the government stated that it would use "minimum force" against the protesters, on November 30 alone two people were killed, and dozens more were wounded during the confrontation.[494]

# 5 BRUTE FORCE SECURITY IMPACT PATTERNS

CAREFULLY EXAMINING THE STATE-INITIATED brute force case study outcomes reveals persistent patterns of success and failure. After flagging security dangers from overuse and underuse of force, this chapter identifies the conditions under which state-initiated brute force works best, highlighting standards from which deviations could be measured and comparatively evaluated to determine the wisdom of force use. Identified initiator and target attributes linking to successful outcomes merit much higher policy priority than common but low-impact force legitimacy concerns.

Tables 5.1 through 5.10 provide a comparative overview of these findings through twenty indicators of the external and internal brute force case backgrounds, initiator profiles, target profiles, power ratios, and strategic outcomes. The case backgrounds identify the force initiator, force target, challenge dates, and force provocation. The initiator profiles identify the initiator's purpose/rationale, force misperception, force commitment, and force restraint. The target profiles identify the target's disruptive elements, societal order, tactical fluidity, and response capacity. The power ratios identify the initiator's coercive advantage, domestic support level, exposure to outside intervention, and degree of violent target resistance. The strategic outcomes identify the initiator's force effectiveness (short-run and long-run) and force legitimacy, and the case's force aftermath (action–reaction cycles and regional contagion) and future prospects.

**Table 5-1. External brute force case backgrounds.**

| Case name | Force initiator | Force target | Challenge dates | Force provocation |
|---|---|---|---|---|
| American drone strikes in Pakistan and Yemen | United States | Terrorist leaders | 2009–present | Unprovoked extermination of terrorist targets |
| American invasion of Afghanistan | United States | Taliban/al-Qaeda | October 2001–2014 (estimated end) | Immediate response to 9/11 terrorist attacks |
| American invasion of Iraq | United States | Saddam Hussein regime | March 2003– December 2011 | Last resort after failed diplomacy and economic sanctions |
| American killing of Osama Bin Laden | United States | Head of al-Qaeda | May 2011 | Long-awaited retaliation against al-Qaeda leader |
| French intervention in Mali | France | Mali rebels | January–May 2013 | Response to request for assistance from Malian government |
| Israeli invasion of Lebanon | Israel | Hezbollah | July 2006 | Immediate response to killing and capturing of Israeli soldiers |
| Israeli destruction of Syrian nuclear facility | Israel | Syrian nuclear plant | September 2007 | Preemptive strike against dangerous enemy |
| NATO coercion in Libya | NATO (multilateral) | Muammar el-Qaddafi regime | March–October 2011 | Last resort U.N.-sanctioned protection of protesters from state reprisals |
| North Korean sinking of South Korean Ship | North Korea | South Korean naval vessel | March 26, 2010 | Unacknowledged and unprovoked destructive attack |
| Russian invasion of Georgia | Russia | Georgian regime | August 2008 | Immediate response to turmoil in Russia-leaning South Ossetia |

**Table 5-2. External brute force initiator profiles.**

| Case name | Purpose/rationale | Force misperception | Force commitment | Force restraint |
|---|---|---|---|---|
| American drone strikes in Pakistan and Yemen | Deterrence threat eradication | Overestimation of violence reduction | High | Low |
| American invasion of Afghanistan | Compellence revenge | Underestimation of tribal traditions and corruption | Medium | High |
| American invasion of Iraq | Deterrence/compellence dictator overthrow | Overestimation of postforce peaceful compliance | Medium | High |
| American killing of Osama Bin Laden | Deterrence threat eradication | Underestimation of Pakistani collusion | High | Low |
| French intervention in Mali | Deterrence/compellence suppressing revolt | Underestimation of postforce turmoil | Medium | High |
| Israeli invasion of Lebanon | Deterrence retaliation | Underestimation of Hezbollah resiliency | High | Low |
| Israeli destruction of Syrian nuclear facility | Deterrence preemption | Underestimation of regional repercussions | High | Low |
| NATO coercion in Libya | Deterrence/compellence humanitarian aid | None | Medium | High |
| North Korean sinking of South Korean ship | Deterrence muscle-fexing | Underestimation of identified culpability | Low | Low |
| Russian invasion of Georgia | Deterrence/compellence controlling bordering area | None | High | Low |

**Table 5-3. External brute force target profiles.**

| Case name | Disruptive elements | Societal order | Tactical fluidity | Response capacity |
|---|---|---|---|---|
| American drone strikes in Pakistan and Yemen | Multiple | Resilient (Pakistan) Nonresilient (Yemen) | High | High |
| American invasion of Afghanistan | Multiple | Nonresilient | High | High |
| American invasion of Iraq | Multiple | Nonresilient | Medium | High |
| American killing of Osama Bin Laden | Single | Resilient | High | High |
| French intervention in Mali | Multiple | Nonresilient | Low | Low |
| Israeli invasion of Lebanon | Single | Resilient | High | Medium |
| Israeli destruction of Syrian nuclear facility | Single | Resilient | Low | Low |
| NATO coercion in Libya | Single | Nonresilient | Low | High |
| North Korean sinking of South Korean ship | None | Resilient | Low | Medium |
| Russian invasion of Georgia | Single | Resilient | Low | Low |

**Table 5-4. External brute force power ratios.**

| Case name | Coercive advantage | Domestic support | Outside intervention | Violent resistance |
|---|---|---|---|---|
| American drone strikes in Pakistan and Yemen | High | Initially high, later medium | None | Low |
| American invasion of Afghanistan | High | Initially high, later low | Small foreign military support for United States | High |
| American invasion of Iraq | High | Initially medium, later low | Small foreign military support for United States | High |
| American killing of Osama Bin Laden | High | High | None | None |
| French intervention in Mali | High | High | Small foreign military support for United States | High |
| Israeli invasion of Lebanon | High | Initially high, later medium | Low | High |
| Israeli destruction of Syrian nuclear facility | High | High | Low (American collusion) | None |
| NATO coercion in Libya | High | Medium | None (outside multilateral coalition) | High |
| North Korean sinking of South Korean ship | Low | Unknown | None | None |
| Russian invasion of Georgia | High | High | None (but expected by Georgia) | Medium |

**Table 5-5. External brute force strategic outcomes.**

| Case name | Force effectiveness | | Force legitimacy | Force aftermath | | Future prospects |
|---|---|---|---|---|---|---|
| | Short-run | Long-run | | Tit-for-tat cycle | Regional contagion | |
| American drone strikes in Pakistan and Yemen | Killing of terrorists | Fear/violence/retaliation attempts | Global disapproval of government action | Low | Medium (others acquiring drones) | Bright |
| American invasion of Afghanistan | Defeat of the Taliban | Stalemate/quagmire | Global disapproval of government action | High | High (Pakistan) | Bleak |
| American invasion of Iraq | Overthrow of the Hussein regime | Turmoil | Global disapproval of government action | High | Medium (Iran) | Mixed |
| American killing of Osama Bin Laden | Death of al-Qaeda leader | Reduction of global terrorist activity | Global approval of government action | Low | Low | Bright |
| French intervention in Mali | Quelling rebel activity | Beginning of new guerrilla-type conflict | Global approval of government action | Medium | Medium | Mixed |
| Israeli invasion of Lebanon | Death and destruction in southern Lebanon | Solidification of support for Hezbollah | Global disapproval of government action | High | Low | Mixed |
| Israeli destruction of Syrian nuclear facility | Destruction of nuclear plant | Stalling of syrian nuclear program | Global approval of government action | Low | Low | Bright |
| NATO coercion in Libya | Overthrow of the Qaddafi regime | Low-level turmoil of government action | Global approval | Low | Low | Bright |
| North Korean sinking of South Korean ship | Destruction of naval vessel | Increased mutual hostility and threat | Global disapproval of government action | Low | Low | Bleak |
| Russian invasion of Georgia | Death and destruction in northern Georgia | Anger and resentment | Global disapproval of government action | Low | Medium | Mixed |

**Table 5-6. Internal brute force case backgrounds.**

| Case name | Force initiator | Force target | Challenge dates | Force provocation |
|---|---|---|---|---|
| Bahraini crackdown on dissidents | Bahraini government | Internal dissidents | February 14, 2011–present | Popular antiregime protests |
| Chinese repression of dissidents | Chinese government | (1) Tibetans and (2) internal dissidents | (1) Spring 2008–present (2) February 2011–present | Popular antiregime protests |
| Egyptian repression of dissidents | Egyptian government | Internal dissidents | January 25–February 12 2011 | Popular antiregime protests |
| Greek repression of dissidents | Greek government | Internal protesters | May 2010–present | Popular antiregime protests |
| Indian repression of Kashmir separatists | Indian government | Kashmir protesters | Summer 2008–summer 2010 | Popular antiregime protests |
| Mexican coercion against drug lords | Mexican government | Drug lords | 2007–present | Widespread drug cartel violence |
| Myanmar repression of Dissidents | Myanmar government | Internal dissidents | August–September 2007 | Popular antiregime protests |
| Sudanese repression of dissidents | Sudanese government | (1) People in Darfur (2) Internal dissidents | (1) 2003–2010 (2) June 2012–present | Popular antiregime protests |
| Syrian repression of rebels | Syrian government | Internal dissidents | March 2011–present | Popular antiregime protests |
| Thai repression of dissidents | Thai government | Internal dissidents | March 14, 2010–May 20, 2010 | Popular antiregime protests |

**Table 5-7. Internal brute force initiator profiles.**

| Case name | Purpose/rationale | Force misperception | Force commitment | Force restraint |
|---|---|---|---|---|
| Bahraini crackdown on dissidents | Deterrence maintenance of regime control | Underestimation of dissidents' persistence | Medium | Low |
| Chinese repression of dissidents | Deterrence maintenance of regime control | Underestimation of global attention | High | Low |
| Egyptian repression of dissidents | Deterrence maintenance of regime control | Underestimation of dissidents' persistence | Medium | Medium |
| Greek repression of dissidents | Deterrence maintenance of regime control | Underestimation of global attention | High | Medium |
| Indian repression of Kashmir separatists | Deterrence maintenance of regime control | Underestimation of dissidents' persistence | Medium | Medium |
| Mexican coercion against drug lords | Deterrence/compellence elimination of drug violence | Underestimation of easy replacement of drug lords | High | Medium |
| Myanmar repression of dissidents | Deterrence maintenance of regime control | Underestimation of dissidents' persistence | High | Low |
| Sudanese repression of dissidents | Deterrence maintenance of regime control | Underestimation of dissidents' persistence | High | Low |
| Syrian repression of rebels | Deterrence maintenance of regime control | Underestimation of dissidents' military strength | High | None |
| Thai repression of dissidents | Deterrence maintenance of regime control | Underestimation of dissidents' persistence | High | Medium |

**Table 5-8. Internal brute force target profiles.**

| Case name | Disruptive elements | Societal order | Tactical fluidity | Response capacity |
|---|---|---|---|---|
| Bahraini crackdown on dissidents | Single | Resilient | Low | Low |
| Chinese repression of dissidents | Multiple | Resilient | Low | Low |
| Egyptian repression of dissidents | Single | Nonresilient | High | High |
| Greek repression of dissidents | Single | Resilient | High | Medium |
| Indian repression of Kashmir separatists | Single | Resilient | Low | Low |
| Mexican coercion against drug lords | Multiple | Resilient | High | High |
| Myanmar repression of dissidents | Single | Resilient | Low | Low |
| Sudanese repression of dissidents | Multiple | Nonresilient | Medium | Medium |
| Syrian repression of rebels | Multiple | Nonresilient | High | High |
| Thai repression of dissidents | Single | Resilient | Low | Low |

**Table 5-9. Internal brute force power ratios.**

| Case name | Coercive Advantage | Domestic support | Outside intervention | Violent resistance |
|---|---|---|---|---|
| Bahraini crackdown on dissidents | High | Low | Saudi Arabian military aid to Bahraini government | Low |
| Chinese repression of dissidents | High | Medium | None | Low |
| Egyptian repression of dissidents | Medium | Low | Foreign economic and military aid to protesters | Low |
| Greek repression of dissidents | High | Medium | None | Medium |
| Indian repression of Kashmir separatists | High | Medium | None | Medium |
| Mexican coercion against drug lords | Low | High | American military aid to Mexican government | High |
| Myanmar repression of dissidents | High | Low | None | Low |
| Sudanese repression of dissidents | High | Medium | Low | High |
| Syrian repression of rebels | Medium | Low | Foreign economic and military aid to rebels | High |
| Thai repression of dissidents | High | High | None | Low |

**Table 5-10. Internal brute force strategic outcomes.**

| Case name | Force effectiveness | | Force legitimacy | Force aftermath | | Future prospects |
|---|---|---|---|---|---|---|
| | Short-run | Long-run | | Tit-for-tat cycle | Regional contagion | |
| Bahraini crackdown on dissidents | Effective crackdown | Continued turmoil | Global disapproval of government action | Low | Low | More confrontation |
| Chinese repression of dissidents | Effective crackdown | Continued turmoil | Global disapproval of government action | Low | Low | More confrontation |
| Egyptian repression of dissidents | Effective crackdown | Government overthrow | Global disapproval of government action | Low | High | Political instability |
| Greek repression of dissidents | Effective crackdown | Continued turmoil | Global acceptance of government action | Medium | Medium | More confrontation; economic woes |
| Indian repression of Kashmir separatists | Effective crackdown | Continued turmoil | Global disapproval of government action | Medium | Low | More confrontation |
| Mexican coercion against drug lords | Semieffective Crackdown | Continued turmoil | Global approval of government action | High | High | More confrontation; drug lords move out |
| Myanmar repression of dissidents | Effective crackdown | Continued turmoil | Global disapproval of government action | Low | Low | More confrontation |
| Sudanese repression of dissidents | Effective crackdown | Continued turmoil | Global disapproval of government action | High | Low | More confrontation |
| Syrian repression of rebels | Effective crackdown | Civil war | Global disapproval of government action | High | High | Government overthrow |
| Thai repression of dissidents | Effective crackdown | Continued turmoil | Global disapproval of government action | Medium | Low | More confrontation |

## BRUTE FORCE OVERUSE AND UNDERUSE DANGERS

Risks of negative military, political, economic, and social consequences emerge from state overreliance or underreliance on brute force. Figure 5-1 displays these dangers. Overall, brute force overuse affects human security more, and brute force underuse affects state security more.

### Dangers of State Overreliance on Brute Force

Significant perils are associated with force overuse. Great powers seem particularly prone to force overuse, for "relatively abundant military resources make decision makers more likely to use force."[1] The military dangers of force overuse are militarization of societies and consequent promotion of insecurity, escalation of arms races and force-related expenditures and the spread of instruments of violence to those without proper aggressive restraint, martyr creation inspiring further defiant disruptive behavior (evident in the Kashmir, drone strike, and bin Laden killing case studies), and inability to maintain strategic advantage due to the formation of opposing military alliances (in response to perceived threat). Although state-initiated brute force can increase citizens' physical and psychological security, if an area is full of coercive heavily armed government military or police, physical security among the masses may be maintained, but their psychological security is endangered because these uniformed security personnel may be reminders of continuing threat; and—if the armed troops are non-native—"the very presence of foreign combat forces can provoke insurgent attack and undermine the legitimacy of the host government."[2] Linking to both domestic gun control and international arms control debates, although militarization could positively increase deterrence of internal violence and prospects of international peace, such militarization could also increase internal violent social turmoil and international violent conflict: One side assumes that "the only way to stop a bad guy with a gun is with a good guy with a gun,"[3] while the other side believes that managing disorder through arms is inherently destabilizing.[4]

The political dangers of force overuse are breakdown of the social contract between the rulers and the ruled, moral outrage and perceived illegitimacy of authority, difficulty in politically gauging threat thresholds, hollowness of negotiation, and regime fragility and failure. Force overuse can signal state political weakness—reinforcing global images of illegitimacy—and shaky foundations of regime control; for example, inadequate governance is commonly identified as a leading cause of today's wars.[5] Force overuse can imply

**Figure 5-1.** Brute force overuse and underuse dangers.

the failure of (1) deterrence[6] and (2) power to achieve ends peacefully, where states are inept in applying or honing other policy instruments. Always relying on the "heavy hand" of force against uncooperative foes could signal a form of state failure—because "it can no longer count on the fabric of shared values to hold it together, the basis of state authority in such situations then shifts to the unstable solution of coercion."[7]

Socioeconomic dangers from force overuse abound. The economic dangers are financial decline, widening of the internal rich–poor gap, and resource diversion away from basic needs (linked to the "guns-versus-butter" trade-off, although defense is but one of many areas with equally valid resource demands). The social dangers are promotion of popular discontent, psychological disorientation, and outmigration pressures. Brute force can backfire through bottom-up disruptions to the human security status quo: Brute force can inadvertently generate human costs, such as when initiators' abuse and torture of detainees or callous disregard for civilian life and infrastructure stimulates force targets' adoption of new tactics, including unconventional violence against civilians and recruitment of new supporters.[8] Force may foster temporary security, but unless people derive benefits from coercion, instability is likely to follow.

Brute force's emotional intensity may lead to a nightmare scenario:

> Adversaries' attempts to kill, disable, or hurt each other risk turning what may have started as a conflict over particular objectives into a contest of destruction, arousing a fanatic passion to win at all costs. And when such a determination to win takes over, the results are almost entirely the product of brute strength and the intensity of emotion generated, not the result of the pragmatic, legal, and moral merits of the initial competing claims.[9]

Force overuse could lead both political leaders and private citizens to conclude that no amount of coercion is adequate to guarantee attaining one's ends, triggering a spiraling bloody action–reaction cycle involving mutual escalation of military expenditures and violent carnage, with little hope of ever gaining the enduring peace and stability originally desired. Confronting force with force (such as using soldiers against suicide bombers) can fail during asymmetric confrontations begun by ruthless armed nonstate groups.[10]

Moral dilemmas arise from brute force overreliance involving the guilt and anguish of initiators violating basic principles of human decency; an inability to forgive or reconcile with enemies whose previous force use created painful memories of mass atrocities; or irresolvable ambiguities about proportionality of force—whether or not the amount of force applied was appropriate. From a global image standpoint, risks emerge of being resented as a bully or characterized as illegitimate, as spreading fear rather than trust, as neglecting diplomacy, or as brushing aside fundamental justice issues. With unilateral force use, then regardless of justification global reactions are often that the act was impulsive lacking appropriate consultation.

### Dangers of State Underreliance on Brute Force

Force underuse also generates risks. The military dangers are heightened vulnerability to internal and external coercive disruption, ineffective self-defense to protect national sovereignty, emergence of a perceived power vacuum inviting violent aggression, and assumed weakness and inability to deter adversaries. The political dangers are (1) low credibility of promises and threats by states with little track record of backing up words with coercive actions, leading to commit questions, or the "boy who cried wolf" syndrome, where—without actual force application—threats seem hollow; (2) difficulty in determining political outcomes of confrontations; (3) reduced global status and influence due to hesitation, confusion, or ambivalence about national security interests; and (4) empowering of internal and external adversaries, including antiregime terrorists and insurgents and antagonistic states. The economic dangers are dependence on foreign sources for economic protection and inadequate domestic arms manufacturing in case of direct attack. The social dangers are inability to stop state coercive oppression of citizens (including genocide) and handicaps in promoting peace and social stability in the long run.

To prevent major security breaches, political leaders "must guard against permitting prudent caution morphing into crippling timidity."[11] Outside states may read force underuse as a deficiency: For example, Middle Eastern leaders often interpret American foreign policy restraint as a sign of weakness.[12] Moreover, some positive ends may never be achieved if brute force is underused—the "employment of force can convince adversaries to cease and desist or physically prevent them from undertaking actions that would be even more dangerous."[13] Force may be necessary to prevent an aggressive and ruthless dictator commanding a large army from rampaging across the world—"when barbarians and other rogues threaten, time and time again it has been found that there is no substitute for military power."[14] Force may also be vital for self-defense, to protect a state's autonomy when it is being invaded. Finally, force may be needed not only to establish or restore a predictable continuous top-down authority structure but also sometimes to promote bottom-up protection of the affected population. If force is not used in such circumstances, strategic outcomes may be uncertain: Relying on softer means of influence can leave doubt about mission success, for within today's global anarchic system "old fashioned 'hard kills,' provided they can be monitored, do not have this difficulty."[15] Overall, "the perils of military action have to be balanced against the costs and risks of inaction":[16] "Using force can injure the very noncombatants U.S. forces want to protect (and shape), but failure to use force in some circumstances may allow adversary forces to escape or prevail, leading to a lack of belief in friendly force capabilities to overcome the foe" and possible further harm to the civilian population.[17]

Moral dilemmas arise from state underuse of brute force. Although most observers assume that military force is more inhumane than economic sanctions, in reality economic sanctions often can end up starving to death the most deprived civilians, while military force usually targets combatants or military facilities—thus "it may be morally preferable to use limited military force against carefully targeted military objectives *before* applying such an indiscriminate weapon as general economic sanctions."[18] Relying too heavily on diplomacy, which often extensively relies on deception and manipulation, can create a long-run atmosphere of distrust and even hostility. Eschewing force can indirectly hurt human security, condemning innocent civilians to needless ongoing pain and suffering; when brute force could alleviate severe mistreatment of innocent people, failure to do so could be considered immoral.

## INITIATOR ATTRIBUTES LINKED TO BRUTE FORCE SUCCESS

As Figure 5-2 derives from the cases, the initiator attributes most linked to brute force success are attainable purpose, credible commitment, unified resolve, and forward thinking. These conditions are rarely evident all together. Nonetheless, they point the way toward improved initiator force management.

### Attainable Purpose

Brute force works best when the strategic purpose is narrow, tangible, and well defined, not ambiguous, broad, constantly changing, or ill suited to the military skill set. Although some might consider these standards unrealistic in

## Attainable Purpose

Brute force undertaken with narrow tangible objectives such as leadership decapitation is more likely to be successful than brute force with broad vague objectives such as instilling political democracy or enhancing social justice.

Brute force undertaken for goals for which the military was designed, entailing killing people and destroying property, is more likely to be successful than brute force with other goals, such as those entailing social work and nation building.

## Credible Commitment

Brute force undertaken with high staying power, such as within high-interest neighboring areas part of an initiator's sphere of influence, is more likely to be successful than brute force with low staying power, such as within low-interest distant areas not part of an initiator's sphere-of-influence.

Brute force undertaken with an ability and willingness to employ all appropriate coercive tools is more likely to be successful than brute force operating under tight political constraints or with few such tools available.

## Unified Resolve

Brute force undertaken with wide support within a state's government and its citizenry is more likely, particularly within democracies, to be successful than brute force evidencing internal division of opinion, apathy, confusion, or emotional desperation.

Brute force undertaken with state armed forces unwaveringly loyal to the national government is more likely to be successful than brute force involving state armed forces with mixed loyalties or sympathy for the force target.

## Forward Thinking

Brute force undertaken with advance planning for stabilizing postforce reconstruction efforts and protection of the affected population is more likely to be successful than brute force without such planning, probably triggering a violent action-reaction cycle.

Brute force undertaken with significant forethought about isolating and localizing postforce political, economic, and cultural impacts is more likely to be successful than brute force without such planning, probably triggering contagious regional violence.

**Figure 5-2.** Initiator attributes linked to brute force success.

today's world, they represent an ideal from which deviations can be evaluated. Often mission goals are confused or poorly tuned to the ongoing predicament. Because force is inappropriate for some strategic purposes, it becomes crucial "to identify objectives that can be achieved only by military force, and the limitations on the use of force beyond them,"[19] realizing that success entails not just force quality or quantity but also understanding the political context.[20]

Force-initiating political leaders often overestimate (1) outsiders' accurate recognition of their political plight and purpose, (2) the versatility of soldiers in undertaking potentially conflicting roles on the battlefield (a misperception less common among military leaders), and (3) the clarity and appropriateness of their communication and objectives. For American political leaders, persistent force use seems to be due to overoptimism about their ability to accomplish an overly broad range of strategic purposes.[21] Given exaggerated expectations of offensive and defensive tangible and symbolic force payoffs, overconfident force initiators may overestimate the ease of achieving objectives through military means. If the force used is foreign military intervention from a source unfamiliar with or alienated from the force target, then obstacles multiply: Such force is unsuited to security if it promotes purposes not valued or needed by the affected society. Overall, policy makers can waste lots of money and effort building up force capabilities for nearly impossible to attain strategic objectives.

Brute force undertaken with narrow tangible objectives such as leadership decapitation is more likely to be successful than brute force with broad vague objectives such as instilling political democracy or enhancing social justice. Many states, including Israel and the United States, feature leadership decapitation in their counterterrorist strategies.[22] Aggregate leadership decapitation studies suggest effectiveness: One study finds that killing militant leaders is more likely to achieve security goals than is capturing them,[23] whereas another study finds that leadership decapitation significantly increases the mortality rate of subversive groups.[24] Force appears well suited to narrow goals such as getting rid of a dictator, exemplified by NATO in Libya, or eradicating terrorist leaders, exemplified by the American drone strikes and the killing of Osama bin Laden. Although leader decapitation is often morally objectionable and globally illegitimate, it can be popular internally and externally if facing ruthless tyrants. In contrast, force appears unsuited to broad goals such as achieving democracy in Iraq, stability in Afghanistan, or social justice in Thailand, due to the complexity of needed nonmilitary transformation.

Brute force undertaken for goals for which the military is designed, entailing killing people and destroying property, is more likely to be successful than brute force with other goals, such as social progress and nation building. Military force works better when used for traditional purposes for which soldiers have prepared—with a decisive comparative advantage over other means—rather than unorthodox purposes outside of their normal training. New recruits (within countries having voluntary conscription) joining the armed services do not usually do so in the hope of using their skills to build civil society, engage in social work, or change a country's values. Although hostile military interventions' greatest political impact may be to help democratize nondemocratic force targets,[25] using force to achieve social goals does a lot worse than to achieve objecting matching military training.[26] For example, the successful Russian invasion of Georgia had purposes in tune with the advantages of military force, although the less successful American invasions of Afghanistan and Iraq did not. In attempting to transform political systems, there may be neither a functioning electoral system nor credible moderate local leaders with indigenous political support,[27] political corruption may persist,[28] and conducting fair elections may be daunting.[29] Nonetheless, states often use force for purposes for which it is not designed, even with its sizable costs: Political leaders who believe that coercion is still the ultimate arbiter in international relations frequently ask military force to stretch and attain political, social, and economic progress because this kind of mission objective is now in vogue.

### Credible Commitment

Brute force works best when force initiators are committed to use any means necessary and to remain in force confrontations as long as it takes to accomplish the designated objectives. However, states applying force often lack commitment or misjudge how force targets perceive their commitment, leading to dismal outcomes with puny payoffs. Force is likely to be unsuccessful if a state is unwilling or unable to apply a sufficient magnitude and duration of force or if antagonistic groups or states have greater resources, will, legitimacy, or effectiveness than force initiators. Although normally one would expect that states possessing huge military advantages over targets would just have to "saber rattle" through coercive threats to achieve their ends,[30] the cases of Russia with Georgia, United States with Iraq, and NATO with Libya show that the mere threat of force was insufficient to trigger compliance because the force targets misestimated the probability of force use; its magnitude, scope, and duration; or the availability of outside assistance: Iraq and Libya erroneously thought that the West lacked commitment, and Georgia erroneously thought that it would receive substantial Western military aid. Although fear of counterforce through deterrence can discourage aggression, "this discouragement is far from complete and reliable."[31] Force initiators' failings often stem from their overestimation of (1) weapons capabilities signaling force potential and force potential signaling force use; (2) value of advanced war-fighting technology, with an aversion to expanding types of force used; (3) sufficiency of force superiority for mission success; and (4) ability to overcome any obstacle and expectations for huge strategic gains. Remote or peripheral security challenges, or severe restraints on coercive approaches, often lead to weak or irrelevant attempts to instill fear or induce concessions.

Even when overwhelming brute force is applied—where the force ratio dramatically favors the initiator over the target—the case studies indicate that rarely was the result more than short-term military objectives achievement against an adversary, leaving long-term political purposes unfulfilled: "Despite their immense war-fighting capacity, major power states have failed to attain their primary political objective in almost 40 percent of their military operations against weak state and nonstate targets since 1945."[32] Illustrating the limits of an external quick sledgehammer approach are (1) in the 1950s, the French applied disproportionate brute force in counterinsurgency operations in Algeria, ultimately causing the failure of the military campaign against the National Liberation Front there;[33] and (2) in 2003, the American "shock-and-awe" attack in the Iraq War proved to be indecisive. Non-Western states' internal force use—even when overwhelming—has also been handicapped:

> Paradoxically, a ruler's reliance on repression may also be the source of the regime's greatest weakness. Repression is costly. Regimes must pay police and soldiers to do their jobs—and as the risk of the job goes up, the pay must also increase to keep these workers coming back. Politically, repression can undermine the legitimacy of the government, while simultaneously creating even more grievances against the government—grievances that, if widely shared, can cost a dictator his throne.[34]

The poverty and external dependence of many developing states using internal repression may impede their success, exemplified by the Mexican government's application of force against the drug lords, where even short-term effectiveness was in doubt. The success obstacle here appears to be less the amount of force applied and more the durability of force and the unyielding will to combine it with other influence instruments.

Brute force undertaken with high staying power, such as within nearby high-interest areas that are part of an initiator's sphere of influence, is more likely to be successful than brute force with low staying power, such within distant low-interest areas outside of an initiator's sphere of influence (often with predetermined quick exit strategies). Although military victory can sometimes occur rapidly, achieving postforce strategic objectives usually takes considerable time. The force use by Russia in Georgia, China in Tibet, and India in Kashmir exemplify the advantages of long-term staying power. Having force targets close by within one's spheres of influence can also lower chances of outside intervention.

Brute force undertaken with an ability and willingness to use all appropriate coercive tools is more likely to be successful than brute force operating under tight political constraints or with few such tools available. Diverse security challenges require a diverse force arsenal. However, states often discover that they lack or are unwilling to use certain coercive options due to force constraints, such as casualty aversion or collateral damage worries embedded in enlightened democratic norms. The ability of centralized autocratic regimes such as Russia and China to use any means necessary to quell dissidents or constrain neighbors contrasts sharply with Western states' severe morality or public opinion concerns. Ultimately brute force's "utility to liberal Western societies is menaced by the imprudent measure of their imprudent enthusiasm for placing constraints upon their use of it"—"our contemporary determination to employ force justly and decently is in some danger of imperiling the prospects for success in military missions."[35] Thus key brute force options can be off the table for legitimacy reasons:

> To convince the targets that opposition is hopeless, the brutal approach must be consistently murderous and unrelenting, not just episodically callous. But deliberate and sustained terror is not an option for the United States even if it works. Americans are capable of premeditated slaughter of civilians under extraordinary circumstances like the strategic bombing campaigns of World War II, but not in idealistic interventions assumed to be for the benefit of the contested populations.[36]

Paradoxically, brute force's unattractiveness to the West can be an incentive for enemies to persist in aggressive action.[37] Although successful in defeating Qaddafi, NATO's force tactics in Libya were severely constrained by legitimacy concerns. Ironically, force use by Western states—particularly the

United States—has recently often been more likely than that by others to gen-erate vocal international criticism.

## Unified Resolve

Brute force works best when agreement exists within a force initiator among the mass public, government officials, and uniformed soldiers about the mis-sion's value. For internal legitimacy, particularly within democracies, a criti-cal prerequisite is a force-initiating state's citizenry's willingness to make major sacrifices for the cause. Brute force may be unsuccessful if there is little consensus within the government or society about a military mission's prior-ity or viability.

Many states apply force in ways that are perceived internally as not care-fully adapted and tuned to conform to the transformed global security set-ting, or as blatantly violating enlightened principles endorsed, leading to the absence of national government or domestic public consensus emerging behind the action undertaken. Force initiators often overestimate the legal-ity and legitimacy of their actions as well as onlookers' unwavering support and admiration for force outcomes. Sometimes force initiators alter existing laws to make their force use appear to be legally sanctioned: This tendency is exemplified by the American PATRIOT Act, implemented to facilitate force use after the 9/11 terrorist attacks, and by draconian regulations in India's Kashmir and Thailand's "Red Shirt" crackdowns, shielding soldiers and po-lice from prosecution yet allowing them to arrest any demonstrator suspected of disturbing the peace. Outsiders frequently perceive this altered legality of state force use as highly arbitrary.

Brute force undertaken with wide national support within a state's gov-ernment and citizenry is more likely, particularly within democracies, to be successful than brute force evidencing internal division of opinion, apathy, or confusion. The justification is that unified resolve associates with high na-tional morale for using force, conducive to making sacrifices when necessary for mission accomplishment. When force confrontations go in unplanned directions, such domestic support seems crucial. The Israeli destruction of the Syrian nuclear facility highlights advantages from such unified resolve. Although the sizable costs of applying force would logically seem to restrict its use to when consensus national support exists, the cases suggest that West-ern states' force use with halfhearted resolve can be due to divisions among government officials and private citizens over its desirability. These states are often caught between recognizing that the enemies they face are ruthless and acknowledging that public concerns about domestic casualties prevent applying the force necessary for success. Over time, the domestic public may become impatient with force's high human costs and inadequate payoffs and begin demanding troop withdrawal and military operation termination. The American wars in Afghanistan and Iraq vividly illustrate this pattern.

Brute force undertaken with state armed forces unwaveringly loyal to the national government is more likely to be successful than brute force involving state armed forces with mixed loyalties or sympathy for the force target. Without fierce loyalty by the armed forces, when the going gets rough—due either to tough combat or to external criticism—desertion and defection rates can skyrocket, and then force effectiveness and legitimacy can plummet. Often state internal crackdowns backfire "when the soldiers and police enforcing regime brutality can relate to the protestors in some way."[38] If government soldiers or police agree with an internal protest, then they can connect with the mass frustration, and the operation can be undermined. The divided loyalty of the Egyptian army, due to soldiers' sympathy with protesters' concerns and disaffection with state authorities, ultimately was a key contributor to the downfall of the Mubarak regime and its failed force use. In many of this study's cases, mass loyalties run deeper to subnational tribal, religious, or ethnic groups than to state regimes. To forestall this, Iran established the Iranian Revolutionary Guard Corps (IRGC)—to have an armed force separate from the regular military whose regime loyalty is unquestioned, no matter how horrific their orders. In such cases, a state may choose to make examples of disloyal members of their military, sometimes by torturing them or killing their families.

### Forward Thinking

Brute force works best when a force initiator thinks carefully not only about how to apply force but also about how to deal with what transpires afterward. This forethought involves minimizing the postforce action–reaction cycles and regional contagion and maximizing peaceful postforce political, economic, and social reconstruction. Managing postforce aftershocks helps human security as well as state security and regional and global security as well as national interests. Strategic failure can result from underestimating the need for contingency postforce planning. Force initiators often too blithely assume that "everything will fall nicely into place" after military victory.

States often apply brute force in ways that involve little advanced planning for postforce aftershocks, which often surprise them. Despite recent debacles, the emphasis is still on winning confrontations, not mopping up afterward or establishing long-term political stability.

As the case findings confirm, many force initiators shortsightedly ignore postforce reconstruction until after a violent confrontation ends, eliminating the opportunity to apply force so as to facilitate a smooth aftermath. A common assumption is that little can be done during confrontations to control what happens afterward, accompanied by reluctance to change fighting tactics to ease postforce challenges. Even when there is openness to forestalling postforce aftershocks, they are often misunderstood or misestimated due to poor intelligence. Many policy makers overestimate the postforce ease of transforming a target's political system, transferring power to local authorities and avoiding action–reaction cycles and regional contagion. The postforce "vacuum of authority" could intensify verbal barbs and hostile acts within targets, as people jockey for position and influence while simultaneously resenting the initiator.[39]

Brute force undertaken with advance planning for stabilizing postforce reconstruction and protecting the affected population is more likely to be successful than brute force with little such planning, often triggering action–reaction cycles. Careful force planning, avoiding overestimating targets' passive submissiveness, can minimize the chances of destabilizing retaliation. Exemplifying the dire consequences of inadequate planning of this type are the indecisive Afghanistan and Iraq war outcomes[40] and the government crackdowns in Syria and Sudan becoming full-blown civil wars.

Brute force undertaken with advanced planning for isolating and localizing postforce political, economic, and cultural impacts is more likely to be successful than brute force with little such planning, probably triggering regional contagion. American military operations planning is especially weak at minimizing postforce regional contagion: Although the American military attempts to ascertain likely downstream contagion impacts of military action, they are not very adept at it, and civilian leaders often disregard or downplay these postforce consequences. Whereas Americans' traditionally short time horizons—reflecting impatience and demanding immediate results—can promote greater short-term military success compared to other cultures, the result can also blind the United States to potential long-run contagion consequences. Globally, this is a weak area for many states. The case studies indicate that many force initiators do not think enough about possible regional contagion or inflammation of ethnically, religiously, or racially connected populations. The absence of French planning for postforce reconstruction and regional contagion in its Mali invasion shows how unconcern about the aftermath of military force use can be debilitating even after its success. Although such advanced planning does not guarantee forestalling undesired outcomes, the chances of ensuing action–reaction cycles and regional contagion tend to drop.

## TARGET ATTRIBUTES LINKED TO BRUTE FORCE SUCCESS

Besides initiator characteristics, target attributes play a key role in brute force outcomes. As Figure 5.3 shows, the target attributes most associated in the cases with force success are a single disruptive element, resilient societal order, stable predictable tactics, low response capacity, and contained local friction. This combination of ideal target conditions is rare in today's world.

### Single Disruptive Element

Brute force undertaken where only a single centralized disruptive element exists within a force target is more likely to be successful—due to the lower probability of security provocations—than brute force undertaken with multiple independent disruptive elements within a force target. Geographically dispersed unruly parties can be key obstacles to force effectiveness, simply shifting a threat from one place to another[41] rather than managing it. Exemplifying this challenge are the external American invasion of Afghanistan facing resistance from the Taliban, al-Qaeda, and various extremist groups and China and Sudan coercively facing different kinds of internal dissidents.

### Resilient Societal Order

Brute force undertaken where a force target has a resilient societal order—in which postforce stability is easy to restore—is more likely to be successful than if brute force is undertaken where a force target has unmitigated societal chaos devoid of meaningful infrastructure. Force is likely to be unsuccessful if force targets have a governance vacuum or deep societal infrastructure deficiencies. Within weak or fragile states, internal turmoil may be unending if governments are inept or cannot provide basic needs to citizens. Force may fail if the instability scope is primarily societal rather than strictly governmental—especially if the greatest needs are the development of civil society, the injection of economic stimulus, or the provision of essential services.

---

**Single Disruptive Element**

Brute force undertaken where only a single disruptive element exists within a force target is more likely to be successful—due to the lower probability of security provocations—than brute force undertaken with multiple disruptive elements within a force target.

**Resilient Societal Order**

Brute force undertaken where a force target has resilient societal order is more likely to be successful than if brute force is undertaken where the force target has unmitigated societal chaos devoid of meaningful infrstructure.

**Stable Predictable Tactics**

Brute force undertaken where the opposition in a force target is relatively static and predictable in its strategy and tactics is more likely to be successful than if brute force is undertaken against highly adaptive and changeable opposition within a force target.

**Low Response Capacity**

Brute force undertaken where a force target has a low capacity to respond coercively or noncoercively to a force initiator is more likely to be successful than brute force undertaken where a force target has a high capacity to respond coercively or noncoercively to a force initiator.

**Contained Local Friction**

Brute force undertaken where political frictions within a force target are isolated and contained is more likely to be successful than if brute force is undertaken where local frictions transcend national boundaries and involve neighboring groups and states.

---

**Figure 5-3.** Target attributes linked to brute force success.

Whatever target compliance is desired would be thwarted without an effective local body to implement it in an orderly way. If there is little stable resilient societal infrastructure, then force outcomes can be dismal: The 2003 American invasion of Iraq reveals postforce societal disorder impeding postforce stability, and the American drone strikes against terrorists in Yemen seemed doomed from the outset—due to the country's failed state status—in altering the regime's willingness to harbor such disruptive groups.

### Stable Predictable Tactics

Brute force undertaken where the opposition in a force target is relatively static and predictable in its strategy and tactics is more likely to be successful than if brute force is undertaken against highly adaptive and changeable opposition within a force target. Force may flounder if a force target's strategy and tactics adapt quickly to changing circumstances—enemies of the West constantly adjust their tactics to exploit weaknesses and vulnerabilities in existing defenses and force structures. When in irregular confrontations, states "are confronted by a range of difficult-to-deter actors struggling in a dynamic strategic landscape in which escalation thresholds are fluid and difficult to ascertain";[42] then force can easily fall flat. Due to relatively static predictable opposition, the Bahraini repression of internal dissidents was an ideal circumstance for state force use whereas, in contrast, the constant reevaluation of tactics by drug lords in Mexico and terrorists in Pakistan and Yemen makes them tough force compliance targets.

### Low Response Capacity

Brute force undertaken where a force target has a low capacity to respond coercively or noncoercively to a force initiator is more likely to be successful than brute force undertaken where a force target has a high capacity to respond coercively or noncoercively to a force initiator. Force often fails if force targets have the capability and will to respond strongly with tangible support from other parties, as an unending action–reaction cycle may commence. Target retaliation capacity must incorporate the specter of military allies intervening—although NATO was able to use brute force successfully in Libya because Qaddafi had no allies, the West prudently decided not to intervene militarily in Syria due to tangible Russian military support for Assad's regime. If this interactive friction crosses a critical threshold, then violent warfare—such as the 2006 Israel–Lebanon War—seems likely to ensue.

### Contained Local Friction

Brute force undertaken where local frictions within a force target are isolated and contained is more likely to be successful than if brute force is undertaken where local frictions transcend national boundaries and involve neighboring groups and states. However, globalization pressures are making it increasingly difficult to isolate or contain local disruptions. Having a dispute spread nearby to foreign sympathizers with common ideological views or ethnic identification can impede long-term force success. Isolated and contained friction lessens chances of thwarting long-range strategic objectives. External interference seems less likely to occur under these conditions, and state initiator forces do not need to be spread so thin if security impacts are successfully contained.

To illustrate this pattern, (1) the isolated and contained brutal Myanmar government crackdown contributed to its success, although (2) the uncontrolled contagion in the Middle Eastern Arab Spring protests and (3) the ties of the Mexican drug lords to illicit activity elsewhere in the region exacerbated effective force management.

## COMMON BUT LOW-IMPACT FORCE LEGITIMACY CONCERNS

The case study patterns challenge much prevailing conventional wisdom about brute force legitimacy. The three clusters of widely stressed elements deemed least impactful, summarized in Figure 5-4, pertain to (1) force framing, (2) force execution, and (3) force reaction. Although legitimacy concerns do have a major impact on force success, they do so in ways other than many observers expect.

### Force Framing

Self-Defense   The case findings do not support the common claim—due to the significance of stability maintenance—that brute force for defensive purposes is more successful than that for offensive purposes. This claim's logic is often applied to asymmetric conflict, assuming that defensive protection of citizens from harm works better than offensive attempts to wipe out terrorist cells.[43] Force initiators may try to justify aggression by characterizing it as defensive; for example, Russia portrayed its 2008 attack on Georgia as simply defending the citizens of South Ossetia from an unprovoked Georgian aggression.

However, many force initiators' defensive claims lack credibility, and global observers differ in interpreting coercion as offensive or defensive. Due to inherent subjectivity, labeling a force purpose as "defensive" against perceived dangers does not raise its global legitimacy. This term is bandied about so loosely, with identified threats so indirect, that many observers may still see the action as "offensive" in every sense.

Last Resort   The case findings also do not support the common claim—due to the importance of coercion not being used impulsively —that brute force used as a last resort is more successful than that used right off the bat. Many analyses (including the Weinberger Doctrine) assert that global approval increases when states use force strictly as a last resort, linked to the "just war" tradition:[44] Particularly advanced industrial societies argue that force should

**Force Framing**

*Self-Defense*
Despite the significance of stability maintenance, little success difference emerges between brute force undertaken with a defensive orientation and that with an offensive orientation.

*Last Resort*
Despite the importance of coercion not being used impulsively, little success difference emerges between brute force undertaken as a last resort and that undertaken as an early option.

**Force Execution**

*Humanitarian Purpose*
Despite the value of using brute force for morally acceptable ends, little success difference emerges between brute force undertaken for humanitarian purposes and that for other purposes.

*Rights Protection*
Despite the common outrage at gratuitous violence, little success difference emerges between brute force undertaken with restraint respecting human rights and that without such restraint.

**Force Reaction**

*Nonviolent Resistance*
Despite the pervasiveness of global support for nonviolent resistance, little success difference emerges between brute force eliciting violent responses and that eliciting nonviolent responses.

*Global Praise*
Despite the worth of outside coercive support, little success difference emerges between brute force eliciting strong global verbal approval and that eliciting global verbal condemnation.

**Figure 5-4.** Common but low-impact force legitimacy concerns.

be used as a last resort,[45] only after every other reasonable alternative has failed. Despite the 2003 Iraqi invasion being a preemptive attack, the United States defended it as a last-resort measure, given failed political and economic sanctions.

However, frequently the consideration of nonmilitary options has been largely cosmetic, and global legitimacy has not risen and international community resentment has not fallen just because noncoercive alternatives were tried first. At least in the twenty-first century, states have rarely initiated force as a true last resort. Moreover, once states chose to use force, their flexibility and willingness to negotiate often diminished. American President George H. W. Bush's 1991 Gulf War external force use illustrates this rigidity:

> Once the president sets his jaw and has a singleness of purpose that military action is the right way to do it, he won't be diverted from it by somebody worrying about "Why don't we wait and see if something better happens?"; his experience is that something better is not likely to happen, and you could lose your momentum and resolve by delaying the process.[46]

Similarly, after internal force use, the Thai government rebuffed dissident pleas to negotiate or bring in outside mediation.

Using force only as a last-resort can be costly:[47]

> Waiting until other policies have failed may limit or forfeit the opportunity to use force effectively. The passage of time may mean the loss of surprise and the loss of initiative while giving the adversary opportunity to prepare military and politically for the battle to come. Also, waiting for diplomacy or, as is often the case, economic sanctions to work can allow people and other interests to suffer dearly.[48]

Despite the need for caution in using force, early action can sometimes be better than waiting until one comes under attack, because going second can be disadvantageous—a first strike by an opponent could be disarming and severely limit or even prevent any response. Regarding the 2007 Syrian construction of a nuclear reactor, had Israel waited to use force until diplomacy failed, force effectiveness might have been minimal. Force initiators' overestimation of a successful force use's global approval occurs regardless of their application of non-military options beforehand. Notably, "the great strategic lesson of the 1930s is that early military action is far more preferable than a last-resort use of force against that very rare, powerful enemy who is both politically unappeasable and militarily undeterrable."[49]

### Force Execution

Humanitarian Purpose   The case findings do not support the common claim—due to the value of using coercion for morally acceptable ends—that brute force used for humanitarian purposes is more successful than that used for other purposes. This finding is ironic, because many analysts contend that humanitarian needs provide the soundest justification for brute force intervention, represented in the U.N. "responsibility to protect" norm.[50] For example, despite the role of oil interests, the NATO intervention in Libya was defended on such humanitarian grounds. Often identifying force as an instrument of justice, Western states believe that their values of democracy and freedom are universal and that everyone—regardless of distinctive cultural traditions—should enjoy these benefits.

However, state-initiated force often serves the government's national interests, not directly citizens' interests, as mass populations' values may differ sharply from those of their governments. Even when force use is intended for humanitarian purposes, global legitimacy may not rise, and such coercion can have a negative impact on human security, such as when coercive interventions "harm relief operations and the fragile attempts at peace accords."[51] To those affected, it matters little whether collateral damage is accidental or intentional.

The West faces particular challenges in this regard. When its humanitarian force use seems too arbitrary, its moral underpinnings can unravel: For example, the United States is often accused of exhibiting a "double standard" in its reactions to overseas democratic protests—supporting those facing anti-American dictators but opposing those facing pro-American dictators—and this accusation allows Syrian regime supporters to argue that American opposition to the Assad regime's repression "is not based on a universal commitment to human rights and democracy, but simply a means to destabilize a country whose leadership has not been supportive of Western interests."[52] Western states often are accused of "cultural imperialism"—imposing their values on others although ignoring local beliefs and the U.N. principle of self-determination of peoples. Western force use may stop brutal genocides or remove cruel tyrants, but it may not promote freedom or civil society:

> There are those who oppose such intervention not so much because it involves violations of state sovereignty, but because it involves the use of armed force. The concern here is that humanitarian intervention is merely a new justification for the militarism that pervades our societies and our political structures. . . . Furthermore, the destruction, human suffering and loss of life resulting from any military action can undermine the humanitarian objectives of armed intervention.[53]

This perceived counterproductive clash between force use and humanitarian intervention[54] supports the "anti-militarist view of armed humanitarian intervention as a self-contradictory principle or doctrine."[55] At its worst, well-intentioned military intervention can destroy human security, as the United States and the United Nations "have learned at great cost."[56]

Rights Protection   The case findings also do not support the common claim—due to the common outrage at gratuitous violence—that brute force involving great restraint and few human rights violations is more successful than that with little restraint and significant human rights violations. If a force initiator's government military or police chooses to engage in gratuitous violence—"acts of physical, face-to-face violence that transgress shared norms about the proper treatment of persons and bodies"[57]—not directly advancing mission objectives, the impact can certainly sometimes be counterproductive: Resentment, anger, and perceived force illegitimacy may dramatically escalate both during and following confrontations. For these reasons, although in the past American armed forces have been accused of engaging in barbaric atrocities during battlefield encounters,[58] the American military is now required by law to use the absolute minimum necessary force to achieve mission objectives. Flagrant human rights violations—often triggered by emotional hatred or fear—can cause force failure, for global watchdogs may highlight them and call for international remedial action. For example, Assad's soldiers in Syria committing barbarous acts of violence against the opposition, well beyond what military necessity would entail, undercuts government legitimacy. Although such action tries to intimidate opponents and break their will, it can lead to escalating violence and global resentment.

However, if one emphasizes simply short-term compliance, then occasionally unrestrained coercion can be effective[59] and even sometimes seen as legitimate. The most common response by state force initiators violating human rights has been to deny either the existence of these violations or their culpability for them. Because conflicting reports emerge about what actually transpires in the midst of bloody confrontations, the call for force restraint often goes unheeded. In many of the case studies, pursuing vital national interests trumps restraint regarding human rights violations, with more direct human rights violations in the internal than the international cases. Although many international force uses elicited cries to the global community about alleged human rights violations, including requests to the International Criminal Court or International Court of Justice to review actions taken, in only one case—the Israeli invasion of Lebanon—did force use end due to concerted global action (through a U.N. cease-fire). Thus, despite global rhetoric, enlightened global norms and international customary law—linked to legitimacy—appear too weak to restrain internal and external force use. Furthermore, if the target of state-initiated brute force has engaged in sufficiently heinous violent acts and is consequently widely despised, then government troops engaging in unrestrained coercion against it can be viewed as legitimate even when human rights violations occur, as exemplified by the Mexican government crackdown against the drug lords.

### Force Reaction

Nonviolent Resistance   The case findings do not support the common claim—due to the pervasiveness of global support for nonviolent resistance—that brute force use eliciting violent responses is more successful than that eliciting nonviolent responses. Undergirding internal nonviolent resistance movements is the claim that coercive "repression only backfired when the movements remained nonviolent in spite of regime provocations":[60]

> Armed resistance can terrify people not yet committed to the struggle, making it easier for a government to justify violent repression and use of military force in the name of protecting the population. The use of force against unarmed resistance movements, on the other hand, usually creates greater sympathy for the government's opponents.[61]

Supporting such views is contrasting the short-term success of the peaceful Egyptian protesters to the short-term struggles of armed Syrian rebels.

However, although force target nonviolence attracts more global sympathy today than in the past, nonviolence alone is still inadequate for a force target to reap substantial outside tangible military or economic support. For example, in Bahrain, Myanmar, and Kashmir, not only did state brute force work against largely nonviolent protesters, but these protests also failed to draw the kind of global attention that generated significant foreign aid. Although nonviolent force targets may receive some global backing, the cases show that it has usually been insufficient to thwart force initiators. In the end, sometimes outsiders interpret an organized and coherent violent target response to state-initiated brute force as a legitimate reaction to brutal unjust repression, and sometimes this target violence can provide a more effective form of resistance to state force than widespread foreign sympathy.

Global Praise   The case findings also do not support the common claim—due to the value of outside support—that brute force use with high global verbal approval is more successful than that with high global verbal condemnation. This claim emphasizes the value of global praise for legitimacy and ultimately success in force use. This contention assumes that stinging global rebukes prevent force success. However, in most of the cases, the global community's verbal reaction—support or opposition—did not prove pivotal in determining force outcomes. Outside powers do not usually intervene militarily unless the force target is strategically value to them.[62] Despite the global spread of democracy, enlightened values, and Internet-based awareness of oppression, world public opinion by itself has failed to restrain force use. The global mass public is notoriously fickle about force:

> Governments are under constant public pressure, on one hand, to do something or to intervene in situations where fundamental human rights are being violated, but on the other, they seem to have reason to fear that their citizens will not have the endurance to suffer the consequences and the casualties that action might require, thus forcing them to make U-turns in their policies, which may detract from their credibility.[63]

Perhaps not surprisingly, in many of the cases involving internal force use—particularly Bahrain, China, Myanmar, and Thailand— outside verbal criticism of state force initiators and verbal sympathy for nonstate force targets were insufficient to prompt meaningful outside restraining action, especially in the forms of military or economic intervention. Although conventional media and Internet sources often criticize unilateral state-initiated force, this criticism's restraining impact is usually negligible. Especially if a national government's force use is speedy and successful, applied internally or within accepted spheres of influence, or targeting strategically unimportant external targets, it seems unlikely to upset the global community. So many states choose to apply force in the face of existing or anticipated outside criticism because they do not believe tangible outside punishment will follow, despite force targets' tendency to overestimate global obligations to assist them. The cases thus confirm realpolitik force initiator skepticism that vocal outrage has no teeth, with global community reactions fleeting, fundamentally unconcerned, and ultimately noncommittal. Exemplifying this cynical attitude was Russia's invasion of Georgia in 2008:

Indeed, the culture shock to liberal Westerners on witnessing the exercise of brute force, can have a political value for reason of its shocking political incorrectness. Consider the highly aggressive pre-planned use of military power by Russia against U.S.-leaning Georgia in 2008. For all the negative commentary that Moscow attracted from abroad, the net balance of consequences between costs and political rewards probably was significantly weighted in favor of the rewards.[64]

Meaningful force restraint simply does not result from verbal criticism alone.

## CONCLUDING THOUGHTS

The case study analysis of twenty-first-century brute force use reveals some depressing realities. First, the circumstances under which force is most effective and legitimate are those that seem least likely to exist within the current global security setting. Second, the circumstances under which force has been used are not those most conducive to long-term strategic successes. Third, often state-initiated brute force promotes key security trade-offs: It may enhance national security at the expense of regional security or world order, and it may enhance state security at the expense of human security. Fourth, most major brute force uses during this time period are unilateral (NATO's intervention in Libya is a key exception), undertaken without significant consultation with other parties to determine their advisability. Fifth, prevailing conventional wisdom about brute force legitimacy needs significant refinement. Finally, although being sensitive to brute force dangers is important, identifying occasions of force overuse or underuse is difficult: One might describe the American involvement in the 2001 Afghanistan War as force underuse and the 2008 Russian invasion of Georgia as force overuse, but such designations would be highly tentative and subjective due to the differing modes and amounts of force applied.

Nonetheless, identifying twenty-first-century brute force success patterns may help to isolate areas where corrections are most desperately needed and provide hope for more appropriate future force use. Although resort to force may be frequently instinctive, primitive, and barbaric, one could imagine a decision calculus determining force use that is much more appropriate in its conclusions, purposes, modes of application, and ultimate outcomes. The force initiator and force target attributes associating with success, derived from the case studies and not totally out of reach in today's world, could help security policy makers determine exactly when and how brute force should be implemented. The refinements to conventional wisdom about force legitimacy, also emerging from the cases, could help them more realistically understand the actual functioning parameters—not the idealized lofty rhetoric—of the global security context.

# 6 CONCLUSION

## Promising Security Paths

THIS CONCLUDING CHAPTER TRANSLATES the case patterns into pragmatic policy advice about managing brute force. More specifically, this study derives some broad guidelines before force use and specific recommendations during force use, summarized in Figure 6-1. These suggestions are specially tuned to the twenty-first-century global security setting.

Is it true currently that violence is the only language that bitter enemies understand, as some Israelis claimed after the destruction of the Syrian nuclear facility? If so, then state-initiated brute force may have a crucial signaling role to play in today's world. However, given the mixed case study evidence about force outcomes, this policy instrument cannot be used indiscriminately to communicate with one's foes. Even when the most intense mutual emotional hatred and fear exist between contending adversaries, having state governments rely on force alone to attain mission objectives would seem highly imprudent.

When violence results from brute force, the primary damage is usually not on state security but rather on human security felt by the global masses.[1] This human peril changes the force calculus in two unfortunate ways: Defensively, traditional security responses to threat, such as hardening strategically critical vulnerable targets, often fail when an entire civilian society is at risk; and offensively, political leaders choosing to apply force usually do not suffer directly its most negative consequences. The more democratic values spread around the globe, forcing national governments to respond to their citizens' frustrations, the greater the potential that the outcry deriving from

---

*Policy Guidelines for Initiators before Brute Force Use*

### Considering Broad Implications

Situate brute force within a wider range of influence instruments.
Evaluate the full security repercussions of applying brute force.

### Identifying Coercive Limitations

Expand open public discussion about the restricted value of brute force.
Frame brute force as a transitional short-run local military solution.

### Acquiring Wide Acceptance

Pursue, when feasible, multilateral approval and cooperation.
Forestall deterioration of regional and global state and human security.

---

*Policy Recommendations for Initiators during Brute Force Use*

### Promoting Attainable Purpose

Encompass narrower and more tangible mission goals.
Emphasize vital purposes for which brute force is designed.

### Undertaking Credible Commitment

Increase the staying power of brute force applications.
Incorporate the application of all appropriate coercive tools.

### Encouraging Unified Resolve

Forge strong national support for brute force applications.
Foster loyalty among government armed forces applying brute force.

### Sustaining Forward Thinking

Boost planning for action–reaction cycles.
Bolster forethought about regional contagion effects.

---

**Figure 6-1.** Improving brute force management.

distressing human security problems will serve—for better or worse—as both a trigger and a restraint on state-initiated brute force.

Although some analysts conclude that brute force is obsolete in today's enlightened globalized world, instead recent futility seems to result from states' misapplication of brute force. This misapplication includes failure to apply sufficient force, the right kind of force, or force for a long enough time to achieve its objectives; faulty intelligence or analysis by force initiators; or misguided or poorly chosen force purposes. The most critical force limitations do not revolve around the honor, courage, and fighting skills of soldiers undertaking it. Thus futility may associate more with defective planning and execution by leaders than with inherent force deficiencies. Within the tight constraints of today's global security setting, to be successful brute force use needs to be a lot smarter than in the past (although admittedly the words *smart* and *brute* rarely ought to appear together).

## POLICY GUIDELINES FOR INITIATORS
## BEFORE BRUTE FORCE USE

Broad policy guidelines emerge regarding brute force prior to its application. These are (1) considering broad implications, situating brute force within a wider range of influence instruments and evaluating the full security repercussions of applying brute force; (2) identifying coercive limitations, expanding open discussion about the restricted value of brute force, and framing brute force as a transitional short-run local military solution; and (3) acquiring wide acceptance, pursuing when feasible multilateral approval and cooperation and forestalling deterioration of regional and global state and human security. These clusters of ideas suggest a significant reorientation of strategic doctrine, providing a refashioned overarching rubric within which policy recommendations during force use can be properly implemented.

### Considering Broad Implications

Situate Brute Force Explicitly within a Wider Array of Influence Instruments  To apply brute force prudently, it needs to be properly nested within a wider array of influence instruments. Rather than seeing force as a substitute for diplomacy—as is common in some circles—it would be wiser to view force as one element in a multifaceted process of altering others' behavior. Force cannot alone face the full range of security challenges:

> The problem with a conception centered on force is simple: force is perfect for destroying, and there are indeed many valid targets for destruction—terrorists, murderous regimes, and horrific weapons. But even in the fight against terrorism, force is only one tool among many others. When it comes to other essential tasks: reconstruction, state building, the fight against misery and for

development in the world, the harnessing and conservation of resources, the protection of the environment, force's role is far more humble.[2]

If used imprudently, "to expect to gain and maintain control through military prowess and muscle flexing could turn out to be a dangerous illusion."[3] There is ample evidence that brute force or hard power alone cannot usually accomplish much[4]—even former American Secretary of Defense Donald Rumsfeld recognizes that the global "struggle cannot be won by military force alone, or even principally."[5] The proper resort to brute force assumes that an appropriate tools assessment has occurred beforehand determining that noncoercive soft power options cannot accomplish the goals better;[6] after all, "the proposition that military force is more effective than other power resources is both ambiguous and debatable."[7] Nonetheless, some analysts argue that brute force may render negotiation completely unnecessary—"with enough force, a country may not need to bargain."[8] Indeed, "Americans—not unlike many of their European counterparts—considered war an *alternative* to bargaining, rather than part of an ongoing bargaining process, as in the Clausewitzian view."[9] Overall, force initiators could greatly benefit from using complementary noncoercive alternatives,[10] as negotiation and diplomacy may be essential to resolve the underlying issues of dispute.

The central challenge is figuring out how to craft an optimum combination of hard and soft power, keeping in mind that—due to legitimacy concerns—not every coercive option may actually be on the table, and not every noncoercive option may be effective. Because force is often considered in worst-case predicaments when all other options have failed, determining this combination can be difficult. However, seemingly weak noncoercive options may work better when applied together with coercive tools.

Hard and soft power need to be synchronized to achieve desired compliance, subject to time requirements (because soft power generally takes a lot longer to work). Accompanying force use should be efforts to restore targets back into the international community,[11] with such reintegration not time limited—it is continuously present before, during, and after force use. Key questions include whether the use of soft power should always precede the use of hard power (because using force as a last resort is not always wise); what kinds of hard and soft power are most and least mutually compatible; and what safeguards should guarantee that soft power and hard power used do not undercut each other. Applying soft power during force confrontations needs to overcome the obstacle that force victims may be highly resentful and not wish to talk to force initiators, often addressed through having those personnel using hard power differ from those employing soft power.

Evaluate the Full Security Repercussions of Applying Brute Force Given the complexities surrounding brute force use, with the exception of time-pressured security crises, there should be no "rush to judgment" to determine whether to apply it to cope with threat. Indeed, "what is needed more than ever is care, prudence, and judiciousness in determining prior to its application whether and how to use military force."[12] Prior to force use, this outcome assessment needs to take into account short term and long term, national and global, and military, political, economic, and cultural security impacts. When significant disparities exist among these impacts, the balance of advantages and disadvantages needs careful weighing. This weighing would differ across societies but should not in any case base force use exclusively on short-term national interests. Because virtually every brute force use creates unexpected and unintended consequences, this weighing should pay special attention to possible unexpected security impacts.[13]

It is common to suggest that the best way to fashion the proper role for brute force is to specify the nature of security challenges faced: For example, some analysts think that "it seems obvious that military forces should focus on improving their ability to fight conventional, counter-insurgency, counter-terrorism and stability operations similar to those experienced since 2001."[14] However, such conclusions are controversial due to the constantly changing nature of emerging security challenges—"a look at the past should make anyone hesitate to discuss the future of force,"[15] as charting future threats to suggest future force needs can be truly daunting. Rather than attempting to pinpoint future force requirements, it seems preferable to develop flexibility and adaptability in strategies for confronting the widest range of threats and resulting security outcomes that might demand force use.

### Identifying Coercive Limitations

Expand Open Public Discussion about the Restricted Value of Brute Force Currently within countries there is little open discussion between the government and the public about the opportunities and limitations surrounding brute force. What discussion exists today on this topic is usually hampered by extremist emotional polarized views about the relationship among force, militarization, and violence. Included in these unproductive conversations are rigid opposing assumptions about whether violence is the only effective way to respond to violence, as well as vastly different notions of brute force, force effectiveness, and force legitimacy, often based on misinformation and misperception. For many, a fatalistic acceptance of global violence exists, in part because "a fundamentally flawed and ahistorical understanding of future conflict continues to survive" among many security policy makers and private citizens.[16] Sadly, across the globe, "public discourse on matters military has mostly been delegated to debates on defence spending and the legality and morality of the use of force—whilst discussion of the actual meaning of force, and its utility, has become nearly obsolete."[17]

Before its use, there is a need to find better ways—particularly within democracies—to increase mass public understanding of brute force dynamics. A discriminating awareness needs to develop of its purposes, impacts, and transformational possibilities and limitations, taking into account prevailing societal values within both force initiators and force targets. Misunderstandings of ongoing force trends can be corrected through placing current coercive confrontations in deeper historical perspective.[18] Government officials should explain better to the mass public the political, sociocultural, economic, technological, military–strategic, geopolitical and geostrategic, and historical context behind using force.[19]

A critical need exists for more internal transparency in states laying out certain brute force parameters. This transparency includes (1) avoidance of misleading inflammatory labels placed on threats, such as states engaging in violent crackdowns against peaceful protesters calling them "domestic terrorist attacks" (as in the case of Bahrain), "foreign terrorists" (as in the case of Syria), or "terrorists in disguise" (as in the case of China); and (2) avoidance of depictions of extreme systematic government applications of force against nonviolent targets as "isolated incidents" (as in the case of Greece and Bahrain). The payoff of greater transparency is greater public trust in the national government, comprehension of force logic, and ultimately acceptance of citizen sacrifices that might need to occur on behalf of the state.

Furthermore, the appropriate range of brute force use needs to be placed more explicitly in the context of a well-defined publicly articulated national strategy. Although it is common to view threat as a "force-shaper," with perceived threat dictating force capabilities,[20] instead typically a state's overall defensive strategy should determine force configuration. Without a well-formulated and flexible strategic doctrine, incorporating "coordinated action in diplomacy, propaganda, secret operations, and the entire economic sphere, as well as in military policy,"[21] the critical integrative rubric for coherent security policy is missing, and a public–private discussion could remain disjointed and potentially contradictory. The discussion must include "a constant dialogue between military effort and political goals":[22] It needs to emphasize better communication between military and political personnel as well as between those in the battle zone and those at home. If undertaken properly, the result of such efforts could be improved internal and external force legitimacy.

Frame Brute Force as a Transitional Short-Run Local Military Solution   Brute force can still contribute—and sometimes constitute the primary way—to restoring order, particularly when what is most critical for mission success is transitional military stability within a short time period and confined to a specific target area. In such situations, possessing significant force capabilities and appropriately applying such force can be essential:

> The efficacy of force endures. It must. For in anarchy, force and politics are connected. By itself, military power guarantees neither survival nor prosperity. But it is almost always the essential ingredient for both. Because resort to force is the ultimate card of all states, the seriousness of a state's intentions is conveyed fundamentally by its having a credible military posture. Without it, a state's diplomacy generally lacks effectiveness.[23]

Applications of appropriate levels and types of force can achieve target compliance very quickly, can be instantly understood by antagonists regardless of cultural differences, and can even be deemed legitimate when perceived as being used defensively to restrain aggression. Persistent global anarchy ensures occasions when force is warranted to achieve short-term local military objectives.

At the same time, brute force ought not to be deemed the final solution or step needed to achieve long-range strategic mission objectives. Over time, within an interdependent globalized world, international, transnational, and subnational pressures can undermine desired compliance resulting from force over an unwilling or unenthusiastic target population. So, prior to its use, policy makers need to carefully frame it as a transitional short-run local military solution.

### Acquiring Wide Acceptance

Pursue when Feasible Multilateral Approval and Cooperation   From the outset, force initiators usually can choose between unilateral and multilateral brute

force use. A multilateral strategy—involving coalition approval and cooperation—has a mix of costs and benefits:

> The benefits include international and domestic legitimacy for U.S. military
> actions; influence over the actions of other countries and political movements;
> wartime and postwar burdensharing; easier access to the battlefield; and ac-
> cess to more intelligence. The costs include giving others, who may not share
> U.S. priorities or strategic calculations, a share in political authority and/or
> command over U.S. military operations; delays in undertaking actions that
> may be time-urgent; loss of secrecy; the politicizing of intrawar strategies and
> the distortion of war aims; and the complication of postwar reconstruction
> and stabilization tasks.[24]

The ratio of these costs and benefits varies tremendously depending on the
kind of external or internal brute force application.

Nonetheless, politically and diplomatically, force initiators are on stronger
ground with coalitions. Coalition partners lend their support and participation, better legitimizing the operation in a political sense than if a state were to
go it alone. A coalition shows that a force initiator is not acting only in its own
best interest. For example, President George H. W. Bush displayed diplomatic
skill in putting together the broad coalition for Operation Desert Storm, recognizing the importance of coalition strategy. Military benefits also emerge
because coalition partners contribute their own capabilities, reducing the burden on their own forces, even if the aid is only logistics, intelligence support,
or security for their bases. If force initiators have permission or sanction from
allies, target states, or international organizations to use force, this could be
highlighted to increase its global acceptance.

However, it is usually very difficult to put together a multilateral coalition, and it takes time to do so effectively; so if going multilateral critically
delays a force thrust or dilutes its purpose, then this approach may be counterproductive. Within such an arrangement, partners often want something
in return, and their participation often comes with domestic political costs
for one's political leaders. Operating multinational forces in a unified way is
difficult: Communicating effectively, executing command-and-control, and
undertaking operational planning are more complex, time consuming, and
error prone.

Moreover, absolute insistence on multilateral approaches is often used by
political opponents of a military operation to impede its execution because

they know how hard it is—sometimes impossible—to put them together. So agreeing to go multilateral in a sense gives such opponents a victory. For American force initiatives, Russia, China, and sometimes France can be counted on not only to refuse to participate, but to object diplomatically, vetoing the operation in the U.N. Security Council. For instance, France strongly has objected to any military operation against Iran because such an effort would disrupt French companies' many business ties to Iranian enterprises.

Regardless, today multilateral state-initiated brute force uses seem more successful: "Although multilateralism requires states to forgo their personal interests for the greater global good, this sacrifice grants legitimacy to military action"; and "the cases in which unilateral military action would receive international legitimacy and be deemed a success in both the eyes of the world and the country performing the action are far fewer than those which could be deemed successes if multilateralism was pursued."[25] If force use abroad is truly multilateral—unlike the largely unilateral 2003 American invasion of Iraq and the 2013 French invasion of Mali, which were portrayed as multilateral—then when the primary force initiator disengages or lessens its role in a confrontation, the pressure on force targets for compliance endures. If force use at home is sanctioned multilaterally, the risk of outsiders thwarting the coercive effort may be lessened. The United States in particular has come under attack recently for ignoring or downplaying in its policies the benefits of multilateralism—for example, American President George W. Bush's foreign security policy was called "immersion in irresponsible unilateralism."[26] Many outside observers now persuasively argue that "in a world in which there are now two rising powers (China and India) and one restored power (Russia), the United States can no longer assume that new rules will be entirely to its liking"; and so the United States "better get on board" in a global setting "in which multilateral institutions and diplomacy matter far more than in the past."[27]

Forestall Deterioration of Regional and Global State and Human Security   For brute force to be successful, it cannot sacrifice regional or global security for the sake of promoting strategic objectives consistent with a force initiator's vital national interests, and it cannot sacrifice human security for the sake of promoting strategic objectives consistent with a force initiator's state regime benefits. To view national and regional/global security—or human and state security—as inescapably zero-sum is self-defeating: If force promotes national interests but undercuts regional or global security, or promotes the government but undercuts the citizenry, force initiators will often eventually see any postforce gains eroded. Although force applications often fulfill vital national state interests but worsen long-term stability and human security regionally and globally, circumstances do exist—such as quelling violent unjust internal or external disruption—where national interests and regional/global security—and state security and human security—can be compatible.

Prior to brute force use, any preforce review—either by internal legislative bodies or outside parties—needs to focus on the legitimacy of the force use as well as on mission effectiveness, taking into account both regional/global and human security impacts. Ultimately, external force uses need to be justified through demonstration that the dangers associated with the destabilizing trigger for force use are more crucial than sovereignty violations entailed; internal force uses need to be justified through demonstration that the dangers associated with destabilizing trigger for force use are more crucial than human rights violations entailed. This calculation needs to include an impartial assessment by state force initiators about the probable salience of the force use inside and outside the initiating country.

Although global verbal disapproval alone does not restrain brute force (as noted in Chapter 5's section on common but low-impact force legitimacy concerns), state force initiators should where possible maximize and stress the regional and global force benefits—and the types of pressing problems resolved—to the broader international community.

Policy makers should also try to manage postforce repercussions in ways that not only preserve national interests but also avoid major disruptions to regional and global security. Such an approach would involve implementing policies designed specifically to prevent or contain escalating postforce turmoil.

To accrue global legitimacy, without making rash claims of force promoting global justice, states should stress compatibilities between their actions and enlightened liberal democratic values. Exemplifying this approach is the Greek government's violent crackdown on mass protesters, in which the regime stressed the need to coercively defend its imposition of stark austerity measures to right itself financially, showing the European Union that it was taking the responsible—if highly unpopular and nondemocratic—path. Sometimes force use can be defended in terms of pursuit of noble ideals.

The importance of regional and global security concerns relates to the external security dilemma, where persistent state force use against other states can create regional insecurity due to perceived upset of the status quo balance of power. Global anarchy is responsible for creating this classic security dilemma surrounding force:

> Because there are no institutions or authorities that can make and enforce international laws, the policies of cooperation that will bring mutual rewards if others cooperate may bring disaster if they do not. Because states are aware of this, anarchy encourages behavior that leaves all concerned worse off than they could be, even in the extreme case in which all states would like to freeze the status quo.[28]

Indeed, "many of the means by which a state tries to increase its security decrease the security of others" as "one state's gain in security often inadvertently threatens other."[29] Among powerful states, force-related competition for external influence can easily trigger a counterproductive arms race; even after the end of Cold War bipolarity, regional balances of power still stimulate this kind of competition. Among weaker states, government force use can trigger rising within-state individual and group militarization, worsening the security dilemma by increasing fears from neighbors about the contagion of within-country nonstate violence. Because of growing global communication networks increasing awareness in neighboring states, turmoil can spread more quickly within a region than in the past, particularly when people have common ethnicities or religions or face common hardships or deprivations. Even state force use against its own people can trigger an arms race with neighbors due to regional fears.

Although state-initiated brute force alone is not the best means of promoting humanitarian ends (as noted in as noted in Chapter 5's section on common but low-impact force legitimacy concerns), state force initiators should where possible maximize and stress the human security benefits—and the types of pressing socioeconomic problems resolved—to their domestic citizens resulting from the application of coercion.

Given that force use usually generates significant collateral damage, during violent confrontations policy makers should strive to contain such damage and—after the confrontation ends—to repair whatever damage has occurred. To earn greater domestic legitimacy, force initiators should stress the compatibility of their actions with enlightened liberal democratic values: Illustrating this strategy is the Mexican government's violent crackdown on drug lords, where the regime has emphasized its need to employ draconian coercive measures to reduce the drug violence, thereby demonstrating to its citizens its willingness to do whatever was necessary—regardless of the costs—to promote internal peace and to protect mass welfare.

The importance of human security concerns relates to an internal security dilemma—because the welfare of the people (human security) and the welfare of the political regime (state security) may differ and even be at cross-purposes, national governmental possession and application of force either internally or externally does not necessarily assure mass public safety. Individual and group militarization increases within a country do not always enhance the security of the state regime, and state government increases in military and police forces do not always enhance the security of a country's citizens. The global spread of democracy is responsible—via the concept of a two-way social contract between the rulers and the ruled—for high citizen expectations about ruling regimes' responsibility to provide their protection and to be the primary source of human security, and these high expectations frequently have not been fulfilled within the twenty-first-century global security setting. Due to growing internal communication networks, when states do not fulfill mass security needs, bottom-up frustration and disruption with high levels of human insecurity can spread more quickly within a country than they have in the past; through external communication networks, these dissatisfactions can easily bubble over and create turmoil in neighboring states. State governments no longer possess a near monopoly on instruments of violence and so therefore cannot always maintain internal order and effectively suppress emerging substate disruption, and the proliferation of transnational and subnational threats often outstrips states' ability to protect citizens against them.

## POLICY RECOMMENDATIONS FOR INITIATORS
## DURING BRUTE FORCE USE

Keeping in mind the aforementioned broad policy guidelines, specific recommendations emerge regarding brute force during its use. These interrelated recommendations take into account both force effectiveness and force legitimacy and stem from the force initiator attributes associating with success involving attainable purpose, credible commitment, unified resolve, and forward thinking. These ideas provide tangible clues about how to escape from the stifling pattern of long-run force futility in the twenty-first century.

### Promoting Attainable Purpose

Encompass Narrower and More Tangible Mission Goals    To ensure that states will use brute force only when mission objectives are narrow and tangible, these goals need to be clarified and tightened, tied to the military's comparative advantages, and linked more rigorously to national interests. This effort can be a real challenge, given that "more often than not, states end wars with aims different or additional to the ones with which they started."[30] These tighter mission ends need to apply on every level, extending from the strategic political objectives justifying force use down to the tactical military objectives on the battlefield: "For military commanders whose units are engaged in battle, it often becomes a contest of brute force whose immediate objectives are independent of the reasons of state that brought it on."[31]

Moving in this direction depends on heads of state obtaining better advice from close political advisors, harnessing better the lessons from their own experience, and heeding more the mission-constraining advice of the military leadership, which usually argues for narrow tangible attainable mission objectives. Part of the process in making goals narrower and more tangible is identifying in advance objective metrics for gauging every aspect of mission success. In the midst of a coercive confrontation, intentional comparison and analysis of current objectives and progress to preconfrontation expectations needs to occur on a regular basis.

Emphasize Vital Purposes for Which Brute Force Is Designed    To ensure that brute force is used only for the vital purposes for which it is designed, political leaders must constantly question the need to use brute force for a mission, keeping in mind that this tool is designed for killing people and destruction of property. Strategists taking an overly expansive view of the utility of military operations need to be ignored in favor of those seeking to limit the military mission as narrowly as possible, questioning such amorphous goals as nation building, enhancing partnership capacity, and peacekeeping. Even the common stability promotion goal may frequently represent a mismatch for force: In many developing countries, "development, not deterrence, is the most effective strategy for building safe societies,"[32] and so, if instability sources are multifaceted or deeply rooted in society, then force is unlikely to provide an enduring solution. The optimal purposes for brute force are those where decisive mission success is possible: "If war is sometimes useful, even necessary, a truly decisive outcome is especially valuable; wars with inconclusive outcomes, at least in the authoritative opinion of one of the belligerents, are more likely than not to be renewed in the future."[33]

Both ends and means need reconsideration. Regarding ends, brute force should be used only when vital national interests—involving protection of people, territory, and regime[34]—are at stake. The problem is that heads of state portray this rationale for every force use: For example, "every major US combat intervention overseas since 1945 has been attended by White House declarations of the presence of threatened vital interests."[35] Regarding means, although it is popular to argue that "military forces, their governments and coalitions need to develop improved inter-departmental capabilities for planning and executing statebuilding,"[36] political leaders should not resort to force for strategic objectives outside the military skill set, due to force's comparative disadvantage for purposes such as social work, civil society implantation, or nation building.

### Undertaking Credible Commitment

Increase the Staying Power of Brute Force Applications    To ensure the use of brute force only when it could be applied for as long as it takes (rather than for "speedy-exit" opportunities), perhaps the most important first step is to acquire better intelligence before and during force use about what complications could substantially lengthen (and/or broaden) security threats. That military, political, economic, and social intelligence would include exactly how force use would make a major difference in ongoing confrontations. With appropriate intelligence in hand, force planners could calculate within reasonable probabilities the estimated length of time for force commitment, the amount of soldiers and weapons needed, the required logistical support, and the overall costs—in both money and lives—of the whole enterprise. These steps would help to improve the decision calculus and avoid the pattern that in most of the case force initiators do not go into confrontations with nearly enough staying power.

Announcing early on in a brute force use when it will end or when troops will withdraw should be avoided at all costs. In sidestepping this pitfall, "leaders should also abandon the belief that wars can be waged efficiently with a minimalist approach to the commitment of forces and other resources".[37] "To make non-compliance too costly" to force targets, force initiators often try in vain "to defeat the adversary or deny him his objectives quickly with little cost in terms of blood and treasure."[38] It seems somewhat naïve that "U.S. military men and political leaders typically saw the destruction of an opponent's armed might and the occupation of his capital as marking the end of war."[39] Instead, during and after force use there needs to be adequate commitment— not exclusively through military means—"to whatever postwar responsibilities and resources will be required to restore at least minimal civic life where it has been severely disrupted."[40] Substantial contingency planning about unanticipated disruptions ought to occur during force applications. Perhaps most important, armed with this improved intelligence and awareness of mission success requirements, political leaders should continually revise their calculations about the value of the mission objectives if a security challenge looks as if it is highly likely to require a significantly extended force use.

Incorporate the Application of All Appropriate Coercive Tools   To ensure that brute force will be used only when it involves all appropriate coercive tools (rather than highly constrained force use), government defense ministries could strive to do a better job of providing a wider range of options for heads of state to use when they resort to military instrument of power. Political leaders need a wide assortment of tools and tactical expertise to give them a freer hand in employing force within the existing demanding legal and political constraints. In this regard, it is important to commit sufficient resources to the force effort: "If one accepts war as a legitimate, albeit regrettable, occasional necessity, the overriding purpose of policy cannot be to wage it in as modest a fashion as the enemy permits," for "the nature and dynamics of war are not to be lightly mocked by undercommitment."[41] To know which coercive tools are most appropriate, the aforementioned high-quality intelligence is vital on the noncompliant force target, including about its capabilities, plan, and intentions.[42] In expanding the force tool kit, states need to be prepared for a wide range of coercive confrontations where they can engage in different kinds of force options to pursue national policy goals and in continuous reevaluation and alteration as necessary over time of these options. To be ready, "forces must be able to fight under conditions of uncertainty and be employed in sufficient force and in the right combination to establish security and overwhelm the enemy in their area of operations."[43]

Using all appropriate coercive tools does not mean that state-initiated brute force ought always to strive to apply vastly superior military technology, as "military forces must abandon the dangerous and seductive illusion that technology can solve the problem of future conflict."[44] The case data tables show that most force initiators' sizable coercive advantage had little long-term strategic benefit, indicating the deficiencies of this technocentric approach. In particular, "the characteristics of the U.S. style of warfare—speed, joint-ness, knowledge, and precision—are better suited for strike operations than for translating such operations into strategic successes."[45] Sometimes state-initiated use of overwhelming force backfires in terms of international com-munity reactions: When a force initiator launches a massive unrestrained high-tech strike on a target, outsiders may call this an overreaction and al-most instinctively side with the underdog, as evidenced by Russia's massive external attack on Georgia and Syria's massive internal attack on the rebels. Often states marshalling superior military technology cannot bring this ad-vantage effectively to bear in their violent confrontations: "Massive, rapid, and decisive use of force is virtually impossible in a world of limited and politi-cally messy wars, in a global environment in which nonstate enemies practice protracted irregular warfare as a means of negating the potential effective-ness of America's conventional military supremacy."[46] In contrast to seeking advanced technology, sometimes states are wise to mimic disruptive armed nonstate groups' highly irregular low-tech tactics. In moving toward this kind of "outside-the-box" analysis, defense establishments would need to overcome their institutional bureaucratic inertia—resisting innovation and dismissing ideas requiring significant change in standard operating procedures and rules of engagement: "Even the US Army . . . is finding it difficult to cut completely loose from years of wrongheaded thinking."[47]

### Encouraging Unified Resolve

Forge Strong National Support for Brute Force Applications   To ensure that brute force is used only when there is wide national support within a state's government and its citizenry (as opposed to divided opinion, apathy, or con-fusion) about the desirability and feasibility of a mission, a key prerequisite especially in democracies is support by the mass public about state force use. Fitting within the aforementioned policy guideline of expanding open pub-lic discussion, political leaders should try to increase domestic approval of force uses by clarifying their purposes and means–end calculations, without revealing sensitive tactical details or violating secrecy needs for mission suc-cess: Specifically, this effort should emphasize due process in reaching deci-sions and any international consultation involved, while at the same time assiduously avoiding clumsy manipulation trying to hoodwink citizens about force use. Force should then be employed only if there is assurance that "the interests and values at stake are of sufficient weight—and have sufficient support in the country—to warrant going to war."[48] However, since the Korean War, there have been few if any provocations that produced a strong unified national consensus within the United States for military action; across other state force initiators, the paucity of wide domestic support for many twenty-first-century internal and external uses of brute force is telling.

Altering military parameters can affect domestic public support. If the head of state can truthfully say to the public that a proposed military campaign can be circumscribed in its human, financial, material, and diplomatic cost, this can have a tangible, beneficial effect on public acceptance. The public in most countries will support more strongly their states' involvement in foreign military interventions if these interventions start out and remain limited in their goals, can be completed quickly, and entail low human and financial costs. The more a military campaign oversteps these conditions, the more public acceptance of it will deteriorate. This maxim applies all over the world: greater policy maker awareness of the links between well-implemented military limits and public support would help with domestic approval for U.S. force use, for recent American foreign military interventions have grossly overstepped these bounds with disastrous results; in developing countries, increasing accountability and reducing corruption through reforms of the military and police structures may be essential for greater public support, involving better integration and professionalization of government security officials. Regardless, because such domestic public support is often ephemeral—"assured public support at the beginning of an overseas military intervention can weaken, even evaporate, in the event of military stalemate or defeat"[49]—political leaders need to continuously monitor and reevaluate internal support levels.

Foster Loyalty among Government Armed Forces Applying Brute Force    To ensure that brute force is used only with unwaveringly loyal government armed forces, changes must occur in the recruitment and indoctrination of those executing the mission. If there is voluntary military service, greater emphasis in selection should be not only on the physical skills of recruits but also on their mental and psychological fitness for the mission. Despite the widespread use and value of private military contractors and foreign soldiers for many security purposes, due to loyalty issues they should not be pivotal combat components in critical missions. Military indoctrination and training should explicitly emphasize a mission's value and the needed sacrifices at least as much as obedience to military superiors' orders.

Such loyalty needs particularly careful monitoring when a violent confrontation involves (1) an antagonistic force target whose background or beliefs might appeal to state military personnel (such as in the 2011 Egyptian uprising) or (2) a cause about which domestic public opinion is sharply divided (such as in the Vietnam War). Managing this first concern is exceptionally important when force is used internally against a country's own people. As to the second concern, because high desertion rates or even high rates of posttraumatic stress disorder can occur when soldiers do not understand or support mission objectives, soldiers should be more realistically and comprehensively inoculated against the stress and physical and psychological challenges they will face by being more intensively prepared for the horrors of war. Moreover, tours of duty should be adjusted such that burnout does not occur due to overly long strenuous time commitment on the battlefield without opportunities to recover.

### Sustaining Forward Thinking

Boost Planning for Action–Reaction Cycles    To ensure that advance planning for postforce reconstruction minimizes the chances of a postforce violent action–reaction cycle, there needs to be a renewed state emphasis on learning how to "clean up" after employment of brute force and restore order. Force initiators need to develop fluid adaptive force policies based on future-oriented analysis of evolving action–reaction cycle trends. For military officers, there needs to be more emphasis on downstream consequences in the war colleges and in military higher education institutions. Professional war games[50] and military simulations of projected confrontations need to emphasize more unanticipated second-order and third-order force consequences rather than immediate impacts of strategy and tactics on battle outcomes. Future requirements include better training and recruitment of defense strategists who can creatively and realistically think several moves ahead, game things out, and anticipate how the other side will respond to their moves while simultaneously determining their own next countermoves. These security analysts need to improve assessments of force's broader security implications beyond immediate short-term military impacts on direct participants. Force initiators need to avoid responses that cause opponents to respond violently, eschewing countermeasures that overreact to an existing provocation. Force use may often trigger a defiant sense of aggression among force targets, willing to escalate indefinitely: Exemplifying this tendency in the 2003 Iraq War are American leaders brushing off repeated warnings from their staff that the conventional combat phase could be followed by a violent, uncontrollable domestic insurgency seeking to undercut American security objectives of a democratic government collaboratively overseeing a stable and secure civil order through using Iraqi military and security forces. What is most needed is a concerted political, military, economic, and social effort to defuse the tensions, misperceptions, and antagonisms between contesting parties, and to develop sustainable constrained stable interaction between even the most diehard adversaries.[51]

To minimize the risk of an action–reaction cycle, force initiators need to gain a much deeper understanding of how this violent cycle works in today's global security environment. They need to identify (1) the points early in the cycle where the hostile entrapping interactive pattern can be most easily broken, and (2) the pressures keeping opposing parties from extricating themselves from this cycle even when one or both wish to do so. Armed with this understanding, effective monitoring and policing is vital of postforce internal and external order.[52] Force initiators need to find a balance between restraint and leniency in confronting violent elements: "Unless comprehensive security needs are addressed up front, spoilers will find the weak areas and retain leverage to affect the political outcomes, vitiating the peace."[53] Discovering effective responses other than force to an adversary is a critical component of breaking out of this dangerous tit-for-tat escalation cycle. In particular, "contemplated military operations must be adequately evaluated with respect to both their direct human and material costs and their risk of escalating to more dangerous levels of conflict—and that the prospects of such higher costs must also be factored into the initial assessment of any coercive strategy."[54] Using target-centered threat assessment,[55] reducing the exclusive focus on identifying and punishing the culprit responsible for a confrontation, may help sidestep pernicious mutually escalatory dynamics.

Bolster Forethought about Regional Contagion Effects   To ensure that strategic approaches are found to isolate and localize impacts and to minimize postforce regional contagion effects, more analysis is needed about local tensions spreading to neighbors or regional players providing economic or military aid to contending parties. Analytical approaches stressing bottom-up processes may be best able "to grasp the conflict dynamics that lead to a diffusion of violence and the emergence of a regional conflict system."[56] Ignoring regional contagion is most dangerous when even before force use, a high potential exists for regional turmoil, including powerful outside states with regional strategic interests probably militarily or economically intervening on behalf of force targets. Illustrating these dynamics was the Libyan government's brute force use against its internal rebels: Outside observers were aware of (1) the links between the Libyan rebel activity and the broader Arab Spring movement and (2) the understandable worry by onlooker European states in NATO about the possible cutoff of Libyan oil and massive North African refugee flows, leading to these European states' decision not just to stand by and watch without taking action.

Isolating and localizing brute force impacts entail appropriately attempting to shape media coverage, without (as with forging national support) engaging in manipulative distortion. Because during chaotic violent confrontations normal government and commercial reporting channels are often unreliable, the Internet can be a key target because it can influence global responses—getting news out of the region, information from other countries into the region, and political and operational support for or against an involved party. For the military, the role of the media needs to be an "integral part of planning": When applying force, the goal in shaping media coverage would be to increase the chances that most of the audience "are following your script in the context, and not that of the opponent"—for example, "if you are fighting for the will of the people, however many tactical successes you achieve they will be as naught if people do not think you are winning."[57] With full recognition that most of the media is in the entertainment business,[58] political leaders' goals in explaining force use should be to attain the role of the "narrator" "who explains to the audience what has happened, its significance, and where events might lead."[59] For internal force use, media access can play an important role—Egypt and Myanmar failed to control it, while China, Syria, and Thailand did so, at least initially. For external force use, despite high sensitivity about shaping media coverage of military operations abroad, the American Department of Defense regularly attempts to affect the perceptions of the key players and the public; however, by most accounts Western states have been largely unsuccessful achieving their strategic objectives in such media-shaping efforts. Although preventing outsiders from discovering state brute force use in today's globalized world is difficult, coercive "repression can only backfire when people are aware of—and disgusted by—the regime's abuses."[60]

## A CHANGING PLACE FOR BRUTE FORCE
## IN TODAY'S WORLD

This study has shown that brute force is situated in a very different place in today's world than in the past. Figure 6-2 summarizes the far from ideal setting in which force operates, the truly messy current global security challenge, and the resulting shrinking brute force role. Understanding this transformation seems an essential prerequisite for force success.

### A Far from Ideal Setting

Most people in the world would readily agree that they would prefer to live at a time and in a place where brute force was completely unnecessary, never the best or only way to resolve disputes. They would enjoy more a global setting where widespread international condemnation of any emerging injustices would be in itself sufficient to stop them. If given a choice, they would rather not have to concern themselves with unpleasant issues such as fear, threat, vulnerability, and survival. Often national political leaders manifest these same desires to reconstruct a peaceful global system.[61] Imagining a world without war or brute force can be immensely pleasurable.

However, despite diminishing levels of aggregate global violence and major power warfare, "conflict and confrontation will continue" as long as massive shifts in relative coercive power occur over time,[62] military and police capabilities vary significantly across states, sovereignty and sphere-of-influence ambiguities are evident, core values substantially differ across groups and societies, and global anarchy prevails. Thus a world without brute force seems remote: "So long as security communities, be they states or some other kind of organization, compete for political power and influence, then for so long must war retain its utility as the court of final appeal."[63] Moreover, in international relations "the shape of politics without violence is not necessarily benign."[64]

Political leaders continue to feel attracted or compelled to apply brute force internally and externally, even if they see it as suboptimal:

> If the past be any guide to the future, then military power will remain central to the course of international relations. Those states that do not have the wherewithall to field large forces (for example, Denmark) or those that choose to field forces far smaller than their economies can bear (for example, Japan)

---

**A Far From Ideal Setting**

*Lofty Security Aspirations*
Most people in the world would prefer to live at a time and in a place where brute force was unnecessary, never the best or only way to resolve disputes, and where widespread international condemnation of emerging injustices would be sufficient to stop them.

*Need for Reality Checks*
Brute force use continues due to massive shifts in relative coercive power, differing military and police capabilities, contrasting core values, spreading instruments of violence, freer public expression of dissatisfaction, declining state loyalty, and global anarchy.

---

**A Messy Global Security Challenge**

*Large Perceptual Gaps*
There are an expectation–reality gap between high security expectations and low security performance, a rhetoric–reality gap between avowed enlightened global cooperation and persisting coercive anarchy, and a needs–reality gap between strategic transformation and traditional security responses.

*Need to Bridge Gaps*
Improved global management of brute force necessitates identifying ways to create awareness of these gaps and then finding ways to reduce and eliminate them by fine-tuning brute force to be both effective and legitimate in today's world.

---

**A Shrinking Brute-force Role**

*Tight Coercion Limits*
Brute force works under shrinking circumstances, needing for success to operate within parameters that have substantially narrowed compared to the past, where policy makers make a greater effort to recognize and the contracting circumstances conducive to positive outcomes.

*Need to Overcome Limits*
Given these limits, it appears essential to restrict force use to circumstances where tangible benefits dramatically exceed actual costs, as well as to resist common temptations, avoiding succumbing to the many seductive opportunities for force use.

---

**Figure 6-2.** A changing place for brute force in today's world.

will pay the price. Both will find themselves with less control over their own fate than would otherwise be the case. Those states that field powerful military forces will find themselves in greater control, but also that their great military power can produce unintended effects and that such power is not a solution to all their problems. For both the strong and the weak, however, as long as anarchy obtains, force will remain the final arbiter to resolve the disputes that arise among them.[65]

Despite the high cost of brute force and war,[66] some security challenges remain where using peaceful negotiation and diplomacy alone is both inadequate and dangerous. Although "democracy is spreading, economic interdependence is growing, and international institutions are flourishing," "they cannot wholly fill the political vacuum created by the absence of effective world government and the military power that would accompany it."[67] There are always occasions in both developed and developing countries where (1) states or armed non-state groups seek to engage in aggression either for selfish gain or for causes they deem virtuous, and (2) such aggressors fail to listen to reason and refuse to cease pursuing their offensive action. If force targets attempt to respond to such aggression challenges simply by issuing coercive threats, these threats will eventually become empty if force is never applied.

Because within and across countries privatized security provision is growing,[68] armed nonstate group power is escalating, instruments of violence are spreading, popular dissatisfaction with ruling regimes is more freely expressed, and public identification with and loyalty to the state is declining, both Western and non-Western states seem likely to continue to use brute force for the foreseeable future. It is understandable that, as an institution's power and ability to be the exclusive provider of essential services wanes, it finds force reliance more essential to guarantee compliance with its wishes. As globalization spreads, eroding traditional state sovereignty, policy makers may perceive that they have to resort to coercion to achieve their political ends because they can no longer count on softer means of persuading targets to comply. With the social contract changing within states between the rulers and the ruled regarding security responsibilities, where citizens want more protection but expect less directly from their national governments, "governance (including the use of force) is increasingly 'multilayered'—that is taking place at the level of the central state but also in other supranational, regional and subnational levels and involving not only state but other actors."[69] The impact of this multilayered governance includes that, when using force, states encounter coercive competitors. Recognizing the foibles of force use can prevent government officials from always choosing to resort to force as their response to challenges and help them realize that this policy instrument might not be less ironclad a solution to authority loss and to threatening global turmoil than they initially think.

## A Messy Global Security Challenge

Insights about global system transformation, national might misperception, and modern coercion conundrum, as well as lessons from recent coercive success and failure patterns, combine to highlight within today's global security setting a unique set of brute force management challenges for political leaders. These officials need to make a renewed attempt to gain a deeper understanding of these challenges and then, in formulating and implementing policies, need to investigate ways to improve their ability to address a complex set of fluid circumstances that make successful force use—involving both effectiveness and legitimacy—quite difficult.

Three critical perceptual gaps between state government perceptions and prevailing realities hamper overcoming these security challenges. The first is an expectations–reality gap, as (1) state perspectives incorporating hopeful political leader security aspirations (based on "wishful thinking"), beliefs that the world is a safer place, assumptions that state force promotes justice, and high anticipated force payoffs contrast with (2) the actual global predicament involving depressing global system security tensions, an unsafe world with justified fears and real threats, ominous global "might makes right" exercise of power (inducing caring about just if someone else is strong enough to stop or punish you for your action), and low global strategic force success. The second is a rhetoric–reality gap, as (1) state perspectives incorporating lip service to an enlightened cooperative world community, spreading morality, democracy, and law (inducing caring about civilized self-restraint and protection of human life), more restricted and constrained coercion norms, and vocal focus on policy legitimacy and justice contrast with (2) the actual global predicament involving frequent national brute force application, global anarchy without common security values, less restricted and constrained coercion practices (often covert), and expedient focus on policy effectiveness and stability. The third is a needs–reality gap, as (1) state perspectives involving the needs for a coercive/noncoercive mix, better handling of cultural differences, strategic transformation, and advance long-range planning contrast with (2) the actual global predicament involving military capacity just to kill and destroy, skills only for temporary repression of disruption, perpetuation of traditional security responses, and outcomes deemed surprising and disappointing.

These gaps' roots are inadequate security comprehension, problematic global security trends, and national security policy rigidity. Inadequate security comprehension involves misunderstanding of protection challenges, misperception of brute force and its effectiveness and legitimacy, and confusion about how to attain force target compliance. Problematic global security trends include the wide but incomplete spread of democratic values, tensions between interdependence and national interest, proliferating armed nonstate force disruption (such as terrorism), rapid diffusion of conventional and unconventional weapons technology across porous borders, and acceleration of low-intensity conflicts.[70] National security policy rigidity involves a stubborn reluctance by state political leaders to reexamine strategic posture in light of an altered security context, low adaptability to changing defense challenges, and continuing force misapplication.

Any improvement in the global management of brute force would thus necessitate identifying ways to create awareness of these gaps and finding ways to reduce and eliminate them by fine-tuning force use to maximize effectiveness and legitimacy in today's world. To overcome existing roadblocks, creative "outside-the-box" thinking is essential—any solution to force management needs to find better unorthodox ways to address these gaps. This kind of thinking involves reassessment of both ongoing security policies and the implications for changes in the ways force is employed in today's world, modifying standard operating procedures and commonly accepted strategic premises along the way. As long as many political leaders controlling state-initiated brute force continue to downplay or ignore the tensions embedded within these gaps, they will continue to experience not-so-surprising futility and failure in long-range strategic force outcomes.

This troubling security predicament has thrown a monkey wrench into widespread force effectiveness notions, anticipating that traditional global coercion practices involving superior force and military victory translate into global strategic success. Many onlookers today continue to expect that brute force use will automatically yield tangible political, economic, and social benefits for force initiators and that political leaders due to their vast experience will apply it expertly. However, when states employ force using means and pursuing ends they think appropriate, they often find that they struggle to achieve long-range objectives. Without the presence of diplomacy and other noncoercive security instruments, the notion that state-initiated brute force alone will be a panacea for all modern security ills makes little sense, as the cases suggest at least for the early twenty-first century. Although current security challenges often demand that force effectiveness focus on durable political, social, and economic stability, in practice military defeat of opposing forces in battle continues to be the principal outcome, without the specter of accomplishing the central underlying strategic mission.

At the same time, the current global security setting has tampered with traditional force legitimacy notions, anticipating that enlightened global norms and global public disapproval constrain violent internal and external disruptions. Many onlookers today continue to expect that coercive disruptions will gradually disappear, national governments will feel increasingly restrained internally and externally in their brute force use, and—when force does rear its ugly head—widespread global condemnation of its inherent injustice will automatically bring it to a halt. However, without the application of counterforce, expecting ruthless and determined terrorists, insurgents, warlords, and rogue states to cease violent disruptive activity makes little sense, as the cases suggest at least for the early twenty-first century. Although the global criticism of brute force has intensified, in practice the result has not been state force restraint, as political leaders seem to have few qualms when employing unilateral coercive means to achieve their ends.

### A Shrinking Brute Force Role

Brute force can indeed work in today's world, albeit under shrinking circumstances. Within the current global security setting, the conditions promoting force success have substantially narrowed compared to those in the past. Although it may be too restrictive to suggest that brute force is "more an insurance policy against gross misbehavior by one of the protagonists than a tool that we can use on a daily basis,"[71] policy makers need to make a greater effort to recognize and operationalize the contracting circumstances conducive to positive force outcomes. Within this limited sphere of appropriate application, "war remains, and will continue to be, a useful, indeed a necessary, instrument of policy."[72]

Brute force has clear limits. Even when force use is appropriate, there is no assurance that it will be used properly; yet at the same time its need to be applied carefully and skillfully does not minimize its importance:

> Hard military threat and use are more difficult to employ today than was the case in the past, in part because of the relatively recent growth in popular respect for universal humanitarian values. However, this greater difficulty does

not mean that military force has lost its distinctive ability to secure some political decisions. The quality of justification required for the use of force has risen, which means that the policy domain for military relevance has diminished, but has by no means disappeared.[73]

Prudence is the key to force effectiveness and legitimacy, and searching for a fixed mission success formula is futile due to the diversity of force challenges.

Given these limits, a brute force cost–benefit ratio reappraisal seems essential. State force initiators need to correct their tendency to overstate their benefits and understate force target benefits, to understate their costs and overstate force target costs, and to assume that winners in coercive confrontations will always gain much more than losers. Over time such distortions can directly undermine sound force use analysis.

State force initiators need to modernize their cost–benefit analysis, recognizing that likely force gains are now smaller and likely losses are now larger than in the past, likely force costs are now larger than in the past and larger than for other policy instruments, and winners in coercive confrontations are now likely to end up with larger obligations than losers. Today force initiators need to recognize the difficulties of completely obliterating threats such that they cannot regenerate. Regarding force benefits, for states the rewards from brute force use are "unduly meager," as "the spoils of victory are not what they once were—for example, territory, gold and other natural resources, and glory—but they are still substantial."[74] Regarding force costs, for states they are very high and seem to be rising rapidly:

> Because military force is apt to be exceptionally costly when compared with the employment of the other grand-strategic instruments of policy, typically today its use requires an unusually strong justification. However, to record this reality is not to argue that such force has lost utility, and still less is it to suggest that military force is yesterday's policy weapon. Nonetheless, it is valid to argue that the use of force is more costly today than was the case in the past.[75]

To tighten their projected outcome assessment, state force initiators need to undertake innovative force evaluation, dispassionate rather than tainted by nationalist emotions and ideologies. Often "plans may be hatched by the cool and calculating, but they are likely to be implemented by the passionate and unpredictable."[76] Political leaders may make force decisions in highly charged emotional contexts, such as in security crises eliciting fear of imminent danger or disputes over something of great value,[77] where perspicacious analysis is unlikely and where more objective appraisal might have taken force use off the table.

This brute force cost–benefit reappraisal requires more careful weighing of means versus ends. Most basically, "the price of success must be weighed against the degree of coercion employed,"[78] for trade-offs between coercion and durable stability may impede goal attainment. Force success occurs only through well-planned and well-executed means–ends calculations involving transparency to relevant parties and accurate high-quality intelligence. Military strategy is, after all, "the art of distributing and applying military means to fulfill the ends of policy."[79] State-initiated force use needs to be restricted to those circumstances where the tangible benefits dramatically exceed the actual costs—"given the big obstacles to manipulating military causes to produce political effects, resort to force should be rare in cases where the estimated balance between benefits and costs is close."[80] Regardless of the size of anticipated force payoffs, "it makes no sense to use force if it cannot realize its purposes at an acceptable cost."[81] If, regardless of overarching strategic purpose, what a society most values is using only the most civilized means, then states should rarely if ever employ force as an instrument of foreign or domestic policy. If, in contrast, what a society most values is promoting national and global security ends, then force should play a key role in states' policy arsenal. Killing people and destroying property are truly horrible, but sometimes protecting the freedom and safety of an endangered population makes this otherwise repulsive carnage necessary.

In sum, for success state-initiated brute force now has to fit within an extremely restrictive set of parameters. Prior to its use, in addition to projected benefits needing to dramatically exceed costs, the critical gaps between expectations and reality, rhetoric and reality, and needs and reality must be substantially reduced. Force initiators must make efforts to minimize their all-too-common misperceptions of both the global security predicament and force targets. Moreover, policy makers need to situate force within a wider range of influence instruments, evaluate its full security implications, expand open discussion about its restricted value, frame it as a transitional short-run local military solution, pursue when feasible multilateral approval and cooperation, and forestall deterioration of regional and global state and human security. During its use, states employing force need to incorporate narrower and more tangible mission goals, focus on vital purposes for which it was designed, increase its staying power, employ all appropriate coercive tools, forge strong national support, foster loyalty among government armed forces, reduce action–reaction cycles, and contain regional contagion effects. In doing so, states must make sure to navigate carefully between the security-oriented Scylla and Charybdis perils of overuse and underuse of force.

In the end, state security policy makers need to resist several common temptations, avoiding succumbing to the many and varied seductive opportunities for force use. Regarding force effectiveness, (1) due to belief that force is decisive, having police and military security forces play a much wider range of roles confronting security challenges, regardless of these forces' capacity to do so well or the availability of less costly policy instruments; (2) due to longstanding Westphalian traditions, maintaining the conviction that states always have the preponderance of power in confrontations and that resistance is futile, regardless of the opposition's popularity; and (3) due to blind faith in technology, striving constantly to acquire advanced weaponry to confront enemies, regardless of these violence instruments' appropriateness for managing existing threats. Regarding force legitimacy, (1) due to unawareness of diversity in fairness notions, portraying one's force use as an absolute instrument of justice, regardless of how unconvincing this portrayal is may be to domestic citizens or foreign onlookers; (2) due to (again) persistent Westphalian traditions, assuming that state force use will universally be seen as morally acceptable, regardless of possible objections emanating from those with divergent value systems; and (3) due to the premise that cultural differences affecting basic human desires are insignificant, believing that everyone else wants the same security ends you want, regardless of difficulties in transformation.

## CONCLUDING THOUGHTS

Where resorting to force satisfies "the most stringent criteria of necessity and morality,"[82] and where government leaders possess "greater caution and selectivity in using force as well as greater attention paid to the potential unintended repercussions of military action,"[83] the net security impact can be positive. Brute force could be undertaken in a manner minimizing long-term regional and global turmoil and mass human insecurity, not just maximized for short-term local national interests; pursuing clear ends matching the strengths of military and police power, not just indiscriminately oriented toward trendy aims for which force is usually inappropriate; incorporating sensitively cultural differences and changing challenges, not just implemented in a fixed formulaic manner; reflecting full commitment with robust planning for a wide range of security contingencies, not just pursued impulsively or halfheartedly envisioning one type of outcome; and helping directly to remedy underlying tensions, not just aimed at Band-Aid superficial suppression of immediate disruption. State-initiated internal and external force could be more discriminating, coherent, and comprehensible, effective and legitimate in the eyes of both domestic and international observers, with the long-run aim of reduced frustration and anger surrounding the coercion conundrum paradoxes. Citizens' security expectations of their governments' ability and willingness to protect them could then become more realistic; and government policy makers could experience greater force predictability and fewer disappointments, enhancing opportunities for long-term global peace and durable political, economic, and social stability. In the end, chances could rise that force would remain relevant in the contemporary global security setting, "capable of coping with threats from hostile states as well as non-state actors."[84]

Brute force can be strategically and surgically applied, rather than implemented in the primitive, unrestrained, and barbaric manner witnessed all too often throughout world history. To apply this tool in this way, states should not use force just because they believe that (1) they have the capability to do so, (2) force might achieve their designated objectives, or (3) force might somehow minimize loss of life. The calculus for appropriate force application is necessarily more complex, involving the right combination of force initiator and force target attributes giving brute force precisely the kind of unique comparative advantage to accomplish the designated mission—often in combination with other policy tools—under appropriate circumstances.

If executed properly within suggested parameters, then—with sufficient time and effort—state-initiated brute force can constitute a central element to convert domestic and international fear, hatred, and anger into trust, calm, and cooperation:

> We used "brute military force" in WWII against Germany and Japan to a far greater extent than anything either Afghanistan or Pakistan has seen to date. And yet at the end of the war what we got was "long term peace and stability" with these countries. In fact, we remain allies and friends to this day. It is quite possible to have "brute military force" and "long term peace and stability" at the same time with the same combatants.[85]

If national political and military leaders become more adaptable and open to reexamining their central strategic assumptions,[86] then force use might avoid leaving a chaotic confounding cauldron of carnage in its wake. Although violence and justice are usually incompatible, highly selective and constrained brute force use can occasionally be surprisingly pivotal in fostering the emergence of a stable and progressive world order.

**REFERENCE MATTER**

# NOTES

## Chapter 1

1. Richard K. Betts, *American Force: Dangers, Delusions, and Dilemmas in National Security* (New York: Columbia University Press, 2012), p. 4.

2. Jan Angstrom and Isabelle Duyvesteyn, "War, What Is It Good For?" in Jan Angstrom and Isabelle Duyvesteyn, eds., *Modern War and the Utility of Force: Challenges, Methods and Strategy* (New York: Routledge, 2010), p. 4; and Richard N. Haass, *Intervention: The Use of American Military Force in the Post-Cold War World* (Washington, DC: Carnegie Endowment for International Peace, 1994), p. 1.

3. Robert Jervis, *Force in Our Times* (New York: Columbia University Saltzman Working Paper #15, July 2011), p. 3.

4. Robert J. Art and Kenneth N. Waltz, eds., *The Use of Force: Military Power and International Politics*, 7th edition (Lanham, MD: Rowman & Littlefield, 2009), p. 1; and Micah Zenko and Michael A. Cohen, "Clear and Present Safety: The United States Is More Secure Than Washington Thinks," *Foreign Affairs*, 91 (March/April 2012), p. 79.

5. Robert J. Art, "American Foreign Policy and the Fungibility of Force," *Security Studies*, 5 (Summer 1996), p. 7.

6. Vladimir V. Putin, "A Plea for Caution from Russia," *New York Times* (September 11, 2013); retrieved from www.nytimes.com/2013/09/12/opinion/putin-plea-for-caution-from-russia-on-syria.html?_r=0.

7. F. H. Hinsley, "The Rise and Fall of the Modern International System," *Review of International Studies*, 8 (January 1982), p. 1.

8. Art, "American Foreign Policy and the Fungibility of Force," p. 41.

9. Colin S. Gray, *Fighting Talk: Forty Maxims on War, Peace, and Strategy* (Westport, CT: Praeger Security International, 2007), p. 9.

10. Barry M. Blechman and Stephen S. Kaplan, *Force without War: U.S. Armed Forces as a Political Instrument* (Washington, DC: Brookings Institution, 1978), p. 12.

11. Seyom Brown, *The Illusion of Control: Force and Foreign Policy in the 21st Century* (Washington DC: Brookings Institution Press, 2003), p. 5.

12. See Joseph S. Nye Jr., *The Paradox of American Power: Why the World's Only Superpower Can't Go It Alone* (New York: Oxford University Press, 2002), p. 4; Joseph S. Nye Jr., *Soft Power: The Means to Success in World Politics* (New York: Public Affairs, 2004), p. 5; and Kurt M. Campbell and Michael E. O'Hanlon, *Hard Power: The New Politics of National Security* (New York: Basic Books, 2006), p. 7.

13. Rupert Smith, *The Utility of Force: The Art of War in the Modern World* (New York: Vintage, 2008), p. 8.

14. Carl Von Clausewitz, *On War* (New York: Penguin Books, 1968), chapter 1.

15. Betts, *American Force*, p. 12; and Smith, *The Utility of Force*, pp. 27–28.

16. Colin S. Gray, *Another Bloody Century: Future Warfare* (London: Weidenfeld & Nicolson, 2005), p. 355.

17. *Sustaining U.S. Global Leadership: Priorities for 21st Century Defense* (Washington, DC: U.S. Department of Defense, January 2012), p. 4.

18. Peter Viggo Jakobsen, "Coercive Diplomacy," in Alan Collins, ed., *Contemporary Security Studies*, 2nd edition (New York: Oxford University Press, 2010), p. 286.

19. Peter G. Stillman, "The Concept of Legitimacy," *Polity*, 7 (Autumn 1974), pp. 32–56.

20. See, for example, Roy Godson and Richard Shultz, *Adapting America's Security Paradigm and Security Agenda* (Washington, DC: National Strategy Information Center, 2010), pp. 34–35.

21. Andrew Hurrell, "Legitimacy and the Use of Force: Can the Circle Be Squared?" in David Armstrong, Theo Farrell, and Bice Maiguashca, eds., *Force and Legitimacy in World Politics* (New York: Cambridge University Press, 2005), p. 15.

## Chapter 2

1. See, for example, John Rapley, "The New Middle Ages," *Foreign Affairs*, 85 (May/June 2006), p. 102; Robert Mandel, *Deadly Transfers and the Global Playground: Transnational Security Threats in a Disorderly World* (Westport, CT: Praeger Publishers, 1999), pp. 12–13; Anthony Burke, *Postmodern Conflict: Global Security and Asymmetric War* (forthcoming), chapter 1; Sean Kay, *Global Security in the Twenty-First Century: The Quest for Power and the Search for Peace*, 2nd edition (New York: Rowman & Littlefield Publishers, 2012), p. 241; Rod Thornton, *Asymmetric Warfare: Threat and Response in the Twenty-First Century* (Cambridge, UK: Polity Press, 2007), p. 1; Phil Williams, "New Context, Smart Enemies," in Robert J. Bunker, ed., *Non-State Threats and Future Wars* (Portland, OR: Frank Cass Publishers, 2003), pp. viii, x; Rob

de Wijk, "The Limits of Military Power," *Washington Quarterly*, 25 (2001), pp. 75–92; Paul Rogers, *Losing Control: Global Security in the 21st Century*, 2nd edition (London: Pluto Press, 2002), p. 119; and Robert Mandel, *Global Security Upheaval: Armed Non-State Groups Usurping State Stability Functions* (Stanford, CA: Stanford University Press, 2013), chapter 4.

2. Robert Mandel, *Armies without States: The Privatization of Security* (Boulder, CO: Lynne Rienner Publishers, 2002), p. 7.

3. Phil Williams, "Strategy for a New World: Combating Terrorism and Transnational Organized Crime," in John Baylis, James L. Wirtz, Colin S. Gray, and Eliot Cohen, eds., *Strategy in the Contemporary World*, 2nd edition (New York: Oxford University Press, 2007), p. 193.

4. Colin S. Gray, *Hard and Soft Power: The Utility of Military Force as an Instrument of Policy in the 21st Century* (Carlisle, PA: Strategic Studies Institute, April 2011), pp. 21–22.

5. Seyom Brown, *The Illusion of Control: Force and Foreign Policy in the 21st Century* (Washington DC: Brookings Institution Press, 2003), p. 143.

6. Robert O. Keohane and Joseph S. Nye, *Power and Interdependence*, 2nd edition (New York: Harper Collins Publishers, 1989), pp. 21–29.

7. See, for example, Peter Viggo Jakobsen, "Pushing the Limits of Military Coercion Theory," *International Studies Perspectives*, 12 (2011), p. 166; Colin S. Gray, *Modern Strategy* (New York: Oxford University Press, 1999): p. 99; Dominic D. P. Johnson and Dominic Tierney, "The Rubicon Theory of War: How the Path to Conflict Reaches the Point of No Return," *International Security*, 36 (Summer 2011), pp. 8–9, 15; Rodney Barker, *Making Enemies* (New York: Palgrave Macmillan, 2007), pp. 2, 74–75; and Robert Mandel, *The Meaning of Military Victory* (Boulder, CO: Lynne Rienner, 2006), chapter 4.

8. Robert Jervis, *Perception and Misperception in International Politics* (Princeton, NJ: Princeton University Press, 1976), chapter iv; and Klaus Knorr, "Threat Perception," in Klaus Knorr, ed., *Historical Dimensions of National Security Problems* (Lawrence: University Press of Kansas, 1976), p. 113.

9. Robert Mandel, "Adversaries Expectations and Desires about War Termination," in Stephen C. Cimbala, ed., *Strategic War Termination* (Westport, CT: Praeger Publishers, 1986): p. 177.

10. Ralph K. White, *Nobody Wanted War: Misperception in Vietnam and Other Wars* (Garden City, NY: Doubleday and Company, 1970), pp. 303–305.

11. William Eckhardt, "Civilian Deaths in Wartime," *Bulletin of Peace Proposals* 20 (1989), p. 90.

12. Troy S. Thomas, Stephen D. Kiser, and William D. Casebeer, *Warlords Rising: Confronting Violent Non-State Actors* (Lanham, MD: Lexington Books, 2005), p. 22.

13. J. F. C. Fuller, *Armament and History: The Influence of Armament on History from the Dawn of Classical Warfare to the End of the Second World War* (New York: Da Capo Press, 1998), p. ix.

14. John T. Correll, "Casualties," *Air Force Magazine* 86 (June 2003), p. 51.

15. Ibid., pp. 51–52.

16. Raymond Fisman and Edward Miguel, *Economic Gangsters: Corruption, Violence, and the Poverty of Nations* (Princeton, NJ: Princeton University Press, 2008), pp. 114, 136.

17. Steven Pinker, *The Better Angels of Our Nature: Why Violence Has Declined* (New York: Viking, 2011). See also John Mueller, *The Remnants of War* (Ithaca, NY: Cornell University Press, 2004).

18. Dan Smith, *The Penguin State of the World Atlas*, ninth edition (New York: Penguin Books, 2012), p. 56.

19. Joshua S. Goldstein, *Winning the War on War: The Decline of Armed Conflict Worldwide* (New York: Plume, 2012), p. 4.

20. Smith, *The Penguin State of the World Atlas*, 9th edition, p. 56.

21. Goldstein, *Winning the War on War*, p. 4; and Smith, *The Penguin State of the World Atlas*, 9th edition, p. 56.

22. Goldstein, *Winning the War on War*, pp. 5–6.

23. Pinker, *The Better Angels of Our Nature*, chapter 3.

24. Martha Finnemore, *The Purpose of Intervention: Changing Beliefs about the Use of Force* (Ithaca, NY: Cornell University Press, 2003), p. 141.

25. F. S. Northedge, "The Resort to Arms," in F. S. Northedge, ed., *The Use of Force in International Relations* (New York: The Free Press, 1974), p. 31.

26. Robert Jervis, *Force in Our Times* (New York: Columbia University Saltzman Working Paper #15, July 2011), p. 13.

27. Emil J. Kirchner, "Regional and Global Security: Changing Threats and Institutional Responses," in Emil J. Kirchner and James Sperling, eds., *Global Security Governance: Competing Perceptions of Security in the 21st Century* (New York: Routledge, 2007), p. 3.

28. Smith, *The Penguin State of the World Atlas*, 9th edition, p. 62.

29. Micah Zenko, *Between Threats and War: U.S. Discrete Military Operations in the Post–Cold War World* (Stanford, CA: Stanford University Press, 2010), p. 2; and Brown, *The Illusion of Control*, p. 1.

30. Brown, *The Illusion of Control*, p. 1.

31. Benaisha Daruwalla, "The Wars in Afghanistan and Iraq and US Use of Military Force" (February 18, 2012); available at www.e-ir.info/2012/02/18/what-impact-have-the-wars-in-afghanistan-and-iraq-had-on-the-willingness-to-utilise-military-force-to-advance-us-foreign-policy-objectives/.

32. Brown, *The Illusion of Control*, p. 149.

33. Gregory D. Saxton, "Repression, Grievances, Mobilization, and Rebellion: A New Test of Gurr's Model of Ethnopolitical Rebellion," *International Interactions*, 31 (2005), p. 1.

34. Aziz Choudry, "Military-Industrial Complex and Impacts on the Third World" (November 25, 2008); available at www.aprnet.org/journals-a-policy-papers/volume-16-june-2008/366-military-industrial-complex-and-impacts-on-the-third-world.

35. Alexander Wendt and Michael Barnett, "Dependent State Formation and Third World Militarization," *Review of International Studies*, 19 (1993), p. 342.

36. "What's Your Opinion on the Boston Bombing?" (April 2013); available at http://au.answers.yahoo.com/question/index?qid=20130416103952AAO2t7O.

37. Clark Kent Ervin, *Open Target: Where America Is Vulnerable to Attack* (New York: Palgrave Macmillan, 2006), pp. 24–25.

38. Robert Mandel, *Global Threat: Target-Centered Assessment and Management* (Westport, CT: Praeger Security International, 2008), p. 25.

39. Robert Mandel, *Security, Strategy, and the Quest for Bloodless War* (Boulder, CO: Lynne Rienner Publishers, 2004).

40. *SIPRI Yearbook* (Stockholm: Stockholm International Peace Research Institute, 2002); available at http://projects.sipri.se/milex/mex_trends.html.

41. Smith, *The Penguin State of the World Atlas*, 9th edition, p. 62.

42. William Flavin, "Planning for Conflict Termination and Post-Conflict Success," *Parameters*, 33 (Autumn 2003), p. 96.

43. Wendt and Barnett, "Dependent State Formation and Third World Militarization," p. 322.

44. Paul Collier, "War and Military Expenditures in Developing Countries," *Economics of Peace and Security Journal*, 1 (2006), p. 10.

45. Ibid., p. 10; and Wendt and Barnett, "Dependent State Formation and Third World Militarization," p. 338.

46. Wendt and Barnett, "Dependent State Formation and Third World Militarization," p. 338.

47. Collier, "War and Military Expenditures in Developing Countries," p. 10.

48. Zeev Maoz, *Paradoxes of War* (Boston: Unwin Hyman, 1990), p. 312.

49. Benjamin O. Fordham, "A Very Sharp Sword: The Influence of Military Capabilities on American Decisions to Use Force," *Journal of Conflict Resolution*, 48 (October 2004), p. 654.

50. Mandel, *Armies without States*, p. 88.

51. Michael T. Klare, "The Deadly Connection: Paramilitary Bands, Small Arms Diffusion, and State Failure," in Robert I. Rotberg, ed., *When States Fail: Causes and Consequences* (Princeton, NJ: Princeton University Press, 2004), p. 119.

52. Hassan Vejdani, "Force Has Lost Its Efficacy in International Relations" (May 21, 2012); available at http://www.iranreview.org/content/Documents/Force_Has_Lost_its_Efficacy_in_International_Relations.htm.

53. Mark P. Sullivan, *The Mechanism for Strategic Coercion* (Maxwell Air Force Base, AL: Air University Press, April 1995), p. 5.

54. Anthony Burke, "Paradoxes of Force and Security: Postmodern Conflict" (December 9, 2010); available at http://worldthoughtworldpolitics.wordpress.com/2010/12/09/paradoxes-of-force-and-security/.

55. Maoz, *Paradoxes of War*, p. 253.

56. Dominic D. P. Johnson, *Overconfidence and War* (Cambridge, MA: Harvard University Press, 2004), pp. 4, 36.

57. Robert Jervis, "Theories of War in an Era of Leading-Power Peace," *American Political Science Review*, 96 (March 2002), p. 8.

58. Jan Angstrom and Isabelle Duyvesteyn, "War, What Is It Good For?," in Jan Angstrom and Isabelle Duyvesteyn, eds., *Modern War and the Utility of Force: Challenges, Methods and Strategy* (New York: Routledge, 2010), p. 7.

59. Colin S. Gray, *Another Bloody Century: Future Warfare* (London: Weidenfeld & Nicolson, 2005), p. 355.

60. Burke, *Postmodern Conflict: Global Security and Asymmetric War*, chapter 1.

61. Jakobsen, "Pushing the Limits of Military Coercion Theory," p. 166.

62. Zenko, *Between Threats and War*, p. 3.

63. Burke, "Paradoxes of Force and Security."

64. Burke, *Postmodern Conflict*, chapter 1.

65. Leonard Wibberley, *The Mouse That Roared* (Boston: Little, Brown, & Co., 1955).

66. Richard Hobbs, *The Myth of Victory: What Is Victory in War?* (Boulder, CO: Westview Press, 1979): p. 475.

67. Maoz, *Paradoxes of War*, p. 253.

68. U.S. Army and U.S. Marine Corps, *The U.S. Army/Marine Corps Counterinsurgency Field Manual* (Chicago: University of Chicago Press, 2007), pp. 47–51.

69. Jeffrey Record, *Beating Goliath: Why Insurgents Win* (Washington, DC: Potomac Books, 2007), pp. xii, 132.

70. Colin S. Gray, *Fighting Talk: Forty Maxims on War, Peace, and Strategy* (Westport, CT: Praeger Security International, 2007), p. 109.

71. Anna Simons, "Soft War = Smart War? Think Again," (Philadelphia, PA: Foreign Policy Research Institute E-Notes, April 14, 2012), p. 5; available at www.fpri.org/enotes/2012/201204.simons.soft-war-smart-war.html.

72. Ibid.

73. Colin Powell, *My American Journey* (New York: Random House, 1995), p. 576.

74. Richard Norton-Taylor, "The Futility of Force," *Guardian* (July 31, 2006); available at www.guardian.co.uk/commentisfree/2006/aug/01/iraq.foreignpolicy.

75. See Mandel, *The Meaning of Military Victory*, chapters 1–2 and 5–7.

76. Mueller, *The Remnants of War*, pp. 149–151.

77. Stephen D. Biddle, *Military Power: Explaining Victory and Defeat in Modern Battle* (Princeton, NJ: Princeton University Press, 2004), chapter 1; and Victor Davis Hanson, *Why the West Has Won: Carnage and Culture from Solamis to Vietnam* (London: Faber and Faber, 2001).

78. Dominic Tierney and Dominic Johnson, "Winning and Losing the War on Terror" (Honolulu, HI: Paper presented at the annual meeting of the International Studies Association, March 2005), pp. 36–37.

79. Page Fortna, "Where Have All the Victories Gone? War Outcomes in Historical Perspective" (Honolulu, HI: Paper presented at the annual meeting of the International Studies Association, March 2005), p. 32.

80. Mandel, *The Meaning of Military Victory*.

81. Record, *Beating Goliath*, p. 109.

82. Colin S. Gray, *Defining and Achieving Decisive Victory* (Carlyle, PA: U.S. Army War College Strategic Studies Institute, April 2002), pp. 21–23.

83. Center for Strategic and International Studies and Association of the United States Army, *Meeting the Challenges of Governance and Participation in Post-Conflict Settings* (Washington, DC: Center for Strategic and International Studies and Association of the United States Army monograph, July 8, 2002), p. 7.

84. Andrew M. Mack, "Why Big Nations Lose Small Wars," *World Politics*, 27 (January 1975), pp. 175–200; and Ivan Arreguin-Toft, "How the Weak Win Wars: A Theory of Asymmetric Conflict," *International Security*, 26 (Summer 2001), pp. 93–128.

85. Stuart Albert and Edward C. Luck, eds., *On the Endings of Wars* (Port Washington, NY: Kennikat Press, 1980), p. 243.

86. Carl Osgood, "Bush Administration's Strategic Policy Creates a Conundrum for U.S. Military." *Executive Intelligence Review*, 32 (May 20, 2005); available at www.larouchepub.com/other/2005/3220war_games.html.

87. Burke, *Postmodern Conflict*, chapter 1.

88. Anthony Zinni, "Forum 2003: Understanding What Victory Is," *Proceedings of the United States Naval Institute*, 129 (October 2003), p. 32.

89. Wendela C. Moore, "Stability Operations: A Core Warfighting Capacity?" (2003), p. 10; available at www.ndu.edu/library/n4/n03AMooreStability.pdf.

90. Adam Yarmolinsky, "Professional Military Perspectives on War Termination," in Stuart Albert and Edward C. Luck, eds., *On the Endings of Wars* (Port Washington, NY: Kennikat Press, 1980),

91. Matthias Stiefel, "Rebuilding after War: Lessons from WSP" (Geneva, Switzerland: War-Torn Societies Project, 1999); available at http://wsp.dataweb.ch/wsp_publication/rebu-05.htm.

92. James K. Bishop, "Combat Role Strains Relations between America's Military and its NGOs" (Summer 2003), p. 28; available at www.humanitarian-review.org/upload/pdf/BishopEnglishFinal.pdf.

93. Center for Strategic and International Studies and Association of the United States Army, *Meeting the Challenges of Governance and Participation in Post-Conflict Settings*, p. 1.

94. Richard N. Haass, "Regime Change and Its Limits," *Foreign Affairs*, 84 (July/August 2005), p. 70.

95. Stiefel, "Rebuilding after War."

96. Colin Powell, as quoted in Jeffrey Record, "Back to the Weinberger-Powell Doctrine?," *Strategic Studies Quarterly* (Fall 2007), p. 83.

97. Record, *Beating Goliath*, p. 1.

98. Kori Schake, "The Limits of Limited Force," April 19, 2011; available at www.advancingafreesociety.org/2011/04/19/the-limits-of-limited-force/.

99. Richard N. Haass, *Intervention: The Use of American Military Force in the Post-Cold War World* (Washington, DC: Carnegie Endowment for International Peace, 1994), pp. 72–73.

100. Richard K. Betts, *American Force: Dangers, Delusions, and Dilemmas in National Security* (New York: Columbia University Press, 2012), pp. 152–153.

101. Alexander L. George, "The Role of Force in Diplomacy: Continuing Dilemma for U.S. Foreign Policy"; available at www.pbs.org/wgbh/pages/frontline/shows/military/force/article.html.

102. Haass, *Intervention*, p. 91; and Betts, *American Force*, pp. 297–299.

103. Haass, *Intervention*, p. 94.

104. See Mandel, *Security, Strategy, and the Quest for Bloodless War*; and Charles Knight, Lutz Unterseher, and Carl Conetta, "Reflections on Information War, Casualty Aversion, and Military Research and Development after the Gulf War and the Demise of the Soviet Union," available at www.comw.org/pda/0003refl.html.

105. Colin S. Gray, "The American Way of War: Critique and Implications," in Anthony D. McIvor, ed., *Rethinking the Principles of War* (Annapolis, MD: Naval Institute Press, 2005), pp. 27–33.

106. Scott Sigmund Gartner and Gary M. Segura, "War, Casualties, and Public Opinion," *Journal of Conflict Resolution* 42 (June 1998), p. 279.

107. Peter D. Feaver and Christopher Gelpi, *Choosing Your Battles: American Civil–Military Relations and the Use of Force* (Princeton, NJ: Princeton University Press, 2004), pp. 151–152.

108. Edward N. Luttwak, "Where Are the Great Powers? At Home with the Kids," *Foreign Affairs* 73 (July/August 1994), p. 25.

109. Michael Sheehan, "Military Security," in Alan Collins, ed., *Contemporary Security Studies*, 2nd edition (New York: Oxford University Press, 2010), p. 182.

110. Max Boot, "The Evolution of Irregular War," *Foreign Affairs*, 92 (March/April 2013), p. 113.

111. Gil Merom, *How Democracies Lose Small Wars: State, Society, and the Failures of France in Algeria, Israel in Lebanon, and the United States in Vietnam* (New York: Cambridge University Press, 2003), pp. 19–21, 230–231.

112. Haass, *Intervention*, p. 7.

113. Record, *Beating Goliath*, p. 134.

114. James David Meernik, *The Political Use of Military Force in US Foreign Policy* (Burlington, VT: Ashgate Publishing Company, 2004), p. 242.

115. Edward N. Luttwak, *On the Meaning of Victory: Essays on Strategy* (New York: Simon and Schuster, 1986), p. 289.

116. "Still No. 1," *Economist* (June 30, 2007), pp. 11–12.

117. Haass, *Intervention*, p. 81.

118. Norton-Taylor, "The Futility of Force."

119. Forrest E. Morgan and others, *Dangerous Thresholds: Managing Escalation in the 21st Century* (Santa Monica, CA: The RAND Corporation, 2008), p. 9.

120. Mandel, *Global Threat*, pp. 108–110; and Dean G. Pruitt, "Definition of the Situation as a Determinant of International Action," in Herbert C. Kelman, ed., *International Behavior: A Social-Psychological Analysis* (New York: Holt, Rinehart and Winston, 1965), p. 396.

121. Brown, *The Illusion of Control*, p. 5.

122. Karla Cunningham, "What Is So Extreme about Extreme Violence? Explaining the Escalation in Extreme Violence by Non-State Actors" (Pittsburgh, PA: Presentation at the Conference on "Violent Armed Groups: A Global Challenge," September 16–17, 2010).

123. Barry Buzan, *People, States and Fear: An Agenda for International Security Studies in the Post-Cold War Era*, 2nd edition (Boulder, CO: Lynne Rienner Publishers, 1991), p. 140.

124. Jennifer M. Hazen, "From Social Movement to Armed Group: A Case Study from Nigeria," in Keith Krause, ed., *Armed Groups and Contemporary Conflicts: Challenging the Weberian State* (New York: Routledge, 2010), p. 96.

125. Mandel, *Global Security Upheaval*, chapter 7.

126. Simons, "Soft War = Smart War? Think Again," p. 5.

127. Isabelle Duyvesteyn, "Great Expectations: The Use of Armed Force to Combat Terrorism," in Angstrom and Duyvesteyn, eds., *Modern War and the Utility of Force*, p. 76.

128. Laura K. Donahue, "In the Name of National Security: US Counterterrorism Measures 1960–2000," *Terrorism and Political Violence*, 13 (2001), p. 18.

129. L. Rowell Huesmann, "The Contagion of Violence: The Extent, the Processes, and the Outcomes" (Washington, DC: Address delivered at the National Academies of Sciences' Institute of Medicine's *Global Forum on Violence*, April 29, 2011), p. 1; available at http://rcgd.isr.umich.edu/aggr/articles/Huesmann/2011.Huesmann.The%20Contagion%20of%20Violence.NAS%20Press.pdf.

130. Ibid.

131. Manus I. Midlarsky, Martha Crenshaw, and Fumihiko Yoshida, "Why Violence Spreads: The Contagion of International Terrorism," *International Studies Quarterly*, 24 (June 1980), p. 263.

132. Nadine Ansorg, "How Does Militant Violence Diffuse in Regions? Regional Conflict Systems in International Relations and Peace and Conflict Studies," *International Journal of Conflict and Violence*, 5 (2011), p. 181.

133. Stiefel, "Rebuilding after War."

134. Ansorg, "How Does Militant Violence Diffuse in Regions?," p. 179.

## Chapter 3

1. Peter Bergen and Ketherine Tiedemann, "Washington's Phantom War: The Effects of the U.S. Drone Strike Program in Pakistan," *Foreign Affairs*, 90 (July/August 2011), pp. 12–13; Andrew C. Orr, "Unmanned, Unprecedented, and Unresolved: The Status of American Drone Strikes in Pakistan Under International Law," *Cornell International Law Journal*, 44 (2011), p. 730; and John Walcott and Tony Cappacio, "Drone Strike That Kills Al-Qaeda Leader Leaves Questions," *Bloomberg Business Week* (June 5, 2012), available at www.businessweek.com/news/2012-06-05/drone-strike-that-kills-al-qaeda-leader-leaves-questions.

2. Greg Miller, "Under Obama, an Emerging Global Apparatus for Drone Killing," *Washington Post* (December 27, 2011); available at www.washingtonpost.com/national/national-security/under-obama-an-emerging-global-apparatus-for-drone-killing/2011/12/13/gIQANPdILP_story.html?hpid=z1.

3. Daniel Byman, "Why Drones Work: The Case for Washington's Weapon of Choice," *Foreign Affairs*, 92 (July/August 2013), pp. 32–33.

4. Miller, "Under Obama, an Emerging Global Apparatus for Drone Killing."

5. Jonathan Masters, "Targeted Killings," *Council on Foreign Relations.* (April 30, 2012); available at www.cfr.org/counterterrorism/targeted-killings/p9627.

6. Ibid.

7. Benaisha Daruwalla, "The Wars in Afghanistan and Iraq and US Use of Military Force" (February 18, 2012); available at www.e-ir.info/2012/02/18/what-impact-have-the-wars-in-afghanistan-and-iraq-had-on-the-willingness-to-utilise-military-force-to-advance-us-foreign-policy-objectives/.

8. Boyle, "The Costs and Consequences of Drone Warfare," p. 2.

9. Ibid., p. 3.

10. Masters, "Targeted Killings."

11. Ibid.

12. Bergen and Tiedemann, "Washington's Phantom War," p. 15; and Jane Mayer, "The Predator War," *The New Yorker* (October 26, 2009), p. 45.

13. Walcott and Cappacio, "Drone Strike That Kills Al-Qaeda Leader Leaves Questions."

14. Byman, "Why Drones Work," p. 32.

15. Bergen and Tiedemann, "Washington's Phantom War," pp. 16–17.

16. Ibid., p. 12.

17. Byman, "Why Drones Work," pp. 32–35.

18. Mayer, "The Predator War," p. 41.

19. Audrey Kurth Cronin, "Why Drones Fail: When Tactics Drive Strategy," *Foreign Affairs*, 92 (July/August 2013), pp. 44–45, 51.

20. Walcott and Cappacio, "Drone Strike That Kills Al-Qaeda Leader Leaves Questions."

21. Peter Bergen and Katherine Tiedemann, *The Year of the Drone: An Analysis of U.S. Drone Strikes in Pakistan, 2004–2010* (Washington, DC: New America Foundation, February 24, 2010), p. 4.

22. Masters, "Targeted Killings."

23. Bergen and Tiedemann, "Washington's Phantom War," p. 14.

24. Masters, "Targeted Killings."

25. Boyle, "The Costs and Consequences of Drone Warfare," p. 3.

26. Walcott and Cappacio, "Drone Strike That Kills Al-Qaeda Leader Leaves Questions."

27. Masters, "Targeted Killings."

28. Miller, "Under Obama, an Emerging Global Apparatus for Drone Killing."

29. Jack Goldsmith, "Fire when Ready," *Foreign Policy* (March 19, 2012); available at www.foreignpolicy.com/articles/2012/03/19/fire_when_ready?page=full.

30. Masters, "Targeted Killings."

31. Miller, "Under Obama, an Emerging Global Apparatus for Drone Killing."

32. Goldsmith, "Fire when Ready."

33. Walcott and Cappacio, "Drone Strike That Kills Al-Qaeda Leader Leaves Questions."

34. Masters, "Targeted Killings."

35. Shuja Nawaz, "Drone Attacks inside Pakistan," *Georgetown Journal of International Affairs*, 12 (Summer/Fall 2011), p. 80.

36. Masters, "Targeted Killings."

37. Walcott and Cappacio, "Drone Strike That Kills Al-Qaeda Leader Leaves Questions."

38. Ibid.

39. Peter Bergen and Jennifer Rowland, "CIA Drone War in Pakistan in Sharp Decline," *CNN* (Cable News Network), (March 28, 2012); available at http://edition .cnn.com/2012/03/27/opinion/bergen-drone-decline/index.html?iref=allsearch.

40. Nawaz, "Drone Attacks inside Pakistan," p. 79.

41. Ibid., p. 83.

42. Pir Zubair Shah, "My Drone War," *Foreign Policy* (March/April 2012); available at www.foreignpolicy.com/articles/2012/02/27/my_drone_war.

43. David Kilcullen and Andrew McDonald Exum, "Death from Above, Outrage down Below," *New York Times* (May 16, 2009); available at www.nytimes.com/ 2009/05/17/opinion/17exum.html?pagewanted=all.

44. Paul Harris, "Drone Attacks Create Terrorist Safe Havens, Warns Former CIA Official," *Guardian* (June 5, 2012); available at www.guardian.co.uk/world/2012/ jun/05/al-qaida-drone-attacks-too-broad.

45. Nawaz, "Drone Attacks Inside Pakistan," p. 80.

46. Byman, "Why Drones Work," p. 38.

47. Orr, "Unmanned, Unprecedented, and Unresolved," p. 731.

48. Walcott and Cappacio, "Drone Strike That Kills Al-Qaeda Leader Leaves Questions."

49. Masters, "Targeted Killings."

50. Miller, "Under Obama, an Emerging Global Apparatus for Drone Killing."

51. Masters, "Targeted Killings."

52. Goldsmith, "Fire when Ready."

53. Masters, "Targeted Killings"; and Mandel, *Global Security Upheaval.*

54. Miller, "Under Obama, an Emerging Global Apparatus for Drone Killing."

55. Masters, "Targeted Killings."

56. Goldsmith, "Fire when Ready."

57. Nawaz, "Drone Attacks inside Pakistan," p. 86.

58. Rod Nordland and Salman Masood, "Recent Drone Strikes Strain U.S. Ties with Afghanistan and Pakistan," *New York Times* (November 29, 2013); available at www.nytimes.com/2013/11/30/world/asia/drone-strike-pakistan.html.

59. Leila Hudson, Colin S. Owens, and Matt Flannes, "Drone Warfare: Blowback from the New American Way of War," *Middle East Policy,* 28 (Fall 2011), pp. 122–123, 125.

60. Masters, "Targeted Killings"; and Boyle, "The Costs and Consequences of Drone Warfare," p. 22.

61. Micah Zenko, "10 Things You Didn't Know about Drones," *Foreign Policy* (March/April 2012); available at www.foreignpolicy.com/articles/2012/02/27/10_things_you_didnt_know_about_drones.

62. David Eshel,. "Pillar of Deterrence," *Aviation Week & Space Technology*, 175 (February 25, 2013), p. DT6.

63. Boyle, "The Costs and Consequences of Drone Warfare," p. 1.

64. Mayer, "The Predator War," p. 41.

65. Richard L. Armitage, Samuel R. Berger, and Daniel S. Markey, *U.S. Strategy for Pakistan and Afghanistan* (New York: Council on Foreign Relations Independent Task Force Report #65, 2010), p. 24.

66. Barnett R. Rubin and Ahmed Rashid, "From Great Game to Grand Bargain: Ending Chaos in Afghanistan and Pakistan," *Foreign Affairs*, 87 (November/December 2008), pp. 35–36.

67. Anthony Gregory, *What Price War? Afghanistan, Iraq, and the Costs of Conflict* (Oakland, CA: The Independent Institute, June 2011), p. 4; available at www.independent.org/pdf/policy_reports/2011-05-31-what_price_war.pdf.

68. Steve Coll, "U.S.–Taliban Talks," *New Yorker* (February 28, 2011); available at www.newyorker.com/talk/comment/2011/02/28/110228taco_talk_coll.

69. Jayshree Bajoria, "Is Peace with the Taliban Possible?," *Council on Foreign Relations* (January 13, 2012); available at www.cfr.org/afghanistan/peace-taliban-possible/p27064.

70. Dennis M. Crowley, "The 12-Year War: 73% of U.S. Casualties in Afghanistan on Obama's Watch," *CNS News* (September 11, 2013); available at http://cnsnews.com/news/article/dennis-m-crowley/12-year-war-73-us-casualties-afghanistan-obamas-watch.

71. Ahmed Rashid, *Taliban: Militant Islam, Oil and Fundamentalism in Central Asia* (New Haven, CT: Yale University Press, 2000), p. 176.

72. James A. Schear, Frederick M. Burkle Jr., Michael T. Klare, Joseph McMillan, and Anthony S. Naitsios, "Fragile States and Ungoverned Spaces," in Patrick M. Cronin, ed., *Global Strategic Assessment 2009: America's Security Role in a Changing World* (Washington, DC: Institute for National Strategic Studies, National Defense University, 2009), p. 100; available at www.ndu.edu/inss/index.cfm?secID=8&pageID=126&type=section.

73. Meirav Meshali-Ram, "Afghanistan: A Legacy of Violence? Internal and External Factors of the Enduring Violent Conflict," *Comparative Studies of South Asia, Africa and the Middle East*, 28 (2008), p. 477.

74. Ibid., p. 479.

75. Ibid., p. 477.

76. Gregg.Bruno, "The Taliban in Afghanistan." *Council on Foreign Relations* (August 3, 2009); available at www.cfr.org/publication/10551/taliban_in_afghanistan.html.

77. Richard H. Shultz and Andrea J. Dew, *Insurgents, Terrorists, and Militias: The Warriors of Contemporary Combat* (New York: Columbia University Press, 2006), p. 186.

78. J. Joseph Hewitt, Jonathan Wilkenfeld, and Ted Robert Gurr, *Peace and Conflict 2010* (Boulder, CO: Paradigm Publishers, 2010), p. 124.

79. Stephen Biddle, Fontini Christia, and J. Alexander Thier, "Defining Success in Afghanistan: What Can the United States Accept?," *Foreign Affairs*, 89 (July/August 2010), p. 50; and "Time for Reassessment of US Mission in Afghanistan," *Asian News Network* (June 2, 2011), available at www.asianewsnet.net/home/news.php?sec=3&id=19233.

80. C. Todd Lopez, "Stability Operations Now Part of Army's Core Mission," February 15, 2008; available at www.army.mil/article/7580/stability-operations-now-part-of-armys-core-mission/.

81. U.S. Government Accountability Office, *Military Operations: Actions Needed to Improve DOD's Stability Operations Approach and Enhance Interagency Planning* (Washington, DC: Report to the Ranking Member, Subcommittee on National Security and Foreign Affairs, Committee on Oversight and Government Reform, House of Representatives, Government Printing Office, May 2007), p. 2.

82. Armitage, Berger, and Markey, *U.S. Strategy for Pakistan and Afghanistan*, p. 18.

83. Thomas E. Ricks, "Bull's-Eye War: Pinpoint Bombing Shifts Role of GI Joe" *Washington Post* (December 2, 2001), p. A1.

84. Fred Kaplan, "New Warfare: High-Tech US Arsenal Proves its Worth," *Boston Globe* (December 9, 2001): p. A34.

85. Armitage, Berger, and Markey, *U.S. Strategy for Pakistan and Afghanistan*, p. 3.

86. Ibid., p. ix.

87. Kathy Gannon, "Afghanistan Unbound," *Foreign Affairs*, 83 (May/June 2004), p. 36.

88. Carl Conetta, "Strange Victory: A Critical Appraisal of Operation Enduring Freedom and the Afghanistan War" (Cambridge, MA: Commonwealth Institute Project on Defense Alternatives Research Monograph #6, January 30, 2002), p. 18; available at www.comw.org/pda/0201strangevic.pdf.

89. Jeffrey Record, "The Limits and Temptations of America's Conventional Military Primacy" *Survival*, 47 (Spring 2005), p. 36.

90. Christi Parsons and Kathleen Hennessey, "Obama Moves up Deadline for Afghans to Take Lead Security Role," *Los Angeles Times* (January 11, 2013); available at http://articles.latimes.com/2013/jan/11/news/la-pn-obama-karzai-afghanistan-20130111.

91. Armitage, Berger, and Markey, *U.S. Strategy for Pakistan and Afghanistan*, p. 6.

92. Ibid., p. 11.

93. Athar Mohiudin, "Increasing Difficulties for U.S. in Afghan War," *Huffington Post* (November 25, 2013); available at www.huffingtonpost.com/athar-mohiudin/increasing-difficulties-f_b_4337707.html.

94. Carl Conetta, "Operation Enduring Freedom: Why a Higher Rate of Civilian Bombing Casualties?" (Cambridge, MA: Commonwealth Institute, Project on Defense Alternatives *Briefing Report* #11, January 18, 2002; revised January 24, 2002); available at http://www.comw.org/pda/02010ef.html.

95. Armitage, Berger, and Markey, *U.S. Strategy for Pakistan and Afghanistan*, p. 3.

96. Kenneth Katzman, *Afghanistan: Post-War Governance, Security, and U.S. Policy* (Washington, DC: CRS Report for Congress, August 23, 2006), p. 10; available at http://fpc.state.gov/documents/organization/71863.pdf.

97. Armitage, Berger, and Markey, *U.S. Strategy for Pakistan and Afghanistan*, p. 24.

98. U.S. Department of Defense, *Report on Progress toward Security and Stability in Afghanistan* (Washington, DC: US Government Printing Office, April 2010), p. 5; available at www.defense.gov/pubs/pdfs/Report_Final_SecDef_04_26_10.pdf.

99. Lana Zak and Ben Forer, "Is U.S. Winning in Afghanistan? Gates and Petraeus Won't Say" (June 6, 2011); available at http://abcnews.go.com/International/gates-petraeus-us-winning-afghan-war/story?id=13771705.

100. Donald F. Thompson, "The Role of Medical Diplomacy in Stabilizing Afghanistan," *Defense Horizons* no. 63 (May 2008), p. 3; available at www.fas.org/man/eprint/meddip.pdf.

101. Michael J. McNerney, "Stabilization and Reconstruction in Afghanistan: Are PRTs a Model or a Muddle?," *Parameters* 35 (Winter 2005-2006), p. 36.

102. Armitage, Berger, and Markey, *U.S. Strategy for Pakistan and Afghanistan*, p. 3.

103. Carter Malkasian and J. Kael Weston, "War Downsized: How to Accomplish More with Less," *Foreign Affairs*, 91 (March/April 2012), p. 111.

104. Jonathan Masters, "Debating the Afghan Mission," *Council on Foreign Relations* (June 10, 2011); available at www.cfr.org/afghanistan/debating-afghan-mission/p25256.

105. *Global Unease with Major World Powers: 47-Nation Pew Global Attitudes Survey* (Washington, DC: The Pew Global Attitudes Project, July 27, 2007).

106. Armitage, Berger, and Markey, *U.S. Strategy for Pakistan and Afghanistan*, pp. 25–26.

107. Ibid., p. 26.

108. Johnson, *Overconfidence and War*, p. 265.

109. Kathy Gannon, "Afghanistan Unbound," *Foreign Affairs*, 83 (May/June 2004), pp. 41, 44.

110. Ibid., p. 41.

111. Stephen Biddle, "Ending the War in Afghanistan: How to Avoid Failure on the Installment Plan," *Foreign Affairs*, 92 (September/October 2013), p. 49.

112. Jonathan Masters, "Drawing Down in Afghanistan," *Council on Foreign Relations*, (February 3, 2012); available at www.cfr.org/united-states/drawing-down-afghanistan/p27280.

113. Rubin and Rashid, "From Great Game to Grand Bargain," p. 33.

114. Masters, "Drawing Down in Afghanistan."

115. Ibid.

116. Meshali-Ram, "Afghanistan: A Legacy of Violence?," p. 473.

117. Ibid., p. 480.

118. Mark Sandalow, "Record Shows Bush Shifting on Iraq War: President's Rationale for the Invasion Continues to Evolve," *San Francisco Chronicle* (September 29, 2004), p. A1.

119. "Three Years and Counting," p. 3.

120. "Iraq, Three Years On: Resolve, but No Solution," *Economist*, 378 (March 18, 2006), p. 29.

121. Ned Parker, "The Iraq We Left Behind: Welcome to the World's Next Failed State," *Foreign Affairs*, 91 (March/April 2012), pp. 95–96.

122. Johnson, *Overconfidence and War*, p. 201.

123. Ibid., pp. 206–207.

124. Stephen J. Hedges, "U.S. Using Wrong Tactics: Fighting in Iraq Likely to Stay at Same Level," *Chicago Tribune* (June 17, 2006).

125. Andrew F. Krepinevich Jr., "How to Win in Iraq," *Foreign Affairs*, 84 (September/October 2005), p. 88.

126. Jessica Tuchman Mathews, "Now for the Hard Part," in *From Victory to Success*, p. 51.

127. Paul T. McCartney, "American Nationalism and U.S. Foreign Policy from September 11 to the Iraq War," *Political Science Quarterly*, 119 (Fall 2004), p. 408; and Susan Page, "Poll of Several Countries Finds 'Complete Misperceptions'" *USA Today* (June 23, 2006), p. 7.

128. Rowan Scarborough, "US Rushed Post-Saddam Planning," *Washington Times*, (September 3, 2003).

129. James Fallows, "Blind into Baghdad," *Atlantic Monthly*, 293 (January/February 2004), p. 53.

130. Record, "The Limits and Temptations of America's Conventional Military Primacy," p. 42.

131. Andrew J.Bacevich, Max Boot, Michael Ignatieff, Michael O'Hanlon, and Jonathan Masters, "Was the Iraq War Worth It?" (New York: Council on Foreign Relations, December 15, 2011); available at www.cfr.org/iraq/iraq-war-worth-/p26820.

132. Christopher Preble, "After Victory: Toward a New Military Posture in the Persian Gulf," *Policy Analysis*, no. 477 (June 10, 2003), p. 12.

133. Andrew J. Bacevich, Max Boot, Michael Ignatieff, Michael O'Hanlon, and Jonathan Masters, "Was the Iraq War Worth It?," *Council on Foreign Relations* (December 15, 2011); available at www.cfr.org/iraq/iraq-war-worth-/p26820.

134. Larry Diamond, "What Went Wrong in Iraq" *Foreign Affairs*, 83 (September/October 2004), p. 36.

135. Krepinevich, "How to Win in Iraq," p. 89.

136. U.S. Government Accountability Office, *Rebuilding Iraq: Stabilization, Reconstruction, and Financing Challenges* (Washington, DC: U.S. Government Accountability Office, February 8, 2006), p. 6.

137. Pamela M. Prah, "The War in Iraq: Is the United States Winning?," *CQ Researcher*, 15 (October 21, 2005), p. 885.

138. Krepinevich, "How to Win in Iraq," p. 90.

139. "Iraq at War with Itself," *Economist*, 378 (March 4, 2006), p. 9.

140. "Iraq: Murder Is Certain," *Economist*, 378 (March 4, 2006), p. 49.

141. Jim Wilson, "Smart Weapons under Fire," 180 *Popular Mechanics* (July 2003), pp. 42–43.

142. Tony Karon, "Ten Grim Lessons Learned from the Iraq War," *Time Magazine* (December 16, 2011); available at http://world.time.com/2011/12/16/ten-grim-lessons-learned-from-the-iraq-war/.

143. Diamond, "What Went Wrong in Iraq," p. 42.

144. Meghan L. O'Sullivan, "Troops Are Gone but Iraq War Is Not 'Over,'" *Bloomberg* (December 20, 2011); available at www.bloomberg.com/news/2011-12-21/troops-are-gone-but-iraq-war-is-not-over-meghan-l-o-sullivan.html.

145. Ibid.

146. Frederic Wehrey and others, *The Iraq Effect: The Middle East after the Iraq War* (Santa Monica, CA: RAND Corporation, 2010), pp. xv, 4.

147. O'Sullivan, "Troops Are Gone but Iraq War Is Not 'Over.'"

148. Larry Diamond, *Squandered Victory: The American Occupation and the Bungled Effort to Bring Democracy to Iraq* (New York: Henry Holt and Company, 2005), p. 279.

149. Fallows, "Blind into Baghdad," p. 54.

150. Dexter Filkins, "Suddenly, It's 'America Who?'" *New York Times* (February 6, 2005), section 4, p. 1.

151. Parker, "The Iraq We Left Behind," p. 96.

152. Chaim Kaufman, "Threat Inflation and the Failure of the Marketplace of Ideas: The Selling of the Iraq War," *International Security*, 29 (Summer 2004), p. 5.

153. Jennifer Harper, "Public Ignores Iraq War Naysayers," *Washington Times* (November 24, 2005), p. A01.

154. Dalia Dassa Kaye, "Bound to Cooperate? Transatlantic Policy in the Middle East," *Washington Quarterly*, 27 (Winter 2003–2004), pp. 179–195.

155. Majors Justin Gage, William Martin, Tim Mitchell, and Pat Wingate, "Winning the Peace in Iraq: Confronting America's Informational and Doctrinal Handicaps" (Norfolk, VA: Joint Forces Staff College, September 5, 2003), p. 1; available at www.jfsc.ndu.edu/current_students/documents_policies/documents/jca_cca_awsp/Winning_the_Peace_in_Iraq.doc.

156. Johnson, *Overconfidence and War*, p. 204.

157. Bacevich et al., "Was the Iraq War Worth It?"

158. Parker, "The Iraq We Left Behind," p. 94.

159. Richard N. Haass, "The Iraq War in Perspective," *The Huffington Post* (May 4, 2009); available at www.huffingtonpost.com/richard-n-haass/the-iraq-war-in-perspecti_b_195653.html.

160. Ibid.

161. Neil MacFarquhar, "As Terrorist Strike Arab Targets, Escalation Fears Arise," *New York Times* (April 30, 2004), p. 13.

162. Ekaterina Stepanova, "War and Peace Building," *Washington Quarterly*, 27 (Autumn 2004), p. 130.

163. "Three Years and Counting," *Nation*, 282 (March 27, 2006), p. 3.

164. Wehrey et al., *The Iraq Effect*, pp. xiii–xiv.

165. Ibid., p. xvi.

166. Haass, "The Iraq War in Perspective."

167. Wehrey and others, *The Iraq Effect*, p. 3.

168. Bacevich et al., "Was the Iraq War Worth It?"

169. "Three Years and Counting," p. 3; and Bacevich et al., "Was the Iraq War Worth It?"

170. Steve Jones, "US Foreign Policy After 9/11"; available at http://usforeignpolicy.about.com/od/defense/a/Us-Foreign-Policy-After-9-11.htm.

171. "Osama Bin Laden Dead" (Transcript of President Barack Obama's Speech, May 1, 2011); available at www.whitehouse.gov/blog/2011/05/02/osama-bin-laden-dead.

172. Bill Adair, "In 2008, Obama Vowed to Kill Osama Bin Laden" (May 1, 2011); available at www.politifact.com/truth-o-meter/article/2011/may/01/obama-vowed-kill-osama-bin-laden/.

173. "US Kills Osama Bin Laden," *Arab Times* (May 2, 2011); available at www .arabtimesonline.com/NewsDetails/tabid/96/smid/414/ArticleID/168703/reftab/36/t/ US-kills-Osama-bin-Laden/Default.aspx.

174. "Osama Bin Laden Dead."

175. Ibid.

176. Richard N. Haass, "Terrorism Concerns after Bin Laden," *Council on Foreign Relations* (May 2, 2011); available at www.cfr.org/terrorism/terrorism-concerns-after-bin-laden/p24840.

177. Richard N. Haass, "Beyond Bin Laden," *Project Syndicate* (May 3, 2011); available at www.project-syndicate.org/commentary/beyond-bin-laden.

178. "Osama Bin Laden Dead."

179. Ed Husain, "Bin Laden as 'Martyr': A Call to Jihadists," *CNN* (Cable News Network), (May 4, 2011); available at www.cnn.com/2011/OPINION/05/02/husain .bin.laden/.

180. "Pakistan People Protest against Bin Laden Killing," *China Daily* (May 6, 2011); available at www.chinadaily.com.cn/world/binLadendead/reaction.html.

181. "US Kills Osama Bin Laden."

182. Ibid.

183. Dean Schabner and Karen Travers, "Osama Bin Laden Killed: 'Justice Is Done,' President Says," *ABC News* (May 1, 2011); available at http://abcnews.go.com/ Blotter/osama-bin-laden-killed/story?id=13505703.

184. "US Kills Osama Bin Laden."

185. David Danelo, "Bin Laden's Death and the Moral Level of War" (Philadelphia, PA: Foreign Policy Research Institute E-Notes, May 2011); available at www .fpri.org.

186. John B. Bellinger III, "Bin Laden Killing: The Legal Basis," *Council on Foreign Relations* (May 2, 2011); available at www.cfr.org/terrorism/bin-laden-killing-legal-basis/p24866.

187. "US Kills Osama Bin Laden."

188. Husain, "Bin Laden as 'Martyr': A Call to Jihadists."

189. "US Kills Osama Bin Laden."

190. "Concerns Raised over Shooting of Unarmed Bin Laden," *China Daily* (May 4, 2011); available at www.chinadaily.com.cn/world/binLadendead/2011-05/04/ content_12444472.htm.

191. Ibid.

192. Ibid.

193. "UN Investigators Seek Facts on Bin Laden's Death," *China Daily* (May 6, 2011); available at www.chinadaily.com.cn/world/binLadendead/reaction.html.

194. "Concerns Raised over Shooting of Unarmed Bin Laden."

195. Haass, "Terrorism Concerns after Bin Laden."

196. Nathan Freier, "Bin Laden's Gone: What Now for Defense Policy?" *Center for Strategic and International Studies* (May 4, 2011); available at http://csis.org/publication/bin-ladens-gone-what-now-defense-policy.

197. Haass, "Beyond Bin Laden."

198. Thomas M. Sanderson, *Future of Al-Qaeda* (Washington, DC: Statement before the House Foreign Affairs Committee, Subcommittee on Terrorism, Nonproliferation, and Trade, May 24, 2011), pp. 2–3.

199. Freier, "Bin Laden's Gone: What Now for Defense Policy?"

200. Mushtaq Yusufzai, "Pakistan Aid Workers Pay the Ultimate Price for the Killing of Osama bin Laden," *NBC World News* (June 22, 2013); available at http://worldnews.nbcnews.com/_news/2013/06/22/19043539-pakistan-aid-workers-pay-the-ultimate-price-for-the-killing-of-osama-bin-laden?lite.

201. "Key Dates in French-Led Mali Intervention," *Global Post* (March 11, 2013); available at www.globalpost.com/dispatch/news/afp/130311/key-dates-french-led-mali-intervention.

202. Amit Singh, "France: Why Intervene in Mali and Not Central African Republic?" *Guardian* (February 5, 2013); available at www.guardian.co.uk/world/2013/feb/05/france-centralafrican-republic-mali-intervention.

203. "France Goes It Alone," *Economist* (February 14, 2013); available at www.economist.com/blogs/charlemagne/2013/01/french-foreign-policy.

204. "Mali: French Intervention Hits Drug Running," *Sky News* (UK) (March 11, 2013); available at http://news.sky.com/story/1063100/mali-french-intervention-hits-drug-running.

205. "Mali Intervention: France's Troops to Quit Timbuktu This Week," *Huffington Post World* (February 4, 2013); available at www.huffingtonpost.com/2013/02/04/mali-intervention-france-troops-timbuktu_n_2614680.html.

206. Paul-Simon Handy and Liesl Louw-Vaudran, "Mali: French Plans to Withdraw from Africa Are on Hold," *All Africa* (June 21, 2013); available at http://allafrica.com/stories/201307012071.html.

207. Olivier Roy, "The Intervention Trap," *New Statesman*, 142 (February 1, 2013), p. 23.

208. Singh, "France: Why Intervene in Mali and Not Central African Republic?"

209. "French Intervention in Mali: Causes and Consequences," *Al-Jazeera Center for Studies* (February 11, 2013); available at http://studies.aljazeera.net/en/positionpapers/2013/01/20131201130207376609.htm.

210. James Bloodworth, "French Intervention in Mali Is Not Colonialism" *Independent* (February 8, 2013); available at www.independent.co.uk/voices/comment/french-intervention-in-mali-is-not-colonialism-the-islamists-really-are-our-enemies-8487262.html.

211. "France Goes It Alone."

212. "French Intervention in Mali," *Economist* (February 2, 2013); available at www.economist.com/news/middle-east-and-africa/21571174-france-triumphs-desert-faces-tougher-time-longer-run-where.

213. Roy, "The Intervention Trap," p. 23.

214. "No Quick Fix for Mali: French Troops Can't End Crisis," *Daily Beast* (January 30, 2013); available at www.thedailybeast.com/articles/2013/01/30/no-quick-fix-for-mali-french-troops-can-t-end-crisis.html.

215. A Malian Quagmire? In Defense of French Intervention," *Atlantic* (January 20, 2013); available at www.theatlantic.com/international/archive/2013/01/a-malian-quagmire-in-defense-of-french-intervention/267339/.

216. Baba Ahmed and Krista A. Larson, "Mali Intervention: French Hunting Extremists in Gao," *Huffington Post World* (February 7, 2013); available at www.huffingtonpost.com/2013/02/07/mali-intervention-france-gao_n_2637894.html.

217. Bloodworth, "French Intervention in Mali Is Not Colonialism."

218. Ahmed and Larson, "Mali Intervention: French Hunting Extremists in Gao."

219. Steven Erlanger, "French Intervention in Mali Raises the Threat of Domestic Terrorism, Judge Says," *New York Times* (February 23, 2013); available at www.nytimes.com/2013/02/24/world/europe/french-intervention-in-mali-raises-threat-of-domestic-terrorism-judge-says.html?pagewanted=all&_r=0.

220. "French Intervention in Mali."

221. Bloodworth, "French Intervention in Mali Is Not Colonialism."

222. "Mali Intervention: France's Troops to Quit Timbuktu This Week."

223. Roy, "The Intervention Trap," p. 25.

224. Ibid.

225. Bloodworth, "French Intervention in Mali Is Not Colonialism."

226. Ibid.

227. "Mali Intervention: France's Troops to Quit Timbuktu This Week."

228. "French Intervention in Mali: Causes and Consequences."

229. Abdulateef Al-Mulhim, "Mali Intervention: No Mercy for France," *Arab News* (February 16, 2013); available at www.arabnews.com/mali-intervention-no-mercy-france.

230. Bloodworth, "French Intervention in Mali Is Not Colonialism."

231. "Key Dates in French-Led Mali Intervention."

232. "French Intervention in Mali."

233. Francois Rihouay, "Serious Human Rights Abuses Pervade in Mali Five Months after French Intervention," *Amnesty International* (June 7, 2013); available at www.amnesty.org/en/news/serious-human-rights-abuses-pervade-mali-five-months-after-french-intervention-2013-06-07.

234. "French Intervention in Mali."

235. Ibid.

236. "No Quick Fix for Mali: French Troops Can't End Crisis."

237. "French Intervention in Mali."

238. Ibid.

239. Ahmed and Larson, "Mali Intervention: French Hunting Extremists in Gao."

240. "French Intervention in Mali."

241. Ibid.

242. Giovanni Faleg, *Castles in the Sand: Mali and the Demise of the EU's Common Security and Defence Policy* (Brussels: Centre for European Policy Studies, January 28, 2013), p. 1.

243. Roy, "The Intervention Trap," p. 23.

244. Erlanger, "French Intervention in Mali Raises the Threat of Domestic Terrorism, Judge Says."

245. "A Malian Quagmire? In Defense of French Intervention."

246. "Mali: French Intervention Hits Drug Running."

247. Faleg, *Castles in the Sand*, p. 1.

248. Elliott Abrams, "Bombing the Syrian Reactor: The Untold Story," *Commentary* (February 2013); available at www.commentarymagazine.com/article/bombing-the-syrian-reactor-the-untold-story/.

249. Leonard S. Spector and Avner Cohen, "Israel's Airstrike on Syria's Reactor: Implications for the Nonproliferation Regime," *Arms Control Today*, 38 (July/August 2008), p. 15.

250. Ibid.

251. Abrams, "Bombing the Syrian Reactor."

252. Daveed Gartenstein-Ross and Joshua D. Goodman, "The Attack on Syria's al-Kibar Nuclear Facility," *InFocus*, 3 (Spring 2009); available at www.jewishpolicycenter.org/826/the-attack-on-syrias-al-kibar-nuclear-facility.

253. Abrams, "Bombing the Syrian Reactor."

254. Ibid.

255. "Syria Target Hit by Israel Was 'Nuclear Site'" *Al Jazeera* (April 29, 2011); available at www.aljazeera.com/news/middleeast/2011/04/201142962917518797.html.

256. Anthony H. Cordesman, *Syrian Weapons of Mass Destruction: An Overview* (Washington, DC: Center for Strategic and International Studies, June 2, 2008), p. 3.

257. Ibid., pp. 4–5.

258. Abrams, "Bombing the Syrian Reactor."

259. David E. Sanger and Mark Mazzetti, "Analysts Find Israel Struck A Syrian Nuclear Project," *New York Times* (October 14, 2007), p. A1.

260. Gartenstein-Ross and Goodman, "The Attack on Syria's al-Kibar Nuclear Facility."

261. Ibid.

262. Ibid.

263. Abrams, "Bombing the Syrian Reactor."

264. Ibid.

265. Ibid.

266. Andrew J. Tabler, "How to React to a Reactor: Using Syria's Nuclear Program to Engage Damascus," *Foreign Affairs Online* (April 19, 2010); available at www.andrewtabler.com/2010/04/how-to-react-to-reactor.html.

267. Elliott Abrams, Eliot Cohen, Eric Edelman, and John Hannah, "The Right Call on the Syrian Threat," *Washington Post* (September 15, 2011); available at www.washingtonpost.com/opinions/the-right-call-on-the-syrian-threat/2011/09/14/gIQAa85eVK_story.html.

268. Erich Follath and Holger Stark, "How Israel Destroyed Syria's Al Kibar Nuclear Reactor," *Spiegel Online International* (November 2, 2009); available at www.spiegel.de/international/world/0,1518,658663,00.html.

269. Abrams, "Bombing the Syrian Reactor."

270. Follath and Stark, "How Israel Destroyed Syria's Al Kibar Nuclear Reactor."

271. Abrams, "Bombing the Syrian Reactor."

272. Follath and Stark, "How Israel Destroyed Syria's Al Kibar Nuclear Reactor."

273. Ibid.

274. Gartenstein-Ross and Goodman, "The Attack on Syria's al-Kibar Nuclear Facility."

275. Follath and Stark, "How Israel Destroyed Syria's Al Kibar Nuclear Reactor."

276. Spector and Cohen, "Israel's Airstrike on Syria's Reactor," p. 15.

277. Ibid., p. 17.

278. Follath and Stark, "How Israel Destroyed Syria's Al Kibar Nuclear Reactor."

279. Ibid.

280. Gartenstein-Ross and Goodman, "The Attack on Syria's al-Kibar Nuclear Facility."

281. Follath and Stark, "How Israel Destroyed Syria's Al Kibar Nuclear Reactor."

282. "Syria 'Had Covert Nuclear Scheme'" *BBC News* (April 25, 2008); available at http://news.bbc.co.uk/2/hi/7364269.stm.

283. Abrams, "Bombing the Syrian Reactor."

284. Anna Newby, "Does Israel's 2007 Attack on Syrian Al Kibar Inform Iran Policy Today?" *Center for Strategic and International Studies* (November 9, 2010); available at http://csis.org/blog/does-israel%E2%80%99s-2007-attack-syrian-al-kibar-inform-iran-policy-today.

285. "Syria 'Had Covert Nuclear Scheme.'"

286. Newby, "Does Israel's 2007 Attack on Syrian Al Kibar Inform Iran Policy Today?"

287. Follath and Stark, "How Israel Destroyed Syria's Al Kibar Nuclear Reactor."

288. Ibid.

289. Gartenstein-Ross and Goodman, "The Attack on Syria's al-Kibar Nuclear Facility."

290. Sanger and Mazzetti, "Analysts Find Israel Struck a Syrian Nuclear Project," p. A1.

291. Follath and Stark, "How Israel Destroyed Syria's Al Kibar Nuclear Reactor."

292. Eshel, "Pillar of Deterrence," p. DT6.

293. Ellen Knickmeyer, "2006 War Called a 'Failure' for Israel; but Panel Refrains from Direct Rebuke of Premier," *Washington Post* (January 31, 2008), p. A14.

294. Ibid.

295. Charles Krauthammer, "A Moment to Be Seized in Lebanon," *Washington Post.* (August 18, 2006), p. A21.

296. Christine Harnieh and Roger Mac Ginty, "A Very Political Reconstruction: Governance and Reconstruction in Lebanon after the 2006 War," *Disasters,* 33 (March 2009), pp. 104–105. See also Roger Mac Ginty, "Reconstructing Post-War Lebanon: A Challenge to the Liberal Peace?" *Conflict, Security and Development,* 7 (2007), pp. 459–461.

297. Paul Salem, "The Future of Lebanon," *Foreign Affairs,* 85 (November/December 2006), p. 14.

298. Ibid., p. 13.

299. Byman, "Should Hezbollah Be Next?," p. 58.

300. Edward P. Djerejian, "From Conflict Management to Conflict Resolution," *Foreign Affairs,* 85 (November/December 2006), pp. 41–42.

301. Augustus Richard Norton, *Hezbollah* (Princeton, NJ: Princeton University Press, 2007), pp. 32–35.

302. Alexus G. Grynkewich, "Welfare as Warfare: How Violent Non-State Groups Use Social Services to Attack the State," *Studies in Conflict & Terrorism,* 31 (2008), p. 361.

303. Staff, "Hezbollah (a.k.a. Hizbollah, Hizbu'llah)," *Council on Foreign Relations Online* (New York: Council on Foreign Relations, June 8, 2009); available at www.cfr.org/publication/9155/hezbollah.html?breadcrumb=%2F

304. Greg Myre and Steven Erlanger, "Clashes Spread to Lebanon as Hezbollah Raids Israel," *New York Times* (July 12, 2006), p. A1.

305. Daniel Byman, "Should Hezbollah Be Next?" *Foreign Affairs,* 54 (November/December 2003), p. 58.

306. Diane E. Davis, "Irregular Armed Forces, Shifting Patterns of Commitment, and Fragmented Sovereignty in the Developing World" (September 2009), p. 26; available at http://hdl.handle.net/1721.1/51817.

307. Roy Godson and Richard Shultz, *Adapting America's Security Paradigm and Security Agenda* (Washington, DC: National Strategy Information Center, 2010), pp. 13–14.

308. Ibid., p. 7.

309. Michael Crawford and Jami Miscik, "The Rise of Mezzanine Rulers: The New Frontier for International Law," *Foreign Affairs*, 89 (November/December 2010), pp. 124–125.

310. Eshel, "Pillar of Deterrence," p. DT8.

311. Knickmeyer, "2006 War Called a 'Failure' for Israel," p. A14.

312. "Among Militia's Patient Loyalists, Confidence and Belief in Victory," *Washington Post* (August 3, 2006), p. A01.

313. Knickmeyer, "2006 War Called a 'Failure' for Israel," p. A14.

314. Ibid.

315. Steven Erlanger and Richard A. Oppel Jr., "A Disciplined Hezbollah Surprises Israel with Its Training, Tactics and Weapons," *New York Times* (August 7, 2006), p. A8.

316. Ibid.

317. Byman, "Should Hezbollah Be Next?" p. 58.

318. "Who Will Disarm Hezbollah?" *Spiegel Online* (August 16, 2006); available at www.spiegel.de/international/the-un-force-who-will-disarm-hezbollah-a-432019 .html.

319. Crawford and Miscik, "The Rise of Mezzanine Rulers," p. 124.

320. Sabrina Tavernise, "Turmoil in the Mideast: Beirutis Try to Plumb the Abyss between Elegance and Chaos," *New York Times* (July 25, 2006), p. A11.

321. Sharon Behn, "U.S., Hezbollah Vie to Rebuild for Lebanese: Hope to Win Public Opinion," *The Washington Times* (August 18, 2006); and Paul Richter, "Cease-Fire in the Middle East," *Los Angeles Times* (August 17, 2006).

322. Judith Palmer Harik, *Transnational Actors in Contemporary Conflicts: Hizbullah and Its 2006 War with Israel* (Cambridge, MA: Program on Humanitarian Policy and Conflict Research, Harvard University, March 9–10, 2007), p. 18; available at www.tagsproject.org/publications.

323. John Kifner, "Hezbollah Leads Work to Rebuild, Gaining Stature," *New York Times* (August 16, 2006), p. A1.

324. Nezar AlSayyad, "Foreword," in Howayda Al-Harithy, ed., *Lessons in Post-War Reconstruction: Case Studies from Lebanon in the Aftermath of the 2006 War* (London: Routledge, 2010), p. ix.

325. Grynkewich, "Welfare as Warfare," p. 363; and "Poll Finds Overwhelming Majorities in Lebanon Support Hezbollah, Distrust U.S." (August 2, 2006), available at www.worldpublicopinion.org/pipa/articles/brmiddleeastnafricara/236.php?nid= &id=&pnt=236&lb=brme.

326. David B. Rivkin Jr. and Lee A. Casey, "Israel Is Within Its Rights," *Washington Post* (July 26, 2006), p. A17.

327. "As Mideast Smoke Clears, Political Fates May Shift," *Washington Post* (August 13, 2006), p. A10.

328. Ibid.

329. Abrams, "Bombing the Syrian Reactor."

330. Harnieh and Mac Ginty, "A Very Political Reconstruction," p. 106.

331. AlSayyad, "Foreword," p. viii.

332. Harnieh and Mac Ginty, "A Very Political Reconstruction," p. 107.

333. Ibid., p. 106.

334. "Aid Conference Raises $7.6 Billion for Lebanon," *New York Times* (January 26, 2007), p. A8.

335. "Hard Choices and Right Choices in the Mideast," *Washington Post* (August 15, 2006), p. A12.

336. Salem, "The Future of Lebanon," p. 13.

337. Byman, "Should Hezbollah Be Next?," p. 59.

338. Ibid., pp. 59–60.

339. Ivo H. Daalder and James G. Stavridis, "NATO's Victory in Libya," *Foreign Affairs*, 91 (March/April 2012), p. 2.

340. Varun Vira and Anthony H. Cordesman, *The Libyan Uprising: An Uncertain Trajectory* (Washington, DC: Center for Strategic and International Studies, June 20, 2011), pp. 10–11.

341. Daalder and Stavridis, "NATO's Victory in Libya," p. 3.

342. NATO, *Operation Unified Protector Final Mission Stats* (Brussels, Belgium: North Atlantic Treaty Organization Public Diplomacy Division Fact Sheet, November 2, 2011).

343. Daalder and Stavridis, "NATO's Victory in Libya," p. 6.

344. Ibid., p. 4.

345. Vira and Cordesman, *The Libyan Uprising*, p. 47.

346. Adam D. M. Svensen, "NATO, Libya Operations and Intelligence Co-Operation—A Step Forward," *Baltic Security and Defence Review*, 13 (2011), p. 54.

347. Ibid., p. 55.

348. Clark A. Murdock and Becca Smith, *The Libyan Intervention: A Study in U.S. Grand Strategy* (Washington, DC: Center for Strategic and International Studies Global Forecast, 2011), p. 62.

349. Heather A. Conley and Uttara Dukkipati, "Leading from the Front: Europe and the New Libya," *Center for Strategic and International Studies* (September 1, 2011); available at http://csis.org/publication/leading-front-europe-and-new-libya.

350. Ibid.

351. Vira and Cordesman, *The Libyan Uprising*, p. 6.

352. Anders Fogh Rasmussen, "NATO after Libya: The Atlantic Alliance in Austere Times," *Foreign Affairs*, 90 (July/August 2011), p. 2.

353. Vira and Cordesman, *The Libyan Uprising*, p. 7.

354. Ibid., p. 53.

355. Daalder and Stavridis, "NATO's Victory in Libya," p. 3.

356. Brian Knowlton, "In Libyan Conflict, European Power Was Felt," *New York Times* (October 20, 2011); available at www.nytimes.com/2011/10/21/world/europe/in-libyan-conflict-european-power-was-felt.html?_r=0.

357. Daalder and Stavridis, "NATO's Victory in Libya," p. 2.

358. Ian Brzezinski, "Lessons from Libya: NATO Alliance Remains Relevant," *National Defense* (November 2011), p. 18.

359. Daalder and Stavridis, "NATO's Victory in Libya," p. 3.

360. Ellen Hallams and Benjamin Schreer, "Towards a 'Post-American' Alliance? NATO Burden-Sharing after Libya," *International Affairs*, 88 (2012), p. 321.

361. Brzezinski, "Lessons from Libya," p. 18.

362. Adel Darwish, "Libya: Where Will the Chips Fall?" *The Middle East* (October 2011), p. 15.

363. Conley and Dukkipati, "Leading from the Front."

364. Tracey Shelton, "After Gaddafi: Two Years On, Libyans Don't Have Much to Celebrate," *Global Post* (October 23, 2013); available at www.globalpost.com/dispatch/news/regions/middle-east/131023/two-years-after-gaddafi-libya-revolution-anniversary.

365. Hallams and Schreer, "Towards a 'Post-American' Alliance?," pp. 323–324.

366. Michael Clarke, *Curious Victory for NATO in Libya* (London: Royal United Services Institute, 2011); available at www.rusi.org/analysis/commentary/ref:C4E53CF030EB3B/.

367. Vira and Cordesman, *The Libyan Uprising*, p. 53.

368. Daalder and Stavridis, "NATO's Victory in Libya," p. 4; and Brzezinski, "Lessons from Libya," p. 18.

369. Ben Barry, "Libya's Lessons," *Survival*, 53 (2011), p. 11.

370. Daalder and Stavridis, "NATO's Victory in Libya," pp. 5–6.

371. Brzezinski, "Lessons from Libya," p. 18.

372. Geir Ulfstein and Hege Føsund Christiansen, "The Legality of the NATO Bombing in Libya," *International and Comparative Law Quarterly*, 62 (January 2013), p. 162.

373. Vira and Cordesman, *The Libyan Uprising*, pp. 54–55.

374. Richard Porritt, "Libya Militias 'Torture Gaddafi Supporters to Death in Camps,'" *Evening Standard (London)* (February 16, 2012), p. 24.

375. Shelton, "After Gaddafi."

376. Darwish, "Libya: Where Will the Chips Fall?," p. 13.

377. Vira and Cordesman, *The Libyan Uprising*, p. 58.

378. Conley and Dukkipati, "Leading from the Front."

379. Chris Stephen, "Libya's Promised Reconstruction Bonanza Fails to Materialise," *Guardian* (August 25, 2012); available at www.theguardian.com/business/2012/aug/26/libya-reconstruction-bonanza-fails-to-materialise.

380. Catherine Cheney, "In Libya, Post-Conflict Phase Is More Construction Than Reconstruction," *World Politics Review* (April 6, 2012); available at www.worldpoliticsreview.com/trend-lines/11817/in-libya-post-conflict-phase-is-more-construction-than-reconstruction.

381. Darwish, "Libya: Where Will the Chips Fall?," p. 16.

382. Borzou Daragahi, "Libya's Oil Production Hostage to Political Unrest," *Financial Times* (November 18, 2013); available at www.ft.com/cms/s/0/d60a85e2-4dde-11e3-8fa5-00144feabdc0.html#axzz2n66Rbl1C.

383. Darwish, "Libya: Where Will the Chips Fall?," p. 13.

384. Cheney, "In Libya, Post-Conflict Phase Is More Construction Than Reconstruction."

385. Richard Falk, "Libya after Qaddafi," *The Nation* (November 14, 2011), p. 4.

386. Reginald Dale, "Libya: U.S. Still Needs Europe," *Center for Strategic and International Studies* (June 6, 2012); available at http://csis.org/blog/libya-us-still-needs-europe.

387. Hallams and Schreer, "Towards a 'Post-American' Alliance?," p. 324.

388. Brzezinski, "Lessons from Libya," p. 19.

389. Hallams and Schreer, "Towards a 'Post-American' Alliance?," p. 314.

390. Bill Powell, "The Torpedo Attack: Will North Korea be Punished?," *Time* (May 19, 2010); available at www.time.com/time/world/article/0,8599,1990289,00.html.

391. "ROK and US Military Pay Tribute to Fallen ROK's *Cheonan* Crew Members"; available at www.dvidshub.net/news/103632/rok-and-us-military-pay-tribute-fallen-roks-cheonan-crewmembers#.UVCEtBfCbTo#ixzz2OZY6vKpw.

392. See, for example, Tanaka Sakai, "Who Sank the South Korean Warship *Cheonan*? Destabilization of the Korean Peninsula," *Asia-Pacific Journal* (May 24, 2010), available at www.globalresearch.ca/who-sank-the-south-korean-warship-cheonan-destabilization-of-the-korean-peninsula/19375; and Stephen Gowans, "The Sinking of the *Cheonan*: Another Gulf of Tonkin Incident?." (May 20, 2010); available at http://gowans.wordpress.com/2010/05/20/the-sinking-of-the-cheonan-another-gulf-of-tonkin-incident/.

393. Brad Lendon, "S. Korea's Final Report Affirms *Cheonan* was Sunk by N. Korean Torpedo," *CNN* (September 13, 2010); available at www.cnn.com/2010/WORLD/asiapcf/09/13/south.korea.cheonan.report/index.html.

394. Powell, "The Torpedo Attack."

395. Ibid.

396. Ibid.

397. Kim Eun-jung, "*Cheonan* Anniversary—Naval Drill," *Global Post* (March 25, 2013); available at www.globalpost.com/dispatch/news/yonhap-news-agency/130325/cheonan-anniversary-naval-drill-0.

398. "Seoul Insists on N. Korea Apology before Dialogue," *Korea Herald* (April 18, 2011); available at www.koreaherald.com/national/Detail.jsp?newsMLId=20110418000733.

399. Larry Shaughnessy, "U.S. and South Korea See More North Korean Provocations Looming," *CNN* (October 28, 2011); available at http://articles.cnn.com/keyword/cheonan.

400. Eun-jung, "*Cheonan* Anniversary—Naval Drill."

401. Leo Lewis, "South Korea Bans All Trade with North over *Cheonan* Attack," *Times (London)* (May 24, 2010); available at www.timesonline.co.uk/tol/news/world/asia/article7134810.ece.

402. Powell, "The Torpedo Attack."

403. Eun-jung, "*Cheonan* Anniversary—Naval Drill."

404. Ibid.

405. Ibid.

406. Park Boram, "*Cheonan* Sinking—3rd Anniversary," *Global Post* (March 17, 2013); available at www.globalpost.com/dispatch/news/yonhap-news-agency/130316/news-focus-cheonan-sinking-3rd-anniversary.

407. Eun-jung, "*Cheonan* Anniversary—Naval Drill."

408. Boram, "*Cheonan* Sinking—3rd Anniversary."

409. Jack Kim and Louis Charbonneau, "South Korea Will Retaliate at North if Attacked, Military Says," *Huffington Post World* (March 6, 2013); available at www.huffingtonpost.com/2013/03/06/south-korea-retaliate-north-korea-attacked_n_2817596.html.

410. Jim Nichol, *Russia–Georgia Conflict in August 2008: Context and Implications for U.S. Interests* (Washington, DC: Congressional Research Service Report for Congress, March 3, 2009), p. 3.

411. Svante E. Cornell, Johanna Popjanevski, and Niklas Nilsson, *Russia's War in Georgia: Causes and Implications for Georgia and the World* (Washington, DC and Stockholm, Sweden: Central Asia–Caucasus Institute & Silk Road Studies Program Joint Center, August 2008), pp. 5–13.

412. Charles King, "The Five-Day War: Managing Moscow after the Georgia Crisis," *Foreign Affairs*, 87 (November/December 2009), p. 2.

413. Marek Menkizak, "Russian Invasion of Georgia: Developments, Objectives and Consequences," *East Week* (Center for Eastern Studies, August 19, 2008); available at www.osw.waw.pl/en/publikacje/eastweek/2008-08-20/russian-invasion-georgia-developments-objectives-and-consequences.

414. "Five Years On, Georgia Makes Up with Russia," *BBC News* (June 24, 2013); available at www.bbc.co.uk/news/world-europe-23010526.

415. Nichol, *Russia–Georgia Conflict in August 2008*, p. 15.

416. Cornell, Popjanevski, and Nilsson, *Russia's War in Georgia*, p. 4.

417. Nichol, *Russia–Georgia Conflict in August 2008*, pp. 9–10.

418. Ibid., pp. 12–13.

419. Cornell, Popjanevski, and Nilsson, *Russia's War in Georgia*, p. 24.

420. "Five Years On, Georgia Makes Up with Russia."

421. Rachel Martin, "Russia's Georgia Invasion May Be about Oil," *ABC News* (August 16, 2008); available at http://abcnews.go.com/Business/story?id=5595811.

422. Menkizak, "Russian Invasion of Georgia"; and Cornell, Popjanevski, and Nilsson, *Russia's War in Georgia*, pp. 3–4.

423. Nichol, *Russia–Georgia Conflict in August 2008*, p. 15.

424. Menkizak, "Russian Invasion of Georgia."

425. Ibid.

426. King, "The Five-Day War," p. 3.

427. Menkizak, "Russian Invasion of Georgia."

428. Ibid.

429. Nichol, *Russia–Georgia Conflict in August 2008*, pp. 11–12.

430. Ibid., pp. 13, 16.

431. Ibid., p. 28.

432. Menkizak, "Russian Invasion of Georgia."

433. Cornell, Popjanevski, and Nilsson, *Russia's War in Georgia*, p. 28.

434. Ibid., p. 3.

435. Stephen Sestanovich, "What Has Moscow Done? Rebuilding U.S.–Russian Relations," *Foreign Affairs*, 6 (November/December 2008), p. 25.

436. King, "The Five-Day War," p. 9.

437. Ibid., p. 10.

438. Cornell, Popjanevski, and Nilsson, *Russia's War in Georgia*, p. 25.

439. Nichol, *Russia–Georgia Conflict in August 2008*, p. 13.

440. Ibid., p. 18.

441. King, "The Five-Day War," pp. 6, 7.

442. Ibid., p. 8.

443. Nichol, *Russia–Georgia Conflict in August 2008*, p. 8.

444. Cornell, Popjanevski, and Nilsson, *Russia's War in Georgia*, p. 26.

445. King, "The Five-Day War," pp. 2–3.

446. Luke Harding and Ian Traynor, "Russians March into Georgia as Full-Scale War Looms," *Guardian* (August 11, 2008); available at www.guardian.co.uk/world/2008/aug/11/georgia.russia13.

447. Nichol, *Russia–Georgia Conflict in August 2008*, p. 25.

448. Ibid., p. 1.

449. Menkizak, "Russian Invasion of Georgia."

450. Ibid.

451. Ibid.

452. King, "The Five-Day War," p. 3.

453. Ibid., p. 6.

454. Nichol, *Russia–Georgia Conflict in August 2008*.

455. "Five Years on, Georgia Makes up with Russia;" and Georgy Dvali and Aleksandr Reutov, "Georgia Denied Diplomatic Relations with Russia," *Current Digest of the Russian Press*, 65 (March 14, 2013), pp. 19–20.

456. King, "The Five-Day War," p. 8.

457. Thaddeus G. McCotter, "Russia's Invasion of Georgia," *Washington Times* (August 11, 2008); available at www.washingtontimes.com/news/2008/aug/11/russias-invasion-of-georgia-what-to-do-about-mosco/.

458. Sestanovich, "What Has Moscow Done?" p. 28.

459. Menkizak, "Russian Invasion of Georgia."

460. Nichol, *Russia–Georgia Conflict in August 2008*, p. 1.

461. Denis Corboy, William Courtney, and Kenneth Yalowitz, "Calming the Roiling Caucasus," *The New York Times* (June 3, 2012); available at www.nytimes.com/2012/06/04/opinion/clinton-in-the-roiling-caucasus.html.

462. Ibid.

## Chapter 4

1. Gwynne Dyer, "The Politics behind Bahrain Crackdown," *Welland Tribune* (March 2, 2013); available at www.wellandtribune.ca/2013/03/01/the-politics-behind-bahrain-crackdown.

2. Patrick Cockburn, "The Footage That Reveals the Brutal Truth about Bahrain's Crackdown," *Independent* (March 18, 2011); available at www.independent.co.uk/news/world/middle-east/the-footage-that-reveals-the-brutal-truth-about-bahrains-crackdown-2245364.html.

3. Derek Lutterbeck, "Arab Uprisings, Armed Forces, and Civil–Military Relations," *Armed Forces & Society*, 39 (January 2013), p. 43.

4. Amitabh Pal, "U.S. Still Acquiescing in Bahraini Crackdown," *Progressive* (February 15, 2013); available at www.progressive.org/u-s--still-acquiescing-in-bahraini-crackdown.

5. Kareem Fahim, "Citing Violence, Bahrain Bans All Protests in New Crackdown," *New York Times* (October 30, 2012); available at www.nytimes.com/2012/10/31/world/middleeast/bahrain-bans-all-protests-in-new-crackdown.html?_r=0.

6. Fahim, "Citing Violence, Bahrain Bans All Protests in New Crackdown."

7. Stephen Zunes, "Bahrain's Arrested Revolution," *Arab Studies Quarterly*, 35 (Spring 2013), pp. 155, 156.

8. Fahim, "Citing Violence, Bahrain Bans All Protests in New Crackdown."

9. Ibid.

10. Ibid.

11. Pal, "U.S. Still Acquiescing in Bahraini Crackdown."

12. "Bahrain Inquiry Confirms Rights Abuses," *Al Jazeera* (November 23, 2011); available at www.aljazeera.com/news/middleeast/2011/11/20111123125645404851.html.

13. Zunes,"Bahrain's Arrested Revolution," p. 149.

14. Ibid.

15. Pal, "U.S. Still Acquiescing in Bahraini Crackdown."

16. Seth G. Jones, "The Mirage of the Arab Spring: Deal with the Region You Have, Not the Region You Want," *Foreign Affairs*, 92 (January/February 2013), pp. 57–58.

17. Dyer, "The Politics behind Bahrain Crackdown."

18. Fahim, "Citing Violence, Bahrain Bans All Protests in New Crackdown."

19. "Bahrain: Crackdown after Clashes," *New York Times* (February 14, 2012); available at www.nytimes.com/2012/02/15/world/middleeast/bahrain-crackdown-after-clashes.html.

20. Zunes, "Bahrain's Arrested Revolution," p. 154.

21. "Bahrain Activists in 'Day of Rage,'" *Al Jazeera* (February 14, 2011); available at www.aljazeera.com/news/middleeast/2011/02/2011214925802473.html.

22. Zunes, "Bahrain's Arrested Revolution," p. 154.

23. "Clashes Rock Bahraini Capital," *Al Jazeera* (February 17, 2011), available at www.aljazeera.com/news/middleeast/2011/02/201121714223324820.html; and "Bahrain Protests: Police Break Up Pearl Square Crowd," *BBC News* (February 17, 2011), available at www.bbc.co.uk/news/world-middle-east-12490286.

24. Fahim, "Citing Violence, Bahrain Bans All Protests in New Crackdown."

25. "Bahrain: Crackdown after Clashes."

26. Pal, "U.S. Still Acquiescing in Bahraini Crackdown."

27. "Bahrain: International Reaction to Violent Crackdown," *Front Line Defenders*; available at www.frontlinedefenders.org/node/14237

28. Zunes, "Bahrain's Arrested Revolution," pp. 159–160.

29. "Arrests Follow Deadly Bahrain Crackdown," *Al-Jazeera* (March 17, 2011); available at www.aljazeera.com/news/middleeast/2011/03/201131733318735470.html.

30. "Bahrain: International Reaction to Violent Crackdown."

31. Justin Elliott, "Revealed: American Arms Sales to Bahrain Amid Bloody Crackdown," *Guardian* (January 15, 2013); available at www.guardian.co.uk/world/2013/jan/15/americas-arms-sales-bahrain-crackdown.

32. Zunes, "Bahrain's Arrested Revolution," p. 158.

33. Fahim, "Citing Violence, Bahrain Bans All Protests in New Crackdown."

34. Ibid.

35. Pal, "U.S. Still Acquiescing in Bahraini Crackdown."

36. "HRW urges EU to Pressure Bahrain to Free Political Prisoners," *Press TV* (June 29, 2013); available at www.presstv.ir/detail/2013/06/29/311385/eu-urged-to-push-bahrain-on-prisoners/.

37. Andrew Hammond, "Bahrain Used 'Excessive Force' in Crackdown," *Reuters* (November 23, 2011); available at www.reuters.com/article/2011/11/23/us-bahrain-violence-idUSTRE7AM0VB20111123.

38. Fouad Ajami, "The Arab Spring at One," *Foreign Affairs*, 91 (March/April 2012), p. 61.

39. Zunes, "Bahrain's Arrested Revolution," p. 150.

40. Kristin Diwan, "Bahrain in Egypt's Shadow," *Atlantic Council* (September 27, 2013); available at www.atlanticcouncil.org/blogs/menasource/bahrain-in-egypt-s-shadow.

41. Dyer, "The Politics behind Bahrain Crackdown."

42. Lobsang Sangayby Sangay, "On Fire in Tibet," *Washington Post* (November 4, 2011), p. A19.

43. Edward Wong, "Reports of 2 Tibetans Killed by Chinese Officers," *The New York Times* (April 23, 2011); available at www.nytimes.com/2011/04/24/world/asia/24tibet.html.

44. Sangay, "On Fire in Tibet," p. A19.

45. "China Must End Crackdowns after Self-Immolations in Tibet," *Amnesty International* (June 1, 2012); available at www.amnesty.org/en/news/china-must-end-crackdown-after-self-immolations-tibet-2012-06-01.

46. Ibid.

47. Chi-Chi Zhang, "China Cracks down on Unrest Ahead of Tibetan Holiday," *CNN* (Cable News Network), (January 30, 2012); available at http://articles.cnn.com/2012-01-30/asia/world_asia_china-tibetans-crackdown_1_tibetans-chinese-security-forces-chinese-authorities?_s=PM:ASIA.

48. Ian Johnson, "Despite Intimidation, Calls for a 'Jasmine Revolution' in China Persist," *The New York Times* (February 23, 2011); available at www.nytimes.com/2011/02/24/world/asia/24china.html.

49. Michael Sainsbury, "China Bullying Foreign Media—Australian Government Condemns Violent Crackdown," *The Australian* (March 7, 2011), p. 28.

50. Archer Wang and Scott Savitt, "In China, Strolling for Reform," *New York Times* (March 4, 2011); available at www.nytimes.com/2011/03/05/opinion/05iht-edsavitt05.html.

51. David Pierson, "Online Call for Protests in China Prompts Crackdown," *Los Angeles Times* (February 26, 2011), available at http://articles.latimes.com/2011/

feb/26/world/la-fgw-china-crackdown-20110227; and "Crackdown Swift on 'Jasmine Revolution' Call," *Tibetan Review*, 46 (March 2011), pp. 22–23.

52. Jeremy Page and James T. Areddy, "World News: China Mobilizes against Activists," *Wall Street Journal* (February 28, 2011), p. A6.

53. Austin Ramzy, "State Stamps Out Small 'Jasmine' Protests in China," *Time Magazine* (February 21, 2011); available at www.time.com/time/world/article/0,8599, 2052860,00.html.

54. Melinda Liu, "China: What Protests?" *Newsweek*, 157 (February 14, 2011); available at www.thedailybeast.com/newsweek/2011/02/06/china-what-protests.html.

55. Sainsbury, "China Bullying Foreign Media," p. 28.

56. Ibid.

57. Ibid.

58. Ibid.

59. Sangay, "On Fire in Tibet," p. A19.

60. "China Must End Crackdowns after Self-Immolations in Tibet."

61. Gillian Wong, "Chinese Police Fire into Crowd of Tibetan Protesters, Say Witnesses," *Christian Science Monitor* (January 24, 2012); available at www .csmonitor.com/World/Latest-News-Wires/2012/0124/Chinese-police-fire-into-crowd-of-Tibetan-protesters-say-witnesses.

62. "Chinese Say 'Trained Separatists' Responsible for Tibetan Violence." *Voice of America* (January 31, 2012); available at www.voanews.com/content/chinese-officials-say-trained-separatists-responsible-for-tibetan-violence-138469539/151402.html.

63. Simon Denyer, "In Tibet, Protests against Chinese Rule Grow," *Washington Post* (April 2, 2012), p. A08.

64. Edward Wong, "In Crackdown by Chinese, a New Arrest," *New York Times* (March 30, 2011); available at www.nytimes.com/2011/03/31/world/asia/31china.html.

65. Ibid.

66. Page and Areddy, "World News: China Mobilizes against Activists," p. A6.

67. Andrew Jacobs, "China Extends Hand and Fist to Protesters," *New York Times* (June 1, 2011); available at www.nytimes.com/2011/06/02/world/asia/02mongolia .html?pagewanted=all.

68. Page and Areddy, "World News: China Mobilizes Against Activists," p. A6.

69. Keith B. Richburg, "China Tamps down Middle East-Inspired Protests before They Can Gain Momentum," *Washington Post* (February 27, 2011); available at www.washingtonpost.com/world/chinese_police_face_down_middle_east_style_ protests/2011/02/27/AB5qyZJ_story.html.

70. Ramzy, "State Stamps out Small 'Jasmine' Protests in China."

71. David Whitehouse, "Repression and Dissent in China," *Socialist Worker* (May 22, 2012); available at http://socialistworker.org/2012/05/22/repression-and-dissent-china.

72. Damian Grammaticas, "Calls for Protests in China Met with Brutality," *BBC News* (February 28, 2011); available at www.bbc.co.uk/news/world-asia-pacific-12593328.

73. Eunice Yoon, "Getting Harassed by the Chinese Police," *CNN* (Cable News Network), (February 28, 2011); available at http://business.blogs.cnn.com/2011/02/28/getting-harassed-by-the-chinese-police/.

74. Denyer, "In Tibet, Protests against Chinese Rule Grow," p. A08.

75. Kurt Achin, "Tibetan Exile Officials Warn Chinese Violence against Protesters 'Unsustainable,'" *Voice of America* (January 30, 2012); available at www.voanews.com/tibetan-english/news/Tibetan-Exile-Officials-Warn-Chinese-Violence-Against-Protesters-Unsustainable-138318749.html.

76. Guobin Yang, "China's Gradual Revolution," *New York Times* (March 13, 2011); available at www.nytimes.com/2011/03/14/opinion/14Yang.html.

77. Ibid.

78. Ibid.

79. Sangay, "On Fire in Tibet," p. A19.

80. Ibid.

81. Ibid.

82. Sainsbury, "China Bullying Foreign Media," p. 28.

83. Andrew Jacobs, "China Puts Some Places off Limits to Journalists," *New York Times* (March 1, 2011), p. A4.

84. Edward Wong, "Human Rights Advocates Vanish as China Intensifies Crackdown," *New York Times* (March 11, 2011); available at www.nytimes.com/2011/03/12/world/asia/12china.html?_r=2.

85. Wong, "Reports of 2 Tibetans Killed by Chinese Officers."

86. Zhang, "China Cracks down on Unrest ahead of Tibetan Holiday."

87. Joseph A. Bosco, "Tiananmen 2.0? Freedom Is Coming to China—One Way or Another," *Christian Science Monitor* (March 2, 2011); available at www.csmonitor.com/Commentary/Opinion/2011/0302/Tiananmen-2.0-Freedom-is-coming-to-China-one-way-or-another.

88. "China Must End Crackdowns after Self-Immolations in Tibet."

89. *"I Saw It with My Own Eyes": Abuses by Chinese Security Forces in Tibet, 2008–2010* (New York: Human Rights Watch, July 2010), p. 2.

90. Pierson, "Online Call for Protests in China Prompts Crackdown."

91. Zhang, "China Cracks Down on Unrest ahead of Tibetan Holiday."

92. Yang, "China's Gradual Revolution."

93. Ibid.

94. See, for example, Ben Neary, "Many Injured, Held in Crackdown on Massive Protest in Dege County," *Tibetan Review*, 47 (May–June 2012), p. 8.

95. Paul Eckert, "Swagger, Insecurity Feed China Crackdown," *Reuters* (January 18, 2012); available at www.reuters.com/article/2012/01/18/us-china-usa-dissident-idUSTRE80H2DW20120118.

96. "Activist Inspires Hope even as Chinese Repression Grows," *USA Today* (March 25, 2013); available at www.usatoday.com/story/news/world/2013/03/25/chinese-dissident-town/2013489/.

97. Ibid.

98. Steve Hess, "From the Arab Spring to the Chinese Winter: The Institutional Sources of Authoritarian Vulnerability and Resilience in Egypt, Tunisia, and China," *International Political Science Review*, 34 (June 2013), p. 268.

99. Dina Shehata, "The Fall of Pharaoh," *Foreign Affairs*, 90 (May/June 2011), p. 26.

100. Erica Chenoweth, "Backfire in the Arab Spring," in *Revolution and Political Transformation in the Middle East: Government Action and Response* (Washington, DC: Middle East Institute, August 2011), p. 24.

101. Ajami, "The Arab Spring at One," p. 58.

102. Thanassis Cambanis, "Egypt's Revolutionary Elite and the Silent Majority," in *Revolution and Political Transformation in the Middle East: Agents of Change* (Washington, DC: Middle East Institute, August 2011), p. 38.

103. Chenoweth, "Backfire in the Arab Spring," p. 24.

104. Ibid.

105. "Clashes Break out in Egypt Demonstrations," *CNN Wire* (May 4, 2012); available at http://articles.cnn.com/2012-05-04/africa/world_africa_egypt-protests_1_egypt-demonstrations-tahrir-square-nile-tv?_s=PM:AFRICA.

106. Cambanis, "Egypt's Revolutionary Elite and the Silent Majority," p. 37.

107. Ajami, "The Arab Spring at One," p. 63.

108. Lisa Anderson, "Demystifying the Arab Spring," *Foreign Affairs*, 90 (May/June 2011), p. 4.

109. Ajami, "The Arab Spring at One," p. 58.

110. Ibid., pp. 62–63.

111. Roger Hardy, "Egypt Protests: an Arab Spring as Old Order Crumbles?," *BBC News* (February 2, 2011); available at www.bbc.co.uk/news/world-middle-east-12339521.

112. Barak Barfi, "Ties That Bind: The Social Pillars of Arab Authoritarian Regimes," in *Revolution and Political Transformation in the Middle East: Government Action and Response* (Washington, DC: Middle East Institute, August 2011), p. 14.

113. Ibid., p. 14.

114. Chenoweth, "Backfire in the Arab Spring," p. 25.

115. Ibid.

116. "Sacrifices Are Higher Than Societal Gains a Year after Arab Spring: Human Rights Report," *Al-Ahram Gate* (June 9, 2012); available at http://english.ahram.org.eg/NewsContent/2/0/44286/World/0/Sacrifices-are-higher-than-societal-gains-a-year-a.aspx.

117. Ahmed Younis and Mohamed Younis, "Most Egyptians Believe Continued Protests Are Bad for Country; Egyptians Were Growing Less Optimistic about Their Lives Post-Mubarak before Monday's Vote," *Gallup Poll News Service* (November 28, 2011); available at www.gallup.com/poll/151001/Egyptians-Believe-Continued-Protests-Bad-Country.aspx.

118. Chenoweth, "Backfire in the Arab Spring," p. 24.

119. Lutterbeck, "Arab Uprisings, Armed Forces, and Civil–Military Relations," pp. 38–39.

120. Stephen Zunes, "The Power of Strategic Nonviolent Action in Arab Revolutions," in *Revolution and Political Transformation in the Middle East: Agents of Change* (Washington, DC: Middle East Institute, September 2011), p. 11.

121. Srdja Popovic and Kristina Djuric, "People Power: The Real Force behind the 'Bad Year for Bad Guys,'" in *Revolution and Political Transformation in the Middle East: Agents of Change* (Washington, DC: Middle East Institute, September 2011), p. 16.

122. Ibid., p. 16.

123. Yochi J. Dreazen, "Mubarak's Departure Raises Tough Questions for U.S., Israel," *National Journal* (February 1, 2011); available at www.nationaljournal.com/mubarak-s-departure-raises-tough-questions-for-u-s-israel-20110201.

124. Zunes, "The United States and the Arab Pro-Democracy Insurrections," p. 8.

125. Hardy, "Egypt Protests."

126. Zunes, "The United States and the Arab Pro-Democracy Insurrections," p. 8.

127. "Sacrifices Are Higher than Societal Gains a Year after Arab Spring: Human Rights Report."

128. Chenoweth, "Backfire in the Arab Spring," pp. 27–28.

129. Shadi Hamid, ""The Rise of the Islamists," *Foreign Affairs*, 90 (May/June 2011), p. 46.

130. Ajami, "The Arab Spring at One," p. 63.

131. Patrick Kingsley, "Egyptian Activists Fear Crackdown on Islamists Will Widen to Other Dissidents," *Guardian* (September 8, 2013); available at www.theguardian.com/world/2013/sep/08/egyptian-activists-crackdown-islamists-widen.

132. Brenda Stoter, "Blast from the Past for Egyptian Dissidents," *al-Jazeera* (October 7, 2013); available at www.aljazeera.com/indepth/features/2013/10/blast-from-past-for-egyptian-dissidents-2013107113914374587.html.

133. Omar Ashour, "Egypt's New Revolution Puts Democracy in Danger," *Guardian* (July 6, 2013); available at www.theguardian.com/commentisfree/2013/jul/07/egypt-revolution-democracy-in-peril.

134. Jonathan Marcus, "Egypt's Political Unrest Causes Regional Concern," *BBC News* (July 8, 2013); available at www.bbc.co.uk/news/world-middle-east-23228297.

135. Zunes, "The United States and the Arab Pro-Democracy Insurrections," pp. 9, 10.

136. Dimitris Dalakoglou, "The Crisis before 'The Crisis': Violence and Urban Neoliberalization in Athens," *Social Justice*, 39 (March 2013), p. 34.

137. Liz Alderman, "Bomb Attacks in Greece Raise Fear of Radicalism," *New York Times* (January 20, 2013); available at www.nytimes.com/2013/01/21/world/europe/bomb-attacks-in-greece-raise-fear-of-revived-radicalism.html?pagewanted=all.

138. "Thousands across Greece Protest Austerity, " *Deutsche Welle* (February 20, 2013); available at http://dw.de/p/17hm3.

139. Amnesty International, *Police Violence in Greece: Not Just "Isolated Incidents"* (London: Amnesty International, 2012), p. 10.

140. Alderman, "Bomb Attacks in Greece Raise Fear of Radicalism."

141. Dalakoglou, "The Crisis before 'The Crisis,'" p. 33.

142. Sylvia Poggioli, "Violence at Both Ends of Political Spectrum Threatens Greece," *NPR News* (February 4, 2013); available at http://tristatesradio.com/post/violence-both-ends-political-spectrum-threatens-greece.

143. "Greece Police Tear Gas Anti-Austerity Protesters," *BBC News* (May 1, 2010); available at http://news.bbc.co.uk/1/hi/world/europe/8655711.stm.

144. Alderman, "Bomb Attacks in Greece Raise Fear of Radicalism."

145. Dalakoglou, "The Crisis before 'The Crisis,'" p. 24.

146. Alderman, "Bomb Attacks in Greece Raise Fear of Radicalism."

147. Ibid.

148. Poggioli, "Violence at Both Ends of Political Spectrum Threatens Greece."

149. "Transcript of a Press Briefing by Caroline Atkinson, External Relations Department, International Monetary Fund" (May 26, 2011); available at www.imf.org/external/np/tr/2011/tr052611.htm.

150. Alderman, "Bomb Attacks in Greece Raise Fear of Radicalism."

151. Amnesty International, *Police Violence in Greece*, p. 7.

152. *State Violence in Greece: An Alternative Report to the United Nations Committee against Torture* (Athens: Report from The World Organisation against Torture, Greek Helsinki Monitor, Minority Rights Group–Greece, and the Coordinated Organizations and Communities for Roma Human Rights in Greece, October 20, 2011), pp. 1–33.

153. Amnesty International, *Police Violence in Greece*, p. 7.

154. Ibid.

155. Alderman, "Bomb Attacks in Greece Raise Fear of Radicalism."

156. Poggioli, "Violence at Both Ends of Political Spectrum Threatens Greece."

157. Timothy Garton Ash, "The Crisis of Europe: How the Union Came Together and Why It's Falling Apart," *Foreign Affairs*, 91 (September/October 2012), p. 14.

158. Dan Bilefsky, "Three Reported Killed in Greek Protests," *New York Times* (May 6, 2010); available at www.nytimes.com/2010/05/06/world/europe/06greece.html.

159. Mark Blyth, "The Austerity Delusion: Why a Bad Idea Won Over the West," *Foreign Affairs*, 92 (May/June 2013), p. 42.

160. Poggioli, "Violence at Both Ends of Political Spectrum Threatens Greece."

161. Alderman, "Bomb Attacks in Greece Raise Fear of Radicalism."

162. Emma Clark, "Students Riot across Italy in Protest over Austerity Measures as Greek Shipyard Workers Demonstrate in Support of Arrested Strikers," *Daily Mail* (October 5, 2012); available at www.dailymail.co.uk/news/article-2213535/Students-riot-Italy-protest-austerity-measures-Greek-shipyard-workers-demonstrate-support-arrested-strikers.html.

163. Lydia Polgreen, "Unusual Summer of Political Calm Is Enjoyed by a Disputed Region," *New York Times* (August 10, 2011), p. A4.

164. Lydia Polgreen, "4 Killed as Indian Forces Try to Quell Protests in Kashmir," *New York Times* (August 14, 2010), p. A4.

165. Cody M. Poplin, "The Conflict in Kashmir: An Examination of Security Imperatives for the United States," *Global Security Studies*, 2 (Fall 2011), p. 23.

166. George Arney, "Non-violent Protest in Kashmir," *BBC News* (October 14, 2008); available at www.bbc.co.uk/worldservice/news/2008/10/081016_kashmir_arney_dm.shtml.

167. Syed Shoaib Hasan, "Why Pakistan Is 'Boosting Kashmir Militants,'" *BBC News* (March 3, 2010); available at http://news.bbc.co.uk/2/hi/south_asia/4416771.stm.

168. Lydia Polgreen, "Indian Forces Face Broader Revolt in Kashmir," *New York Times* (August 13, 2010), p. A1.

169. Emily Wax, "A Message in a Hail of Stones: Kashmir's Young Take up a Traditional Weapon in the Fight for Autonomy from India," *Washington Post* (July 17, 2010), p. A06.

170. Polgreen, "Indian Forces Face Broader Revolt in Kashmir," p. A1.

171. Wax, "A Message in a Hail of Stones," p. A06.

172. Emily Wax, "Tensions High in Kashmir a Day after Fatal Clashes," *Washington Post* (September 15, 2010), p. A12.

173. Ibid.

174. Jim Yardley, "3 Protesters Are Killed In Kashmir," *New York Times* (September 19, 2010), p. A20.

175. Polgreen, "4 Killed as Indian Forces Try to Quell Protests in Kashmir," p. A4.

176. Yardley, "3 Protesters Are Killed In Kashmir," p. A20.

177. Wax, "A Message in a Hail of Stones," p. A06.

178. Wax, "Tensions High in Kashmir a Day after Fatal Clashes," p. A12.

179. Jim Yardley, "After Protests, India Calls for Easing of Security Measures in Kashmir," *New York Times* (September 26, 2010), p. A14.

180. Polgreen, "Indian Forces Face Broader Revolt in Kashmir," p. A1.

181. Eric S. Margolis, "The World's Most Dangerous Border—Kashmir," *Washington Report on Middle East Affairs* (March 2013); available at www.wrmea.org/wrmea-archives/542-washington-report-archives-2011-2015/march-2013/11700-the-world-s-most-dangerous-border-kashmir.html.

182. Wax, "Tensions High in Kashmir a Day after Fatal Clashes," p. A12.

183. Ibid.

184. Polgreen, "Unusual Summer of Political Calm Is Enjoyed by a Disputed Region," p. A4.

185. Poplin, "The Conflict in Kashmir," p. 24.

186. Polgreen, "Unusual Summer of Political Calm Is Enjoyed by a Disputed Region," p. A4.

187. Ibid.

188. "Digest," p. A08.

189. Simon Denyer, "In Kashmir, Indian Army's Grip Still Tight," *Washington Post* (December 8, 2011), p. A08.

190. Wax, "Tensions High in Kashmir a Day after Fatal Clashes," p. A12.

191. Ibid.

192. Ibid.

193. Polgreen, "Unusual Summer of Political Calm Is Enjoyed by a Disputed Region," p. A4.

194. Ibid.

195. Denyer, "In Kashmir, Indian Army's Grip Still Tight," p. A08.

196. Polgreen, "Unusual Summer of Political Calm Is Enjoyed by a Disputed Region," p. A4.

197. Polgreen, "4 Killed as Indian Forces Try to Quell Protests in Kashmir," p. A4.

198. Polgreen, "Unusual Summer of Political Calm Is Enjoyed by a Disputed Region," p. A4.

199. Polgreen, "4 Killed as Indian Forces Try to Quell Protests in Kashmir," p. A4.

200. Denyer, "In Kashmir, Indian Army's Grip Still Tight," p. A08.

201. Hari Kumar, "Quick Action In Kashmir after Death Of Protester," *New York Times* (January 4, 2012), p. A9.

202. Yardley, "After Protests, India Calls for Easing of Security Measures in Kashmir," p. A14.

203. Polgreen, "Unusual Summer of Political Calm Is Enjoyed by a Disputed Region," p. A4.

204. Ibid.

205. Ibid.

206. Kumar, "Quick Action in Kashmir after Death of Protester," p. A9.

207. Hasan, "Why Pakistan Is 'Boosting Kashmir Militants.'"

208. Poplin, "The Conflict in Kashmir," p. 23.

209. Denyer, "In Kashmir, Indian Army's Grip Still Tight," p. A08.

210. "Musharraf Pushes Kashmir Proposal," *BBC News* (December 5, 2006); available at http://news.bbc.co.uk/2/hi/south_asia/6208660.stm.

211. Poplin, "The Conflict in Kashmir," p. 25.

212. Polgreen, "Indian Forces Face Broader Revolt in Kashmir," p. A1.

213. Wax, "A Message in a Hail of Stones," p. A06.

214. Ibid.

215. Poplin, "The Conflict in Kashmir," p. 27.

216. John Diamond, "Taliban, al-Qaeda Linked to Kashmir," *USA Today* (May 29, 2002); available at www.usatoday.com/news/world/2002/05/29/taliban-kashmir.htm.

217. Polgreen, "Unusual Summer of Political Calm Is Enjoyed by a Disputed Region," p. A4.

218. Poplin, "The Conflict in Kashmir," pp. 25–26.

219. Yardley, "After Protests, India Calls for Easing of Security Measures in Kashmir," p. A14.

220. Jason Burke, "Four Killed in Kashmir Protests against Alleged Qur'an Desecration," *Guardian* (July 18, 2013); available at www.theguardian.com/world/2013/jul/18/kashmir-indian-forces-protesting-quran-desecration.

221. "Kashmir Protests Erupt in Srinagar as Anti-India Separatists Clash with Police," *Huffington Post World* (September 20, 2013); available at www.huffingtonpost.com/2013/09/20/kashmir-protests_n_3961608.html.

222. Margolis, "The World's Most Dangerous Border—Kashmir."

223. Anderson Cooper, "The War Next Door: Homeland Security Secretary Says Every American Has a Stake in Mexico's War against Murderous Gangs" (New York: *60 Minutes*—CBS Television Program—March 1, 2009); available at www.cbsnews.com/stories/2009/02/26/60minutes/main4831806.shtml.

224. Patricio Asfura-Heim and Ralph Espach, "The Rise of Mexico's Self-Defense Forces," *Foreign Affairs*, 92 (July/August 2013), p. 143.

225. Vanda Felbab-Brown, *Calderón's Caldron: Lessons from Mexico's Battle against Organized Crime and Drug Trafficking in Tijuana, Ciudad Juárez, and Michoacán* (Washington, DC: Brookings Institution Latin American Initiative, September 2011), p. iv.

226. O'Neil, "Mexico–U.S. Relations—What's Next?," pp. 69–70.

227. Phillip Caputo, "The Fall of Mexico," *The Atlantic Magazine* (December 2009); available at www.theatlantic.com/magazine/archive/2009/12/the-fall-of-mexico/7760/?single_page=true.

228. June S. Beittel, *Mexico's Drug Trafficking Organizations: Source and Scope of the Rising Violence* (Washington, DC: Congressional Research Service, January 7, 2011), p. 3.

229. Robert C. Bonner, "The New Cocaine Cowboys: How to Defeat Mexico's Drug Cartels," *Foreign Affairs*, 89 (July/August 2010), p. 36.

230. David A. Shirk, *The Drug War in Mexico: Confronting a Shared Threat* (New York: Council on Foreign Relations Special Report #60, March 2011), p. 3.

231. Ibid., p. 8.

232. Marcos Pablo Moloeznik, "Organized Crime, the Militarization of Public Security,and the Debate on the 'New' Police Model in Mexico," *Trends in Organized Crime*, 16 (January 2013), pp. 177, 178.

233. Shannon O'Neil, "Mexico–U.S. Relations—What's Next?," *Americas Quarterly* (Spring 2010), p. 69.

234. Shirk, *The Drug War in Mexico*, p. 3.

235. Beittel, *Mexico's Drug Trafficking Organizations*, p. ii.

236. Francisco E. González, "Mexico's Drug Wars Get Brutal," *Current History* (February 2009), p. 72.

237. O'Neil, "Mexico–U.S. Relations—What's Next?," p. 70.

238. Shirk, *The Drug War in Mexico*, pp. 9–10.

239. Vanda Felbab-Brown, *The Violent Drug Market in Mexico and Lessons from Colombia* (Washington, DC: Brookings Foreign Policy Paper #12, March 2009), p. 6.

240. O'Neil, "Mexico–U.S. Relations—What's Next?," p. 72.

241. Beittel, *Mexico's Drug Trafficking Organizations*, p. 4.

242. O'Neil, "Mexico–U.S. Relations—What's Next?," p. 72.

243. Shirk, *The Drug War in Mexico*, p. 4.

244. Ibid., p. vii.

245. Ibid., p. 5.

246. O'Neil, "Mexico–U.S. Relations—What's Next?," p. 71.

247. Ewen MacAskill, "FBI Deployed by US to Fight Mexican Drug Lords," *Guardian* (March 25, 2009), p. 18.

248. O'Neil, "Mexico–U.S. Relations—What's Next?," p. 71.

249. Shannon O'Neil, "Mexico's Candidates Vow a Different Kind of Drug War," *CNN* (Cable News Network), (June 26, 2012); available at www.cnn.com/2012/06/25/opinion/oneil-mexico-election-drug-strategy/index.html.

250. Shirk, *The Drug War in Mexico*, p. vii.

251. Felbab-Brown, *Calderón's Caldron*, p. iv.

252. Patrick Radden Keefe, "Mexico's New Drug War: Catch and Release?," *New Yorker* (September 10, 2013); available at www.newyorker.com/online/blogs/comment/2013/09/mexicos-new-drug-war-catch-and-release.html.

253. Beittel, *Mexico's Drug Trafficking Organizations*, p. 23.

254. Felbab-Brown, *Calderón's Caldron*, p. 37.

255. Ibid.

256. Bonner, "The New Cocaine Cowboys: How to Defeat Mexico's Drug Cartels," p. 41.

257. Lisbeth Diaz, "Crime Crackdown Created More Drug Cartels," *Reuters* (December 18, 2012); available at www.reuters.com/article/2012/12/19/us-mexico-drugs-idUSBRE8BI01E20121219.

258. Mark Stevenson, "In Mexico, Extortion Soars Amid Crackdown on Drugs," *Huffington Post World* (October 14, 2013); available at www.huffingtonpost.com/2013/10/14/mexico-extortion_n_4097989.html.

259. George W. Grayson, "Will Bloodshed Mar the July 1, 2012 Election?" (Philadelphia, PA: Foreign Policy Research Institute E-Notes, June 2012), p. 2; available at www.fpri.org.

260. Beittel, *Mexico's Drug Trafficking Organizations*, p. 18.

261. Aimee Rawlins, "Mexico's Drug War," *Council on Foreign Relations* (December 13, 2011); available at www.cfr.org/mexico/mexicos-drug-war/p13689.

262. Caputo, "The Fall of Mexico."

263. Shirk, *The Drug War in Mexico*, p. 10.

264. Randal C. Archibold, "In Mexico Drug War, Massacres, but Claims of Progress," *New York Times* (February 2, 2011); available at www.nytimes.com/2011/02/02/world/americas/02mexico.html?ref=felipecalderon.

265. Shirk, *The Drug War in Mexico*, p. 10.

266. Felbab-Brown, *Calderón's Caldron*, p. 39.

267. Keefe, "Mexico's New Drug War."

268. Beittel, *Mexico's Drug Trafficking Organizations*, pp. 21, 23.

269. Eric Farnsworth, "Let's Stop 'Conflict Drugs' in Central America," *Huffington Post* (September 30, 2011); available at www.as-coa.org/article.php?id=3667.

270. Joshua E. Keating, "Mexico's Drug War Moves South," *Foreign Policy* (December 2011); available at www.foreignpolicy.com/articles/2011/11/28/the_stories_you_missed_in_2011?page=0,2.

271. Beittel, *Mexico's Drug Trafficking Organizations*, p. 25.

272. John P. Sullivan, *From Drug Wars to Criminal Insurgency: Mexican Cartels, Criminal Enclaves and Criminal Insurgency in Mexico and Central America, and Their Implications for Global Security* (Valley Cottage, NY: Vortex Working Paper #6, March 2012), p. 32.

273. González, "Mexico's Drug Wars Get Brutal," p. 76.

274. Sullivan, *From Drug Wars to Criminal Insurgency*, p. 36.

275. Caputo, "The Fall of Mexico."

276. Asfura-Heim and Espach, "The Rise of Mexico's Self-Defense Forces," pp. 143–144.

277. Moni Basu and Kocha Olarn, "Change in Myanmar? Prisoner Amnesty Begins," *CNN* (Cable News Network), (October 12, 2011); available at www.cnn .com/2011/10/12/world/asia/myanmar-prisoner-release/index.html?iref=allsearch.

278. "Myanmar Soldiers Fire Weapons, Tear Gas into Crowds of Protesters," *New York Times* (September 27, 2007); available at www.nytimes.com/2007/09/27/world/ asia/27iht-27myanmar-wire.7656649.html.

279. Seth Mydans, "Myanmar Generals Intensify Crackdown to Rein in Protests," *New York Times* (September 26, 2007); available at www.nytimes.com/2007/09/26/ world/asia/26iht-myanmar.4.7648200.html.

280. Daniel Pepper, "Aftermath of a Revolt: Myanmar's Lost Year," *New York Times* (October 4, 2008); available at www.nytimes.com/2008/10/05/weekinreview/05pepper .html?_r=1.

281. "Myanmar Soldiers Fire Weapons, Tear Gas into Crowds of Protesters."

282. Seth Mydans, "Months after Protests, Myanmar Junta in Control," *New York Times* (December 8, 2007); available at www.nytimes.com/2007/12/08/world/ asia/08myanmar.html.

283. Glenn Kessler, "India's Halt to Burma Arms Sales May Pressure Junta," *Washington Post* (December 30, 2007), p. A29.

284. Mydans, "Months after Protests, Myanmar Junta in Control."

285. "Authorities Clamp Down on Christians" (January 21, 2012); available at www.compassdirect.org/english/country/burma/restrictions.

286. "Burma: Inside the Saffron Revolution," *PBS* (September 25, 2008); available at www.pbs.org/frontlineworld/rough/2008/09/burma_the_saffr.html.

287. "Aftermath of a Revolt."

288. "Myanmar Soldiers Fire Weapons, Tear Gas into Crowds of Protesters."

289. Mydans, "Myanmar Generals Intensify Crackdown to Rein in Protests."

290. Mydans, "Months after Protests, Myanmar Junta in Control."

291. Ibid.

292. Ibid.

293. Ibid.

294. Ibid.

295. Ibid.

296. Ibid.

297. Pepper, "Aftermath of a Revolt."

298. Ibid.

299. Basu and Olarn, "Change in Myanmar?"

300. Nehginpao Kipgen, "Myanmar Dissidents' Release Calculated," *Global News* (June 5, 2013); available at www.globaltimes.cn/content/786780.shtml#.UdPcQPlnHXQ.

301. Andrew Woodcock, "No More Political Prisoners: Myanmar," *The Austrailian* (July 16, 2013); available at www.theaustralian.com.au/news/latest-news/no-more-political-prisoners-myanmar/story-fn3dxix6-1226679907770.

302. Basu and Olarn, "Change in Myanmar?"

303. Pepper, "Aftermath of a Revolt."

304. Ibid.

305. *Burma's "Saffron Revolution" Is Not Over: Time for the International Community to Act* (Brussels, Belgium: International Federation for Human Rights, December 2007), p. iv.

306. Mydans, "Months after Protests, Myanmar Junta in Control."

307. Pepper, "Aftermath of a Revolt."

308. "Authorities Clamp Down on Christians."

309. Mydans, "Months after Protests, Myanmar Junta in Control."

310. Pepper, "Aftermath of a Revolt: Myanmar's Lost Year."

311. Basu and Olarn, "Change in Myanmar?"

312. "Burma's Bloody Silence; While the Regime Crushes Popular Protests, the U.N. Security Council Prepares to . . . Listen to a Report . . . ," *Washington Post* (October 5, 2007), p. A20.

313. Andrew Buncombe, "Burma: Inside the Saffron Revolution," *The Independent* (September 27, 2007); available at www.independent.co.uk/news/world/asia/burma-inside-the-saffron-revolution-403645.html.

314. Kessler, "India's Halt to Burma Arms Sales May Pressure Junta," p. A29.

315. "Burma's Bloody Silence," p. A20.

316. "Myanmar Soldiers Fire Weapons, Tear Gas into Crowds of Protesters."

317. Mydans, "Months after Protests, Myanmar Junta in Control."

318. Ibid.

319. Ibid.

320. Basu and Olarn, "Change in Myanmar?"

321. "Myanmar's Courts Subvert Rule of Law, Activists Say," *New York Times* (December 3, 2011); available at www.nytimes.com/2011/12/04/world/asia/myanmar-uses-law-to-stifle-dissent-activists-say.html.

322. Basu and Olarn, "Change in Myanmar?"

323. Mydans, "Months after Protests, Myanmar Junta in Control."

324. Ibid.

325. Bertil Lintner, "China behind Myanmar's Course Shift," *Asia Times Online* (October 19, 2011); available at www.atimes.com/atimes/Southeast_Asia/MJ19Ae03.html.

326. "Myanmar, ICRC Vow Future Cooperation," *Global Times* (January 1, 2013); available at www.globaltimes.cn/content/755937.shtml.

327. Hu Yongqi and Li Yingqing, "Myanmar to Expand Cooperation with China," *China Daily* (August 20, 2013); available at http://usa.chinadaily.com.cn/world/2013-08/20/content_16906064.htm.

328. Armin Rosen, "Sudan on the Brink," *World Affairs*, 175 (July 2012), p. 57.

329. *Darfur Documents Confirm Government Policy of Militia Support* (New York: Human Rights Watch Briefing Paper, July 19, 2004), pp. 2–3.

330. "16 U.N. Workers Abducted in Western Sudan," *Washington Post* (June 6, 2004), p. A26.

331. *Entrenching Impunity: Government Responsibility for International Crimes in Darfur* (New York: Human Rights Watch, December 2005), p. 2.

332. *"They Shot at Us as We Fled": Government Attacks on Civilians in West Darfur* (New York: Human Rights Watch, May 2008), p. 2.

333. "Sudan's Darfur Conflict," *BBC News* (February 23, 2010); available at http://news.bbc.co.uk/2/hi/africa/3496731.stm.

334. Michele Kelemen, "Just a Few Months Old, S. Sudan Already in Turmoil" *National Public Radio* (January 15, 2012); available at www.npr.org/2012/01/15/145188077/just-a-few-months-old-s-sudan-already-in-turmoil.

335. "South Sudan Resumes Oil Output after Ending Row with Sudan over Transit Fees," *Reuters* (April 7, 2013); available at www.infopetro.com/news/viewnews.asp?id=14433.

336. Ibid.

337. Jeffrey Gettleman, "Is the Arab Spring Ready to Sweep Sudan? Dissent Grows Rapidly, but Analysts Are Skeptical Government Will Collapse," *International Herald Tribune* (July 7, 2012), p. 4.

338. Ibid.

339. Isma'il Kushkush,"Protesters and the Police Clash in Sudan," *New York Times* (July 7, 2012); available at www.nytimes.com/2012/07/07/world/africa/in-sudan-protesters-clash-with-the-riot-police.html.

340. Gettleman, "Is the Arab Spring Ready to Sweep Sudan?," p. 4.

341. Ibid.

342. "Sudan—Violent Crackdown on Protesters—Rein in Security Forces, Release or Charge Detainees," *All Africa* (Human Rights Watch) (June 26, 2012); available at http://allafrica.com/stories/201206261205.html.

343. "Sudan Detains Anti-Government Protesters," *Al Jazeera* (June 30, 2012); available at www.aljazeera.com/news/africa/2012/06/2012630144383598.html.

344. Susan Trimel, "Sudanese Authorities Must End Violent Crackdown on Protesters, End Impunity for Abuses," *Amnesty International* (July 11, 2012); available

at www.amnestyusa.org/news/press-releases/sudanese-authorities-must-end-violent-crackdown-on-protesters-end-impunity-for-abuses.

345. "South Sudan Resumes Oil Output after Ending Row with Sudan over Transit Fees."

346. "Sudan—Violent Crackdown on Protesters."

347. "Sudan's Darfur Conflict."

348. "Sudanese Police Crackdown on Growing Protests," *CNN* (Cable News Network), (June 24, 2012); available at http://articles.cnn.com/2012-06-24/africa/world_africa_sudan-protests_1_protests-south-sudan-sudanese-police?_s=PM:AFRICA.

349. Gettleman, "Is the Arab Spring Ready to Sweep Sudan?," p. 4.

350. Kushkush,"Protesters and the Police Clash in Sudan."

351. Zeina Khodr, "Opposition Hopes Soar over Sudan Protests," *Al Jazeera* (July 3, 2012); available at www.aljazeera.com/indepth/features/2012/07/201272743659532.html.

352. Gettleman, "Is the Arab Spring Ready to Sweep Sudan?," p. 4.

353. Alexander Dziadosz, "Sudanese Protest over Cuts amid Security Crackdown," *Chicago Tribune* (June 23, 2012); available at http://articles.chicagotribune.com/2012-06-23/news/sns-rt-us-sudan-protestbre85l16k-20120622_1_sudanese-protest-spending-cuts-protests-spread.

354. Gettleman, "Is the Arab Spring Ready to Sweep Sudan?," p. 4.

355. Khodr, "Opposition Hopes Soar over Sudan Protests."

356. Gettleman, "Is the Arab Spring Ready to Sweep Sudan?," p. 4.

357. Ibid.

358. Ibid.

359. Khodr, "Opposition Hopes Soar over Sudan Protests."

360. Nicholas Bariyo, "Sudanese Troops Clash with Rebels," *Wall Street Journal* (July 3, 2012); available at http://online.wsj.com/article/SB10001424052702304299704577504283424566736.html?mod=googlenews_wsj.

361. Khodr, "Opposition Hopes Soar over Sudan Protests."

362. Ibid.

363. Gettleman, "Is the Arab Spring Ready to Sweep Sudan?," p. 4.

364. "Unnoticed Genocide," *Washington Post* (February 25, 2004), p. A25.

365. *Entrenching Impunity*, p. 1.

366. *Darfur Documents Confirm Government Policy of Militia Support*, p. 3.

367. "Sudan's Darfur Conflict."

368. "Unnoticed Genocide," p. A25.

369. "Sudan Detains Anti-Government Protesters."

370. U.S. Condemns Crackdown on Sudan Anti-Government Protests," *Al Arabiya News* (June 27, 2012); available at http://english.alarabiya.net/articles/2012/06/27/222996.html.

371. Ibid.

372. William Davison, "U.S. Urges Sudan, South Sudan to Talk or Face Economic Turmoil," *Bloomberg* (July 18, 2012); available at www.bloomberg.com/news/2012-07-18/u-s-urges-sudan-south-sudan-to-talk-or-face-economic-turmoil.html.

373. "Sudan Detains Anti-Government Protesters."

374. "Sudan—Violent Crackdown on Protesters."

375. Trimel, "Sudanese Authorities Must End Violent Crackdown on Protesters, End Impunity for Abuses."

376. Ibid.

377. "Sudanese Police Crackdown on Growing Protests."

378. "Sudan—Violent Crackdown on Protesters."

379. "Sudan Crackdown on Independent Newspapers," *Guardian* (July 19, 2012); available at www.guardian.co.uk/media/greenslade/2012/jun/19/press-freedom-sudan.

380. Trimel, "Sudanese Authorities Must End Violent Crackdown on Protesters, End Impunity for Abuses."

381. "Sudan Detains Anti-Government Protesters."

382. Khodr, "Opposition Hopes Soar over Sudan Protests."

383. Dziadosz, "Sudanese Protest over Cuts amid Security Crackdown."

384. "Sudan Detains Anti-Government Protesters."

385. Khodr, "Opposition Hopes Soar over Sudan Protests."

386. "Sudanese Police Crackdown on Growing Protests."

387. Mark Landler, "U. S. Pushes for Global Eye on South Sudan Conflict," New York Times (July 29, 2013); available at www.nytimes.com/2013/07/30/us/us-pushes-for-global-eye-on-south-sudan-conflict.html?_r=0.

388. Nicholas Bariyo, "Sudan Asks Rebels to Pause for Talks." *Wall Street Journal* (April 30, 2013) available at http://online.wsj.com/article/SB10001424127887323528404578452732599885290.html.

389. Khodr, "Opposition Hopes Soar over Sudan Protests."

390. "U.S. Condemns Crackdown on Sudan Anti-Government Protests."

391. Stephanie Hanson, "Sudan, Chad, and the Central African Republic," *Council on Foreign Relations* (January 2, 2007); available at www.cfr.org/sudan/sudan-chad-central-african-republic/p12309.

392. Radwan Ziadeh, "The Syrian Revolution: The Role of the 'Emerging Leaders,'" in *Revolution and Political Transformation in the Middle East: Agents of Change*, p. 43.

393. Nicholas Blanford, "With Qaddafi's Death, World Attention Turns to Syria," *Christian Science Monitor* (October 21, 2011); available at www.csmonitor.com/World/Middle-East/2011/1021/With-Qaddafi-s-death-world-attention-turns-to-Syria.

394. Ziadeh, "The Syrian Revolution," p. 44.

395. Jansen, "Syria Torn between Armed and Peaceful Struggle."

396. Ziadeh, "The Syrian Revolution," p. 44.

397. Ibid., p. 43.

398. Ibid.

399. Jonathan Masters, "Syria's Crisis and Global Response," *Council on Foreign Relations* (October 28, 2012); available at www.cfr.org/syria/syrias-crisis-global-response/p28402#p1.

400. "France Urges Action on Syria, Says 120,000 Dead," *Alliance News* (September 25, 2013); available at www.lse.co.uk/AllNews.asp?code=loegkpgo&headline=France_urges_action_on_Syria_says_120000_dead.

401. Andrew J. Tabler, "Syria's Collapse," *Foreign Affairs*, 92 (July/August 2013), p. 90.

402. Michael Jansen, "Syria Torn between Armed and Peaceful Struggle," *Irish Times*. (March 16, 2012), p. 12; available at www.irishtimes.com/newspaper/world/2012/0316/1224313394428.html.

403. Ibid.

404. Ibid.

405. Ajami, "The Arab Spring at One," p. 61.

406. Jansen, "Syria Torn between Armed and Peaceful Struggle."

407. Ajami, "The Arab Spring at One," p. 62.

408. Jim Muir, "Syria Crisis: Gulf States Recognize Syria Opposition," *BBC* (November 12, 2012); available at www.bbc.co.uk/news/world-middle-east-20295857.

409. Ibid.

410. Jansen, "Syria Torn between Armed and Peaceful Struggle."

411. Ibid.

412. Chenoweth, "Backfire in the Arab Spring," p. 28.

413. Ajami, "The Arab Spring at One," p. 62.

414. Blanford, "With Qaddafi's Death, World Attention Turns to Syria."

415. Deborah Jerome, "Countering Syria's Ramadan Offensive," *Council on Foreign Relations* (August 4, 2011); available at www.cfr.org/syria/countering-syrias-ramadan-offensive/p25582.

416. Tony Badran, "How Assad Stayed in Power—and How He'll Try to Keep It," *Foreign Affairs Online* (December 1, 2011); available at www.foreignaffairs.com/articles/136707/tony-badran/how-assad-stayed-in-power%E2%80%94and-how-hell-try-to-keep-it.

417. Neil MacFarquhar, "Assad Denies Government Role in Massacre, Blaming Terrorism," *New York Times* (June 4, 2012), p. A4.

418. "UN Human Rights Probe Panel Reports Continuing 'Gross' Violations in Syria," *UN News Centre* (May 24, 2012); available at www.un.org/apps/news/story.asp?NewsID=42079#.Up9xCtJDvAc.

419. Michael R. Gordon and Eric Schmitt, "Russia Sends More Advanced Missiles to Aid Assad in Syria," *New York Times* (March 16, 2013); available at www.nytimes .com/2013/05/17/world/middleeast/russia-provides-syria-with-advanced-missiles .html?hp&pagewanted=all&_r=0.

420. Ajami, "The Arab Spring at One," p. 62.

421. Badran, "How Assad Stayed in Power—and How He'll Try to Keep It."

422. Matt Spetalnick, "U.S. Accuses Assad on Chemical Weapons, Plans Military Aid to Rebels," *Reuters* (June 13, 2013); available at www.reuters.com/article/2013/06/13/ us-syria-crisis-usa-idUSBRE95C1AB20130613.

423. "Syrian Chemical Attack: What We Know," *BBC News* (September 24, 2013); available at www.bbc.co.uk/news/world-middle-east-23927399.

424. Spetalnick, "U.S. Accuses Assad on Chemical Weapons, Plans Military Aid to Rebels."

425. Loveday Morris, "Battling on Two Fronts, Moderate Syrian Rebels Struggle for Funding, Lose Fighters," *Washington Post* (October 18, 2013); available at www .washingtonpost.com/world/middle_east/battling-on-two-fronts-moderate-syrian-rebels-struggle-for-funding-lose-fighters/2013/10/17/fa9232e6-359e-11e3-89db-8002ba99b894_story.html.

426. John Jackson, "An Egyptian Summer," in *Revolution and Political Transformation in the Middle East: Agents of Change* (Washington, DC: Middle East Institute, August 2011), p. 30.

427. Barfi, "Ties that Bind," p. 17.

428. Ibid.

429. "Hillary Clinton Hails Defection of Syria Military Official," *USA Today* (July 6, 2012); available at www.usatoday.com/news/world/story/2012-07-06/ syrian-opposition-no-fly-zone/56053692/1.

430. Ziadeh, "The Syrian Revolution," p. 43.

431. Ajami, "The Arab Spring at One," pp. 60, 62.

432. Peter Gelling and Tracey Shelton, "In Syria, One Man's Terrorist Is Another Man's Freedom Fighter," *Global Post* (March 4, 2013); available at www .globalpost.com/dispatch/news/regions/middle-east/syria/130303/syria-terrorist-terrorism-al-nusra-suqur-al-sham-rebels-bashar-al-assad.

433. Ziadeh, "The Syrian Revolution," p. 43.

434. Marc Fisher, "Embattled Assad Embraces Pariah Status," *Washington Post* (June 17, 2012), p. A01.

435. Ajami, "The Arab Spring at One," p. 62.

436. Chenoweth, "Backfire in the Arab Spring," p. 23.

437. Tabler, "Syria's Collapse," p. 90.

438. Gordon and Schmitt, "Russia Sends More Advanced Missiles to Aid Assad in Syria."

439. Oliver Holmes, "Syrian Reconciliation Thwarted by Savagery," *Huffington Post World* (May 13, 2013); available at www.huffingtonpost.com/2013/05/15/syria-reconciliation-thwarted-by-savagery_n_3276958.html.

440. Liz Sly, "Doomsday Scenario if Syria Fails," *Washington Post* (May 1, 2011); available at www.washingtonpost.com/world/unrest-in-syria-threatens-regional-stability/2011/05/01/AF3OQtUF_story.html.

441. Jansen, "Syria Torn between Armed and Peaceful Struggle."

442. Paul Salem, "Can Lebanon Survive the Syrian Crisis" (December 11, 2012); available at http://carnegieendowment.org/2012/12/11/can-lebanon-survive-syrian-crisis/escs.

443. Blanford, "With Qaddafi's Death, World Attention Turns to Syria."

444. Tabler, "Syria's Collapse," p. 91; and Con Coughlin, "The Syrian Civil War Is Breeding a New Generation of Terrorist," *Telegraph* (December 3, 2013), available at www.telegraph.co.uk/news/worldnews/middleeast/syria/10491523/The-Syrian-civil-war-is-breeding-a-new-generation-of-terrorist.html.

445. Masters, "Syria's Crisis and Global Response."

446. "Thailand's Political Crisis," *CNN* (Cable News Network), (May 17, 2010); available at http://edition.cnn.com/2010/WORLD/asiapcf/05/17/thailand.crisis.explainer/index.html?hpt=C1.

447. "Bangkok Death Toll Rises amid Bloody Red-Shirt Clashes," *BBC News* (May 15, 2010); available at http://news.bbc.co.uk/2/hi/asia-pacific/8684164.stm.

448. Thilo Thielke, "Death in Bangkok: The Day the Thai Army Moved In," *Spiegel Online* (May 24, 2010); available at www.spiegel.de/international/world/death-in-bangkok-the-day-the-thai-army-moved-in-a-696422.html.

449. Ibid.

450. Erik Cohen, "Contesting Discourses of Blood in the 'Red Shirts' Protests in Thailand," *Journal of Southeast Asian Studies*, 43 (June 2012), pp. 221–226.

451. Thielke, "Death in Bangkok."

452. *Descent into Chaos: Thailand's 2010 Red Shirt Protests and the Government Crackdown* (New York: Human Rights Watch, May 2011), p. 10.

453. "Bangkok Death Toll Rises amid Bloody Red-Shirt Clashes."

454. Adrees Latif and Damir Sagolj, "Bangkok under Curfew after Fresh Violence," *Reuters* (May 19, 2010); available at www.reuters.com/article/2010/05/19/us-thailand-idUSTRE64C0L620100519.

455. Thielke, "Death in Bangkok."

456. Latif and Sagolj, "Bangkok under Curfew after Fresh Violence."

457. Eric Talmadge, "Thai Government Declares Protest Violence Mostly Quelled," *Huffington Post* (May 20, 2010); available at www.huffingtonpost.com/2010/05/20/thai-government-declares-_n_583116.html.

458. *Descent into Chaos*, p. 4.

459. Andrew Higgins, "Thai Officials Use a Powerful Visual to Explain Violence," *Washington Post* (May 23, 2010); available at www.washingtonpost.com/wp-dyn/content/article/2010/05/22/AR2010052203166.html.

460. *Descent into Chaos*, p. 4.

461. "Thailand's Political Crisis."

462. "Bangkok Death Toll Rises amid Bloody Red-Shirt Clashes."

463. Thielke, "Death in Bangkok."

464. Thomas Fuller, "Thai Protesters Shut Down Parts of Bangkok," *New York Times* (March 16, 2010), p. A4.

465. Thielke, "Death in Bangkok."

466. Fuller, "Thai Protesters Shut Down Parts of Bangkok," p. A4.

467. Thielke, "Death in Bangkok."

468. Thomas Fuller, "Arson and Riots as Thai Military Quells Protests," *New York Times* (May 20, 2010), p. A1.

469. Andrew Higgins, "Thailand Reestablishes a Tenuous Calm," *Washington Post* (May 21, 2010), p. A10.

470. Jim Taylor, "Remembrance and Tragedy: Understanding Thailand's 'Red Shirt' Social Movement," *Journal of Social Issues in Southeast Asia*, 27 (2012), p. 143.

471. Thielke, "Death in Bangkok."

472. Jason Szep and Ambika Ahuja, "Thailand Toughens Stand against Spiraling Protests," *Reuters* (May 16, 2010); available at www.reuters.com/article/2010/05/16/us-thailand-idUSTRE64CoL620100516.

473. "Bangkok Death Toll Rises amid Bloody Red-Shirt Clashes."

474. Szep and Ahuja, "Thailand Toughens Stand against Spiraling Protests."

475. Ben Doherty, "Redshirts War of Civil War as Thai Troops Told to Shoot on Sight," *Guardian* (May 15, 2010); available at www.guardian.co.uk/world/2010/may/15/redshirts-warn-civil-war-thai-troops.

476. Andrew Higgins, "Thai Government, Protesters Appear Unwilling to Yield," *Washington Post* (May 18, 2010), p. A10.

477. "Bangkok Death Toll Rises amid Bloody Red-Shirt Clashes."

478. Ibid.

479. Szep and Ahuja, "Thailand Toughens Stand against Spiraling Protests."

480. *Descent into Chaos*, p. 5.

481. Ibid., pp. 5–7.

482. Ian MacKinnon and Damien McElroy, "Ten Killed in Thailand as Police Join Red Shirt Protest," *Telegraph* (May 14, 2010); available at www.telegraph.co.uk/news/worldnews/asia/thailand/7725645/Ten-killed-in-Thailand-as-police-join-Red-Shirt-protest.html.

483. "Thai Curfew Extended as Cleanup Begins," *CBC News* (Canadian Broadcasting Corporation), (May 20, 2010); available at www.cbc.ca/news/world/story/2010/05/20/thailand-bangkok-curfew.html.

484. Thielke, "Death in Bangkok."

485. "Thai Curfew Extended as Cleanup Begins."

486. Latif and Sagolj, "Bangkok under Curfew after Fresh Violence."

487. Ibid.

488. Andrew Higgins, "Bangkok's Residents Join Cleanup Efforts," *Washington Post* (May 24, 2010), p. A10.

489. Thomas Fuller and Seth Mydans, "Thai General Shot: Army Moves to Face Protesters," *New York Times* (May 13, 2010); available at www.nytimes.com/2010/05/14/world/asia/14thai.html?_r=1&hp.

490. Fuller, "Thai Protesters Shut Down Parts of Bangkok," p. A4.

491. Ibid.

492. "Thailand's Political Crisis."

493. Somroutai Sapsomboon, Pimnara Pradubwit, and Praphan Jindalertudomdee, "PM Urged to Condemn Attack by Red Shirts," *The Nation* (June 16, 2013); available at www.nationmultimedia.com/politics/PM-urged-to-condemn-attack-by-red-shirts-30208409.html.

494. "Thai Troops Deployed amid Bangkok Protests," *BBC News* (December 1, 2013); available at www.bbc.co.uk/news/world-asia-25173348.

## Chapter 5

1. Benjamin O. Fordham, "A Very Sharp Sword: The Influence of Military Capabilities on American Decisions to Use Forc." *Journal of Conflict Resolution*, 48 (October 2004), p. 633.

2. Jeffrey Record, *The American Way of War: Cultural Barriers to Successful Counterinsurgency* (Washington, DC: CATO Paper #577, September 1, 2006), p. 16.

3. National Rifle Association Executive Vice President Wayne LaPierre, as quoted in "NRA: 'Only Way to Stop a Bad Guy with a Gun Is with a Good Guy with a Gun'" (December 21, 2012); available at http://washington.cbslocal.com/2012/12/21/nra-only-way-to-stop-a-bad-guy-with-a-gun-is-with-a-good-guy-with-a-gun/.

4. Fareed Zakaria, "The Case for Gun Control," *Time* (August 20, 2012); available at www.time.com/time/magazine/article/0,9171,2121660-1,00.html.

5. John Mueller, *The Remnants of War* (Ithaca, NY: Cornell University Press, 2004), p. 172.

6. Patrick C. Bratton, "When Is Coercion Successful? And Why Can't We Agree on It?," *Naval War College Review*, 58 (Summer 2005), p. 102.

7. Troy S. Thomas and William D. Casebeer, *Violent Systems: Defeating Terrorists, Insurgents, and Other Non-State Adversaries* (Colorado Springs, Colorado: USAF Academy, U.S. Air Force Institute for National Security Studies INSS Occasional Paper 52, March 2004), p. 11; and Donald Snow, *Uncivil Wars: International Security and the New Internal Conflicts* (Boulder, CO: Lynne Rienner Publishers, 1996), p. 35.

8. Anthony Burke, "Paradoxes of Force and Security: Postmodern Conflict" (December 9, 2010); available at http://worldthoughtworldpolitics.wordpress.com/2010/12/09/paradoxes-of-force-and-security/.

9. Seyom Brown, *The Illusion of Control: Force and Foreign Policy in the 21st Century* (Washington DC: Brookings Institution Press, 2003), p. 154.

10. Troy S. Thomas, Stephen D. Kiser, and William D. Casebeer, *Warlords Rising: Confronting Violent Non-State Actors* (Lanham, MD: Lexington Books, 2005), p. 218.

11. Jeffrey Record, "Back to the Weinberger-Powell Doctrine?," *Strategic Studies Quarterly* (Fall 2007), p. 80.

12. Bernard Lewis, *The Shaping of the Modern Middle East* (New York: Oxford University Press, 1994).

13. Brown, *The Illusion of Control*, p. 5.

14. Colin S. Gray, *Fighting Talk: Forty Maxims on War, Peace, and Strategy* (Westport, CT: Praeger Security International, 2007), p. 98.

15. Colin S. Gray, *Another Bloody Century: Future Warfare* (London: Weidenfeld & Nicolson, 2005), p. 323.

16. Stephen E. Miller, "Gambling on War: Force, Order, and the Implications of Attacking Iraq" (Paper Prepared for Pugwash Meeting No. 276—Workshop on Terrorism and Weapons of Mass Destruction, Como, Italy, September 26–28, 2002), p. 4.

17. Todd C. Helmus, Christopher Paul, and Russell W. Glenn, *Enlisting Madison Avenue: The Marketing Approach to Earning Popular Support in Theaters of Operation* (Santa Monica, CA: RAND National Defense Research Institute, 2007), p. 50.

18. David Fisher, "The Ethics of Intervention," *Survival*, 36 (Spring 1994), p. 54.

19. Rupert Smith, *The Utility of Force: The Art of War in the Modern World* (New York: Vintage, 2008), p. 400.

20. Colin S. Gray, *Hard and Soft Power: The Utility of Military Force as an Instrument of Policy in the 21st Century* (Carlisle, PA: Strategic Studies Institute, April 2011), p. 16.

21. Micah Zenko, *Between Threats and War: U.S. Discrete Military Operations in the Post-Cold War World* (Stanford, CA: Stanford University Press, 2010), p. 3.

22. Bryan C. Price, "Targeting Top Terrorists: How Leadership Decapitation Contributes to Counterterrorism," *International Security*, 36 (Spring 2012), p. 9.

23. Patrick B. Johnson, "Does Decapitation Work? Assessing the Effectiveness of Leadership Targeting in Counterinsurgency Campaigns," *International Security*, 36 (Spring 2012), pp. 50, 75.

24. Price, "Targeting Top Terrorists," pp. 11, 22.

25. Jeffrey Pickering and Emizet F. Kisangani, "Political, Economic, and Social Consequences of Foreign Military Intervention," *Political Research Quarterly*, 59 (September 2006), pp. 363–376.

26. See, for example, Michael Mandelbaum, "Foreign Policy as Social Work," *Foreign Affairs*, 75 (January/February 1996), pp. 16–32.

27. Minxin Pei, "Lessons of the Past," in *From Victory to Success: Afterwar Policy in Iraq* (New York: Carnegie Endowment for International Peace, 2003), p. 53.

28. Center for Strategic and International Studies and Association of the U.S. Army, *Meeting the Challenges of Governance and Participation in Post-Conflict Settings* (Washington, DC: Center for Strategic and International Studies and Association of the United States Army monograph, July 8, 2002), p. 7.

29. Phebe Marr, "Occupational Hazards: Washington's Record in Iraq," *Foreign Affairs*, 84 (July/August 2005), p. 181.

30. Máire A. Dugan, "Coercive Power," in Guy Burgess and Heidi Burgess, eds., *Beyond Intractability* (Boulder: University of Colorado Conflict Research Consortium, September 2003); available at www.beyondintractability.org/essay/threats.

31. Gray, *Another Bloody Century*, p. 365.

32. Patricia L. Sullivan, "War Aims and War Outcomes: Why Powerful States Lose Limited Wars," *Journal of Conflict Resolution*, 51 (June 2007), p. 519.

33. Aaron Edwards, "Deterrence, Coercion and Brute Force in Asymmetric Conflict: The Role of the Military Instrument in Resolving the Northern Ireland 'Troubles,'" *Dynamics of Asymmetric Conflict*, 4 (November 2011), p. 228.

34. Erica Chenoweth, "Backfire in the Arab Spring," in *Revolution and Political Transformation in the Middle East: Government Action and Response* (Washington, DC: Middle East Institute, August 2011), p. 29.

35. Gray, *Hard and Soft Power*, p. 48.

36. Richard K. Betts, *American Force: Dangers, Delusions, and Dilemmas in National Security* (New York: Columbia University Press, 2012), p. 151.

37. Gray, *Hard and Soft Power*, p. 10.

38. Chenoweth, "Backfire in the Arab Spring," p. 29.

39. Anne Garrels, "Covering the War in Iraq" (Boston: John F. Kennedy Library and Foundation, September 29, 2003); available at www.cs.umb.edu/jfklibrary/forum_garrels.html.

40. Kurt M. Campbell and Michael E. O'Hanlon, *Hard Power: The New Politics of National Security* (New York: Basic Books, 2006), p. 9.

41. Audrey Kurth Cronin, *How Terrorism Ends: Understanding the Decline and Demise of Terrorist Campaigns* (Princeton, NJ: Princeton University Press, 2009), p. 143.

42. Forrest E. Morgan, Karl P. Mueller, Evan S. Medeiros, Kevin L. Pollpeter, and Roger Cliff. *Dangerous Thresholds: Managing Escalation in the 21st Century* (Santa Monica, CA: The RAND Corporation, 2008), p. 132.

43. Ibid.

44. Michael Walzer, *Just and Unjust Wars*, 4th edition (New York: Basic Books, 2006).

45. Grant T. Hammond, "Paradoxes of War," *Joint Force Quarterly* (Spring 1994), p. 7; available at www.dtic.mil/doctrine/jel/jfq_pubs/jfq0404.pdf.

46. Jack Nelson, "The Use of Military Force—Last Resort to Some Is Standard Option in President's View," *Los Angeles Times* (March 15, 1991); available at http://community.seattletimes.nwsource.com/archive/?date=19910315&slug=1271797.

47. Isabelle Duyvesteyn, "War, What Is It Good for . . . ," in Angstrom and Duyvesteyn, *Modern War and the Utility of Force* (London: Routledge, 2010), p. 271.

48. Richard N. Haass, *Intervention: The Use of American Military Force in the Post-Cold War World* (Washington, DC: Carnegie Endowment for International Peace, 1994), p. 89.

49. Jeffrey Record, "Back to the Weinberger-Powell Doctrine?," *Strategic Studies Quarterly* (Fall 2007), p. 91.

50. U.N. Office of the Special Adviser on the Prevention of Genocide, "The Responsibility to Protect"; available at www.un.org/en/preventgenocide/adviser/responsibility.shtml.

51. Derek S. Reveron and Kathleen A. Mahoney-Norris, *Human Security in a Borderless World* (Boulder, CO: Westview Press, 2011), p. 217.

52. Stephen Zunes,"Bahrain's Arrested Revolution," *Arab Studies Quarterly*, 35 (Spring 2013), pp. 162–163.

53. Iain Atack, "Ethical Objections to Humanitarian Intervention," *Security Dialogue*, 33 (2002), pp. 281–282.

54. Kenneth Campbell, "The Role of Force in Humanitarian Intervention," *Airman-Scholar* 3 (Spring 1997), pp. 20–27.

55. Atack, "Ethical Objections to Humanitarian Intervention," p. 290.

56. Reveron and Mahoney-Norris, *Human Security in a Borderless World*, p. 220.

57. Lee Ann Fujii, "The Puzzle of Extra-Lethal Violence," *Perspectives on Politics*, 11 (June 2013), p. 410.

58. See, for example, Nick Turse, *Kill Anything That Moves: The Real American War in Vietnam* (New York: Metropolitan Books, 2013).

59. Fujii, "The Puzzle of Extra-Lethal Violence," pp. 413, 419.

60. Chenoweth, "Backfire in the Arab Spring," p. 27.

61. Zunes, "Bahrain's Arrested Revolution," pp. 152–153.

62. Paul K. Huth, "Major Power Intervention in International Crises, 1918–1988," *Journal of Conflict Resolution*, 42 (December 1998), pp. 747, 749.

63.  Philip Everts, "When the Going Gets Rough: Does the Public Support the Use of Military Force?" *World Affairs*, 162 (Winter 2000), p. 91.

64.  Gray, *Hard and Soft Power*, p. 44.

## Chapter 6

1.  Anthony Burke, "Paradoxes of Force and Security: Postmodern Conflict" (December 9, 2010); available at http://worldthoughtworldpolitics.wordpress.com/2010/12/09/paradoxes-of-force-and-security/.

2.  Stanley Hoffmann, *Force, Legitimacy, and Order* (Washington, DC: The Brookings Institution, February 2005), p. 2; available at www.brookings.edu/fp/cuse/analysis/hoffmann20050201.pdf.

3.  Seyom Brown, *The Illusion of Control: Force and Foreign Policy in the 21st Century* (Washington DC: Brookings Institution Press, 2003), p. 1.

4.  Robert J. Art, "American Foreign Policy and the Fungibility of Force," *Security Studies*, 5 (Summer 1996), p. 23.

5.  Donald Rumsfeld, *Quadrennial Defense Review* (Washington, DC: U.S. Government Printing Office, February 2006), p. 9.

6.  Brown, *The Illusion of Control*, p. 163.

7.  David Baldwin, *Paradoxes of Power* (New York: Basil Blackwell, 1989), p. 153.

8.  Thomas C. Schelling, *Arms and Influence* (New Haven, CT: Yale University Press, 1966), p. 1.

9.  Antulio J. Echevarria II, *Toward an American Way of War* (Carlisle, PA: U.S. Army War College Strategic Studies Institute, March 2004), p. 1.

10.  Mark P. Sullivan, *The Mechanism for Strategic Coercion* (Maxwell Air Force Base, AL: Air University Press, April 1995), pp. v, 3.

11.  F. S. Northedge, "The Resort to Arms," in F. S. Northedge, ed., *The Use of Force in International Relations* (New York: The Free Press, 1974), p. 28.

12.  Brown, *The Illusion of Control*, p. 143.

13.  Colin S. Gray, *Fighting Talk: Forty Maxims on War, Peace, and Strategy* (Westport, CT: Praeger Security International, 2007), p. 18.

14.  H. R. McMaster, "On War: Lessons to be Learned," *Survival*, 50 (February–March 2008), p. 25.

15.  Robert Jervis, *Force in Our Times* (New York: Columbia University Saltzman Working Paper #15, July 2011), p. 1.

16.  McMaster, "On War," p. 28.

17.  Rupert Smith, *The Utility of Force: The Art of War in the Modern World* (New York: Vintage, 2008), p. 11.

18.  McMaster, "On War," p. 28.

19.  Gray, *Fighting Talk*, p. 3.

20. Daniel Smith, Marcus Corbin, and Christopher Hellman, *Reforging the Sword: Forces for a 21st Century Security Strategy* (Washington, DC: Center for Defense Information, September 2001), p. 55.

21. Edward N. Luttwak, *Strategy: The Logic of War and Peace*, revised edition (Cambridge, MA: Belknap Press of Harvard University Press, 2001), p. 260.

22. Colin S. Gray, *Another Bloody Century: Future Warfare* (London: Weidenfeld & Nicolson, 2005), p. 334.

23. Robert J. Art, "To What Ends Military Power?," *International Security*, 4 (Spring 1980), p. 35.

24. Seyom Brown, *Multilateral Constraints on the Use of Force: A Reassessment* (Carlisle, PA: Strategic Studies Institute, March 2006), p. v.

25. Audrey M. Calkins, "Multilateralism in International Conflict: Recipe for Success or Failure?"; available at www.thepresidency.org/storage/documents/Calkins/Calkins.pdf.

26. John Dumbrell,. "Unilateralism and 'America First'? President George W. Bush's Foreign Policy," *Political Quarterly* 73 (2002), pp. 279–287.

27. Margaret P. Karns, "Multilateralism Matters Even More," *SAIS Review*, 28 (Summer–Fall 2008), pp. 3, 13.

28. Robert Jervis, "Cooperation under the Security Dilemma," *World Politics*, 30 (January 1978), p. 167.

29. Ibid., pp. 169–170.

30. Jeffrey Record, "Back to the Weinberger-Powell Doctrine?," *Strategic Studies Quarterly* (Fall 2007), p. 91.

31. Brown, *The Illusion of Control*, p. 5.

32. Paul Collier, "War and Military Expenditures in Developing Countries," *Economics of Peace and Security Journal*, 1 (2006), p. 10.

33. Gray, *Another Bloody Century*, p. 339.

34. See Robert Mandel, "What Are We Protecting?", *Armed Forces & Society* 22, (Spring 1996), pp. 335–355.

35. Record, "Back to the Weinberger-Powell Doctrine?," p. 90.

36. McMaster, "On War," p. 27.

37. Ibid.

38. Peter Viggo Jakobsen, "Coercive Diplomacy," in Alan Collins, ed., *Contemporary Security Studies*, 2nd edition (New York: Oxford University Press, 2010), p. 283.

39. Echevarria, *Toward an American Way of War*, p. 1.

40. Brown, *The Illusion of Control*, p. 170.

41. Gray, *Another Bloody Century*, pp. 334, 339.

42. Gray, *Fighting Talk*, p. 68.

43. McMaster, "On War," p. 28.

44. Ibid., p. 26.

45. Echevarria, *Toward an American Way of War*, p. 16.

46. Record, "Back to the Weinberger-Powell Doctrine?," p. 92.

47. McMaster, "On War," p. 26.

48. Brown, *The Illusion of Control*, p. 156.

49. Record, "Back to the Weinberger-Powell Doctrine?," p. 91.

50. See Martin van Creveld, *Wargames: From Gladiators to Gigabytes* (Cambridge, UK: Cambridge University Press, 2013).

51. Robert Mandel, *Global Threat: Target-Centered Assessment and Management* (Westport, CT: Praeger Security International, 2008), p. 110.

52. Gray, *Fighting Talk*, p. 20.

53. Center for Strategic and International Studies and Association of the U.S. Army, *Play to Win: Final Report of the Bi-Partisan Commission on Post-Conflict Reconstruction* (Washington, DC: Center for Strategic and International Studies and Association of the U.S. Army, January 2003), p. 7.

54. Brown, *The Illusion of Control*, p. 152.

55. Mandel, *Global Threat*, p. 110.

56. Nadine Ansorg, "How Does Militant Violence Diffuse in Regions? Regional Conflict Systems in International Relations and Peace and Conflict Studies," *International Journal of Conflict and Violence*, 5 (2011), p. 183.

57. Smith, *The Utility of Force*, p. 400.

58. Gray, *Another Bloody Century*, p. 339.

59. Smith, *The Utility of Force*, p. 401.

60. Erica Chenoweth, "Backfire in the Arab Spring," in *Revolution and Political Transformation in the Middle East: Government Action and Response* (Washington, DC: Middle East Institute, August 2011), p. 28.

61. F. H. Hinsley, "The Rise and Fall of the Modern International System," *Review of International Studies*, 8 (January 1982), p. 4.

62. Ibid., p. 8.

63. Gray, *Another Bloody Century*, p. 340.

64. Jervis, *Force in Our Times*, p. 28.

65. Art, "To What Ends Military Power?," p. 27.

66. Gray, *Another Bloody Century*, p. 361.

67. Art, "American Foreign Policy and the Fungibility of Force," p. 7.

68. Robert Mandel, *Armies without States: The Privatization of Security* (Boulder, CO: Lynne Rienner Publishers, 2002).

69. Anna Leander, *Eroding State Authority? Private Military Companies and the Legitimate Use of Force* (Rome: Rubbettino, 2006), p. 10.

70. Robert Mandel, *The Changing Face of National Security: A Conceptual Analysis*, (Westport, CT: Greenwood Press, 1994), chapter 1.

71. Daniel Serwer, "The Limits of Military Power" (October 14, 2011); available at www.peacefare.net/?p=5165.

72. Gray, *Another Bloody Century*, p. 340.

73. Colin S. Gray, *Hard and Soft Power: The Utility of Military Force as an Instrument of Policy in the 21st Century* (Carlisle, PA: Strategic Studies Institute, April 2011), pp. vi–vii, 47–48.

74. Ibid., pp. 7–8, 10.

75. Ibid., p. 21.

76. Lawrence Freedman, *The Transformation of Strategic Affairs* (London: International Institute for Strategic Studies Adelphi Paper #379, 2006), p. 36.

77. Máire A. Dugan, "Coercive Power," in Guy Burgess and Heidi Burgess, eds., *Beyond Intractability* (Boulder, CO: University of Colorado Conflict Research Consortium, September 2003); available at www.beyondintractability.org/essay/threats.

78. Jakobsen, "Coercive Diplomacy," p. 285.

79. B. H. Liddell Hart, *Strategy*, 2nd edition (New York: Praeger, 1967), p. 335.

80. Richard K. Betts, *American Force: Dangers, Delusions, and Dilemmas in National Security* (New York: Columbia University Press, 2012), p. 269.

81. Richard N. Haass, *Intervention: The Use of American Military Force in the Post-Cold War World* (Washington, DC: Carnegie Endowment for International Peace, 1994), p. 87.

82. Brown, *The Illusion of Control*, p. 151.

83. Record, "Back to the Weinberger-Powell Doctrine?," p. 94.

84. McMaster, "On War," p. 20.

85. John Kerry, "The Road Home from Kabul," *Foreign Policy* (June 24, 2011); available at www.foreignpolicy.com/articles/2011/06/24/the_road_home_from_kabul

86. See Colin S. Gray, *Perspectives on Strategy* (New York: Oxford University Press, 2013), pp. 29–30.

# INDEX

"Absolute war" (Carl Von Clausewitz), distinguished from brute force use, 7

Action-reaction cycle, 32, 33–34, 64, 97–98, 125, 133, 140–141, 165, 180, 189, 190, 191, 193, 220–221, 231

Adaptability, in brute force use. *See* Flexibility, in brute force use

Afghanistan: war (2001), 19, 22, 26, 43–49, 51, 73, 184, 185, 190, 191, 201; American drone strikes against, 36

Aggression: link to brute force, 7, 181; difficulties of pinpointing aggressor, 34; justification of aggression as defensive, 194; ubiquitousness of, 225

Algeria, target of French brute force, 186

Alliances, 90–94, 105, 178, 193. *See also* Multilateralism

Anarchy, 1, 3, 10, 11, 15, 34, 53, 65, 164, 182, 209, 213, 223, 224, 225

Arab Spring uprisings, 32, 35, 53, 81, 88, 108, 109, 113, 114, 116, 124, 125, 149, 155, 156, 157, 162, 194, 222

Armed nonstate groups: acceptability of violence, 43, 63; growth in power of, 41, 67–68, 225, 227; irregular tactics of, 218; susceptibility to action-reaction cycles, 33–34

Arms control, 4, 178

Arms race, 20–21, 98, 178, 213

Asymmetric confrontation, 24–25, 85, 194

Autonomy: desire for, 19, 70, 99, 115, 131–132, 149, 151, 182; disruptive impact of, 120, 135; sacrifice of, 16

Backfire effects, associated with brute force, 21, 38, 39–41, 58, 74, 78, 87, 116, 122, 127–128, 199, 218, 223

Bahrain, internal repression of dissidents, 108–112, 193, 199, 200, 208

Barbarity, 18, 137, 161, 201

Bin Laden, Osama, killing of, 15, 30, 43, 60–68, 178, 184

Brutality, general discussion, 30, 33; link to brute force, 8

Brute force: conditions when it succeeds and fails, 2, 168–202, 228, 230–231, 232; controversies surrounding, 1; challenges, 3; defensive versus offensive orientation, 194; definition of, 6–9, 208; desirability of a world without brute force, 223; flexibility of, 62, 84, 94, 196, 207; futility of, 2, 14, 22, 25, 204–205, 215, 227; general value of, 23–24, 209; as an insurance policy, 228; limitations, 2, 205, 206, 207–209, 224, 228–229; need for improvement, 205, 208; notion of "major" brute force use, 5; overuse and underuse dangers, 178–182; pejorative associations with, 7; policy recommendations concerning, 205–223; scope of this study, 2–6; security implications of, 6; severity of, 2–3, 6–7; shrinking role of, 2, 223, 224, 228–231; similarities between internal and external brute force use, 5; strategic purpose of, 182–185, 204, 215–216